D1270789

Animal Models of Human Emotion and Cognition

Animal Models of Human Emotion and Cognition

**Edited by Marc Haug
and Richard E. Whalen**

AMERICAN PSYCHOLOGICAL ASSOCIATION
WASHINGTON, DC

Published by
American Psychological Association
750 First Street, NE
Washington, DC 20002

Copies may be ordered from
APA Order Department
P.O. Box 92984
Washington, DC 20090-2984

In the U.K., Europe, Africa, and the Middle East, copies may be ordered from
American Psychological Association
3 Henrietta Street
Covent Garden, London
WC2E 8LU England

Typeset in Century Schoolbook by EPS Group Inc., Easton, MD

Printer: Edwards Brothers, Inc., Ann Arbor, MI
Cover Designer: Berg Design, Albany, NY
Technical/Production Editor: Anne Woodworth

Library of Congress Cataloging-in-Publication Data
Animals models of human emotion and cognition / [edited by] Marc Haug
    and Richard E. Whalen.—1st ed.
        p.   cm.
    Includes bibliographical references and index.
    ISBN 1-55798-583-9
    1. Psychology, Comparative.   2. Human behavior—Animal models.
I. Haug, M. (Marc)   II. Whalen, Richard E.
BF671.A55   1999
156—dc21   99-30612
                                                                    CIP

British Library Cataloguing-in-Publication Data
A CIP record is available from the British Library.

Printed in the United States of America
First Edition

Contents

Acknowledgments

We would like to take this opportunity to acknowledge the contributions of a number of individuals who provided valuable review commentary on the chapters: M. Carlier, P. Mormède, and R. Dantzer (France); M. Martinez (Spain); J. Archer, R. J. Rodgers, and C. Frith (United Kingdom); H. Mittelstaedt (Germany); R. Hudson, A. DeCasper, F. Robinson, J. L. Gariepy, A. J. Figueredo, S. Pellis, R. Cairns, L. Nadel, B. Murray, T. Zentall, V. Lolordo, and A. Ellenbroek (United States); and L. Rodgers (Australia).

We are also greatly indebted to the American Psychological Association Books Acquisition, Development, and Production staff members for their constant support, and in particular, we would like to express our gratitude to Mary Lynn Skutley, Judy Nemes, and Anne Woodworth. They took care of innumerable details that helped make the editing of this book possible.

After these expressions of sincere thanks, however, both editors must assure the reader emphatically that any errors or other shortcomings in this book are ours alone.

Marc Haug and Richard E. Whalen

Contributors

Enrico Alleva, Section of Behavioural Physiopathology, Laboratorio di Fisiopatologia di Organo e di Sistema, Istituto Superiore di Sanità, Rome, Italy

James R. Anderson, Department of Psychology, University of Stirling, Stirling, Scotland

Claude Aron, Institut d'Histologie de la Faculté de Médecine, Université Louis Pasteur, Strasbourg, France

D. Caroline Blanchard, Pacific Biomedical Research Center and Department of Anatomy, John A. Burns School of Medicine, University of Hawaii, Honolulu

Robert J. Blanchard, Department of Psychology and Békésy Laboratory of Neurobiology, University of Hawaii, Honolulu

Bela Bohus, Department of Animal Physiology, University of Gröningen, Haren, The Netherlands

Claude Bonnet, Laboratoire des Systèmes Biomécaniques, Université Louis Pasteur, Strasbourg, France

David L. Braff, Department of Psychiatry, School of Medicine, University of California, San Diego

Paul F. Brain, School of Biological Sciences and Department of Psychology, University of Wales, Swansea, United Kingdom

Sietse F. de Boer, Department of Animal Physiology, University of Gröningen, Haren, The Netherlands

Delphine Dépy, Centre National de la Recherche Scientifique, Centre de Recherche en Neurosciences Cognitives, Marseille, France

Anne J. H. de Ruiter, Department of Animal Physiology, University of Gröningen, Haren, The Netherlands

Christopher A. Duva, Department of Psychology, University of British Columbia, Vancouver, British Columbia, Canada

Joël Fagot, Centre National de la Recherche Scientifique, Centre de Recherche en Neurosciences Cognitives, Marseille, France

Gordon G. Gallup, Jr., Department of Psychology, State University of New York at Albany

Mark A. Geyer, Department of Psychiatry, School of Medicine, University of California, San Diego

Olivier Gosselin, UMR 7521, Université Louis Pasteur, Strasbourg, France

Carolyn Granier-Deferre, Laboratoire Cognition et Développement, Université René Descartes, Paris

Guy Griebel, CNS Research Department, Synthelabo Recherche, Bagneux, France

Marc Haug, Laboratoire d'Ethologie et Neurobiologie, Université Louis Pasteur, Strasbourg, France

Mark Hebert, Pacific Biomedical Research Center, University of Hawaii, Honolulu

Pierre Karli, Faculté de Médecine, Université Louis Pasteur, Strasbourg, France

Jaap M. Koolhaas, Department of Animal Physiology, University of Gröningen, Haren, The Netherlands

Tom J. Kornecook, Department of Psychology, University of British Columbia, Vancouver, British Columbia, Canada

Jean-Pierre Lecanuet, Laboratoire Cognition et Développement, Université René Descartes, Paris

Lynne Marrow, School of Biological Sciences and Department of Psychology, University of Wales, Swansea, United Kingdom

Stephen C. Maxson, Biobehavioral Sciences, University of Connecticut, Storrs

Ralph R. Miller, Department of Psychology, State University of New York at Binghampton

Dave G. Mumby, Department of Psychology, Concordia University, Montreal, Quebec

Philippe Oberling, Faculté de Médecine, INSERM U405, Université Louis Pasteur, Strasbourg, France

J. Bruce Overmier, Department of Psychology, University of Minnesota, Minneapolis

Lewis Petrinovich, Department of Psychology, University of California, Riverside

John P. J. Pinel, Department of Psychology, University of British Columbia, Vancouver, British Columbia, Canada

David J. Sanger, CNS Research Department, Synthelabo Recherche, Bagneux, France

Lisa M. Savage, Department of Psychology, State University of New York at Binghampton

Benoist Schaal, Laboratoire du Comportement Animal, Station de Physiologie de la Reproduction, INRA, Nouzilly, France

Whitney A. Sweeney, Department of Psychology, State University of New York at Binghampton

Neil R. Swerdlow, Department of Psychiatry, School of Medicine, University of California, San Diego

Jacques Vauclair, Centre National de la Recherche Scientifique, Centre de Recherche en Neurosciences Cognitives, Marseille, France

Augusto Vitale, Section of Comparative Psychology, Laboratorio di Fisiopatologia di Organo e di Sistema, Istituto Superiore di Sanità, Roma, Italy

Christian Werhrahn, Max-Planck-Institut fur Biologische Kybernetik, Tuebingen, Germany

Richard E. Whalen, Department of Psychology, University of California, Riverside

Animal Models of Human Emotion and Cognition

1

Introduction

Marc Haug and Richard E. Whalen

Humans owe a debt to animals that predates recorded history. Since ancient times, we have used animals to herd, to pull, and to plow. Many centuries later, as modern empirical science has established itself, animals have provided us with information about skeletal structure and the nature of bodily organs. This information has formed a basis for speculations about the behavioral capacities of animals and, ultimately, about evolution.

Over the years, two distinct but interrelated lines of research have developed. One line has focused on the animals themselves: how they are constructed, how they interact with each other and with their environment, how they shape their environments, and how changing environments in turn shape the evolution of species. The second line of research—our current area of concern—has focused on how information derived from studying animals can be applied to the human condition. Animal research thus has become a foundation of modern medical and behavioral science.

During the nineteenth century, investigators used animals to further their understanding of the nervous system. They came to understand what nerves are, how they work, and how they are interconnected. It is difficult to believe that concepts of the synapse and the reflex arc are of such recent origin, but these concepts revolutionized the study of the brain and its regulation of behavior. Investigators also began to learn how the brain integrates sensory information and how the hypothalamus and related structures are involved in the regulation of basic behavioral and bodily functions such as hunger, thirst, sex drive, and aggression. This led to investigations of the role of the brain in truly complex activities such as learning and perception. Such studies continue to explain the complex processes that govern our behavior.

Psychological science is now enriched by findings from other flourishing disciplines. Through studies of animals such as fruit flies, the biological sciences have enabled us to apply genetic concepts to human behavior, and advances in the neurosciences help us to understand how our nervous system controls behavior. Animal studies appear to hold out promise for the understanding and treatment of a number of behavioral disorders, including anxiety, depression, addiction, Alzheimer's disease, and Parkinson's disease.

Despite these past and continuing contributions, many general psychologists remain unaware of the crucial role that animal studies play in understanding human behavior. Possibly the most important reason for this is the fundamental change in the structure of academia that occurred in the late 1960s in the United States. In the decades before 1970, animal laboratories were quite common in psychology departments in the United States, and these usually taught undergraduate and graduate courses in animal behavior, sensory psychology, and physiological psychology. Such courses are much less common today.

In the early 1970s, students of animal behavior and the nervous system realized their common interests and the need for interdisciplinary cooperation. The Society for Neurosciences was formed and rapidly became the nexus for research interactions. Departments of neuroscience and psychobiology were formed, but their home was more likely to be in a medical school or a biological science program than it was to be in a behavioral science program. Graduate students who in the past had regularly enrolled in physiological psychology programs abandoned psychology for neuroscience, and animal-based components of psychology departments withered on the vine. Thus, most psychology students today are not exposed to the contributions of animal scientists to the behavioral science endeavor. And, of course, although neuroscience has flourished as an independent discipline, the study of cognitive processes also has flourished within the behavioral sciences, thereby accelerating the divergence of the behavioral and neuroscience communities.

The goal of this book is twofold. We hope that the chapters gathered together here will demonstrate that theories based on animal studies of brain, behavior, and cognition are indeed providing new insights and new directions for research on human function; we hope also to promote a dialogue between animal and human researchers that will lead to increased understanding of the complex issues involved in modeling human behavior. We have organized the chapters under five general themes: Part I—foundations, Part II—psychiatric and emotional disorders, Part III—development, Part IV—cognition, and Part V—aggression as one specific behavioral system.

Part I covers important background material against which the subsequent chapters need to be viewed. In chapter 2, Overmier provides an interesting overview of how the use of animals as models of human behavior has been refined over the years. The chapter also addresses the crucial question of what, precisely, is meant by the term *model*. Overmier points out that a model is not considered a claim of identity with that which is being modeled, but rather that is a convergent set of several kinds of analogies between the target real-world phenomenon and the system being studied as a model.

Petrinovich, in chapter 3, acknowledges the ethical issues that arise out of experimentation that uses animals. This issue has always been of concern to the general public, as is evidenced by the actions of animal rights activists. However, the cloning of Dolly the ewe, which made newspaper and television headlines, brought ethics issues to the center of public, scientific, and political consciousness once more. We do not wish to extend the polemics of the animal rights proponents. We do feel, however, that this is an appropriate time to ask questions about the current relevance of hypotheses and theories emerging from animal research for understanding the human condition.

Petrinovich reviews the major issues surrounding the use of animals in scientific research. His essay proposes a "utilitarian" position on the use of animals, which seeks to minimize any necessary pain and suffering on their part while maximizing the associated benefits to humankind. This kind of approach has long been used to justify animal studies directed toward finding therapies for cancer, AIDS, heart disease, obesity, and so forth and has generally received broad public support. On the other hand, animal studies of emotional and psychiatric disorders have received less public support. Perhaps this is because Freud's enormous influence on Western thinking has left a residue of belief that emotional disorders are largely the result of the environment, that is, of "nurture." By this, we mean that Freud led people to believe that disorders such as depression result from a person's interactions with parents, siblings, and the community in general and that curing such disorders must come from a close interaction with a psychoanalyst or similar talk therapist. This is true in spite of the facts that lithium has long been used to control manic–depressive disorder and that Prozac is one of the most widely prescribed drugs to control emotional lability. Petrinovich, furthermore, dismantles the current philosophical stance on animal rights by reducing the very concept of rights to a corollary of the social contractarian position, which would clearly exclude any applicability to nonhuman animals. Finally, he shows the major inconsistencies in the internal logical coherence of the animal rights position by detailing the ad hoc nature of the various special pleadings required to make their position appear even minimally reasonable to the general public.

In chapter 4, Karli ponders the affective aspects of human nature from a neurobiologist's perspective. In the initial pages of his chapter, he outlines the basic argument that there are three domains of human nature— biological, social, and self-conscious—and that these are necessarily linked together by sharing the same brain. The proposal that knowledge about affective processes, in contrast to knowledge about cognitive processes, is particularly important for understanding the nature of human nature is of special interest. Karli then contrasts cognitive and emotional controls on behavior. Animal studies are critical if we are to understand the human brain and control of affective processes, the maintenance of homeostasis and social interactions. For example, the natural tendency of a rhesus monkey is to react to humans with a combination of fear and rage. If a small piece of brain tissue called the *amygdala* is removed, the monkey becomes calm and often hypersexual. Does the rage behavior shown by some humans reflect some dysfunction in the amygdala? Another example might be *bonding*, the close attachment between infants and parents. We know that this process of affective interlocking is often crucial for the survival of the infant as well as for his or her ability to form normal social interactions with peers. What brain mechanisms are involved that allow appropriate development? Only brain studies of animals will permit insights into these processes. The chapter points to reciprocal integration across domains, suggesting that when this integration is disrupted, there seems to be something wrong with the brain circuitry.

The goal of Part II is to provide a sampling of the kinds of strategies that animal investigators have used to obtain information that may help alleviate psychiatric and emotional disorders. Most scientists who work with animals generally do so because of the belief that their research will be relevant to humankind. This is especially the case in psychopharmacology, where psychiatric disorders have been modeled in animals to better understand brain functioning and offer conditions to discover new therapies.

As described in chapter 5, by Brain and Marrow, recent years have seen major expansion in the number of behavioral paradigms that might serve as simulations within which to investigate aspects of human neuroses and psychoses. They point out that although validated nonanimal alternatives are emerging in such areas as toxicology, attempts to assess the biological basis of human mental disease and to develop appropriate drugs for its treatment are still largely dependent on animal models. In their chapter, Brain and Marrow examine the ethics of using animals in such investigations and discuss the characteristics of useful animal models of human neurosis and psychosis. A number of experiments in which rodents are used to model anxiety, hostility, and depression are described and evaluated.

Relatedly, Griebel and Sanger, in chapter 6, seek to isolate components of defensive behavior in mice by means of drugs that have been used clinically to control generalized anxiety disorder and panic disorder. By using a variety of drugs that have different effects on different neurotransmitter systems, Griebel and Sanger hope to understand the different emotional states associated with defensive behaviors.

Although the use of animal models readily lends itself to the study of anxiety, schizophrenia—one of the most complex disabling disorders—has been resistant to analysis. The next two chapters contain findings that show promise in helping researchers better understand the disruptions in attentional mechanisms that have long been associated with schizophrenia. For years, investigators have used animals in a training procedure termed *latent inhibition* to model for the attentional deficits of schizophrenia. In chapter 7, Oberling, Gosselin, and Miller critically review this model, proposing that current theories of latent inhibition need modification. The major conclusion of the chapter is that the latent-inhibition paradigm does not measure attention but use of context and that use of context is probably the key problem in schizophrenia.

The eyeblink startle response habituates more slowly in people with schizophrenia than in normal controls, and there is also an increased peak startle latency in those with schizophrenia. In addition, if a preliminary auditory signal is applied, control participants show a reduced startle response (prepulse inhibition) when compared with patients with schizophrenia. Geyer, Braff, and Swerdlow, in chapter 8, have used prepulse inhibition in rats to investigate, pharmacologically, the neurotransmitter mechanisms that are deficient in people with schizophrenia and to implicate the neurotransmitter dopamine. These findings already have prompted clinical tests of new antipsychotic drugs. However, Geyer et al. briefly mention that prepulse inhibition is disturbed not only in schizophrenia but also in Huntington's chorea and various attention deficit disorders and that to date, there is no evidence that the prepulse deficit in schizophrenia is in some way different from the deficit in other disorders.

Part III focuses on animal studies of developmental processes in humans. Evidence is accumulating to show that the circuitry of the mammalian brain can be reorganized by experience throughout the lifetime of an individual. It is now well established that there are multiple mechanisms of plasticity and that experiences that affect brain morphology and, in turn, brain functioning and behavior include a broad category of events interacting with the developing brain in its environment, both internal and external.

Developmental psychologists, biologists, and pediatricians have been steadily pushing back the age at which we have to consider the sensory and behavioral competence of young vertebrates, both human and non-human. This has been accompanied by the development of ingenious instrumentation and a range of elegant behavioral paradigms appropriate for investigating organisms at the earliest ages. The point has now been reached in which, to more fully understand early developmental processes in mammals, it is necessary to access and experiment within the context of the prenatal environment. Growing awareness of the importance of prenatal events for understanding the course of postnatal development is of obvious relevance to the biomedical and behavioral sciences and is also of theoretical importance because of further blurring of the old but enduring nature-versus-nurture dichotomy. Because of the obvious ethical and practical difficulties of penetrating this most intimate of spheres in the human, animal models are of particular importance. In this context in chapter 9, Schaal, Lecanuet, and Granier-Deferre, quite remarkably, have studied the detection and effects of prenatal sensory stimulation in developing animals and humans. Focusing on chemosensory and auditory stimuli, they show the value of animal studies for understanding human development. Animal and human neonates respond differentially to chemosensory stimuli from their own amniotic fluid, as opposed to control stimuli. Schaal et al.'s studies have an important implication in showing that the human fetus is capable of long-term sensory (olfactory) retention.

Bonnet and Wehrhahn, in chapter 10, focus their attention on the development of human vision. In this domain, animal studies have increased our understanding of how the human visual system is constructed. This, in turn, enables researchers to ask more complex questions about human perception. Focusing particularly on motion detection, Bonnet and Wehrhahn trace visual detection from the eye, through the thalamus to the cerebral cortex, discussing what one can learn about the human brain and the hierarchical nature of visual cortical organization by studying the frog.

In chapter 11, Aron investigates bisexuality. He states that despite the organizational effects of androgens in the perinatal period, males of some mammalian species show the capacity to spontaneously display feminine behavior in adulthood. In extended studies, he notes that progesterone is unable to increase the lordosis response in estrogen-primed males but that, by contrast, orchidectomized animals are not only capable of displaying lordosis after estrogen treatment but also sensitive to the facilitory effects of exogenous or endogenous progesterone. He reports that in the absence of any hormonal or surgical manipulation, male rats may display strain-dependent heterotypic sexual responses to mounts by other males, thus suggesting the impermanence of the organizational effects of androgens on male sexual behavior. Aron demonstrates also that a common behavioral system sensitive to the activational effects of ovarian hormones, which involves both the hypothalamus ventromedial nucleus and the different amygdaloid nuclei, subserves the display of lordosis in male as well in female rats. Finally, he finds that in contrast to unexposed animals, castrated rats treated with ovarian hormones (estradiol and progesterone) show lordosis more frequently in response to appropriate male odors. However, the main objective of Aron's work is to evaluate, in the light of experimental and physiopathological data, the respective roles of hormonal, environmental, and organizational factors in the determinism of sexual orientation in humans. Human data are reviewed on 5α-reductase deficiency in pseudohermaphrodites, in which individuals are said to change their gender identity and role at puberty. Aron suggests that under favorable cultural conditions, the perinatal organizational effects of androgens may overcome the influences of environmental factors. Aron cautions, however, that one should not underestimate the potency of environmental influences, making reference to the number of girls masculinized at birth by the congenital adrenal hyperplasia condition who go on to be heterosexual women after corrective surgery. The main question raised by this chapter is to what extent the use of an animal model may lead to a better understanding of human sexuality. It lays emphasis on the fact that sexual orientation in rodents has been conclusively shown to depend on a balance between organizational and environmental factors. In the absence of any other evidence, why then disregard the biological background of behavioral bisexuality in humans?

Humans clearly have a highly developed sense of visual self-perception. Anderson and Gallup have chosen this interesting area as the topic of chapter 12, in which they investigate self-recognition in nonhuman primates. Their evidence indicates that although some nonhuman and most human primates come to understand that a reflection or photograph can be an image of themselves, monkeys do not self-recognize. These findings permit the construction of a framework in which the comparative study of social cognition can be approached systematically.

Sensation and cognition are inextricably linked. The next four chapters in Part IV focus on another aspect of the perception–cognition continuum: memory processes. As the population now lives longer than in earlier generations, we are seeing an increased incidence of memory loss in such disabling conditions as nonspecific senility and Alzheimer's disease. Because many years may pass before investigators can examine the brains of amnesiacs, it has been difficult to determine the exact nature of the lesion that led to the amnesia. Thus, they have turned to animals.

In recent years, animal models have brought about major advances to the understanding of the role of the medial temporal lobe structures in memory and amnesia. In chapter 13, Duva, Kornecook, and Pinel trace the development of a new view of the relative contributions of the various medial temporal lobe structures to object-recognition memory. They also demonstrate the critical role played in this understanding by the comparative study of different animal models of medial temporal lobe amnesia.

In chapter 14, which explores the ways in which investigators use animal models of global amnesia to study memory, Mumby discusses the critical brain damage in amnesia, the types of memory that are affected, and etiological factors, and he cautions against simple conclusions regarding the anatomical underpinnings of amnesia and against assumptions that a given task, when applied to humans and to rats or monkeys, is measuring the same process.

In the 1940s and 1950s, learning theory was in its heyday. Hull, Tolman, Miller, and colleagues received great attention, and students trained during that period received a broad grounding in the psychology of learning. Then, with the discovery of electrical self-stimulation of the brain, studies of learning took a very biological bent. In chapter 15, Overmier, Savage, and Sweeney demonstrate that the mode of thought characteristic of the learning theory days continues to yield valuable information. They describe a new learning principle, called the *differential outcomes* phenomenon, which appears to involve activation of a form of prospective memory. This has already shown considerable clinical promise in aiding those with learning and memory problems.

Finally, memory functions, like many neural functions, are not symmetrically distributed in the human brain. Broca's (1861) demonstration of hemispheric specialization of language function is probably the best known example. In chapter 16, Vauclair, Fagot, and Dépy demonstrate that in spite of a long-lasting view to the contrary, hemispheric lateralization is not unique to humans and is not limited to language function. They describe the methods used by neuropsychologists and psychologists to investigate functional lateralization and discuss the limitations, as well as some of the interesting revelations, of such studies.

Part V focuses on aggression. Scientists have, for decades, attempted to replicate emotional illness in man with animal models. In the area of aggression, most researchers are familiar with experimental paradigms such as social isolation, footshock, and brain-stimulation-induced aggression in rats as well as muricidal behavior, that is, mouse killing, by rats. Parallels have been drawn between septal-induced aggression in animals and humans with certain forms of brain dysfunction, as analogies have been drawn between footshock- or isolation-induced aggression in rats and hyperirritable states in humans, ranging from hyperkinetic syndromes to the hypervigilant states accompanying paranoid or paranoid–psychotic states. Scientists must, however, be circumspect in generalizations from research on a particular group of organisms given the vast genetic diversity that surrounds them.

Koolhaas, de Boer, de Ruiter, and Bohus, in chapter 17, address the usefulness of animal aggression models of stress research by first discussing the rationale for using animal models, their limitations, and common misperceptions about the ways in which such models can and should be used. The core of the chapter examines individual vulnerability to stress pathology, using two lines of laboratory research on aggression in male rats and mice. Their findings indicate that animals' socially adaptive capacities play an important role in maintaining stable social groups, whereas the failure of socially adaptive capacities in individual animals may lead to serious forms of stress pathology. Because almost all vertebrate species, including human beings, are social creatures, Koolhaas et al. suggest that the social stress processes and coping styles observed in rats, mice, and several other species may be a primitive reflection of similar processes in human beings.

In chapter 18, Maxson takes a more direct approach to genes and aggression, using modern technology to specify particular genes or gene groups that may be involved in aggression in mice and in humans. This approach, Maxson argues, allows direct inferences about the pathways from gene to behavior. In most cases, the genes involved are those that regulate neurotransmitter function. Homologous genes in mice and humans also may allow the development of realistic animal models of human aggression.

Research on aggression among animals raises a number of ethical concerns. Vitale and Alleva, in chapter 19, discuss studies of aggression in rodents and nonhuman primates in the light of these issues. They note that ethical concerns are, of necessity, quite different when studying animals in a confined laboratory environment versus in the natural environment, where field biologists must observe neutrality. (For example, infanticide, which does occur in the natural environment, would generally be prevented in the laboratory.) Vitale and Alleva propose various laboratory guidelines that should be used to prevent destructive interactions that might be observed in the field.

In chapter 20, Blanchard, Hebert, and Blanchard take a step back and look at aggression research in its social context. They point out that animal and human researchers on aggression have traditionally been unable to "make meaningful impressions on each other's understanding of the behaviors on which they focus" (p. 297). This situation has been aggravated by a number of issues, including the political incorrectness of discussing the biological elements of aggression. Lamenting the lack of development of a unified view of aggression, Blanchard et al. suggest that a way to avoid gridlock might be to conceive of aggression as consisting of many different neurobehavioral systems, at least some of which show considerable evidence of continuity between nonhuman mammals and people.

We believe that these chapters provide exemplary material both for researchers and for teachers of experimental courses and their students. We also hope that this volume will stimulate teachers to search out animal studies, to illustrate the biological and evolutionary basis of human behavior. If we can promote a greater understanding of the important role that animal studies play in understanding human behavior, we shall have achieved our goal.

Part I ———————————

Foundations

2

On the Nature of Animal Models of Human Behavioral Dysfunction

J. Bruce Overmier

The Dark Ages were so designated because in Europe there were substantial religious and social prohibitions against activities that might yield new information or new perspectives. These prohibitions applied to the use of animals for dissection as part of anatomical study, and medicine stagnated for nearly a millennium. Yet, although this prohibition on the study of the anatomy and physiology of animals passed with the coming of the Age of Enlightenment, the church still limited what we might infer about humans from the study of animals. This was captured formally in Descartes' seventeenth-century philosophical doctrine of mind–body dualism: The mental life of humans was set apart from that of animals. This metatheoretic belief system plagues us to this day (Dennett, 1991; Koestler, 1967), despite the seminal contributions of Charles Darwin and Herbert Spencer, who argued the continuity of emotions and mind from animals to man and the potential value of a comparative psychology.

It was Pavlov, following Sechenov's dicta on the objective study of the mind, who was most instrumental in breaking the conceptual barriers to animal models in psychology, with his materialistic application of conditioned reflex methodology. Pavlov was not only the first to suggest that we might learn about the function of the mind from the objective study of behavior, but he was also the first to suggest that experimentally induced behavioral dysfunctions might indeed be informative to the study of human mental dysfunction. We are all familiar with the famous Shenger-Krestinova (1921) appetitive classical conditioning experiments with dogs involving a series of increasingly difficult discriminations between a circle and an ellipse in which the animals' behavior finally became so agitated and erratic that the dysfunction was designated *experimental neurosis*. Many are less familiar with the follow-up work in which Krasnogorski (1925) carried out similar experiments with children in an auditory dis-

I wish to thank Susan Mineka and Robert Murison for their constructive criticisms on an earlier draft of this chapter. This chapter was originally published in *Bibliographies in Psychology: Number 12. Animal Models on Human Pathology: A Bibliography of a Quarter Century of Behavioral Research, 1967–1992* (pp. vii–xiv) edited by J. Bruce Overmier and Patricia D. Burke, 1992. Washington, DC: American Psychological Association. Copyright 1992 by the American Psychological Association. Reprinted by permission of the author.

crimination task—and with somewhat similar results. Moreover, Pavlov and his associates found bromide salts to be an effective "therapy" for *both* the dogs and the children (see Babkin, 1938).

There followed a number of efforts to create what we call animal models of psychopathology. The works of two of Pavlov's American students are most readily recognized in this regard. There was Gantt's 12-year series of experiments with the neurotic dog, Nick (Gantt, 1944). And there was the work of Liddell, at the Cornell Behavior Farm, in which young goats and sheep were subject to defensive classical conditioning in either the presence or absence of their mothers; this work eventuated in Liddell's intriguing little book, *Emotional Hazards in Animals and Man* (1956).

The important observations made by Gantt and Lidell that maladaptive behavior patterns analogous to human neuroses could be conditioned—that is, in essence taught—inspired a number of others to explore the possibility of a new scientific study of psychopathology based in animal research. Two important exemplars are Maier's (1949) research with rats, in which being challenged with unsolvable problems caused behavioral fixations that he considered a form of *compulsivity*, and Masserman's (1943) brief punishment of cats' consummatory behavior that caused persistent avoidant behavior that he thought a form of *phobic neuroses*, which he showed were treatable by *environmental press*—a type of extinction procedure. The latter is significant for contemporary clinical psychologists because it was Masserman's research that prompted Wolpe (1958) to his experiments with cats from which he derived the principles for *reciprocal inhibition* therapy so widely and effectively used today to treat phobias. Whether the experimental procedures were in fact a scientifically valid basis for the inferences Wolpe drew in regard to appropriate therapy may be argued at length elsewhere (e.g., Mineka, 1985). Nonetheless, the heuristic value of animal models is clearly established in contemporary psychology by this exemplar, and it also encouraged others to pursue animal models research in their study of psychopathology (which will be returned to) as well as other applied issues such as self-control (e.g., Mahoney & Bandura, 1972).

Animal models offered a promise to treat psychopathology, not as bizarre distortions of behavior, but rather as involving lawful processes whose principles and mechanisms we could come to understand scientifically—to move psychiatry into the modern age. These experimental models of neuroses, or *experimental neurosis*, were seen as critically important as a counter influence to earlier kinds of mythological and anecdotal speculations about the causal factors and to Freudian analysis in human psychopathology that led to treatments such as bleeding the evil humors away for depression, castration as a "treatment" for masturbation, and confinement in an orgone box for neuroses.

A substantial portion of the research efforts in all areas of psychology involves the use of models, and clinical psychology should not be any different if such models can give purchase on phenomena at issue. One sees reliance on models that are mechanical (e.g., cochlear models for audition), conceptual (layered network models of brain function), process-oriented (computer models of thinking), as well as biological (the invertebrate *aplysia* model of vertebrate learning) as only a few types of models (and exemplars among literally hundreds of models) in psychology (Bekesy, 1960; Schmajuk & DiCarlo, 1992; Wagman, 1991; and Byrne & Berry, 1989, respectively as examples). Models are basic and powerful tools in science. The aeronautical scientist builds a miniature airplane for testing in a wind tunnel; the chemical scientist imagines electrons in shared planetlike orbits around atomic nuclei. These two types of models (one physical and one conceptual) aid in the discovery of useful principles for addressing real-world problems such as optimal wing shape for speed or how smooth a shape molecules will take when bonded to the wing's surface.

Models are equally important in biological and behavioral sciences, and this accounts in part for why so much research has been and continues to be done with animals in psychology. Explicit contemporary uses of animal models in psychology are more accepted and less controversial in research on neural mechanisms of learning (Kandel, 1979), perceptual–cognitive mechanisms (Goldman-Rakic, 1987), the mysteries of memory dysfunction in aging populations (e.g., Kesner & Olton, 1990; Lister & Weingartner, 1991; Squire & Zola-Morgan, 1985), mechanisms of drug abuse by humans (Siegel, 1983), and psychopharmacology (Willner, 1991) than they are in addressing behavioral issues in psychopathology (Davey, 1981; Mineka & Zinbarg, 1991). And these models are fundamental components of the successes in those areas where they have been applied. So why is there so substantial a conceptual resistance to their use in understanding human psychopathology? Indeed, the question seems even more cogent given that the existing limited uses of such models have in fact led to development of new therapies for phobias (Stampfl & Levis, 1967; Wolpe, 1958) and depression (Klein & Seligman, 1976). I believe that the bases for this resistance are that (a) there is a lingering Cartesian dualism and (b) the structure and function of models—and animal models in particular—are not well understood. The former has been addressed by Dennett (1991) among others; the latter we address below.

Elements of Models

The key word for understanding models is *analogy*. A model is not considered a claim of identity with that which is being modeled. Rather, a model is a convergent set of several kinds of analogies between the "target" real-world phenomenon to be understood and the system that is being studied as a model for the target phenomenon. Two key kinds of analogies involved are (a) *initial analogy* and (b) *formal analogy*.

To understand the interplay of these different kinds of analogies in the modeling process, we need to note that any phenomenon we wish to model is not "just a thing" arising *deus ex machina*, but the consequence of causal relationships between levels of factors—perhaps unknown factors—in the real world. Similarly, then, any potentially useful model will involve a set of causally related factors. These causal chains of factors in both the target domain and the model domain may be several steps long. Models arise from the claims of correspondence between factors in the two domains. The two domains can have obvious similarities, as between a miniature airplane and a Boeing 747, or they can be dissimilar, as between the ball-and-stick arrays in molecular chemistry that represent the genetic substance DNA and the molecule itself.

Now let us consider the animal models case in psychology where there are both similarities and differences. One might note that some set of dysfunctional physiological and behavioral symptoms characterize patients with a given psychiatric disorder (e.g., refractory but elevated steroids, inability to cope with challenges, and distortions of memory); one might further note that animals exposed to some drug or to some experimental learning treatment exhibit behaviors that are similar to those behavioral symptoms of the patients. A hypothesis that the dysfunctional behavior of the animal and the dysfunctional behavior of the patient were similar in important ways would constitute an initial analogy in the modeling process. An additional hypothesis might be that the patient's dysfunctional physiological symptom is related to the animal's drug-induced physiological state; this would be a second initial analogy. The degree of *descriptive* similarity between the two sets of behaviors or between the two physiological states would constitute the degree of *material or conceptual equivalences*.

Now if a relation between the patient's physiology and the patient's behavior is hypothesized to parallel the empirical causal relation between the animal's physiology and its behavior, a formal analogy can be drawn between these two parallel, within-domain relations. It is this formal analogy—the hypothesized parallelism of causal relations in the two domains—that constitutes a functional model. Indeed, this is exactly how many models in psychology have arisen such as the amphetamine-based model of schizophrenia (Bell, 1965) or the cholinergic depletion model of Korsakov's syndrome (Overstreet & Russell, 1984); development of other models emphasized environmental and learning history as causal factors rather than drug history (e.g., the avoidance model of phobias, Mowrer, 1947; the learned-helplessness model of depression, Seligman, 1975; and the opponent process model of addictions, Solomon & Corbit, 1974). These are only five examples among many models.

The degree of descriptive similarity between the elements in an initial analogy constitutes the degree of *material equivalence*—sometimes confusingly referred to as "material analogy" (Overmier & Patterson, 1988). But material equivalence is often simply out of the question for some modeling efforts. In such cases, one may rely upon additional theoretical notions to place elements for an initial analogy into correspondence. This then is *conceptual equivalence*. Conceptual equivalences may also vary in degree depending on how many theoretical transformations are required to set the elements of the initial analogy into correspondence. Adrenal cortical outputs in a rat (corticosterone) and a human (cortisol) are not identical, but have a very high degree of material equivalence. On the other hand, a rat's pressing of a lever and a human's engaging in grocery shopping must be put into correspondence on the basis of a conceptual equivalence: Both are instrumental acts of food procurement. This reconceptualization seems straightforward enough; although some such shopping is certainly engaged in for reasons other than food-getting, the same is true for rats' lever pressing. However, placing inescapable electric shocks received by dogs into correspondence with failure by humans to solve anagrams requires several conceptual transformations: Minimally, one must first conceive of failure to be as aversive event as shock; then, these aversive events must be seen as functionally equivalent; and finally, the behavior of the dog in the presence of the shock must be conceived of as directed problem-solving behavior. Clearly, the conceptual distance here is greater than in the case of food procurement. Although there is often a preference for material equivalence or close conceptual equivalence (perhaps because it does not strain one's intellectual powers much, although it may be a substantial technical challenge), it is important to note the greater material or conceptual distance does not directly influence the validity or value of a model. Validity and value inhere in the degree to which the formal analogy provides correct information.

It should be clear now that an initial analogy alone is not a functional model; assuming that an initial analogy is a model is a common mistake. A true model involves both initial analogies and formal analogies, and the power of the modeling process is that one can use the known and explicated casual relations in one domain (typically the model domain, but it can work both ways [e.g., Blackman, 1983; Dorworth & Overmier, 1977]) as a guide for finding parallel relations in the second domain.

Some scientists (e.g., Abramson & Seligman, 1977, and McKinney, 1974) require that a large number of formal analogy parallels be proved, all involving substantial material equivalence, before a claim of a model be made. This requirement emphasizes the important representative functions of models (e.g., for development of drug therapy) to the exclusion of their heuristic and evidentiary functions important for learning about the causal and sustaining mechanisms of the dysfunction. Two very important points need to be made here: First, material analogy is not critical to the functional validity of a model; mathematical equations are often powerful models which when processed by computers generate knowledge about systems' behavior—even human decision systems—but without material equivalence. Material equivalence between elements is akin to *face validity*; although it offers promise, it ensures nothing. Second, if we wait until all the causal relations in each domain are fully and independently explicated before we set them into formal analogies, then the model yields little or no evidentiary power for new understanding.

The exemplar psychological models, already noted, all began with an initial analogy being made between behaviors—a so-called *symptomological match*. One can immediately see why this would be so: When two things have the same form, we often assume they are functionally similar, perhaps even homologous. But one might well argue that finding such similarities in symptoms between species is a very chancy process—possibly a misleading one, although subject to empirical testing within the modeling process. This is because each species brings its own evolved propensities and biological constraints on its behavior to the test arena. Different behaviors in different species could serve the same function although common behaviors could serve different functions. Thus, it is conceivable that two different species (e.g., humans and rats) might have opposite dysfunctional behavioral manifestations arising from the same underlying physiological or psychological state. For example, one might freeze, whereas the other might show agitation; yet these two forms of behavior could be part of a useful initial analogy despite their lack of material equivalence. Although, in actual practice, this has not proved a common problem, it does suggest an alternative approach to choosing one's initial analogy.

One might well choose to put into initial correspondence etiological factors rather than symptoms (e.g., see Cullen, 1974, for illustrations). This strategy is common in medical research and is based upon the assumption that etiology and therapy are necessarily linked because in some diseases the causes also sustain the disease process, as in the case of bacterial infection. In contrast, in psychology, we have found that the sustaining conditions for some behavioral processes are often different from those that led to their development. Korsakov's syndrome and phobias seem to be exact exemplars of this. On the other hand, posttraumatic stress disorder (PTSD) may prove to be a case requiring an approach based on an etiological initial analogy if one seeks an animal model of the consequences of traumatic stress, because the reported human symptoms tend to take the form of thought disruptions, flashbacks, and other symptoms that are not directly observable in animals (Basoglu & Mineka, 1992; Foa, Zinbarg, & Rothbaum, 1992; Pitman, 1988, 1989; Saporta & VanderKolk, 1992).

It is perhaps also worth noting here that one area of application that assumes that etiology and therapy are not inextricably linked is operant behavior modification. This form of treatment also has as one of its metatheoretic assumptions the generality of the behavioral principles studied in the laboratory—and commonly with animals (Brown, Weinckowski, & Stolz, 1975; Davey, 1981; Skinner, 1972). And, operant behavior modification has proved a successful basis for treatments of a wide range of behavioral dysfunctions (illustrated in Feldman & Broadhurst, 1976; Krasner & Ullman, 1965; and the articles published in the *Journal of Applied Behavior Analysis*). But the conceptual origins of behavior modification are to be found in Watson's early effort to "teach a phobia" to Little Albert (Watson & Raynor, 1920) and Mary Cover Jones's treatment of Peter for such "fears" (Jones, 1924). Although this work was with children, it was nonetheless an instance of modeling.

Final Considerations

The foregoing has tried to show that animal models have been and continue to be a ubiquitous component of psychological research into human dysfunction. The space provided here has allowed merely for an introduction to the structure and functions of models and the correlated considerations in the use of models. The interested reader is directed to key analytic discussions (Bond, 1984; Fox, 1971; Hanin & Usdin, 1977; Henn & McKinney, 1987; Hinde, 1976; McKinney, 1988; Overmier & Patterson, 1988; Russell, 1964; VonCranach, 1976; Willner, 1986), illustrative critical evaluations of particular models (Costello, 1978; Eysenck, 1979; Green, 1983; Kaufman, 1973; Katz, 1981; Maser & Seligman, 1977; Mineka, 1985; Willner, 1984), and interesting historical reviews (Abramson & Seligman, 1977; Babkin, 1938; Broadhurst, 1960; Cook, 1939; Mowrer, 1947; Richter, 1957; Wolpe, 1952; Zubin & Hunt, 1967). Review of these will put into better perspective the approximately 2,000 items in the following bibliography.

It is also appropriate to note that this modeling process is not always as clearly understood as it should be by either its proponents or its detractors. Unfortunately, some detractors also criticize contemporary animal modeling efforts based on an outdated grasp of the current state of knowledge about animal learning and behavior (Mineka, 1985, gives instances of this). Criticisms based on poor appreciation of the process or outdated information should not be allowed to dissuade either those wishing to use such models or those who provide the funds for such research.

This is not to say that the use of animal models is without its share of problems (e.g., Kornetsky, 1977; Rollin & Kesel, 1990). The model-building process is fraught with difficulties—conceptual, analogic translational, empirical, interpretive, and extensional—but then so is *all* research.

Behavioral dysfunctions and psychiatric disorders must be studied if we are to bring relief to the literally tens of millions of sufferers. And until we have some significant grasp on the processes involved, we are ethically deterred from some classes of research with human subjects and patient populations—in particular those experimenting with etiologies or with therapies that involve physiological changes not yet understood. This grasp is to be gained only through the use of animal models.

There are also ethical considerations in the use of animals for such research. We are obligated to ensure that we fully understand the modeling process and that the analogies in the model we are developing are sound and will pass the test of review by other scientists with a relevant knowledge base. Even such models may sometimes involve necessarily the induction of distress—after all, it appears that physical and emotional distress is involved in the etiology of many common forms of human dysfunctional behavior. When the protocol properly requires the induction of distress, we should not shirk from this if there is not an equally effective alternative. This is because the failing to do appropriate research also carries with it significant costs in future human suffering.

References

Abramson, L. Y., & Seligman, M. E. P. (1977). Modeling psychopathology in the laboratory: History and rationale. In J. D. Maser & M. E. P. Seligman (Eds.), *Psychopathology: Experimental model* (pp. 1–27). San Francisco: Freeman.

Babkin, B. P. (1938). Experimental neuroses in animals and their treatment with bromides. *Edinburgh Medical Journal, 45*, 605–619.

Basoglu, M., & Mineka, S. (1992). The role of uncontrollable and unpredictable stress in post-traumatic stress responses in torture survivors. In M. Basoglu (Ed.), *Torture and its consequences: Current treatment approaches* (pp. 182–225). London: Cambridge University Press.

Bekesy, G. von (1960). *Experiments in hearing.* New York: McGraw-Hill.

Bell, D. S. (1965). Comparison of amphetamine psychosis and schizophrenia. *British Journal of Psychiatry, 111*, 701–707.

Blackman, D. E. (1983). On cognitive theories of animal learning: Extrapolations from humans to animals? In G. C. L. Davey (Ed.), *Animal models of human behaviour: Conceptual, evolutionary, and neurobiological perspectives* (pp. 37–50). Bristol, England: Wiley.

Bond, N. (1984). Animal models in psychopathology: An introduction. In N. Bond (Ed.), *Animal models of psychopathology* (pp. 1–21). Sydney, Australia: Academic Press.

Boulton, A. A., Baker, G. B., & Martin-Iverson, M. T. (Eds.). (1991). *Animal models in psychiatry.* Clifton, NJ: Humana Press.

Broadhurst, P. L. (1960). Abnormal animal behavior. In H. J. Eysenck (Ed.), *Handbook of abnormal psychology* (pp. 726–763). New York: Basic Books.

Brown, B. S., Weinckowski, L. A., & Stolz, S. B. (1975). *Behavior modification: Perspective on a current issue* (Publication No. ADM 75-202). Washington, DC: U.S. Department of Health Education and Welfare.

Byrne, J. H., & Berry, W. O. (Eds.). (1989). *Neural models of plasticity.* New York: Academic Press.

Cook, S. W. (1939). A survey of methods used to produce 'experimental neurosis.' *American Journal of Psychiatry, 95*, 1259–1276.

Costello, C. G. (1978). A critical review of Seligman's laboratory experiments on learned helplessness and depression in humans. *Journal of Abnormal Psychology, 87*, 21–31.

Cullen, J. H. (Ed.). (1974). *Experimental behavior.* Dublin, Ireland: Halsted Press.

Davey, G. (Ed.). (1981). *Applications of conditioning theory.* London: Methuen.

Dennett, D. C. (1991). *Consciousness explained.* New York: Little, Brown.

Dorworth, T., & Overmier, J. B. (1977). On learned helplessness: The therapeutic effects of electroconvulsive shocks. *Physiological Psychology, 5*, 355–358.

Eysenck, H. J. (1979). The conditioning model of neurosis (plus commentaries). *Behavioral & Brain Sciences, 2*, 155–199.

Feldman, M. P., & Broadhurst, A. (Eds.). (1976). *Theoretical and experimental bases of the behaviour therapies.* London: Wiley.

Foa, E., Zinbarg, R., & Rothbaum, B. (1992). Uncontrollability and unpredictability in post-traumatic stress disorder: An animal model. *Psychological Bulletin, 112*, 218–238.

Fox, M. W. (1971). Towards a comparative psychopathology. *Zeitschrift fur Tierpsychologie, 29*, 416–437.

Gantt, W. H. (1944). *Experimental basis of neurotic behavior.* New York: Hoebner.

Goldman-Rakic, P. S. (1987). Circuitry of primate prefrontal cortex and regulation of behavior by representational knowledge. In F. Plum (Ed.), *Handbook of physiology: The nervous system: Vol. V. Higher cortical function* (pp. 373–417). Bethesda, MD: American Physiological Society.

Green, S. (1983). Animal models for schizophrenia. In G. C. L. Davey (Ed.), *Animal models of human behaviour* (pp. 315–337). Chichester, England: Wiley.

Hanin, I., & Usdin, E. (Eds.). (1977). *An animal model in psychiatry & neurology.* Oxford, England: Pergamon Press.

Henn, F. A., & McKinney, W. T. (1987). Animal models in psychiatry. In H. Y. Meltzer (Ed.), *Psychopharmacology: The third generation of progress* (pp. 687–695). New York: Raven Press.

Hinde, R. A. (1976). The use of differences and similarities in comparative psychopathology. In G. Serban & A. Kling (Eds.), *Animal models in human psychobiology* (pp. 187–202). New York: Plenum.

Jones, M. C. (1924). The elimination of children's fears. *Journal of Experimental Psychology, 7*, 382–390.

Kandel, E. R. (1979). Cellular insights into behavior and learning. *Harvey Lectures, 73*, 19–92.

Kaufman, I. C. (1973). Mother–infant separation in monkeys—an experimental model. In J. P. Scott & E. Senay (Eds.), *Separation and depression*. Washington, DC: American Association for the Advancement of Science.

Katz, R. J. (1981). Animal models of human depressive disorders. *Neuroscience & Biobehavioral Reviews, 5*, 231–246.

Kesner, R. P., & Olton, D. S. (1990). *Neurobiology of comparative cognition*. Hillsdale, NJ: Erlbaum.

Klein, D. C., & Seligman, M. E. P. (1976). Reversal of performance deficits in learned helplessness and depression. *Journal of Abnormal Psychology, 85*, 11–26.

Koestler, A. (1967). *The ghost in the machine*. London: Hutchinson.

Kornetsky, C. (1977). Animal models: Promises and problems. In I. Hanin & E. Usdin (Eds.), *Animal models in psychiatry and neurology* (pp. 1–7). Oxford, England: Pergamon Press.

Krasner, L., & Ullman, L. (Eds.). (1965). *Research in behavior modification*. New York: Holt, Rinehart & Winston.

Krasnogorski, N. I. (1925). The conditioned reflexes and children's neuroses. *American Journal of Diseases of Children, 30*, 753–768.

Liddell, H. S. (1956). *Emotional hazards in animals and man*. Springfield, IL: Thomas.

Lister, R. G., & Weingartner, H. J. (1991). *Perspectives in cognitive neuroscience*. New York: Oxford University Press.

Mahoney, M. J., & Bandura, A. (1972). Self-reinforcement in pigeons. *Learning & Motivation, 3*, 293–303.

Maier, N. R. F. (1949). *Frustration: The study of behavior without a goal*. New York: McGraw-Hill.

Maser, J. D., & Seligman, M. E. P. (Eds.). (1977). *Psychopathology: Experimental models*. San Francisco: Freeman.

Masserman, J. H. (1943). *Behavior and neurosis*. Chicago: University of Chicago Press.

McKinney, W. T. (1974). Animal models in psychiatry. *Perspectives in Biology and Medicine, 17*, 529–541.

McKinney, W. T. (1988). *Models of mental disorders: A new comparative psychiatry*. New York: Plenum Press.

Mineka, S. (1985). Animal models of anxiety based disorders: Their usefulness and limitations. In A. H. Tuma & J. D. Maser (Eds.), *Anxiety and anxiety disorders* (pp. 199–244). Hillsdale, NJ: Erlbaum.

Mineka, S., & Zinbarg, R. (1991). Animal models of psychopathology. In C. E. Walker (Ed.), *Clinical psychology: Historical and research foundations* (pp. 51–86) New York: Plenum Press.

Mowrer, O. H. (1947). On the dual nature of learning—A reinterpretation of "conditioning" and "problem solving." *Harvard Educational Review, 17*, 102–148.

Overmier, J. B., & Patterson, J. (1988). Animal models of human psychopathology. In P. Simon, P. Soubrie, & D. Wildlocher (Eds.), *Selected models of anxiety, depression, and psychosis* (pp. 1–35). Basel, Switzerland: Karger.

Overstreet, D. H., & Russell, R. W. (1984). Animal models of memory disorders. In A. A. Boulton, G. B. Baker, & M. T. Martin-Iverson (Eds.), *Animal models in psychiatry: Neuromethods* (Vol. 19, pp. 315–368). Clifton, NJ: Humana Press.

Pitman, R. K. (1988). Post-traumatic stress disorder, conditioning and network theory. *Psychiatric Annals, 18*, 182–189.

Pitman, R. K. (1989). Post-traumatic stress disorder, hormones, and memory. *Biological Psychiatry, 26*, 221–223.

Richter, C. P. (1957). On the phenomenon of sudden death in animals and man. *Psychosomatic Research, 19*, 191–198.

Rollin, B. E., & Kesel, M. L. (Eds.). (1990). *The experimental animal in biomedical research: Vol I.* Boca Raton, FL: CRC Press.

Russell, R. W. (1964). Extrapolation from animals to man. In H. Steinberg (Ed.), *Animal behaviour and drug action* (pp. 410–418). London: Churchill.

Saporta, J. A., & VanderKolk, B. A. (1992). Psychobiological consequences of severe trauma. In M. Basoglu (Ed.), *Torture and its consequences: Current treatment approaches* (pp. 151–181). London: Cambridge University Press.

Schmajuk, N. A., & DiCarlo, J. J. (1992). Stimulus configuration, classical conditioning, and hippocampal function. *Psychological Review, 99,* 268–305.

Seligman, M. E. P. (1975). *Helplessness: On death, dying, and depression.* San Francisco: Freeman.

Shenger-Krestinova, N. R. (1921). Contributions to the question of differentiation of visual stimuli and the limits of differentiation by the visual analyser of the dog. *Bulletin of the Lesgaft Institute of Petrograd, 3,* 1–43.

Siegel, S. (1983). Classical conditioning, drug tolerance, and drug dependence. In Y. Israel, F. B. Glaser, H. Kalant, R. E. Popham, W. Schmidt, & R. G. Smart (Eds.), *Research advances in alcoholism and drug problems* (Vol. 7). New York: Plenum.

Skinner, B. F. (1972). What is psychotic behavior? In *Cumulative record: A selection of papers* (3rd ed.). New York: Appleton-Century-Crofts.

Solomon, R. L., & Corbit, J. D. (1974). An opponent process theory of motivation: I. The temporal dynamics of affect. *Psychological Review, 81,* 119–145.

Squire, L., & Zola-Morgan, S. (1985). The neuropsychology of memory: New links between humans and experimental animals. *Annals of the New York Academy of Sciences, 444,* 137–149.

Stampfl, T., & Levis, D. (1967). Essentials of implosive therapy: A learning theory based on psychodynamic behavioral therapy. *Journal of Abnormal Psychology, 28,* 496–503.

VonCranach, M. (1976). *Methods of inference from animal to human behaviour.* Chicago: Aldine.

Watson, J. B., & Raynor, R. (1920). Conditioned emotional reactions. *Journal of Experimental Psychology, 3,* 1–14.

Wagman, M. (1991). *Artificial intelligence and human cognition: A theoretical intercomparison of two realms of human intellect.* New York: Praeger.

Willner, P. (1984). The validity of animal models of depression. *Psychopharmacology, 83,* 1–16.

Willner, P. (1986). Validation criteria for animal models of human mental disorders: Learned helplessness as a paradigm case. *Progress in Neuro-Psychopharmacological & Biological Psychiatry, 10,* 677–690.

Willner, P. (1991). *Behavioural models in psychopharmacology.* London: Cambridge University Press.

Wolpe, J. (1952). Experimental neuroses as learned behavior. *British Journal of Psychology, 43,* 243–268.

Wolpe, J. (1958). *Psychotherapy by reciprocal inhibition.* Stanford, CA: Stanford University Press.

Zubin, J., & Hunt, H. F. (1967). *Comparative psychopathology: Animal and human.* New York: Grune & Stratton.

3

Justifying the Research Agenda

Lewis Petrinovich

Discussions regarding the permissibility of research using animals are often clouded by a number of terminological, philosophical, and substantive confusions that make it difficult to reach any clear conclusions, let alone agreements. One terminological confusion involves what the term *research* refers to. A second confusion involves what organisms are covered by the term *animal* and what qualities differentiate those organisms that are to be given special consideration as animals from those that are not.

Three basic ideas in moral philosophy that have implications regarding ethical decisions are discussed. These ideas concern the nature of rights, utilitarianism, and social contractarianism. This discussion is followed by a brief consideration of how evolutionary principles can focus issues to provide a biological grounding for morality. Issues in the philosophy of science are discussed: What is the relationship between theory and data, how is scientific change produced, and how can the merits of research be evaluated before it is conducted? A decision model is presented that can focus discussions regarding the permissibility of research studies. Finally, I consider specific objections to research using animals. I have considered many of these issues at length in three recent books (Petrinovich, 1995, 1996, 1999), and detailed arguments as well as basic references can be found in those three books.

Defining Research

The term *research* refers to a myriad of activities that belong in distinct categories that often are intermingled. One category is the study of basic theoretical principles in evolution and biology, with others being applied biomedical research, techniques used to develop drugs, and procedures used to test toxicity of new compounds.

For example, studies of the locus of receptor sites for various compounds in the nervous system and the way actions of these compounds are translated to produce physiological effects are at the basic theoretical level. When events at this level are understood, it is possible to identify sites in the cell where certain classes of drugs act and to understand how neurotransmitters function, which makes it possible to apply theory to develop agents that have specific effects on targeted physiological systems.

Studies of processes involved in cellular proliferation and the identification of the genetic mechanisms that regulate them have astounding implications for biomedical science. Much basic genetic research is done with fruit flies, mice, and rats, and the results have been generalized to understand the processes leading to the development of human breast and ovarian cancer (see Petrinovich, 1995, 1999). The results of genetic studies of cancer testify to the power of basic research that capitalizes on known genetic similarities in gene functioning in species ranging from fruit flies to mice, rhesus monkeys, and humans. Basic biomedical research has been highly successful and is leading to the successful treatment of many physiological defects.

Although most appreciate the value of potential applications of biomedical research, there have been strong objections to research done with no thought of immediate payoff but intended only to develop points important to theory. The charge is made that animals suffer to indulge the curiosity of scientists, whose main interest is to further their prestige, promote professional careers, or enhance their economic well-being (Fox, 1990; Ryder, 1989; Singer, 1990). Such objections can be countered by considering issues in the philosophy of science that relate to scientific change—a point that is discussed below.

A separate category of research is biomedical research done with a direct interest in application. Extensive medical advances have depended on animal research and otherwise would have been unlikely to occur. These advances include research on aging, including Alzheimer's disease; AIDS; anesthesia; familial studies of genetic transmission of disease; development of neurological procedures to treat behavior disorders; diseases and defects of the cardiovascular system; childhood diseases; convulsive disorders; diabetes; organ transplantation; Parkinson's disease; problems in reproductive biology; and the treatment of spinal cored injuries. This list could run to several pages. Animal research has contributed to the alleviation of human and animal suffering. Although many animal rights activists have expressed doubt regarding the value of animal research—and some (e.g., Francione, 1995) have suggested there is strong evidence that animal experimentation has retarded medical progress—it is doubtful that even the most radical champions of animal welfare would abandon what has been learned from research using animals, especially if it could benefit their children and kin.

Many animals have been used to extract products and to develop drugs for biomedical research and therapy; to produce a wide range of antisera, vaccines, and antibodies used for research, diagnosis, and therapy. Rowan (1984) has estimated that between 1% and 5% of all laboratory animals are used each year to diagnose diseases such as tuberculosis, diphtheria, and brucellosis and to diagnose pregnancy. It has been estimated that vaccination against six common diseases prevents the deaths of 3.2 million children worldwide each year (Russell & Nicoll, 1996). In my view, statements made by animal liberation advocates regarding the negligible value of research reflect an inability to understand biomedical science, a deliberate distortion of findings, and politically motivated misstatements regarding data, as well as a view that changing environmental conditions and influencing the values of the community and social policy makers would be more effective. Many of these tactics are unfortunate because they tend to harden lines of dispute, to fuel suspicions both of researchers and of their opponents, and to lead to political power moves that progress on the weight of "might makes right."

The pharmaceutical industry has used laboratory animals to test the toxicity of drugs, pesticides, cosmetics, and toiletries. It was estimated that in 1990, 3.2 million animals were used to test pharmaceuticals in the European community (MacKenzie, 1992) but very few to test products other than pharmaceuticals (such as cosmetic ingredients). In the Netherlands in 1987, 42% of all experiments qualified as fundamental research (40% in the United States), 47% was for vaccine and drug production and testing (26% in the United States), 6% was for toxicity testing (20% in the United States), 4% was for education and training (7% in the United States), and 1% was for other purposes (7% in the United States; Orlans, 1993). Opponents of animal research often unfairly cite the excesses that have occurred in toxicological testing to typify and indict all physiological and biomedical research.

Many of the most objectionable toxicological procedures, such as the Draize eye test to determine the toxicity of a substance by applying it to the eyes of rabbits, have been replaced almost completely by alternative testing methods using tissue preparations, bacterial materials, basic chemical reactions, or computer simulations. The scientific community agrees that testing should adhere to the ideals of what is referred to as the 3 Rs: replacement of the use of animals whenever possible, refinement of procedures to diminish the amount and degree of pain, suffering, and stress experienced by animals, and reduction of the number of animals tested (see Smith & Boyd, 1991).

There is general confusion regarding the degree to which one can rely on the exclusive use of in vitro procedures that do not involve the use of intact animals or use only tissues or cells. Many antivivisectionists tend to overstate the current availability of replacement alternatives, whereas scientists tend to overemphasize their limitations (Smith & Boyd, 1991). Although results based on in vitro procedures cannot be generalized uncritically to in vivo ones—whether at the level of basic biophysical and biochemical events or at levels involving total organismic functioning—it is possible to test theoretical models that certain variables are important using in vitro preparations before proceeding to test intact animals.

In my view, animal liberation activists have misrepresented the realities involved in basic research by conflating all categories of studies using animals, which tars the entire research enterprise by the presentation of emotional discussions of procedures used by industry to test such things as cosmetics. There are ethical concerns regarding many procedures that have been used, in product development and testing, such as the Draize test and the LD-50 test (the dosage that kills 50% of the animals). Research and commercial communities shirked their responsibilities, and many bad practices were tolerated for much too long. Significant advances have been made to develop adequate alternatives, and the amount of testing has been reduced. Ethical questions are also addressed regarding whether the benefits of developing certain products are enough to justify the costs to animals.

Defining Animals

Although there have been strong objections to using cats, dogs, nonhuman primates, and horses, few research procedures involve these animals. It has been estimated variously that 200–225 million (Rollin, 1992) or 50–150 million (Ryder, 1989) animals are used for research annually throughout the world. The United States accounts for about 100 million of these: 50 million mice, 20 million rats, and 30 million others, which includes 200,000 cats and 450,000 dogs (Rollin, 1992). The U.S. Department of Agriculture reported a sharp reduction in the use of dogs and cats in 1994: Only 32,610 cats and 101,090 dogs were used in research, which probably is a more accurate current estimate, being based on required institutional reports ("USDA Report," 1995). In the United Kingdom in 1989, 84% of animals in all research procedures were rodents (of these 53% were mice and 27% rats), birds accounted for 8%, reptiles and amphibians 0.3%, and mammals other than rodents 5% (Smith & Boyd, 1991). These other mammals included rabbits 65% of the time, with sheep, dogs, pigs, cattle, nonhuman primates, cats, ferrets, horses, donkeys, and mules used less than 2% of the time.

Over 100 million cows, pigs, and sheep and 5 billion poultry are raised and slaughtered each year in the United States, indicating that by far the greatest harm to animals occurs in the agricultural area, which is almost completely unregulated. Such figures make it difficult to accept the claim made by Rollin (1992) that the greatest potential for the diminution of animal suffering is in the realm of animal experimentation. I suspect this hyperbole is in the interest of pressing the case against animal experimentation to make it more dramatic and also reflects a belief that it is unlikely animals will cease to be consumed as food.

Considerable inconsistency exists regarding what should be included within the category of *animal*. This is an especially important problem for the animal rights advocates, because they depend on the basic assumption that animals have stipulated rights. The leading animal rights advocate, Tom Regan (1983), has suggested that *animal* means "mammal" (p. 173) or "terrestrial mammals" (p. 240), later including all mammals less than 1 year of age who have developed the characteristics that qualify them as being a subject, of a life—a status that entails more than being alive and conscious (p. 391). This status requires that animals must have beliefs and desires, perception, memory, a sense of the future, preferences, welfare interests, and a psychophysical identity over time (p. 243). Elsewhere, he relaxed the definition of *animal* to include chickens and turkeys, which do not satisfy the subject-of-a-life criterion (p. 349), and finally concluded that it is difficult to draw the line. In a chapter published 6 years later,

Regan (1989) still found it difficult to decide where one should draw the line between those who are and who are not subjects of a life. Because Regan's theory hinges on his idea that all animals meeting the criteria for a subject of a life have an inherent value that must be respected equally, whenever there is any at all, it is critical to decide what organisms are included to make any sense of his ideas.

The influential animal liberationist, Peter Singer (1975), has fewer problems in this regard because he has proposed clear functional criteria that any individual organism must meet to have moral equality. These criteria include the capacities to feel pain and to suffer. He has stipulated that all animals (human and nonhuman) have an equal capacity to suffer, and as such, they all have an equivalent moral standing. I speak to the philosophical positions of Regan and Singer below.

It is difficult to understand how animal advocates assign relative moral standing and value. Most of the statements made in opposition to research have little relevance because the animals they most often discuss—nonhuman primates and common pets such as cats and dogs—are used relatively little and increasingly less and less.

Rights

The idea that organisms have rights that should be respected by everyone has considerable intuitive appeal. A large number of positive and negative rights have been assigned by different people, ranging from those involving primary aspects of existence to ones that reflect secondary interests. Lomasky (1987) has classified rights into three basic types: legal, which are defined by a body of law and institutional regulations; moral, which assume different forms given the norms of specific cultures; and natural, which are independent of any particular social structure but presuppose that there is some sociality. The major problem with rights language is to determine the priority and relative importance of different rights. Rights tend to be stipulated primitives, and different individuals often stipulate contradictory basic principles. The concept of rights should be restricted to the realm of laws and institutional regulations, and moral rights should be grounded on natural biological principles embedded in the evolutionary fabric.

Animals have rights in Regan's (1983) view, and these rights confer a moral standing making it impermissible to use nonhuman animals in any way that infringes rights. Animals possess awareness to the extent they can experience pleasure, feel pain, and suffer. Few in the scientific community would quarrel with this view, and many would agree that individual animals have inherent value. Even fewer would agree, however, with the argument that all animals (human and nonhuman) that have any inherent value have equal value. Regan has emphasized an important distinction regarding moral *agents* (those who meet all of the subject-of-a-life criteria, constitute the moral community, and have direct duties toward all individuals in that community) and moral *patients* (those who lack the prerequisites that allow them to be held morally accountable for what they do in terms of right and wrong). It has been argued that no one who cannot understand and claim it can have a right (Midgley, 1983), and I agree with this position, although I disagree that rights language is useful in other than a legal sense.

Formal justice requires equality for all individuals because all have equal inherent value, according to Regan (1983). The stipulated basis to have rights is the individual's inherent value; it should not be considered as only a receptacle of different amounts of inherent value. Inherent value is an absolute characteristic that either exists or not. If all animals have equal inherent value, it is not permissible to conduct research if it compromises the animal's rights. This has led Regan to an abolitionist position regarding the permissibility of animal research.

Regan (1983) rejects utilitarianism because it permits an inadmissible aggregation of value, not respecting the equal inherent value of all with moral standing. He develops principles to use when making decisions but uses a category he calls "special considerations" (p. 322) to avoid counterintuitive conclusions. This category includes obligations that are incurred through voluntary agreements regarding the duties and responsibilities involved in a social contract, a decreased responsibility toward those who voluntarily engage in hazardous endeavors, instances when a historical background has placed individuals in their present predicament because their basic rights were violated in the past, and moral bonds between friends and family members.

These special considerations cause a sense of uneasiness because there is no consistency regarding when a basic moral right can be overruled by the invocation of an ad hoc special consideration. These special considerations, and the manner in which they are invoked, at times sneak in utilitarian calculations (by whatever name), to favor kin and friends when difficult decisions are to be made, and to avoid conclusions that violate deep moral intuitions. I suggest it is more satisfactory to accept evolutionary factors as basic (rather than special) considerations to develop a more consistent and rational basis for moral theory.

Utilitarianism

A basic aspect of classical utilitarianism is to attain pleasure and to avoid pain, making it necessary to establish the levels of costs and benefits aggregated across individuals. Aggregation could lead to undesirable levels of inequality between individuals, however. A major problem for utilitarianism is to determine the relative goodness of outcomes for any individual and to determine the relative goodness of the same outcome for different individuals.

Singer (1975, 1990) favors a preference utilitarianism emphasizing the importance of considering hopes, plans, and future goals to determine the value of a life. These preferences are to be considered without considering an organism's species membership. The basic criterion for moral standing is sentience: All sentient individuals are entitled to equal consideration. Singer maintains that all animals have an equal capacity to suffer and that this equal capacity establishes an equivalent moral standing, with the wrongness of killing animals framed in terms of a preference to continue living rather than dying.

Singer (1975) has popularized the concept of *speciesism*, which exists whenever the interests of one's own species are allowed to override the greater interests of members of other species. He has asserted that speciesism is identical in pattern to the evils inherent in racism and sexism. In his view, the interests of animals ought to be given equal consideration with like interests of humans. Singer is a reformer rather than an abolitionist regarding the permissibility of conducting animal research. If the benefit is great enough for an individual animal or human, then he believes it is permissible to inflict a lesser harm on another.

Social Contractarianism

The idea of a social contract can be extended to the behaviors of all individuals who constitute a community, and these contracts can be grounded in evolved tendencies that promote ultimate reproductive success. The conception of a social contract can be couched in evolutionary terms: Certain proximate behaviors have evolved because they increase the likelihood of successful mating, reproduction, and nurturance of young; they enable individuals to reach a reproductive stage to continue the process of propagating genes. These behavioral tendencies can be characterized in terms of cooperation, communication, mutualism, and reciprocation: the behaviors that bind a society together.

Rawls's (1971) influential theory of justice falls within the social contract tradition because it emphasizes the importance of doing one's part whenever one accepts goods provided by social institutions (Feinberg, 1989). Rawls invoked a difference principle when considering the distribution of surplus resources: The position of the better-off is to be improved only if it is necessary to improve the position of the worse-off. Decisions cannot permit lesser life prospects for some in order that there be a greater sum of advantages for the aggregate. This argument avoids many of the undesirable inequalities of an unqualified aggregation of utilitarian value.

There is a principle of reciprocity that has been instilled in people to detect cheaters, which has been found in very human culture for which the appropriate information is available. Behaviors that support reciprocity have evolved to allow humans to survive, reproduce, and flourish and to satisfy some of the requirements for a just society. This account of justice establishes a link between a rational acceptance of emotional bonds that have been forged to enhance social cooperation, and at the ultimate evolutionary level, their use promotes the individual realization of utilitarian goals.

The Evolutionary Argument

Rights views are suspect for four reasons: (a) It is not clear what it is that grounds rights and makes one right take precedence over another, beyond a reliance on stipulation; (b) only those who are able to understand the concept of rights can be held to the duties and responsibilities of rights holders, making it impossible to ascribe rights to moral patients; (c) there is no compelling reason to accept the proposition that because organisms have some rights, all have equal rights; and (d) in marginal cases involving impaired or immature humans, special considerations must be invoked to avoid unsatisfactory outcomes.

The animal liberation position, with its emphasis on a preference utilitarianism based on interests, is more acceptable, but the concept of speciesism is not analogous to the morally impermissible sexism and racism. The species is a basic biological concept because it focuses attention on the actions of interbreeding individuals that share characteristics that permit them to adapt to the demands of the environment. Environmental demands shape species characteristics that can be quite different from those possessed by other species. Animals of all species show a clear preference for their own kind: They prefer to associate and mate with their own species; they fight alongside their own kind against members of a foreign species to secure resources; and they defend the young of their species. There is, however, pronounced intraspecies warfare and killing that is peculiar to chimpanzees and humans (Wrangham & Peterson, 1996).

Racism is on a different basis: It is not necessary to know a person's race to know how one should treat that person (beyond respecting certain social customs), but it is essential to know the species of an animal to know how to treat it to permit it to survive (should we make arrangements for it to swim, fly, burrow, or climb?). Race is not one of the characteristics that meaningfully dictate basic needs or determine the quality of treatment due an organism. Sexism is also quite different from speciesism: Although there are many differences between men and women, the distribution of physiological and mental characteristics for the two sexes reveals a high degree of overlap (except for matters most directly related to reproduction).

There is great overlap between different groupings of humans in just about any physical and behavioral characteristic, whereas the differences between humans and animals admit to very little overlap, except certainly in reproductive matters and cognitive abilities. The charge that speciesism is akin to racism and sexism is not warranted. The species concept is a basic biological entity that involves meaningful differences that determine how an individual is to be treated.

Moral agency confers full moral standing, and that standing depends on a cognitive test; a moral agent must understand that some actions can be either right or wrong, understand causation, have a theory of mind at a level sufficient to understand the cognitive states of others, and be able to realize there are duties toward persons who are not moral agents, as well as responsibilities due to all nonhuman moral patients.

A stage of personhood that stands intermediate between that of a moral agent and that of a moral patient occurs at birth—an event that is of major emotional, cognitive, and social importance, which signals the start of the public life of the offspring (Petrinovich, 1995). At birth, the human neonate is responded to as a member of the human community. She or he begins to develop behavioral characteristics, such as language and emotional attachments, that are appropriate in the community within which she or he will live. From an evolutionary standpoint, the development of a social community based on kinship is the primary event that is the biological underpinning of all species. Biological mechanisms have been structured to promote the cooperation and communication required to further the reproductive interests of individuals. It intuitively is natural for humans to favor members of their own species, kin, and community when moral decisions are to be made. Singer (1981) has agreed that the core of ethics has a biological basis common to humans everywhere and that this core is based on the emotional bonding between a neonate and members of the community, especially the mother (Petrinovich, 1995, 1999). Kinship obligations are strong aspects of evolved human nature, and to violate these obligations is considered to be unnatural. It is understandable that we favor the interests of our species over the welfare of animals of other species, just as we favor the welfare of our kin and members of our community and develop norms of reciprocity with others.

The Pursuit of Science

The concept of scientific progress should be considered when deciding whether basic research using animals is permissible: How can it be decided that something is worth knowing and that knowing it would be a sufficient advance in knowledge to warrant research? What are the limits of the generalizability of research findings, and can results found with one species be generalized to understand another?

Some opposed to animal research have attacked the scientific enterprise in general and have raised specific concerns regarding the permissibility of using animals. Science should not be viewed as presenting truth in some abstract sense, nor should it be viewed as an epistemologically superior form of knowledge, according to Francione (1995). Because there are subjective influences in science, the entire enterprise is flawed and not trustworthy. He has noted that facts cannot be formulated in the absence of theory—or, as Popper (1979) has stated it, there is a great deal of planning and preparation involved in observing; to ask someone to observe is absurd. Observation always involves selecting an object, a definite task, an interest, a point of view, and a problem. In this trivial sense, all facts are tainted with subjectivist bias, but for this reason elaborate procedural safeguards are used to ensure against bias, observations are made using more than one method, and tests of hypotheses are framed in terms of plausible competitive alternatives.

A theory is a network of basic and auxiliary hypotheses, and it is unlikely that any single observation is going to reject a theory. Matters should not be construed in terms of true or false; it should not be concluded that because something is not totally objective it is totally subjective. There is a property called *verisimilitude*: As investigations proceed, theories and hypotheses will be developed that have a greater truth-likeness, and as Darwin (1871) reminded, with failure at least one path toward error is closed, and the road to truth is often opened at the same time.

Singer (1990) and Rollin (1989, 1992) have often complained that scientists are too involved in pursuing their narrow interests and selfish goals. In the interest of objectivity, reliance should be placed on the disinterested observations of neutral observers who have no vested interests. It would be the height of folly to entrust the progress of science to observers not trained in the techniques and procedures required to make certain kinds of observations, who are not informed regarding the niceties of experimental design and statistical analysis. Objectivity should not be equated with ignorance.

It is not possible to decide that a novel research direction is a profitable one until a step has been taken. It has been asserted that to justify causing pain to animals, an investigator must prove that the research is necessary and is moving toward a worthwhile goal. When new phenomena are being studied, however, it is never possible to make such a guarantee in advance. Scientific progress occurs when one can explain more things better using fewer basic assumptions. A new approach might not be profitable, or it could be the breakthrough of the century—it is not possible to decide until one looks.

Bateson's Decision Model

A conceptual scheme to drive the process of evaluating research projects was developed by Bateson (1992). Pain, distress, and anxiety generated by scientific research on animals were the issues that most exercise the public, and he proposed a "decision cube" (p. 33) to conceptualize the factors to decide whether a research project should be conducted. On one dimension of the cube was the degree of animal suffering, scaled from low to high. A second dimension was the quality of the research, also scaled from low to high, and on the third was the likelihood of benefit, scaled from low to high. Although Bateson framed this third dimension in terms of medical benefit, Emlen (1993) suggested it would be better to characterize it in terms of scientific value, that is, the conceptual importance of the question being asked and the likelihood that the results could be generalized to other species. He considered this latter point especially important, because fewer experiments would have to be done using different species if the studies were designed with a focus on the question of generalizability.

Bateson (1992) proposed that high levels of animal suffering should be tolerated only when both research quality and probability of benefit were high and suggested that very high levels of animal suffering might well be unacceptable, regardless of the high quality of the research and the high probability of benefit.

Any high-quality research would be permissible that involved little or no animal suffering, even if the research had no potential benefit and was intended only to enable scientists to understand phenomena. Bateson (1992) emphasized that the decision cube was not an exercise in crass utilitarianism because the relative costs and benefits did not depend on a common currency or a balancing of incommensurable properties. Rather, it provided a set of rules to decide whether research should proceed. The boundaries for making a positive or negative decision would not be static. The aim was to encourage research that had maximum benefit and minimal cost, and fair-minded people, even though they had started from completely different moral positions, could find ways to reach agreement.

I endorse his belief that fair-minded people could use rational methods to reach agreements to enhance the likelihood of attaining benefits while minimizing costs, even though those with different moral positions might not be completely satisfied. The value of the proposed exercise is to highlight problems to be faced. Although those with different moral positions have strong disagreements over what constitutes high and low degrees of suffering by animals, a dialogue can be joined that could reduce costs without diminishing benefits, even though there is a level of disagreement regarding basics. The UK Working Party (Smith & Boyd 1991), of which Bateson was a member, have identified factors that could be involved to conceptualize degree of suffering and level of benefit. They have applied the scheme to seven case studies, an analysis of which supports the merit of the approach. Using this explicit model makes it possible for those with different conceptual and technical abilities to contribute to limited aspects of the evaluation, allowing all to contribute something of value to the final decision process.

Specific Criticisms and Responses

In the remaining pages, I briefly list and discuss a few specific objections to research using animals.

1. Animal liberationists have been especially critical of psychological research on animals. Many of their indictments of bad experimentation consist of lists of "stupid and useless" psychological experiments (see Rollin, 1992, chap. 3; Singer, 1990, chap. 2), accompanied by descriptions of procedures they consider offensive. Although some are extreme, it is the importance of the theoretical issues addressed that is critical, not those procedures used to manipulate variables. Coile and Miller (1984) surveyed every article (608) appearing between 1979 through 1983 in the four American Psychological Association journals that report animal research. It

had been charged that the tools of the experimental psychologist were mutilation, castration, agony, starvation, and insanity, but not one article surveyed used such procedures. Singer (1990) claimed that one of the most common ways of experimenting in the field of psychology was to apply shock to animals, a position seconded by Rowan (1984). Coile and Miller found that only 10% of the studies used shock. It is misleading to imply that such procedures typify experimental psychology. Miller (1985) listed benefits to humans that resulted from psychological research with animals—including treatment of urinary and fecal incontinence, behavior therapy to treat eating disorders, rehabilitation of neuromuscular disorders, relief of stress and pain, testing of drugs, understanding deficits of memory that occur with aging, and the development of biofeedback procedures to treat a host of behavioral disorders. Other benefits include rehabilitation from the effects of stroke, head injury, spinal cord injury, and Alzheimer's disease; improved communication with severely retarded children; early detection of eye disorders in children; and treatment for alcoholism, obesity, substance abuse, hypertension, chronic migraine headaches, lower back pain, and insomnia (Baldwin, 1993). Even this cursory list gives the lie to charges that psychological research is stupid and useless activity by sadistic experimenters.

2. Feeney (1987) enhanced the rate and extent of recovery from hemiplegia in rats, and research suggests that it might be possible to heal extensive spinal cord damage (Cheng, Cao, & Olson, 1996). Although these experiments caused extreme harm and suffering to animals (rats and mice), these costs should be balanced against the benefits that would be realized by paraplegics and those suffering severe spinal cord damage, who now have no hope of recovery. Personally, I have no difficulty justifying such research.

3. A large number of studies of genes involved in cancer testify to the power of research that capitalizes on genetic similarities across species (e.g., Holt et al., 1996; Johnson et al., 1996). These studies are based on an understanding of mechanisms of cell proliferation and of the consequences when basic control mechanisms fail, allowing cells to proliferate. It should be possible not only to predict the likelihood of many forms of cancer and to detect their presence but also to develop treatments to stop runaway cell proliferation.

4. The fetal malformations that were produced when the drug thalidomide was taken by pregnant women have been widely cited as a failure of the animal drug-testing program. The attack is based on the claim that the drug had been extensively tested in pregnant dogs, cats, rats, monkeys, hamsters, and chickens, and no deformities were produced (e.g., Singer, 1990). However, the drug had not been tested in pregnant animals; such testing began only when human defects were reported, which led to regulations being es-

tablished to require more thorough animal tests whenever a drug
was to be used by pregnant women (Rowan, 1984).

5. Antivivisectionists have claimed the only cause of polio is the oral
    polio vaccine. Presently, the incidence of polio due to the vaccine
    is 1 in 1 million doses, hardly a major factor (Hilleman, 1995). The
    effectiveness of the vaccination program is attested to by the fact
    that before introduction of the vaccines (1950–1954), the average
    incidence of reported polio in the United States was 24.8 per
    100,000 population; after the introduction of the vaccines (1964),
    it was 0.1 per 100,000 (Koch & Koch, 1985).

    Monkeys were abused during transport from the field to lab-
    oratories during the race to be first to develop an effective vaccine.
    It has been estimated that over a million monkeys died during
    transport, but this waste was overlooked at the time and excused
    by a sense of public urgency. It is agreed that these unethical prac-
    tices should not have been permitted, and now there are safe-
    guards to prevent a recurrence. It is wise to examine the record
    and exploit the lessons provided by it, if the aim is to benefit an-
    imals rather than to distort it for ideological purposes.

All of these cases support the conclusion that arguments should concern questions of how to minimize costs to animals and determine whether
even minimal costs justify benefits to humans and other animals. Some
probably would not be moved by appeals to eliminate crippling diseases
such as childhood polio. For example, Fox (1990) questioned the use of
animals to develop chemotherapy on the grounds that it only averts a few
thousand of the 400,000 deaths from cancer that occur in the United
States each year. Others believe such research efforts should continue because although 90% of people diagnosed with cancer in 1913 died, in 1960,
the figure was 70%; in 1970, it was 60%; and in 1990, it was only 50%
(Russell & Nicoll, 1996).

Conclusion

Research scientists should neither take the paternalistic high road as the
sole arbiters of research excellence nor concede the moral high ground to
philosophers. Scientists have special technical competencies required to
understand and perform experiments and are able to design experiments
that control unwanted variables and to evaluate the likelihood of alternative explanations. Many scientists, however, do not understand the in-
tricacies of experimental design and statistical analysis at a sufficient
depth for them to design more powerful experiments using fewer animals,
and the inadequacies in training that produces this lack of statistical competence should be corrected.

Issues in moral philosophy are complex and contain many hidden
snares for the unwary. Philosophers are superb at developing, probing, and
arguing complex issues—that is their primary business. A recent upsurge

in the field of bioethics is bringing ethical principles to bear on issues that are of concern to society. Scientists should pay close attention to discussions among applied ethicists and philosophers of science, to better appreciate the implicit assumptions on which research is based.

Many philosophers and scientists share the general public's concerns that the welfare of animals should be respected; active discussions and a refinement of regulations to maintain animals should continue. Decisions should be made regarding the relative value of different kinds of animals, and the relative costs and benefits of proposed research should be evaluated. These costs and benefits not only should be viewed at the level of economics and their pragmatic value but also must allow for the value of achieving better understanding along with an appreciation that practical benefits often occur with a deeper understanding.

The establishment of regulations regarding animal care and the formation of institutional animal care and use committees have been positive outcomes of dialogues between animal welfare advocates and the scientific community. Many rules and regulations are odious and bothersome to scientists who were accustomed to having complete freedom and control regarding such matters. I believe that the sciences have profited from careful considerations and justifications that now are required to perform procedures that harm sentient animals. The research world is a better place as a result, and however one measures it, the utilitarian benefits of scientific research have been enhanced by this deeper concern for the welfare of research animals.

References

Baldwin, E. (1993). The case for animal research in psychology. *Journal of Social Issues, 49,* 121–131.

Bateson, P. (1992). Do animals feel pain? *New Scientist, 134*(1818), 30–33.

Cheng, H., Cao, Y., & Olson, L. (1996). Spinal cord repair in adult paraplegic rats: Partial restoration of hind limb function. *Science, 273,* 510–513.

Coile, D. C., & Miller N. E. (1984). How radical animal activists try to mislead humane people. *American Psychologist, 39,* 700–701.

Darwin, C. (1871). *The descent of man.* New York: D. Appleton.

Emlen, S. T. (1993). Ethics and experimentation: Hard choices for the field ornithologist. *Auk, 110,* 406–409.

Feeney, D. M. (1987). Human rights and animal welfare. *American Psychologist, 42,* 593–599.

Feinberg, J. (1989). Rawls and intuitionism. In N. Daniels (Ed.), *On reading Rawls* (pp. 108–123). Stanford, CA: Stanford University Press.

Fox, M. W. (1990). *Inhumane society.* New York: St. Martin's Press.

Francione, G. L. (1995). *Animals, property, and the law.* Philadelphia: Temple University Press.

Hilleman, M. R. (1995). Viral vaccines in historical perspective. *Developments in Biological Standardization, 84,* 107–116.

Holt, J. T., Thompson, M. E., Szabo, C., Robinson, B. C., Arteaga, C. L., King, M. C., & Jensen, R. A. (1996). Growth retardation and tumour inhibition by BRCAI. *Nature Genetics, 12,* 298–302.

Johnson, R. L., Rothman, A. L., Xie, J., Goodrich, L. V., Bare, J. W., Bonifas, J. M., Quinn, A. G., Myers, R. M., Cox, D. R., Epstein, E. H., Jr., & Scott, M. P. (1996, June 14). Human homolog of *patched*, a candidate gene for the basal cell nerves syndrome. *Science, 272,* 1668–1671.

Koch, F., & Koch, G. (1985). *The molecular biology of poliovirus.* Vienna, Austria: Springer-Verlag.

Lomasky, L. E. (1987). *Persons, rights, and the moral community.* New York: Oxford University Press.

MacKenzie, D. (1992). The laboratory rat's guide to Europe. *New Scientist, 134*(1821), 29–31.

Midgley, M. (1983). *Animals and why they matter.* Athens: University of Georgia Press.

Miller, N. E. (1985). The value of behavioral research on animals. *American Psychologist, 40,* 423–440.

Orlans, F. B. (1993). *In the name of science.* New York: Oxford University Press.

Petrinovich, L. (1995). *Human evolution, reproduction, and morality.* New York: Plenum.

Petrinovich, L. (1996). *Living and dying well.* New York: Plenum.

Petrinovich, L. (1999). *Darwinian dominion: Animal welfare and human interests.* Cambridge, MA: MIT Press.

Popper, K. R. (1979). *Objective knowledge* (Rev. ed.). Oxford, England: Oxford University Press.

Rawls, J. (1971). *A theory of justice.* Cambridge, MA: Harvard University Press.

Regan, T. (1983). *The case for animal rights.* Berkeley: University of California Press.

Regan, T. (1989). Ill-gotten gains. In G. Langley (Ed.), *Animal experimentation* (pp. 19–41). New York: Chapman & Hall.

Rollin, B. E. (1989). *The unheeded cry.* Oxford, England: Oxford University Press.

Rollin, B. E. (1992). *Animal rights and human morality.* Buffalo, NY: Prometheus Books.

Rowan, A. N. (1984). *Of mice, models, and men.* Albany: State University of New York Press.

Russell, S. M., & Nicoll, C. S. (1996). A dissection of the chapter "Tools for research" in Peter Singer's *Animal liberation. Proceedings of the Society for Experimental Biology and Medicine, 211,* 109–138.

Ryder, R. D. (1989). *Animal revolution.* Oxford, England: Basil Blackwell.

Singer, P. (1975). *Animal liberation.* New York: Avon Books–Discus Printing.

Singer, P. (1981). *The expanding circle.* New York: Farrar, Straus & Giroux.

Singer, P. (1990). *Animal liberation* (Rev. ed.). New York: Avon Books.

Smith, J. A., & Boyd, K. M. (1991). *Lives in the balance.* Oxford, England: Oxford University Press.

USDA report shows further decline in lab animal numbers. (1999, April). *Foundation for Biomedical News, 12,* 2.

Wrangham, R., & Peterson, D. (1996). *Demonic males.* New York: Houghton Mifflin.

4

On the Affective Nature of Human Nature: A Neurobiologist's Reflections

Pierre Karli

A neurobiologist who studies brain–behavior relationships and strives to reach a deeper understanding of their actual mode(s) of functioning is almost necessarily led to think about the semantic content of the notion of *human nature*. Insofar as scientists hope that the experimental analysis carried out on some animal species will help to specify the biological determinants of their own personality and behavior, they cannot (should not!) be unaware of the reciprocal relationships between the actual scientific endeavor and some personal convictions. As a matter of fact, the vision scientists have of themselves, of their supposed nature, is bound to somehow orient—unconsciously or more deliberately—the way in which they construct the conceptual framework within which they elaborate their working hypotheses and interpret the results obtained when verifying them. Conversely, the data scientists obtain, the way in which they interpret them, and the generalized conception of brain–behavior relationships they infer from them inevitably contribute to the shaping of their vision of mankind, their nature, their being, and their evolution.

Each scientist has a strong propensity to overvalue the significance of that which she or he intensively searches for and thinks about. Thus, the biologist quite spontaneously refers to the fact that the human being is a living system like any other, and there easily arises the tendency to reduce the human being to its sole biological identity and functioning. When yielding to this tendency, one mutilates the human being by stripping its very nature of some of its major dimensions. On the other hand, it is just as misleading to consider merely the fact that the human being differs in many respects from any other living system and to assert that the notion of human nature refers only to those features thought to be specifically human, such as self-consciousness and free will. One thereby ignores the fact that the potentialities for self-consciousness and free will have emerged, in both the phylogenic and the ontogenetic evolution, from a twofold (biological and cultural) history and that their concrete exercise remains embedded in—and dependent on—a number of biological and social determinations (cf. Karli, 1995).

Even though it may be intellectually uncomfortable, we must endeavor to apprehend the human being as a highly complex, dynamic, and evolving whole. Because the human reality is a greatly heterogeneous one, any single model of man constructed through monodisciplinary investigation and conceptualization is bound to be partial and easily biased. It is important, therefore, to consider that there coexist distinct facets within a living system that acts and evolves as a whole. This obviously requires that studies be carried out on distinct levels of analysis and explanation. These facets, with their respective individuality and identity not only closely interact with each other but also further exert a shaping influence on each other. This means that an analysis of their distinctive characteristics and modes of functioning can be truly meaningful only if we then piece the uncovered features and mechanisms together by specifying those processes through which they get integrated into a coherent whole.

In the multifaceted dialogue that any human being carries on with her or his environments, the brain acts as a common "mediating agency." Within each of the three facets that are distinguished here, the goal strived for is basically the same—namely, to experience pleasant and to avoid unpleasant affective states and emotions. Because affective processes have such an important mobilizing and integrating function throughout the human reality, it is of interest to consider some of the research that has been successfully undertaken to study their neural substrate.

The Human Trinity

To grasp the heterogeneous human reality in a pertinent and helpful way, one may consider that across any life course there progressively emerge, coexist, and interact the three major facets of a human trinity: a *biological individual*, a *social actor*, and a *reflecting and deliberating subject*. Each one of these facets carries on a dialogue with an environment of its own: the living organism's material environment, the actor's social milieu, and the subject's inner world. These three dialogues are easily distinguishable in many respects: Basically, they each aim at the satisfaction of specific sets of needs or desires; they are governed by distinct sets of norms, they face constraints of their own, and they therefore require specific ranges of competencies; they involve the processing—in differing ways—of different kinds of information; they bear distinctive relations to the flow of time as well as to the production of meaning.

Although the distinction set forth above is obviously quite pertinent, it is just as obvious that the three facets with their respective dialogue share one and the same brain. Each dialogue consists of an evolving set of appropriate (i.e., both adapted and adaptive) interactions with a specific environment, and the human brain may thus be considered to take on the mediation of a threefold dialogue that evolves across the life course. Within the brain, the three distinct dialogues can be related, to some extent, with three major levels of integration, organization, and adaptation.

Because the three dialogues share one common mediating agency, they necessarily share also some general modes and some more concrete features of functioning. Whichever needs or desires are to be satisfied, it is the ends, not the means, that are basic. In other words, each dialogue is governed not by a logical or ontological necessity, but by a teleological one. Goal attainment is essential, and the efficiency of any given strategy is regularly evaluated both before and after it is implemented. More generally, there exist within each dialogue two-way relations between the occurring events and the underlying brain functioning. On the one hand, the concrete events of the dialogue depend on both the way in which the individual brain is functioning and the nature of the information the brain is currently carrying and processing. But conversely, these events and their manifold consequences affect in turn brain functioning and information processing. Owing to these reciprocal shaping influences that develop across the life course, the human brain is, much more than that of any other species, both a history-producing and a history-produced dynamic entity. The historical dimension of human life in parallel with that of brain development and functioning can hardly be overemphasized.

As the individual life history progresses and experience accumulates, goal attainment increases in flexibility. Not only can a given goal be attained through diverse means but also hierarchies build up (with more and more abstract goals), and priorities get established that evolve over time. As regards brain development, there occurs a progressive bringing into play of higher anatomical and functional levels that are characterized by an increasing plasticity. Higher order functions subordinate more elementary functions, so that the bottom up causality with which the neurobiologist is quite familiar gets combined with a top-down causality that ensures coherence. The organizing action of a higher global function is specially apparent in the reorganization of an injured brain and in the coordinated restoration of its more elementary functions.

Whatever its concrete objective, any interaction with the environment eventually comes down to getting at something or getting away from something. The three facets of the human trinity have in common these two basic attitudes—namely, that of *appetence* (i.e., desire or appetite) and that of *avoidance*. This is not surprising because the two opposite attitudes and their actual expression are closely related to the two basic goals the biological individual, the social actor, and the self-conscious subject alike strive for: to experience pleasant emotions and affective states and to avoid or put an end to unpleasant ones. Concerning the biological individual, the origins and functions of affect do not essentially differ from those that prevail in other mammalian species. On the other hand, specific origins of affect develop in connection with the specifically human aspects of socialization and social interactions, and even more so as the self-conscious subject strives to construct a personalized inner world. But the mediating and integrating action of affective processes intervenes in essentially the same way within any of the three dialogues, which at the same time reflect and build up a unique human reality, thereby allowing the human being to develop and to function as an integrated and integrating totality.

Before considering in more detail the role played by affective processes, a rather important point must be briefly stressed. Even though a neurobiologist interested in brain–behavior relationships is quite naturally led to focus reflections on the brain as the mediating agency of the human being's dialogue with his or her environments, she or he is fully aware of the fact that the way in which this mediation is concretely effected depends, for the brain's input as well as for its output, on a great diversity of more peripheral biological processes and mechanisms (with their individualized functional characteristics), which can hardly be elaborated on here. Moreover, the human body as a whole is more or less deeply involved in the development of social interactions (e.g., attractiveness, body attitudes, multimodal nonverbal communication) as well as in the construction of a self-concept (viz., body image). In other words, if the brain can be (must be!) extracted from the rest of the body for the purpose of analytic thinking and investigation, its functioning makes full sense only if it is then properly reembodied in the dialoguing individual in his or her entirety.

The Essential Role of Affective Processes

The basal activity of the awake brain generates a spontaneous propensity to act, to engage in actual dealings with the environment. But it is the affective significance, whether innate or acquired, of an object or event that urges the individual to establish a particular relation with the environment or to carry out a particular kind of relational change. It is this affective significance that orients action, that underlies the evaluation of its consequences, and that helps to memorize the resulting experience and to integrate it in a developing autobiographic memory. In the process of relating to the world and, in particular, to other people, affective attributes and feelings play an essential role: If they did not exist, there would be no striving, no goal pursuit, and no goal-oriented action. All along the life course, the functionally adaptive properties of emotions mold and fuel the development and expression of any human personality (cf. Magai, 1996). It is undeniably true that a more thorough knowledge of affect and emotions, of their origins, functions, and dynamics, can tell one as much—if not more—about human nature than the knowledge of cognitive processes. And brain research with its specific level of analysis is here obviously of great interest, for at least two complementary reasons.

First, as Panksepp (1996) rightly emphasizes, emotional processes differ from cognitive ones in that the critical symbolic structures of the former "are deep in the brain, with only shadowy reflections in the external world" (p. 33), whereas the critical structures of the latter "are represented with fidelity in the external world" (p. 33). Second, many neurobiological data concerning affective processes can be extrapolated—with the necessary caution—from an animal brain to the human brain: Unlike many cognitive processes that are closely linked to our collective and individual cultural history, the affective underpinnings of any of the three dialogues of the human trinity are basically the same, with the two superordinate categories of positive and negative affect and the two related categories of neural processes that pervade the entire human brain. Let us consider this assertion in more detail.

Satisfaction of Basic Biological Needs

As a biological individual, the human being needs a mode of brain functioning that allows her or him to survive, to preserve her or his physical integrity, and to maintain the homeostasis of her or his internal milieu. Adequate means of functioning are provided by a species-specific genetic endowment, which all members of the species have in common. Owing to the developing organism's interactions with the environment, the potentialities and constraints inherent in this endowment get expressed in an individualized way. In such a beginning life history, the production of meaning hardly goes beyond the mere epigenetic expression of an individual set of genes. Insofar as the biological significance of various stimuli and situations that elicit behavior are genetically preprogrammed, as are the behavioral strategies themselves, the organism's overt behavior merely fits in with the present moment and its basic biological meaning. Brain functioning and overt behavior that regulate the organism's internal milieu are brought into play from within, and their efficiency is validated through feedback arising also from within, in accordance with the norms of an innate "wisdom of the body" (Cannon, 1932). Specific affective states signal both the existence of some biological need and the satisfaction of that need. Of course, the neurobiologist is well aware of the fact that in animal experiments, the affective (pleasant or unpleasant, appetitive or aversive) character of attributes and states can only be inferred from their effects on overt behavior. But this is not to say that they are mere epiphenomena; on the contrary, they are and act as intervening variables, as signals in their own right (cf. Karli, 1987, 1989b, 1991, 1992, 1996; Kentridge & Aggleton, 1990; Panksepp, 1996).

Within the brain, it is essentially at the level of the upper brainstem and the hypothalmus that behavior is organized and controlled to ensure the satisfaction of the individual's basic biological needs and the defense of his or her physical integrity. It is at this same functional level that two neuronal systems have an important part in orienting the individual's basic attitude and overt behavior: A lateral system underlies appetence, approach, and reward (*reward* system), whereas a medial, periventricular system underlies aversion, flight, or defense (*aversion* system). Any natural or experimental activation of the reward system induces effects that the individual (animal and man alike) strives after, which positively reinforce any behavior giving rise to them (as shown, for instance, by the easy induction of a sustained electrical self-stimulation). Conversely, activation of the aversion system induces effects that the individual tries to avoid (through flight, immobility, or defensive aggression), which negatively reinforce any behavior giving rise to them while positively reinforcing any behavior liable to put an end to them (as shown by the rapid acquisition of switch-off responses to an applied electrical stimulation).[1]

The basal activity as well as the degree of responsiveness of the aversion system is controlled by moderating influences that act on it in a permanent or a more episodic manner and that involve, in particular, GABAergic and opioidergic neurotransmissions through the release of GABA (gamma-aminobutyric acid) and endogenous morphins, respectively (cf. Karli, 1987, 1989c, 1991, 1992; Schmitt & Karli, 1989). By locally acting on one or the other of these neurotransmissions, one can manipulate in a predictable way both the processing of sensory information and the animal's overt behavior (with a marked increase in approach responding or, conversely, in withdrawal and escape responding). For instance, a microinjection, into the rat's periaqueductal gray matter, of a GABA-agonist (which facilitates GABAergic transmission and thereby reinforces the moderating influence exerted on the aversion system) provokes enhanced approach responding to tactile stimulation and a clear facilitation of offensive behaviors in social interactions. Conversely, a microinjection of a GABA-antagonist (with opposite local effects) provokes enhanced withdrawal and escape responding to tactile stimulation and an increased tendency to display defensive behaviors. Such an emotive biasing of input–output relationships corresponds to the induction of an actual affective experience, because an increased activity of the aversion system not only produces an overt flight reaction but further supports associative learning in a place-conditioning paradigm (Di Scala & Sandner, 1989). Moreover, the aversive state induced is not an undifferentiated one: When two distinct sites are stimulated within the aversion system, the rat is quite capable of discriminating between the effects induced by each of these stimulations, and this discrimination of their very nature is still achieved even when their aversive intensity (as measured by the vigor of the escape responses) is identical for both stimulations (Lappuke, Schmitt, & Karli, 1982). These brain structures, processes, and mechanisms undeniably play an important role in orienting the behavior toward objects likely to lead to the satisfaction of some primary need or in inducing a behavior likely

---

[1]It is within the hypothalamus that the two neuronal systems can most easily be distinguished. The reward system can be activated in a predictable way by applying an electrical stimulation to the lateral hypothalamic area. The aversion system lies in a more medial, periventricular location, with two major adjacent components: the medial hypothalamus surrounding the third ventricle and the periaqueductal gray matter surrounding the aqueduct of Sylvius. The rat (or cat, or monkey) rapidly learns to switch on a lateral hypothalamic stimulation by pressing a lever (self-stimulation) and just as rapidly to switch off by this means a stimulation applied to the medial hypothalamus or to the periaqueductal gray matter (switch-off response).

to put an end to an aversive experience generated by some dangerous or otherwise unpleasant situation.

Socialization and Social Life

The species-specific, but always unique, genetic endowment provides the human being not only with the means required to carry on an adapted and adaptive dialogue with the material environment but also with the potential to develop the manifold competencies required to establish, maintain, or modify a series of social relationships. The relational homeostasis that the social being strives to build up and preserve differs from the inner biological homeostasis in that both the incitements and the validating feedback come from without, from the interactions with others (even though, as we shall see later, internally generated affective states play an important mediating role). The norms that govern the dialogue with the social milieu are no longer of a descriptive, innate, and universal character closely linked to a specific kind of biological organization and functioning, but of a normative character that is linked to a particular social and cultural context. In more concrete terms, overt behavior no longer aims at reducing some deviation from an innate set point (e.g., glycemia, osmolarity, central temperature) but aims at reducing some discrepancy between a perceived actual state and a goal state relating to socially determined and currently salient reference values. Owing to the interpretation and symbolization of the experienced social events, the individual life history now generates a meaning of its own that is no longer rigidly preprogrammed. But to the extent that the person readily models his or her conduct on the prevailing conventions and fashions, this meaning may remain more or less implicit, without being thought over in a deliberate search for meaningfulness.

The representations of self that are constructed (that are "co-constructed" with other "selves-in-becoming"; Baxter & Montgomery, 1996, p. 151) in and through social interactions are significant components of any personality. The conceptualization of personality "as a system that mediates the relation of the individual with the environment" and is able "to modulate bottom-up and top-down reciprocal influences" (Caprara, 1996, pp. 15–16) is clearly in accordance with that of the brain as a system that achieves, in socialization and in social life, a two-way mediation across the life span (Karli, 1996). In this social constructivist perspective, personality and brain alike both reflect and shape the dialogue with others. In the development and functioning of personality, the dynamics of affect and emotion play an essential energizing and structuring role. That amounts to saying that the construction and expression of personality can be better grasped through a dynamic, functionalist, and developmental approach rather than through a static, taxonomic, and structuralist one (cf. Caprara, 1996; Magai, 1996).

Very early in the human infant's life, mother and infant "share a code of emotional states," and in their early communication, the primary organizing process appears to be "a mirroring of emotional states, a build-up of mutual feelings" (Trevarthen, 1986, p. 91). Through a continuing general emotional learning process, parent–child interactions are critical "for establishing the individual's basic social knowledge structures and interpersonal response styles" (Strauman, 1996, p. 177). The infant achieves quite rapidly a substantial emotion understanding, and such a capacity to understand others' feelings has a great importance for a wide range of social behavior (cf. Dunn, 1995). Emotion is central to joint attention and social referencing behaviors, to the construction of a shared meaning of experience, and deficits in these mental and behavioral processes lead to "autistic aloneness" (Capps & Sigman, 1996). In the autistic child, deficient capacities for personal relatedness underlie the observed failings in intersubjective engagement (Hobson, 1993).

In social cognition and social behavior across the life course, affective processes ensure a two-way mediation between perception and action (cf. Karli, 1987, 1989b, 1991, 1992, 1995, 1996). On the one hand, it is in particular the association of a historically determined affective significance with the perceived cognitive aspects of a given situation that guides the choice of the behavioral strategy deemed appropriate. An emotionally significant event induces a "change in action readiness" (Frijda, 1996, p. 4) that leads to actual goal-oriented action. On the other hand, the affective experience that results from the comparison of the consequences actually derived from the behavior with those that had been anticipated may modify, in return, both the significance of the situation and the evaluation of the relevance of the strategy used. One may therefore consider that it is largely through this two-way mediation of affective states that an overt social behavior is often both a partial reactualization of the past and a determinant that contributes to shape the motivations of behaviors to follow.

Even though there is no longer any clear-cut and generally accepted definition of its functions and anatomical limits (cf. Kötter & Meyer, 1992), the notion of a *limbic* system undeniably has proved fruitful in the study of the neural substrate of two basic and closely related aspects of socialization and social life, namely, their affective and historical dimensions. Bilateral lesions of the hippocampal formation in the human brain are well known to provoke memory deficits, in particular, a severe deterioration in the capacity to memorize life episodes (cf. Zola-Morgan & Squire, 1993). An appropriate functioning of the hippocampal formation (a nodal component of the brain's memory circuits) is required for the brain to play its role of a history-produced and history-producing dynamic entity without which a socially founded autobiographic memory could hardly get constituted and expressed. Animal research has shown hippocampal functions to be characterized by interindividual variation with regard to both structural (mossy fiber projections) and neurochemical (receptor density) features. This variation is genetically determined (Crusio, Schwegler, & van Abeelen, 1989; Roullet & Lassalle, 1992), but the actual expression of the relevant genes depends on the individual's early interactions with the environment (cf. Karli, 1995).

The hippocampal formation closely interacts with another limbic structure, namely, the amygdaloid nuclear complex. These functional interactions within the brain underlie, in part, the various effects that affective states may have on both storage and retrieval of the content of memory traces as well as on the continuous reconstruction and reappropriation of any autobiographic memory (cf. Fiedler & Forgas, 1988; Stein, Liwag, & Wade, 1996). For instance, an affective state due to the activation of the reciprocal connections between the amygdala and the hypothalamic—reward and aversion—neuronal systems[2] has a twofold effect: some kind of affective filtering of the visual information, with a selective orientation of attention, through the mediation of opioidergic projections from the amygdala onto the visual cortex; a facilitated storage of the information that actually has induced the initial affective state, through the bringing into play of cholinergic neurons (of the basal nucleus of Meynert) that project onto the relevant region of the cerebral cortex (cf. Mishkin & Appenzeller, 1987). More generally, it may be emphasized that in the elaboration and evolution of both social perception and self-knowledge, the combinations of and interactions between cognitive and affective processes are often such that it is difficult to conceive of a means that would allow to clearly disentangle and specify these two categories of processes.

The amygdala, in connection with other brain structures, is deeply involved in the control of social behavior in two related ways: In the face of a given situation, an important step lies in the recognition of its full affective significance through reference to the traces laid down by past experiences, which generates some expectancy and guides the choice of the behavioral strategy deemed appropriate; the thus arising significance may be modulated, in return, by the structuring, personalizing effects of the concrete behavioral interaction with the social environment. Moreover, the amygdala has an essential part in the interplay of appetitive and aversive, positively reinforcing and negatively reinforcing, effects. It is not surprising, therefore, that an appropriate functioning of the amygdaloid nuclear complex is required for the development of well-adapted, outcome-determined social interactions and that throughout an individual life history, amygdaloid lesions severely disrupt socioaffective behavior (cf. Karli, 1987, 1989b, 1991, 1992, 1995, 1996). In the rat, early amygdaloid lesions provoke a lasting hyperreactivity (Eclancher & Karli, 1979), and they further reduce the frequency and duration of social play (Panksepp, Siviy, & Normansell, 1984), which interferes with the development of a well-adapted and efficient behavior style. In the monkey, early temporal lobe lesions (including the amygdala) also have been shown to severely disrupt the development of socioaffective behavior: The animals' behavior

---

[2]Unlike the hypothalamus, the amygdala does not embody clearly distinguishable, spatially segregated components of the neuronal reward and aversion systems. It is nevertheless part of the latter systems in that it is, at the same time, a site from which their hypothalamic components can be brought into play and a site onto which converge and within which interact neural processes that originate in those components.

is quite rigid and inappropriate, and their social interactions are extremely poor (Bachevalier, 1990; Thompson, 1981).

Because the amygdala has an essential part in the mediation of the shaping influence of experience, it is understandable that in the adult animal, amygdaloid lesions often deprive social behavior of some of its history-founded aspects. In the rat, bilateral lesions of the medial amygdala have been found to abolish the aggression-preventing effect of a prior familiarization with mice in the rat–mouse interspecific aggression model (Karli, 1981; Vergnes, 1981) and to markedly attenuate the aggression-preventing effect of a prior defeat experience in the intermale aggression model (Koolhaas, 1984). If amygdaloid lesions are carried out in monkeys living in the wild, the lesioned animals prove incapable of rejoining their group or a neighboring one. They appear to have lost the capacity to adapt their behavior to that of their fellow creatures by referring to experience, in consequence of which their resocialization has become impossible (Kling & Brothers, 1992).

When reflecting on the role played by the amygdala in the control of socioaffective behavior, one should not solely consider its intrinsic functional properties. Many individual features of socioaffective behavior most probably result, in part, from two additional factors: the interactions of the amygdala with other brain structures (e.g., the above-mentioned neural substrates of reward and aversion) and the way in which a number of chemical transmitters and modulators affect the functioning of amygdaloid neurons. For instance, the cat's differential predisposition to respond offensively or defensively to a variety of environmental threats was shown to be linked to synaptic transmission properties between the amygdala and the ventromedial hypothalamus (Adamec, 1991), to an altered excitability of the periaqueductal gray and, possibly, to a modulation of the functioning of the benzodiazepine receptors within the amygdala (Adamec, 1993). Kagan (1996) considers that the human infant's differential profile of reactivity to stimulation, which is predictive of an inhibited or uninhibited profile in the 2nd year of life, can be understood by assuming that the infant is born with either a low or a high threshold of excitability in the amygdala and some of its projections.

In animal research, endogenous opiates (which are known to act, in particular, on limbic structures) have been shown to play an important role in the generation of social emotions and in the processes of interindividual attachment (Panksepp, Siviy, & Normansell, 1985). This evidence with the demonstration that the opiate antagonist naltrexone can benefit autistic children led Panksepp (1996) to consider that an endogenous opioid imbalance is surely one of the facets of autism. But as for other humoral factors (cf. Karli, 1991, 1995, 1996), it is important to emphasize the circular character of many processes in the interplay of brain functioning and behavior: Not only do endogenous opiates indeed contribute to the generation of affective states and the elaboration of their behavioral expression but in return the functioning of the rat's opiate systems has been found to be altered by maternal stress during fetal life (Kinsley, Mann, & Bridges, 1992) as well as by repeated maternal deprivation during the neonatal period (Hoersten, Dimitrijevic, Markovic, & Jankovic, 1993).

There is no obvious reason to consider that the basic affective processes with their energizing and orienting effects, as uncovered in animal studies, should differ in any essential way from those at work in the human brain. On the condition that social behavior is grasped as the outcome of a series of dynamic, interacting, and evolving processes, the two closely related concepts of a mediating personality (with its personalized psychodynamics) and a mediating brain (with its individualized neurodynamics) can be of great interest for animal studies and human studies alike (cf. Karli, 1989a, 1996).

Construction of a Personal Inner World

Through conscious and deliberate efforts to achieve self-knowledge and self-determination, and not just automatically, a full-fledged human subject can develop from a biological individual to a social being and beyond. The subject's quest for autonomy, consistency, explicit meaning, and some kind of transcendency requires a critical evaluation of the prevailing conventions and fashions as well as a sustained effort to keep a sound distance from the manifold incitements arising from the environment. A more sovereign self—staying somewhat aloof from the outer world—is constituted through the building up of a more personalized inner world of ideas, aspirations, projects, values, and beliefs. Any perceived social event or internally rising mental event is then meaningful to the extent that it is relevant to (in accordance with or in discrepancy with) some higher order goal that is linked to the ideal self. This relevance is affectively experienced, and the thus generated and interpreted affective experience is likely to fuel a goal-oriented intentional action.

Even though neurobiological investigation has no real access to consciousness per se, that is, to the first-person nature of the subjective experience, a plausible hypothesis can be put forward as regards the complex neural circuits and mechanisms that generate the contents of consciousness, at least as far as the perceived world—and not self-awareness—is concerned (cf. Gray, 1995). It is worth emphasizing that consciousness and the conscious self have coordinating properties, as they are normally single and unified because of dynamic and integrating interactions between the two cerebral hemispheres (Sperry, 1979), despite the fact that information processing has been found to have differential characteristics within one and the other of these two brain halves.

There is good evidence that the prefrontal cortex—with its privileged development in the human brain, its great plasticity, and its rich reciprocal connections (in particular, with the parietal cortical association areas, the hippocampal formation, the amygdala, and the basal ganglia)—plays an important role in the planning, control, and adaptation of goal-oriented intentional action.[3] Such a role requires that the brain have the capacity to plan and initiate intentional acts while inhibiting any ongoing stereotyped activity, to get free from the influence of any immediate experience with its innate or conditioned significance, to achieve a sequential ordering of action, and to adapt its strategy to changing environmental conditions. Each one of these higher order functions proves more or less severely disrupted in patients bearing prefrontal lesions. As a matter of fact, such lesions are liable to entail a "loss of psychic self-activation" (Laplane, 1990), a release of automatic "imitation and utilization behavior" (Lhermitte, Pillon, & Serdaru, 1986), and a more general "environmental dependency syndrome" (Lhermitte, 1986) reflecting a weakened autonomy, an impaired temporal organization of behavior (Fuster, 1990), and an inability to modify behavior according to a changing environment, which results in an "inadaptation of behavior to goal" (Dubois, Verin, Teixeira-Ferreira, Sirigu, & Pillon, 1994, p. 13).

Quite obviously, the prefrontal cortex with its reciprocal connections is deeply involved not only in the complex cognitive processes of a highly efficient "working memory" (cf. Goldman-Rakic, 1994, p. 114) but also in the related affective and conative processes. This is confirmed by the finding that there are prefrontal neurons the activity of which proves correlated with some expectation, with the recording of a reward or, on the contrary, with that of an error-induced failure (i.e., with motivational aspects; cf. Fuster, 1990). It should be added that a dopaminergic regulation—through the mesocorticolimbic dopaminergic network—is essential for these cognitive, affective, and conative processes to develop, to function, and to interact harmoniously (cf. Le Moal & Simon, 1991).

Conclusion

Because the nature of the human being is that of a multifaceted and integrated, evolving, and integrating totality, it can be fully grasped only through a synthetic biopsychosocial approach that gives due consideration to the dynamics of an individual's development and functioning. The true interest of such an integrated approach of the highly complex human reality is more and more acknowledged by psychologists (e.g., Cairns, 1996; Magnusson, 1990; Magnusson & Törestad, 1993) as well as by psychiatrists (e.g. Ciompi, 1991). Of course, all the material needed to construct a holistic view of human nature is yielded, initially, by rigorous analyses

---

[3]Even though it is somewhat arbitrary to select and mention just a few among the many connections of the prefrontal cortex, it is worth emphasizing that the higher level cognitive–affective processing required for the planning of goal-oriented actions can function only if it continuously receives information concerning the recognition of objects (that involves the hippocampal formation), the detection of their location in space (that involves the parietal cortical association areas), and the recognition of their significance (that involves the amygdala). The connection with the basal ganglia further allows the interruption of any automatic and stereotyped activity currently integrated there.

of the functions and processes that concern one or another facet of the human trinity on both the cerebral and the behavioral–mental sides of the brain–behavior and brain–mind relationships considered. But because these relationships operate within the same brain, they interact and cooperate in ways that can be clarified only through interdisciplinary reflection and research. This is obvious as regards aggressive and, more generally, any socioaffective behavior (cf. Karli, 1991, 1995, 1996). Just as evidently, no single discipline can ever explain how storytelling in social life and the resulting evolution of an autobiographic memory (with all the neural functioning and psychobiological capacities needed to produce adapted speech acts and to memorize meaningful events) with the workings of an intrasubjective imagination contribute to the construction of a self-concept (cf. Hanson, 1986; Nelson, 1995). In such interdisciplinary studies, it is essential to define the scope and limits of each level and mode of explanation.

It also matters to be cautious about generalizing the mediating, structuring, and integrating role of affective processes across the distinct facets of the highly complex and heterogeneous human reality. Each one of the sketched out dialogues of the human trinity constructs and reflects its own central agency with specific contents and a varying degree of active processing of experiences. Because the distinctively human self-concept is at the same time a sociocultural product (with the constraints of some "ought self" built up in a given sociocultural environment) and the product of self-evaluation and self-regulation (with a subjective goal hierarchy and a personal way of linking lower order goals to higher order goals and of evaluating goal attainment), there necessarily arise cross-domain and cross-agency discrepancies. The latter may have adaptive, energizing effects if they are somehow overcome or, on the contrary, may induce maladaptive consequences if they lead to a high degree of anxiety or to a state of depression (cf. Martin & Tesser, 1996).

Even though it is neither self-evident nor easy, the neurobiologist must recognize the primacy, the vital importance, of the mental and behavioral functions and processes that allow a living being to efficiently cope with various situations and events. In more concrete terms, the biologist should refrain from considering that the data obtained in studying brain mechanisms do explain, by themselves, the functioning of the human mind and the production of human attitudes and behaviors. To build valid and promising bridges between behavioral neurobiology and human psychology, it is much more pertinent and fruitful to start from well-defined mental or behavioral processes that are likely to—and actually prove to—operate in similar ways in both animal and human beings, and then to carefully study the underlying brain mechanisms. As emphasized above, affective processes have a mobilizing, orienting, organizing, and integrating function within each facet of the human reality (cf. also Ciompi, 1991), and it is specially in this domain that well-thought-over neurobiological research can yield results that may contribute to better understanding of some aspects of human nature.

References

Adamec, R. E. (1991). Partial kindling of the ventral hippocampus: Identification of changes in limbic physiology which accompany changes in feline aggression and defense. *Physiology and Behavior, 49,* 443–453.

Adamec, R. E. (1993). Partial limbic kindling—Brain, behavior, and the benzodiazepine receptor. *Physiology and Behavior, 54,* 531–545.

Bachevalier, J. (1990). Memory loss and the socio-emotional disturbances following neonatal damage of the limbic system in monkeys: An animal model for childhood autism. In C. A. Tamminga & S. C. Schulz (Eds.), *Advances in psychiatry: Vol. 1. Schizophrenia* (pp. 129–140). New York: Raven Press.

Baxter, L. A., & Montgomery, B. M. (1996). *Relating: Dialogues and dialectics.* New York: Guilford Press.

Cairns, R. B. (1996). Socialization and sociogenesis. In D. Magnusson (Ed.), *The lifespan development of individuals: Behavioral, neurobiological, and psychosocial perspectives* (pp. 277–295). Cambridge, England: Cambridge University Press.

Cannon, W. B. (1932). *The wisdom of the body.* New York: Norton.

Capps, L., & Sigman, M. (1996). Autistic aloneness. In R. D. Kavanaugh, B. Zimmerberg, & S. Fein (Eds.), *Emotion: Interdisciplinary perspectives* (pp. 273–296). Mahwah, NJ: Erlbaum.

Caprara, G. V. (1996). Structures and processes in personality psychology. *European Psychologist, 1,* 14–26.

Ciompi, L. (1991). Affects as central organizing and integrating factors: A new psychosocial/biological model of the psyche. *British Journal of Psychiatry, 159,* 97–105.

Crusio, W. E., Schwegler, H., & van Abeelen, J. H. F. (1989). Behavioral responses to novelty and structural variation of the hippocampus in mice: II. Multivariate genetic analysis. *Behavioural Brain Research, 32,* 81–88.

Di Scala, G., & Sandner, G. (1989). Conditioned place aversion produced by microinjections of semicarbazide into the periaqueductal gray of the rat. *Brain Research, 483,* 91–97.

Dubois, B., Verin, M., Teixeira-Ferreira, C., Sirigu, A., & Pillon, B. (1994). How to study frontal lobe functions in humans. In A.-M. Thierry, J. Glowinski, P. S. Goldman-Rakic, & Y. Christen (Eds.), *Motor and cognitive functions of the prefrontal cortex* (pp. 1–16). Berlin: Springer-Verlag.

Dunn, J. (1995). Children as psychologists: The later correlates of individual differences in understanding of emotions and other minds. *Cognition and Emotion, 9,* 187–201.

Eclancher, F., & Karli, P. (1979). Effects of early amygdaloid lesions on the development of reactivity in the rat. *Physiology and Behavior, 22,* 1123–1134.

Fiedler, K., & Forgas, J. (1988). *Affect, cognition and social behavior.* Toronto, Ontario, Canada: Hogrefe.

Frijda, N. H. (1996). Passions: Emotion and socially consequential behavior. In R. D. Kavanaugh, B. Zimmerberg, & S. Fein (Eds.), *Emotion: Interdisciplinary perspectives* (pp. 1–27). Mahwah, NJ: Erlbaum.

Fuster, J. M. (1990). Behavioral electrophysiology of the prefrontal cortex of the primate. In H. B. M. Uylings, C. G. Van Eden, J. P. C. De Bruin, M. A. Corner, & M. G. P. Feenstra (Eds.), *The prefrontal cortex: Its structure, function, and pathology* (pp. 313–324). Amsterdam: Elsevier.

Goldman-Rakic, P. S. (1994). The issue of memory in the study of prefrontal function. In A. M. Thierry, J. Glowinski, P. S. Goldman-Rakic, & Y. Christen (Eds.), *Motor and cognitive functions of the prefrontal cortex* (pp. 112–121). Berlin: Springer-Verlag.

Gray, J. A. (1995). The contents of consciousness: A neuropsychological conjecture. *Behavioral and Brain Sciences, 18,* 659–722.

Hanson, K. (1986). *The self imagined. Philosophical reflections on the social character of psyche.* New York: Routledge & Kegan Paul.

Hobson, R. P. (1993). *Autism and the development of mind.* Hove, UK: Erlbaum.

Hoersten, S. von, Dimitrijevic, M., Markovic, B. M., & Jankovic, B. D. (1993). Effect of early experience on behavior and immune response in the rat. *Physiology and Behavior, 54,* 931–940.

Kagan, J. (1996). Temperamental contributions to the development of social behavior. In D. Magnusson (Ed.), *The lifespan development of individuals: Behavioral, neurobiological and psychosocial perspectives* (pp. 376–393). Cambridge, England: Cambridge University Press.

Karli, P. (1981). Conceptual and methodological problems associated with the study of brain mechanisms underlying aggressive behaviour. In P. F. Brain & D. Benton (Eds.), *The biology of aggression* (pp. 323–361). Alphen aan den Rijn, The Netherlands: Sijthoff & Noordhoff.

Karli, P. (1987). *L'homme agressif* [The aggressive human being]. Paris: Editions Odile Jacob.

Karli, P. (1989a). Is the concept of "personality" relevant to the study of animal aggression? *European Journal of Personality, 3*, 139–148.

Karli, P. (1989b). Perception, cognition and action: The mediating role of affective states. *Brain Behavior and Evolution, 33*, 153–156.

Karli, P. (1989c). Studies on neurochemistry and behavior. In R. J. Blanchard, P. F. Brain, D. C. Blanchard, & S. Parmigiani (Eds.), *Ethoexperimental approaches to the study of behavior* (pp. 434–450). Dordrecht, The Netherlands: Kluwer.

Karli, P. (1991). *Animal and human aggression* (S. M. Carmona & H. Whyte, Trans.). Oxford, England: Oxford University Press. (Original work published 1987)

Karli, P. (1992). De la perception à l'action: Le rôle médiateur et structurant des états affectifs et des émotions [From perception to action: The mediating and structuring role of affective states and emotions]. In H. Barreau (Ed.), *Le cerveau et l'esprit* (pp. 85–104). Paris: CNRS Editions.

Karli, P. (1995). *Le cerveau et la liberté* [The brain and freedom]. Paris: Editions Odile Jacob.

Karli, P. (1996). The brain and socialization: A two-way mediation across the life course. In D. Magnusson (Ed.), *The lifespan development of individuals: Behavioral, neurobiological and psychosocial perspectives* (pp. 341–356). Cambridge, England: Cambridge University Press.

Kentridge, R. W., & Aggleton, J. P. (1990). Emotion: Sensory representation, reinforcement, and the temporal lobe. *Cognition and Emotion, 4*, 191–208.

Kinsley, C. H., Mann, P. E., & Bridges, R. S. (1992). Diminished luteinizing hormone release in prenatally stressed male rats after exposure to sexually receptive females. *Physiology and Behavior, 52*, 925–928.

Kling, A. S., & Brothers, L. A. (1992). The amygdala and social behavior. In J. P. Aggleton (Ed.), *The amygdala* (pp. 353–377). New York: Wiley-Liss.

Koolhaas, J. M. (1984). The corticomedial amygdala and the behavioral change due to defeat. In R. Bandler (Ed.), *Modulation of sensorimotor activity during alterations in behavioral states* (pp. 341–349). New York: Alan R. Liss.

Kötter, R., & Meyer, N. (1992). The limbic system: A review of its empirical foundation. *Behavioural Brain Research, 52*, 105–127.

Laplane, D. (1990). La perte d'autoactivation psychique [The loss of psychic self-activation]. *Revue Neurologique, 146*, 397–404.

Lappuke, R., Schmitt, P., & Karli, P. (1982). Discriminative properties of aversive brain stimulation. *Behavioral and Neural Biology, 34*, 159–179.

Le Moal, M., & Simon, H. (1991). Mesocorticolimbic dopaminergic network: Functional and regulatory roles. *Physiological Reviews, 71*, 155–234.

Lhermitte, F. (1986). Human autonomy and the frontal lobes: Part II. Patient behavior in complex and social situations: The "environmental dependency syndrome." *Annals of Neurology, 19*, 335–343.

Lhermitte, F., Pillon, B., & Serdaru, M. (1986). Human autonomy and the frontal lobes: Part I: Imitation and utilization behavior: A neuropsychological study of 75 patients. *Annals of Neurology, 19*, 326–334.

Magai, C. (1996). Personality theory: Birth, death, and transfiguration. In R. D. Kavanaugh, B. Zimmerberg, & S. Fein (Eds.), *Emotion: Interdisciplinary perspectives* (pp. 171–201). Mahwah, NJ: Erlbaum.

Magnusson, D. (1990). Personality development from an interactional perspective. In L. A. Pervin (Ed.), *Handbook of personality: Theory and research* (pp. 193–222). New York: Guilford Press.

Magnusson, D., & Törestad, B. (1993). A holistic view of personality: A model revisited. *Annual Review of Psychology, 44*, 427–452.

Martin, L. L., & Tesser, A. (1996). *Striving and feeling: Interactions among goals, affect, and self-regulation*. Mahwah, NJ: Erlbaum.

Mishkin, M., & Appenzeller, T. (1987). The anatomy of memory. *Scientific American, 256*, 62–71.

Nelson, K. (1995). Stories in memory: Developmental issues. *Advances in Social Cognition, 8*, 185–191.

Panksepp, J. (1996). Affective neuroscience: A paradigm to study the animate circuits for human emotions. In R. D. Kavanaugh, B. Zimmerberg, & S. Fein (Eds.), *Emotion: Interdisciplinary perspectives* (pp. 29–60). Mahwah, NJ: Erlbaum.

Panksepp, J., Siviy, S., & Normansell, L. (1984). The psychobiology of play: Theoretical and methodological perspectives. *Neuroscience and Biobehavioral Reviews, 8*, 465–492.

Panksepp, J., Siviy, S. M., & Normansell, L. A. (1985). Brain opioids and social emotions. In M. Reite & T. Field (Eds.), *The psychobiology of attachment and separation* (pp. 3–49). Orlando, FL: Academic Press.

Roullet, P., & Lassalle, J. M. (1992). Behavioural strategies, sensorial processes and hippocampal mossy fibre distribution in radial maze performance in mice. *Behavioural Brain Research, 48*, 77–85.

Schmitt, P., & Karli, P. (1989). Periventricular structures and the organization of affective states and their behavioural expression. *Brain Behavior and Evolution, 33*, 162–164.

Sperry, R. W. (1979). Consciousness, free will and personal identity. In D. A. Oakley & H. C. Plotkin (Eds.), *Brain, behaviour and evolution* (pp. 219–228). London: Methuen.

Stein, N. L., Liwag, M. D., & Wade, E. (1996). A goal-based approach to memory for emotional events: Implications for theories of understanding and socialization. In R. D. Kavanaugh, B. Zimmerberg, & S. Fein (Eds.), *Emotion: Interdisciplinary perspectives* (pp. 91–118). Mahwah, NJ: Erlbaum.

Strauman, T. J. (1996). Self-beliefs, self-evaluation, and depression: A perspective on emotional vulnerability. In L. L. Martin & A. Tesser (Eds.), *Striving and feeling: Interactions among goals, affect, and self-regulation* (pp. 175–201). Mahwah, NJ: Erlbaum.

Thompson, C. I. (1981). Long-term behavioral development of rhesus monkeys after amygdalectomy in infancy. In Y. Ben-Ari (Ed.), *The amygdaloid complex* (pp. 259–270). Amsterdam: Elsevier.

Trevarthen, C. (1986). The structure of motives for human communication in infancy: A ground-plan for human ethology. In J. Lecamus & J. Cosnier (Eds.), *Ethology and psychology* (pp. 91–100). Toulouse, France: Privat.

Vergnes, M. (1981). Effect of prior familiarization with mice on elicitation of mouse-killing in rats: Role of the amygdala. In Y. Ben-Ari (Ed.), *The amygdaloid complex* (pp. 293–304). Amsterdam: Elsevier.

Zola-Morgan, S. M., & Squire, L. R. (1993). Neuroanatomy of memory. *Annual Review of Neuroscience, 16*, 547–563.

Part II

Psychiatric and Emotional Disorders

5

Rodent Models of Human Neuroses and Psychoses

Paul F. Brain and Lynne Marrow

Mice, rats, guinea pigs, hamsters, gerbils, and other rodents account for, by far, the greatest numbers of laboratory vertebrates used. Over 10 million rodents were used in Europe in 1991 (European Community, 1994), and 2.3 million were used in the United Kingdom in 1996 (Home Office, 1997). Although the development of new and validated nonanimal alternatives is growing, especially in areas such as toxicology, an early move to a situation in which whole organism studies are deemed unnecessary seems very unlikely. Further, there are some questions about humans based on animal models that cannot be answered with tissue cultures and computer modeling, and these include all the various attempts to examine and ameliorate mental disease. Rodents will probably be the species of choice in many such cases. Laboratory rats (probably because their size is more conducive to surgical procedures involving the brain) have predominated in terms of annual numbers used in Europe until recently. The arrival of transgenics has, however, seen a comparative explosion in mouse experimentation.

In spite of their distance from humans, rodents have certainly featured very prominently in attempts to assess the biological underpinning of human neuroses and psychoses and (especially) in attempts to develop an armamentarium of drug treatments to treat such conditions.

The above development creates a variety of problems. Many individuals are concerned about the extent to which especially human phenomena (e.g., depression or anger) can be genuinely modeled in animals as far away from the human condition as rats and mice. Indeed, many of the overt written attacks on the appropriateness of using animals in research focus on essentially psychopharmacological investigations including those concerned with mental disease. The argument often is based on the perceived inappropriateness of the questions being asked. Consequently, it seems worthwhile to reexamine the strands of the debates concerning the ethics of using animals at all and how one assesses the validity of an

The work of a number of former students of Paul Fredric Brain, including Alias bin Kamis, Nastiti Kusumorini, and Helena Kurishingal, is quoted here. Support of Medical Research Council Grant G942945IN is gratefully acknowledged.

animal model of a human neurosis or psychosis. In this chapter, we essentially look at the issues surrounding what constitutes a relevant animal "model" of a human neurosis or psychosis. We concentrate particularly on anxiety, hostility, and depression. An increased need for a leap of faith is illustrated by attempts to "model" human social anxiety.

Animal Welfare and Models

This present account does not attempt to cover (by any means) the whole range of situations in which laboratory rodents are used to model human mental disease. In contrast, it takes the tack that it is going to become increasingly more difficult to advocate the use of rodents in this way (because of welfare-related issues) and that to argue successfully for their use, people are going to have to be more restricted in the claims they make. This is simply an extension of the costs (in terms of animal welfare) versus benefits (in terms of educational or scientific gain) analysis that must precede licensing of animal work in countries such as the United Kingdom.

The use of laboratory rodents as models for human neuroses and psychoses at least admits the probability that such animals can be subject to distress or fear. Although it is now well established that laboratory animals such as cats, dogs, primates, and rabbits deserve environmental enrichment to ameliorate some of the negative consequences of restrictive housing, such an enlightened view has been less quick to emerge for laboratory rodents (O'Donoghue, 1994). It is often difficult to establish optimal circumstances for such animals—for example, there is a view that individual housing is deleterious for social species, but conspecific aggression is a common source of pain, distress, and lasting harm in mature male laboratory mice (Brain, 1989, 1990, 1992b, 1997). As pointed out earlier (Brain, 1994b), "simply abolishing events or conditions that acutely change indicators of 'stress' would environmentally impoverish animals and make them less capable of dealing with subsequent 'stressors'" (p. 623). Clearly, *welfare* is a fine balance between environmental enrichment and stress, a process that must take into account species, sex, and strain differences of animals. The view also has been repeatedly expressed (e.g., Brain, 1992a) that chronic pain or distress is more problematic than acute experiences, yet these are precisely the conditions that have to be generated for many of the models of human neuroses and psychoses that use laboratory rodents.

Characteristics of Useful Models

Willner (1984, 1990) has described the procedures he sees as important for validating animal models of psychiatric disorders. He suggests that *predictive validity* (i.e., the drug actions in the model should largely correspond with those in the clinic), *face validity* (i.e., the model and the disorder should have similar diagnostic characteristics), and *construct va-*

lidity (i.e., a convincing theoretical rationale) should all be in place for the model to be truly useful. Difficulties most often seen with face and construct validities as superficial similarities are easy to establish but may be of little real significance.

The usefulness of an animal model of a psychiatric disorder depends on the use to which the model is to be put. To screen new therapeutic drugs, a model does not have to mimic exactly the disorder at which the drugs are targeted. It is simply enough that the effects of drugs on the behavioral changes that constitute the model parallel the effectiveness of the drugs in the face of the clinical condition. However, the simple screening of drugs is only one use to which models are put. The other major use is in the deduction of the neural substrate that underlies the disorder. This aspect of a model's usefulness (predictive validity at the mechanistic level) fundamentally requires that the model have a high degree of construct validity, that is, a high degree of commonality must exist between the condition and the model at the theoretical level.

Rodent Models of Anxiety

Brain, Kusumorini, and Benton (1991) have reviewed some of the developments in models of anxiety that use laboratory rodents. They have suggested that the newer models (based on realistic situations in which anxiety might reasonably be implicated) offer improvements on the older tests.

In the absence of any fully characterized biological indicator, anxiety has been generally measured clinically by the verbal reports of patients. Because of the subjective nature of this condition, suitable animal models have been difficult to design. It is, however, true that animals respond with anxietylike expressions in a variety of situations. Indeed, there have been a number of recent attempts to devise tests for *anxiolytic* (anxiety-reducing) properties of drugs in rodents after predator–prey interactions and exposure of individuals to dominant conspecifics (e.g., D. C. Blanchard, Rodgers, & Blanchard 1990; R. J. Blanchard & Blanchard, 1990). Even if such models cannot be exact replicas of human anxiety, they do appear useful in investigations of the biochemistry of anxiety and in determining the mechanisms of actions of anxiolytic drugs. As noted earlier (in regard to predictive validity), pharmacology is the most common current way of validating a proposed animal test of anxiety (File, 1987). Vellucci (1989) has suggested the following as necessary requirements of animal models of anxiety (see also Treit, 1985): (a) The animal must be sensitive to clinically effective anxiolytics in a dose-dependent manner, (b) the relative potencies of different anxiolytic agents should be similar to those seen clinically, and (c) the tests should distinguish the effects of anxiolytic from nonanxiolytic drugs. Lee (1990) has comprehensively detailed the enormous diversity of laboratory models for anxiety that use rodents. Detailed notes on some of the more commonly used tests follow; some of these will be contrasted in relation to a particular example.

Open Field

This is one of the simplest tests and involves placing a rodent in an unfamiliar area in which ambulation is assessed in relation to photocell beams or lines drawn on the floor. As the rodent crosses each beam or line, a score of one unit of exploratory activity is recorded. Fully automated, computer-assisted videotape systems that distinguish between traversed areas adjacent to walls and those more internal (indicative of reduced anxiety) are now common. The experimenter also often counts the number of fecal boluses deposited because increased defecation is indicative of increased anxiety or emotionality. The ambulation score (especially of internal areas) in such tests may be increased by anxiolytics (Christmas & Maxwell, 1970).

Social Interaction Tests

Elements of anxiety can be identified in rodent social encounter tests with videotaped recordings of the encounters to identify elements such as freezing, stretched attention, and tentative activities (Brain et al., 1991).

Two-Chambered Light–Dark Transition

This test takes into account the rodent's aversion to bright light. The subject is placed in an area consisting of light and dark compartments, and the number of transitions between the two is used as a measure of anxiety. The subject is effectively faced with conflict between a desire to explore a novel area and an aversion to bright light. Anxiolytics significantly increase the number of movements between the compartments (Crawley, 1981).

Elevated-Plus-Maze

This device also involves conflict between exploration and aversion. The apparatus is elevated and consists of two open arms and two closed arms in the form of a cross. The subject is placed on an open arm, generating anxiety due to the mouse's aversion to elevated open spaces. Anxiolytics increase the relative amount of time spent in the open arms (Pellow, 1985).

The elevated-plus-maze is one of the most commonly used tests for the anxiolytic–anxiogenic properties of drugs, and hence it might be assumed that the mechanisms that underlie drug-induced changes in plus-maze behavior are related to the mechanisms that underlie human anxiety. However, the precise effects of drugs on plus-maze behavior are much influenced by details of how the test is applied (Hogg, 1996). Unless we assume that a multiplicity of anxiety states exist with subtly different substrates, the sensitivity of the model to extraneous variables probably means that the test tells us little about the fundamental changes underpinning anxiety in humans (i.e., its predictive validity at the mechanistic level is low). This conclusion receives further support from the fact that the test may produce false positives with certain categories of drugs (see Charrier, Dangoumau, Puech, Hamon, & Thiebot, 1995).

Ultrasonic Distress Calling

Anxiolytic drugs decrease the ultrasonic distress calls emitted by rodent pups separated from their mothers (Gardner, 1985; Insel, Hill, & Mayor, 1986). Claims have been made that the benzodiazepine agonist- and serotonin-antagonist-induced reductions in calls are due to the drugs' sedative, muscle relaxant, or hypothermic actions, but Brain et al. (1991) has ruled out the possibility that decreases in ultrasonic calling are simply related to these effects.

Comparison of models. Lee (1990) has identified the two-chambered light–dark transition, the elevated-plus-maze, and the social interaction tests as some of the most systematically investigated paradigms, and Brain et al. (1991) have advocated the ultrasonic distress-calling test. Table 1 consequently compares ultrasonic calling with these three tests in situations where identical drugs (benzodiazepines and serotonergic drugs) have been assessed.

Table 1 provides data that are promising in terms of the ultrasonic calling test. Most of the compounds that produced reliable anxiolytic or anxiogenic (anxiety-generating) effects in the three tests examined by Lee (1990) generated similar actions on the ultrasonic calling test. Only the benzodiazepine antagonists (Flumazenil and ZK 93426) apparently produced anxiogenic effects in the social interaction test (a test that relies on the fact that initial encounters between unfamiliar conspecifics are anxiety inducing) without modifying ultrasonic calling. The serotonin hypothesis of anxiety holds that decreasing serotonin neurotransmission produces an anxiolytic effect and increasing such transmitter activity promotes anxiety. In studies of drug impact on ultrasonic calling, antagonists of serotonin had anxiolytic effects, in line with the three tests detailed by Lee (1990). In the case of the agonist, 8-OH DPAT (8-hydroxy-2[di-n-propylamino]-tetralin) only the ultrasonic calling test provided evidence of an opposite (i.e., anxiogenic) action, whereas the other tests produced indications of anxiolytic effects. The anxiogenic effect of the serotonergic agonist seen in the ultrasonic calling test is supported by findings with quipazine maleate and DOI-HCl (1[3-chlorophenyl-4-iodophenyl]2-amino propane hydrochloride). Use of the ultrasonic calling test seems to provide a situation that generally accurately distinguishes compounds with anxiolytic and anxiogenic properties. This technique consequently appears to be a reliable method for screening anxiolytic drugs. The test is also relatively simple to carry out and (being automated) does not require substantial training of the operative, but do any of these features make it superior as a rodent model of human anxiety? One could argue that it has ethical advantages

Table 5.1. Comparisons of Benzodiazepine and Serotonergic Receptor-Influencing Drugs on Different Anxiety Tests Using Rodents

	Test			
Compound	Two-chambered light–dark transition	Elevated-plus-maze	Social interaction	Ultrasonic calling
Benzodiazepine				
Agonist				
Diazepam	+	+	+	+
Chlordiazepoxide	+	+	+	+
ZK 91296	ND	ND	+	+
Antagonist				
Flumazenil	ND	ND	−	0
ZK 93426	ND	ND	−	0
Inverse agonist				
FG 7142	−	−	−	−
DMCM	ND	−	ND	−
β-CCM	ND	ND	−	−
Serotonin				
Agonist				
8-OH DPAT	ND	+	+	−
Antagonist				
Ipsapirone	ND	+	+	+
Buspirone	+	+	+	+
Gepirone	ND	+	+	+
Ritanserin	ND	+	+	+
Ondansetron	+	ND	+	+

Note. The data for the first three tests are taken from a review by Lee (1990). + = anxiolytic effects; ZK 91296 = 5-benzgloxy-4-methoxymethyl-beta-carboline-3-carboxylic acid; ND = no data; − = anxiogenic effects; 0 = inactive; ZK 93426 = 5-isopropoxy-4-methyl-beta-carboline-3-carboxylic acid ethyl ester; FG 7142 = N′-methyl-β-carboline-3-carboxamide; DMCM = methyl 6, 7-dimethoxy-4-ethyl-beta carboline-3-carboxylate; β = CCM = methyl-beta-carboline-3-carboxylate; 8-OH DPAT = 8 hydroxy-2[dien-propylamino]tetralin.

(often canceled by subjective protective responses to neonates, because it uses animals presumedly less sentient than adult mice). However, the central nervous systems of newly born mice are by no means fully developed, and thus, these animals may not accurately model adults. Some rodent neonates inhibit distress calling in the presence of potentially dangerous conspecifics or predators. Does this mean that any associated fear or anxiety is lessened?

Rodent Models of Hostility

A very wide range of rodent models of aggression have been repeatedly used in the laboratory (Brain, 1981, 1984, 1986, 1994a; Brain & Haug,

1992; Brain, Miras, & Berry, 1993). *Hostility* is viewed as a tendency to react with threat or attack under inappropriate circumstances or to show excessive aggressiveness. Obviously value judgments are involved in making such distinctions.

The models include the following five types. The first is the *social conflict* model, in which generally intraspecific encounters involve competition for a mate, a territory, social status, or food. Winners increase their relative fitness (breeding potential) by such acts. The conflicts often use strategies that minimize the potential for serious damage. The second, the *parental defense* model, may be intra- or interspecific in nature. The behavior protects the attacker's young or nest sites from potentially destructive intruders. A third type is the *self-defense* model, which may be seen in both inter- and intraspecific situations. The active responses (threat and attack) protect the actor from potential predators or attacking members of their own species. These behaviors are generally seen only if flight or escape is precluded. They involve no injury-limiting strategies. The fourth, the *infanticide* model, involves the killing of (generally) unrelated young. In males, this strategy seems a method of increasing the individual's reproductive fitness, whereas in females, it is generally a response to stress or disturbance. Finally, the fifth type is the *predation* model, which may be inter- or intraspecific responses that involve efficient killing, and they are generally followed by feeding activity. In laboratory rodents, mouse-killing behavior by rats (Karli, 1956) and insect-killing behavior by mice and hamsters (Brain & Al-Maliki, 1978) have been the most studied examples of this approach.

It should be very evident from the above descriptions that *aggression*, as studied with laboratory rodents, is a very heterogeneous set of phenomena. Studies with genetic strains (Jones & Brain, 1987), hormonal manipulations (Brain & Haug, 1992; Brain, Haug, & Alias bin Kamis, 1983), and application of psychoactive drugs (Brain & Al-Maliki, 1979; Brain, Alias bin Kamis, Haug, Mandel, & Simler, 1982; Brain et al., 1993) all strongly confirm that the threat and attack seen in the different rodent tests serve a variety of functions, namely offense, defense, and predation. Having said this, the idea of pure offense and defense cannot easily be supported by the data. Factors such as a change in the nature of the opponent (Brain, Benton, Childs, & Parmigiani, 1981; Martinez, Simon, Castanu, & Brain, 1989), the opponent's sex (Parmigiani, Brain, Mainardi, & Brunoni, 1988), or prior social experiences (Brain & Kamal, 1989) have profound effects on the form of the generated threat and attack. Note also (Brain & Haug, 1992; Brain, 1994a) that many of the rodent models (which are often clearly adaptive responses) do not easily represent human behaviors receiving the label *hostility* (which are generally viewed as maladaptive or inappropriate use of threat or attack in particular situations). Indeed, it has been suggested that animal models with a greater emphasis on defense or predation might be more appropriate than those clearly involving offense. This is because many examples of human hostility can be viewed as excessive defensiveness (often mentally ill people strike out or respond to imagined threats, and hostile people seem to have larger areas of personal space) or an almost predatory response with low arousal (such as the behavior of psychopaths).

Although, for example, a recent study by Martinez-Sanchis, Brain, Salvador, and Simon (1996) attempts to look at the potential impact of anabolic steroids on aggressive behavior in laboratory mice, it is in no sense a model of stanozolol abuse by weight lifters. The only potentially useful information to come out of this animal study would be to establish whether the compound could change mood. The study was stimulated by a claim that steroid-abusing weight lifters have been involved in seemingly unprovoked attacks, but the human complications of concern about body appearance, the relationship between physical power and responding in conflict situations, the relationship between steroid abuse and alcohol ingestion, and steroid abuse as an excuse for behavior cannot be addressed in the animal model. It is our belief that there is a tendency to extrapolate too far when using laboratory rodents in studies directed to furthering our understanding of human hostility. We should recognize that although the studies provide valuable insight about the possibilities of particular biological, situational, or experimental factors changing the propensity for threat or attack in interindividual situations, they tell us little about murder, rape, or war. This is because murder and rape are actually very heterogeneous human phenomena, and war is an organized group activity often involving obedience to authority rather than overt hostility.

Rodent Models of Depression

Human depression is a debilitating phenomenon with major depressive episodes lasting at least 2 weeks and with core symptoms of depressed mood and markedly suppressed interest and a lack of reactivity to pleasurable stimuli. There are often associated symptoms such as weight loss, sleeping disorders, fatigue or loss of energy, feelings of worthlessness, lessened ability to concentrate on mental tasks, and repeated thoughts of death or suicide. This common human condition has been modeled in laboratory rodents by means of a variety of paradigms (reviewed by Willner, 1984). On a variety of features, Willner (1984) found some paradigms to be promising.

The *behavioral despair* model involved rats or mice that were forced to swim in a confined space (e.g., Porsolt, 1981). The paradigm seemed to have potential, but there were doubts about its construct validity, largely based on the assumption that it was a milder version of the learned helplessness paradigm (Seligman & Beagley, 1975). Costela, Tejedar-Real, Mico, and Gibert-Rahola (1995) found that neonatal handling of rats improved their adaptation to the environment, so that they were able to cope with stress in the learned helplessness model of depression more effectively.

In the *chronic unpredictable stress* paradigm (Katz, 1981), rats are subjected to a variety of different stressors, including electric shocks, cold water immersion, and reversal of the light–dark rhythm. It also seemed to have predictive powers, but there was some doubt about the precise relationship between depression and stress in clinical populations.

The *chronic mild stress* (CMS) paradigm (Willner, Muscat, & Papp, 1992) was largely developed as a modification of the chronic unpredictable stress model, having the apparent advantages of removing the need for substantial stressors and concentrating on the loss of the reward principle. This procedure seems to work in mice as well as rats (Monleon et al., 1995) but is, of course, based essentially on manipulations designed to chronically impair well-being in the subjects. Ayensu et al. (1995) found that CMS increased corticosterone responses in Flinders lines of rats as well as reducing their saccharin preference and immune responsiveness.

The CMS model of depression has been designed to induce a state of anhedonia in rodents (as measured by sucrose intake) that mimics, as closely as is possible, the human condition. Anhedonia is a core symptom of depression, as listed in the *Diagnostic and Statistical Manual of Mental Disorders* (4th ed.; American Psychiatric Association, 1994), and is defined as "the decreased capacity to experience pleasure of any sort" (Fawcett, Clark, Scheftner, & Gibbons, 1983). Consequently, claims have been made that CMS can be used to determine the underlying neural mechanisms of anhedonia. Specifically, it has been suggested that anhedonia in rats is mediated by changes in dopamine D_2 receptor sensitivity in the nucleus accumbens. The implication is that anhedonia in humans also reflects a homologous change in the sensitivity of accumbens dopamine receptors.

Some doubt has been cast on the construct validity of the CMS model, however. Hence, Matthews, Forbes, and Reid (1995) have suggested that the changes in sucrose intake after the CMS regime may actually be related to changes in body weight rather than anhedonia, because they found that sucrose intake was decreased in animals that had undergone only food and water deprivation rather than the full CMS regime. Although this possibility has been argued against by Willner, Moreau, Nielsen, Papp, and Sluzewska (1996), it emphasizes the fact that establishing the construct validity of animal models of human psychological states is extremely difficult. The behavioral change in the animal that constitutes the model can arise from a multitude of causes. The problem is that because there is doubt about whether the animals subjected to CMS are actually anhedonic, the claims made about the underlying mechanisms of depression derived from the model must also be in doubt.

The last serious contender for a rodent model of human depression has seemed to be *intracranial self-stimulation* (ICSS) of reward centers, but the paradigm exists in several forms. In one, withdrawal from chronic amphetamine treatment (Leith & Barrett, 1976) is used; in a second, a lesion of the internal capsule in the region of the telencephalic–diencephalic border is carried out (Emrich, 1982); but a third involves no prior treatment (e.g., Fibiger & Phillips, 1981). Willner (1984) has argued that these tests all have a strong basis in that "depression is associated with a low frequency of positive reinforcement, particularly social reinforcement" (p. 10).

Since the Willner (1984) review was written, there has been a further attempt to assess whether *loss of social status* in rats also may produce a valid model of human depression. Rats exposed to CMS were said to behave more submissively when a conspecific intruder was introduced into their home cage (D'Aquila, Brain, & Willner, 1994). Impairment of aggressive behavior resulting from chronic stress had been earlier shown to be reduced by repeated treatment with a range of antidepressive agents (Zebrowska-Lupina, Ossowska, & Klenk-Majevska, 1991). Willner, D'Aquila, Coventry, and Brain (1995) have suggested that weekly defeat by aggressive Tryon Maze Dull rats decreases home cage dominance behavior of previously stable Lister rats as well as their consumption of palatable sucrose solution. Both effects have been normalized by 3 weeks of treatment with the tricyclic antidepressant imipramine. The approach needs much more detailed evaluation before it can be seriously considered an effective model of human depression.

Because this model is still being developed, it is too early yet to make any inferences based on it about the mechanisms that underlie loss of self-esteem in depression. There is still much to do before this model can truly be said to be validated. However, it should be mentioned that the construct validity of the model has recently been challenged (see Marrow & Brain, 1998).

There is considerable debate about the utility of rodent models in this area of research, but some do seem to have benefits for rapidly screening drugs. Whether they can be genuinely claimed to mimic the features of full clinical depression is much less certain. Certainly, some of the paradigms do not appear to work reliably in all laboratories, suggesting that there are aspects that have not been fully explored. All essentially involve considerable impairment of the animal's well-being.

Rodent Models of Social Anxiety

Social phobia, according to Davison and Neale (1978), "is a collection of fears generally linked to the presence of other people. Eating, speaking or virtually any other activity that might be carried out in the presence of others can elicit extreme anxiety" (p. 146). Brain (1995) has examined the features of potential rodent models of this activity and has concluded that such candidates must involve social behavior in a social species and should not be based on hierarchical relationships. Although there are a number of situations in which rodents show high anxiety levels (many of these featured in the section **Rodent Models of Anxiety**), it is actually impossible to establish that a rat or a mouse avoids conspecifics for irrational reasons. Often the responses are clearly adaptive (avoidance of a social dominant by a subordinate is a logical response) or, at least, interpretable in terms of neophobia. We personally feel that social phobia is a condition that is not going to be simply modeled in rats or mice. We can deal with anxiety or avoidance but not rationality.

Conclusion

There are very positive things that one can say about the use of animal models in exploring human neuroses and psychoses. Putting aside the obvious truism that such models have played a pivotal role in the development of a range of much more specific psychoactive drugs than those gaining currency before widespread use of the models, studies with rodents have greatly improved researchers' understanding of the roles of biological and other factors in human mental disease. Most of the studies on the localization of central nervous system lesions in (some) neuroses and psychoses would have been impossible (until very recently) without animal studies. Animal studies are useful also in evaluating the precise impact of genetic and experiential effects in the genesis or predisposition for such conditions. Rodent models have had, however, other more fundamental benefits. To take examples from the hostility literature, the studies with rodents have had a profound impact in changing our appreciation of the concept of hostility. They certainly give more currency to the view that use of threat and attack does not signal a single motivation. These studies emphasize that it is unlikely that a simple physiology underpins all expressions of this behavior and that conflict is a dynamic phenomenon involving changes in both the attacker and the attacked. Most neuroses and psychoses have been found, on examination, to be more complex than their original formulations.

Having said this, we feel that it has become increasingly difficult to defend the use of large numbers of rats and mice as models of human neuroses and psychoses. One reason is clearly rooted in our greater understanding of the behavioral needs of rats and mice and recognition that well-being of large numbers of such animals are chronically impaired in such models. On the cost versus benefit approach to animal experimentation, one has to be very convinced about the potential benefits to humans. This surety is challenged by the plethora of different tests available, often with very different characteristics and outcomes. There needs to be a serious reevaluation of which tests are most useful under a majority of circumstances. Less useful paradigms should be phased out relatively rapidly. The tendency to claim too much on the basis of such tests should also be resisted because it reduces credibility of the whole procedure. The limitations of animal models of human mental conditions should be freely admitted. Perhaps one should hear more about the impact of a certain hormone or drug on defensive threat rather than the compound's antihostility properties? Perhaps one should be happy to accept the predictive properties of a test in drug development without reading too much into other aspects of the model?

It seems that the time has come to perhaps attempt a dispassionate evaluation of the range of rodent models. Clearly, some models are persisted with because people have a vested interest in continuing with a particular model that may have served them well in the past. It seems improbable that we need all the models currently on display (many are said to do the same thing). Obviously the choice of the best models must be a balance between their costs (in terms of pain, suffering, and distress) and their utility (in terms largely of predictive power and reliability). (See Petrinovich's discussion, this volume, of a cost–benefit model for justifying a research agenda.) This evaluation obviously should not simply be done once, but should be part of a rolling program involving the fullest consultation.

References

American Psychiatric Association. (1994). *Diagnostic and statistical manual of mental disorders* (4th ed.). Washington, DC: Author.

Ayensu, W. K., Pucilowski, O., Mason, G. A., Overstreet, D. J., Rezvani, A. H., & Janowsky, D. S. (1995). Effects of chronic mild stress on serum complement activity, saccharin preference and corticosterone levels in Flinders lines of rats. *Physiology and Behavior, 57*, 165–169.

Blanchard, D. C., Rodgers, R. J., & Blanchard, R. J. (1990). Ethopharmacological control of fear and anxiety in the rat. In P. F. Brain, S. Parmigiani, R. J. Blanchard, & D. Mainardi (Eds.), *Fear and defence* (pp. 245–267). Chur, Switzerland: Harwood Academic.

Blanchard, R. J., & Blanchard, D. C. (1990). Anti-predator defence as models of fear and anxiety. In P. F. Brain, S. Parmigiani, R. J. Blanchard, & D. Mainardi (Eds.), *Fear and defence* (pp. 89–108). Chur, Switzerland: Harwood Academic.

Brain P. F. (1981). Differentiation of attack and defense in rodents. In P. F. Brain & D. Benton (Eds.), *Multidisciplinary approaches to aggression research* (pp. 53–78). Amsterdam: Elsevier/North-Holland.

Brain, P. F. (1984). Comments on laboratory-based "aggression tests." *Animal Behaviour, 32*, 1256–1257.

Brain, P. F. (1986). The nature of aggression. In P. F. Brain (Ed.), *Alcohol and aggression* (pp. 1–18). London: Croom-Helm.

Brain, P. F. (1989). Social stress in laboratory mouse colonies. In T. B. Poole (Ed.), *Laboratory animal welfare research: Rodents* (pp. 1–21). Potter's Bar, United Kingdom: University Federation for Animal Welfare.

Brain P. F. (1990). Stress in agonistic contexts in rodents. In R. Dantzer & R. Zayan (Eds.), *Stress in domestic animals* (pp. 73–85). Dordrecht, The Netherlands: Kluwer Academic.

Brain, P. F. (1992a). Behavioural and clinical assessment of pain and distress: Species differences. In G. Perretta (Ed.), *Valutazione e controllo del dolore e del distress negli animali da laboratorio* [Evaluating and control of pain and distress in laboratory animals] (pp. 1–8). Rome: Comitato Italiano per le Scienze degli Animuli da Laboratorio.

Brain, P. F. (1992b). Understanding the behaviours of feral species may facilitate design of optimal living conditions for common laboratory rodents. *Animal Technology, 43*, 99–105.

Brain, P. F. (1994a). Hormonal aspects of aggression and violence. In A. J. Reiss, Jr., & J. A. Roth (Eds.), *Understanding and preventing violence: Volume 2. Biobehavioral influences* (pp. 177–244). Washington, DC: National Academy Press.

Brain, P. F. (1994b). Pain and distress in laboratory animals: What we know and what we assume. In A. M. Goldberg & L. F. M. van Zutphen (Eds.), *World Congress on Alternatives and Animal Use in the Life Sciences: Education, research and testing* (pp. 623–628). New York: Liebert.

Brain, P. F. (1995). Animal modelling of social anxiety. *Journal of Psychopharmacology, 9*(Suppl. 1), 139.

Brain, P. F. (1997). Aggression in laboratory rodents as sources of pain and distress. In P. N. O'Donoghue (Ed.), *Harmonization of laboratory animal husbandry* (pp. 10–14). London: Royal Society of Medicine Press.

Brain, P. F., Alias bin Kamis, Haug, M., Mandel, P., & Simler, S. (1982). Studies on diverse models of aggression in drug research. *Acta Physiologica et Pharmacologica Bulgarica, 8*, 97–105.

Brain, P. F., & Al-Maliki, S. (1978). A comparison of "intermale fighting" in "standard opponent" tests and attack directed towards locusts by "TO" strain mice: Effects of simple experimental manipulations. *Animal Behaviour, 26*, 723–737.

Brain, P. F., & Al-Maliki, S. (1979). Effects of lithium chloride injections on rank-related fighting, maternal aggression and locust-killing responses in naive and experienced "TO" strain mice. *Pharmacology, Biochemistry and Behavior, 10*, 663–669.

Brain, P. F., Benton, D., Childs, G., & Parmigiani, S. (1981). The effect of the type of opponent in tests of murine aggression. *Behavioural Processes, 6*, 319–327.

Brain, P. F., & Haug, M. (1992). Hormonal and neurochemical correlates of various forms of animal "aggression." *Psychoneuroendocrinology, 17*, 1–16.

Brain, P. F., Haug, M., & Alias bin Kamis. (1983). Hormones and different tests for "aggression" with particular reference to the effects of testosterone metabolites. In J. Balthazart, E. Prove, & R. Gilles (Eds.), *Hormones and behavior in higher vertebrates* (pp. 290–304). Berlin: Springer-Verlag.

Brain, P. F., & Kamal, K. B. H. (1989). Effects of prior social experiences on individual aggressiveness in laboratory rodents. *Rassegna di Psychologia, 6*, 37–44.

Brain, P. F., Miras, R. L., & Berry, M. S. (1993). Diversity of animal models of aggression: Their impact on the putative alcohol/aggression link. *Journal of Studies on Alcohol*, Suppl. II), 140–145.

Brain, P. F., Kusumorini, N., & Benton, D. (1991). "Anxiety" in laboratory rodents: A brief review of some recent behavioural developments. *Behavioural Processes, 25*, 71–80.

Charrier, D., Dangoumau, L., Puech, A. J., Hamon, M., & Thiebot M. H. (1995). Failure of CCK receptor ligands to modify anxiety-related behavioural suppression in an operant conflict paradigm in rats. *Psychopharmacology, 121*, 127–134.

Christmas, A. J., & Maxwell, D. R. (1970). A comparison of some benzodiazepines and other drugs on aggressive and exploratory behaviour in mice and rats. *Neuropharmacology, 9*, 17–29.

Costela, C., Tejedar-Real, P., Mico, J. A., & Gibert-Rahola, J. (1995). Effect of neonatal handling on learned helplessness model of depression. *Physiology and Behavior, 57*, 407–410.

Crawley, J. (1981). Neuropharmacological specificity of a simple animal model for the behavioral actions of the benzodiazepines. *Pharmacology, Biochemistry and Behavior, 15*, 695–699.

D'Aquila, P. S., Brain, P., & Willner, P. (1994). Effects of chronic mild stress on performance in behavioral tests relevant to anxiety and depression. *Physiology and Behavior, 56*, 861–867.

Davison, G. C., & Neale, J. M. (1978). *Abnormal psychology* (2nd ed.). London: Wiley.

Emrich, H. M. (1982). A possible role of opioid actions in endogenous depression. In S. Z. Langer, R. Takahashi, T. Segawa, & M. Briley (Eds.), *New vistas in depression* (pp. 233–237). New York: Pergamon Press.

European Community. (1994). *First report from the Commission to the Council and the European Parliament on the statistics on the number of animals used for experimental and other scientific purposes*. Luxembourg: Office of Publications of the Europeran Communities.

Fawcett, J., Clark, D. C., Scheftner, W. A., & Gibbons, R. D. (1983). Assessing anhedonia in psychiatric patients: The Pleasure Scale. *Archives of General Psychiatry, 40*, 79–84.

Fibiger, H. C., & Phillips, A. G. (1981, November). Increased intracranial self-stimulation in rats after long-term administration of desipramine. *Science, 214*, 683–685.

File, S. E. (1987). The contribution of behavioural studies to the neuropharmacology of anxiety. *Neuropharmacology, 26*, 877–886.

Gardner, C. R. (1985). Distress vocalization in rat pups: A simple screening method for anxiolytic drugs. *Journal of Pharmacological Methods, 14*, 181–187.

Hogg, S. (1996). A review of the validity and variability of the elevated plus-maze as an animal model of anxiety. *Pharmacology, Biochemistry and Behavior, 54*, 21–30.

Home Office. (1997). *Statistics of scientific procedures on living animals, Great Britain 1996.* London: Her Majesty's Stationery Office.

Insel, T. R., Hill, J. L., & Mayor, R. B. (1986). Rat pup ultrasonic isolation calls: Possible mediation by the benzodiazepine receptor complex. *Pharmacology, Biochemistry and Behavior, 24*, 1263–1267.

Jones, S. E., & Brain, P. F. (1987). Performances of inbred and outbred laboratory mice in putative tests on aggression. *Behavior Genetics, 17*, 87–96.

Karli, P. (1956). The Norway rat's killing response to the white mouse: An experimental analysis. *Behaviour, 10*, 81–103.

Katz, R. J. (1981). Animal models and human depressive disorders. *Neuroscience and Bio-behavioural Reviews, 5*, 231–246.

Lee, C. (1990). *Behavioural and neurohumoral mechanisms of environmental analgesia in Mus musculus.* Unpublished doctoral dissertation, University of Bradford, Yorkshire, England.

Leith, N. J., & Barrett, R. J. (1976). Amphetamine and the reward system: Evidence for tolerance and post-drug depression. *Psychopharmacology, 46*, 19–25.

Marrow, L. P., & Brain, P. F. (1998). An evaluation of the use of defeat-induced loss of status in the rat as a model of loss of self-esteem and depression in humans. *Aggressive Behavior, 24*, 297–306.

Martinez, M., Simon, V. M., Castano, D., & Brain, P. F. (1989). Effect of type of opponent on aggression in male mice with particular reference to studies with anti-hormones. *Behavioural Processes, 20*, 125–138.

Martinez-Sanchis, S., Brain, P. F., Salvador, A., & Simon, V. M. (1996). Long-term chronic treatment with stanozolol lacks significant effects on aggression and activity in young and adult male laboratory mice. *General Pharmacology, 27*, 293–298.

Matthews, K., Forbes, N., & Reid, I. C. (1995). Sucrose consumption as a hedonic measure following chronic unpredictable mild stress. *Physiology and Behavior, 57*, 241–248.

Monleon, S., D'Aquila, P., Parra, A., Simon, V. M., Brain, P. F., & Willner, P. (1995). Attenuation of sucrose consumption in mice by chronic mild stress and its restoration by imipramine. *Psychopharmacology, 117*, 453–457.

O'Donoghue, P. N. (Ed.). (1994). *The accommodation of laboratory animals in accordance with animal welfare requirements* [Proceedings of an International Workshop at Bundesgesundheitsant, Berlin]. Bonn, Germany: Bundesministerium Fur Ernahrung, Landwirtschaft und Forsten.

Parmigiani, S., Brain, P. F., Mainardi, D., & Brunoni, V. (1988). Different patterns of biting attack generated when lactating female mice (*Mus domesticus*) encounter male and female conspecific intruders. *Journal of Comparative Psychology, 102*, 287–293.

Pellow, S. (1985). Can drug effects on anxiety and convulsions be separated? *Neuroscience & Biobehavioral Reviews, 9*, 55–73.

Porsolt, R. D. (1981). Behavioral despair. In S. J. Enna, J. B. Malick, & E. Richelson (Eds.), *Antidepressants: Neurochemical, behavioral and clinical perspectives* (pp. 121–139). New York: Raven Press.

Seligman, M. E. P., & Beagley, G. (1975). Learned helplessness in the rat. *Journal of Comparative and Physiological Psychology, 88*, 534–541.

Treit, D. (1985). Animal models for the study of anti-anxiety agents: A review. *Neuroscience & Biobehavioral Reviews, 9*, 203–222.

Vellucci, S. V. (1989). Anxiety. In R. A. Webster & C. C. Jordan (Eds.), *Neurotransmitters, drugs and disease* (pp. 394–427). London: Blackwell Scientific.

Willner, P. (1984). The validity of animal models of depression. *Psychopharmacology, 83*, 1–16.

Willner, P. (1990). Animal models of depression: An overview. *Pharmacological Therapy, 45*, 425–455.

Willner, P., D'Aquila, P. S., Coventry, T., & Brain, P. (1995). Loss of social status: Preliminary evaluation of a novel animal model of depression. *Journal of Psychopharmacology, 9*, 207–213.

Willner, P., Moreau, J. -L., Nielsen, C. K., Papp, M., & Sluzewska, A. (1996). Decreased hedonic responsiveness following chronic mild stress is not secondary to loss of body weight. *Physiology and Behavior, 60*, 129–134.

Willner, P., Muscat, R., & Papp, M. (1992). Chronic mild stress-induced anhedonia: A realistic animal model of depression. *Neuroscience & Biobehavioral Reviews, 16*, 525–534.

Zebrowska-Lupina, I., Ossowska, G., & Klenk-Majevska, E. (1991). Chronic stress reduces fighting behaviour in rats: The effect of antidepressants. *Pharmacology Biochemistry and Behavior, 39*, 293–296.

6

The Mouse Defense Test Battery: An Experimental Model of Different Emotional States

Guy Griebel and David J. Sanger

There are few well-accepted animal models of psychiatric disorders. However, a number of animal models of anxiety have been proposed, most of which involve exposure of animals to external (e.g., cues previously paired with footshock) or internal (e.g., drugs) stimuli that are assumed to be capable of inducing anxiety in humans. The actual measures taken include suppression of previously punished activities, conditioned emotional responses, a range of sonic and ultrasonic vocalizations, and social and exploratory behaviors (for reviews, see Sanger, Perrault, Morel, Joly, & Zivkovic, 1991; Treit, 1985).

The suggestion has been made many times that defensive behaviors of lower mammals constitute a significant model for understanding human emotional disorders (e.g., R. J. Blanchard & Blanchard, 1984; see also Brain & Marrow, this volume). Defensive behaviors occur in response to a number of threatening stimuli, including predators, attacking conspecifics, and dangerous objects or situations. Such behaviors can readily be studied in wild rats, which show a complete defensive repertoire in response to danger. In contrast, in laboratory rats, defensive threat and attack behaviors in response to predators have been much reduced through systematic selection for docility by breeders (R. J. Blanchard, Flannelly, & Blanchard, 1986). However, the disadvantages of using wild rats as subjects in laboratory research are obvious. For example, it is clear that the difficulty and cost in obtaining and maintaining these animals are greater than for laboratory rats.

There are reasons to believe that the laboratory mouse has not been so severely selected on the basis of its defensive behaviors. The smaller size of the mouse and its reduced potential to inflict serious wounds, plus the ease of handling mice with a tail pickup, have enabled greater tolerance of defensive attack behavior in this species, and indeed, domesticated

We acknowledge the contribution of Professors D. Caroline and Robert J. Blanchard (University of Hawaii) in offering suggestions and stimulating discussion during the course of this work.

mice often show biting behavior to human handling (R. J. Blanchard, Parmigiani, Agullana, Weiss, & Blanchard, 1995). Thus, it has been demonstrated that mice from four lines—three inbred (BALB/c, C57BL/6, and DBA/2) and one outbred (Swiss)—show intense defense reactions when confronted with an approaching threat stimulus (laboratory rat). They display initial flight, followed by risk assessment (RA), and defense vocalization and biting occur when escape is blocked (Griebel, Sanger, & Perrault, 1997). The concept of RA has emerged from the work of D. C. Blanchard, Blanchard, and Rodgers (1991). These authors have defined RA in terms of orientation toward present or potential threat, often followed by specific approach responses. D. C. Blanchard et al. have demonstrated that RA is associated with gathering of information concerning threat sources. Together, these defense patterns closely resemble those of wild rats, suggesting that mice of these strains do not show the reductions in flight and defensive threat–attack that are typical of laboratory rats. Such findings clearly indicate that the laboratory mouse may be a suitable subject for studies concerned with defensive behaviors.

However, it was not clear in these initial studies whether the responses displayed by the mice were specific to the encounter with a laboratory rat. The idea that defensive reactions might be elicited by any approaching stimulus was addressed by studying the influence of various stimuli on defensive reactions of Swiss mice (Griebel, Blanchard, Jung, & Blanchard, 1995). Briefly, this study demonstrated that when compared with mice approached by a leather glove, mice confronted with an anesthetized or conscious rat displayed potentiated flight responses and defensive threat–attack reactions, whereas RA behavior was generally similar in all three conditions. Furthermore, escape attempts after removal of the stimulus were higher in the rat conditions compared with the leather glove group. In this latter case, however, responses displayed by the leather glove group mice were also higher than those observed in a group that was not exposed to any stimulus, indicating that the leather glove stimulation also elicited defense reactions, albeit at a lower level. Together, these results demonstrate that a rat stimulus elicits higher levels of flight reactions and defensive threat–attack responses than a leather glove stimulus, thereby suggesting that this experimental situation is appropriate for investigating antipredator defense. The aim of the present chapter is to provide evidence that antipredator defense behaviors elicited in mice by the encounter with a rat may be useful to model different aspects of human anxiety.

The Mouse Defense Test Battery

The Mouse Defense Test Battery (MDTB) consists of an oval runway based on that used in the Fear Defense Test Battery with rats (for more details, see R. J. Blanchard, Blanchard, Rodgers, & Weiss, 1990; Griebel, Blanchard, Jung, & Blanchard, 1995). However, specific situational and behavioral components of the Anxiety Defense Test Battery (R. J.

Table 6.1. Defensive Behaviors Elicited in the Mouse by the Exposure to a Rat and the Corresponding Parameters Recorded in the Mouse Defense Test Battery

Defensive behavior	Parameters
Risk assessment	Stops and orientations when the mouse is chased by a rat; approaches followed by withdrawal responses toward the rat, which remains at a constant distance (the mouse is trapped in one part of the runway)
Flight	Avoidance distance and frequency of avoidance when the rat is introduced into the runway apparatus
Defensive threat–attack	Vocalizations, biting, and upright postures on forced contact with the rat
Contextual defense	Escape attempts from the runway after the rat has been removed from the test area

Blanchard et al., 1990), involving reactivity to stimuli associated with potential threat rather than to the actual presence of an approaching predator, are incorporated into the MDTB. Briefly, the MDTB consists of five tests associated either with potential threat (contextual defense) or with the actual presence of an approaching threat (i.e., a rat). The latter focuses on changes in flight, RA, and defensive threat–attack behaviors, whereas the former involves escape attempt responses from the runway cage (see Table 1).

In the contextual defense situation, postpredator escape attempts from the runway cage are dramatically increased when compared with the performance measured before the confrontation with the rat. Similarly, in response to an approaching predator, mice invariably show active flight behavior, and when subjects run to escape the chasing predator, they frequently show RA consisting of an abrupt movement arrest often followed by orientation to the oncoming predator. Furthermore, when mice are constrained in one part of the runway, they often display active RA, consisting of approaches to the predator followed by withdrawals. Finally, defensive threat and attack to the rat occur almost invariably on forced contact (Griebel, Blanchard, Jung, & Blanchard, 1995). This pattern of responding can be quantified using the specific behavioral parameters listed in Table 1.

Evidence That Defense Reactions Relate to Different Emotional States

It has been suggested that defense responses of rats confronted with a predatory stimulus provide an appropriate laboratory model for investigating behavior relevant to human emotional disorders (R. J. Blanchard & Blanchard, 1984). Subsequent investigations with anxiolytic compounds have confirmed this idea (for review, see R. J. Blanchard, Yudko, Rodgers, & Blanchard, 1993). Interestingly, these studies indicated that defense reactions may be used to differentiate between several classes of anxiolytic drugs. For instance, benzodiazepines (BZPs; e.g., diazepam or chlordiazepoxide), serotonin receptor ligands (e.g., buspirone, gepirone, or 8-hydroxy-2-(di-n-propylamino)-tetralin [8-OH-DPAT]), and alcohol produce modification in responding primarily involving RA and defensive threat–attack reactions. Interestingly, these latter responses showed a bidirectional (increase at low doses and decrease at high doses) response to alcohol, indicating some differences between alcohol and BZPs, suggesting that particular patterns of drug effects may map rather precisely onto the target symptoms for specific psychopathologies. Therefore, the relationships between the variety of responses measured in the MDTB become an important issue. Do these different responses provide different measures of the same state, or do they measure distinct states of defensiveness, fear, or anxiety? This question can be approached by (a) performing a factor analysis of the various behavioral defense reactions observed in the battery and (b) comparing the effects of drugs used in the clinical management of different anxiety disorders (i.e., generalized anxiety disorder [GAD] and panic disorder [PD]).

Evidence From Factor Analysis

Factor analyses are commonly used to describe the relationships among different variables and, consequently, to identify specific indexes or factors, such as Anxiety or Locomotor Activity. Performed on the behaviors recorded in the MDTB, this analysis identified three main independent factors (Griebel, Blanchard, & Blanchard, 1996; see Exhibit 1). Factor 1 included cognitive aspects of defensive behaviors that appear to be related to the process of acquiring and analyzing information in the presence of threatening stimuli (i.e., RA). Flight responses loaded heavily on Factor 2 and to a lesser extent on Factor 3. Several defensive threat–attack reactions (i.e., upright postures and biting) and escape attempts loaded highly on Factor 3, indicating that this factor reflects more affective defense reactions. Together, this pattern is consistent with the idea that defense reactions of mice exposed to a threat stimulus relate to different emotional states.

Exhibit 6.1. Main Factor Loadings of the Various Defensive Behaviors in the Mouse Defense Test Battery

Factor 1	Factor 2	Factor 3
Stops	Avoidance distance	Biting
Orientations	Avoidance frequency	Upright postures
Approaches followed by withdrawal responses		Avoidance distance
		Escape attempts

Evidence From Drug Effects

The clinical evidence for a dissociation of GAD and PD, on the basis of drug response, is controversial (Lister, 1991). However, there is general agreement that a range of tricyclic antidepressants, serotonin reuptake inhibitors (SSRIs), inhibitors of monoamine oxidase (MAO inhibitors), the triazolobenzodiazepine alprazolam, and some other high-potency BZPs (e.g., clonazepam) are effective against PD (Burrows, Judd, & Norman, 1993; Priest, Gimbrett, Roberts, & Steinert, 1995). In addition, clinical and basic studies support the involvement of cholecystokinin (CCK) in PD (Bradwejn, Koszycki, Couetoux du Tertre, & Bourin, 1992; Van Megen, Den Boer, & Westenberg, 1994). By contrast, drugs used against GAD, such as the traditional BZP receptor full agonists (e.g., chlordiazepoxide or diazepam) and the serotonin receptor agonist buspirone, are of minimal utility in the treatment of PD (Johnson, Lydiard, & Ballenger, 1995; Klein, 1995; Lader, 1994; Roy Byrne, Wingerson, Cowley, & Dager, 1993).

On the basis of these clinical findings, the drugs investigated in the MDTB were divided into three categories (see Table 2): (a) those used against GAD, including two classical BZPs (chlordiazepoxide and diazepam) and one serotonin receptor agonist (gepirone); (b) those effective or potentially effective against PD, including a tricyclic antidepressant (imipramine), an SSRI (fluoxetine), two reversible MAO inhibitors (moclobemide and befloxatone), and two CCK_B receptor antagonists (PD 135,158 and LY 288513); and (c) those used in the treatment of both GAD and PD, represented by the second-generation BZPs alprazolam and clonazepam.

Effects of compounds used in the treatment of GAD. Results indicated that chlordiazepoxide and diazepam reduced RA activities observed in the

Table 6.2. Drugs Tested in the Mouse Defense Test Battery and Their Clinical Efficacy (if Known) in the Management of Generalized Anxiety Disorder (GAD) and Panic Disorder (PD)

Drug	Action–class	GAD	PD
Alprazolam	Benzodiazepine	+	+
Befloxatone	MAOP-A inhibitor		
Chlordiazepoxide	Benzodiazepine	+	(+)
Clonazepam	Benzodiazepine	+	+
Diazepam	Benzodiazepine	+	(+)
Fluoxetine	Serotonin reuptake inhibitor	−	+
Gepirone	Serotonin agonist	+	−
Imipramine	NA/5-HT reuptake inhibitor	−	+
LY 288513	CCK_B antagonist		
Moclobemide	MAO-A inhibitor		+
PD 135, 158	CCK_B antagonist		

Note. MAO = monoamine oxidase; NA/5-HT = noradrenalin/serotonin; CCK = cholecystokinin; + = demonstrated clinical effects; (+) = effective at high and mostly sedative doses; − = negative or inconclusive effects.

Table 6.3. Effects of Various Drugs Effective Against Generalized Anxiety
Disorders on Defensive Behaviors in the Mouse Defense Test Battery

Drug	Risk assessment		Flight	Defensive threat and attack	Escape attempts
	Chase	Straight alley			
Chlordiazepoxide	↓	–	(↓)	↓	↓
Diazepam	↓	↑	–	↓	↓
Gepirone	–	–	–	↓	↓

Note. ↓ = a decrease in the response; (↓) = a decrease in the response at motor-impairing
doses only; – = ineffective; ↑ = an increase in the response.

chase–flight test, defensive threat–attack reactions induced by physical
contact with the rat, and escape attempts after the rat had been removed
from the test area (see Table 3). Furthermore, diazepam, but not chlordiazepoxide, slightly increased RA responses displayed when subjects were
constrained in one part of the runway. In addition, diazepam failed to
affect flight whereas chlordiazepoxide reduced this behavior, albeit at a
motor-impairing dose (25 mg/kg; spontaneous locomotor activity was measured in the runway apparatus during a 3-min period preceding the exposure to the rat; Griebel, Blanchard, Jung, & Blanchard, 1995; Griebel, Sanger, & Perrault, 1997). Compared with the BZPs, the serotonin
receptor agonist gepirone presented a very similar profile on defensive
threat–attack responses, escape attempts, and flight. The former responses were reduced, whereas flight behavior remained unchanged. By
contrast, gepirone did not decrease the high level of RA responses
when subjects were chased by the rat and did not increase these activities in the straight alley situation (Griebel, Blanchard, Jung, Masuda, &
Blanchard, 1995). Together, these results indicate that defensive threat–
attack reactions and escape attempts show a consistent response to drugs
used in the treatment of GAD regardless of their pharmacological
properties. By contrast, RA responses appear to be mainly modulated by
BZPs.

Effects of compounds used in the treatment of PD. Imipramine, fluoxetine, and the reversible MAO inhibitors were administered both acutely
and chronically because clinical data indicate that long-term treatment is
necessary to achieve therapeutic response. The effects of two potential
antipanic compounds, PD 135,158 and LY 288513, were investigated after
acute treatment.

After single administrations, imipramine, fluoxetine, and both reversible MAO inhibitors did not affect any of the defense responses (see Table
4). Instead, imipramine and fluoxetine potentiated flight responses and
defensive biting (data not shown). In sharp contrast with this profile,
chronic administration of the two drugs decreased both measures. In addition, imipramine and fluoxetine also decreased RA activities when sub-

Table 6.4. Effects of Various Drugs Effective or Potentially Effective Against Panic Disorder on Defensive Behaviors in the Mouse Defense Test Battery

| Drugs | Risk assessment | | Flight | Defensive threat and attack | Escape attempts |
	Chase	Straight alley			
Befloxatone	−	↑	↓	−	−
Fluoxetine	↓	−	↓	↓	↓
Imipramine	↓	−	↓	↓	↓
LY 288513	−	−	↓	−	−
Moclobemide	−	−	↓	−	−
PD 135,158	−	−	↓	−	−

Note. − = ineffective; ↑ = an increase in the response; ↓ = a decrease in the response. Results refer to effects observed after repeated administration of imipramine, fluoxetine, befloxatone, and moclobemide and acute administration of LY 288513 and PD 135,138.

jects were chased by the rat and escape attempts after the removal of the rat (Griebel, Blanchard, Agnes, & Blanchard, 1995). After repeated administration of the two reversible MAO inhibitors moclobemide and befloxatone, a significant reduction in flight was observed. In addition, befloxatone but not moclobemide increased RA responses when mice were constrained in one part of the apparatus facing the rat, which remained at a constant distance (Griebel, Perrault, & Sanger, 1997). Finally, a single administration of PD 135,158 and LY 288513 resulted in a reduction in the flight measure. No other drug effects were observed with these compounds.

Overall, these results showed that antipanic compounds mainly affected flight reactions. Furthermore, some of these compounds (i.e. imipramine, fluoxetine, and befloxatone) partially affected defensive threat–attack responses and RA activities. In addition, the finding of a potentiation in some defense reactions (i.e., flight and bitings) after a single dose of imipramine and fluoxetine fits well with the clinical observation of an exacerbation in anxious responses that may sometimes occur at the beginning of treatment with imipramine or with an SSRI (Westenberg, 1996; Westenberg & Den Boer, 1993).

Effects of compounds used in the treatment of GAD and PD. Alprazolam and clonazepam displayed very similar behavioral profiles in the MDTB (Griebel, Blanchard, Jung, Lee, et al., 1995; Griebel, Sanger, & Perrault, 1996; see Table 5). The drugs reduced flight, defensive threat–attack reactions, and RA activities during the chase–flight test. In addition, they increased RA in the straight alley situation, although the effect of alprazolam was not statistically significant. Thus, these drugs affected a wider range of defense reactions than compounds used against either GAD or PD.

Table 6.5. Effects of Drugs Effective Against Generalized Anxiety and Panic Disorders on Defensive Behaviors in the Mouse Defense Test Battery

Drugs	Risk assessment		Flight	Defensive threat and attack	Escape attempts
	Chase	Straight alley			
Alprazolam	↓	↑	↓	↓	↓
Clonazepam	↓	↑	↓	↓	↓

Note. ↓ = a decrease in the response; ↑ = an increase in the response.

Discussion

The MDTB: Advantages in Using a Multiparameter Test Paradigm

A major concern with traditional animal models of anxiety is that they are in most cases unable to discriminate between anxiolyticlike effects induced by BZPs, serotonin receptor agonists, or SSRIs, although clinical findings strongly indicate differential therapeutic efficacy of these agents, according to the anxiety disorder treated. On the basis of these observations, it is clear that the major advantage of the MDTB is that it provides multiple measures that may be differentially involved in various forms of anxiety. The factor analysis performed on the different defense reactions displayed in the MDTB identified several subsets of defensive behaviors that may ultimately represent different emotional states.

Drug experiments demonstrated that anxiety-relieving compounds generally tend to decrease defensive behaviors. However, note that some responses are specifically or mainly affected by certain drug classes. Thus, BZPs decreased RA activities of mice chased by the rat and defensive threat and attack responses, whereas the serotonin agent gepirone mainly affected contextual defense and defensive threat and attack behaviors. In addition, SSRIs, MAO inhibitors, and CCK$_B$ antagonists have a clearer impact on flight responses than on other defensive reactions. Together, these observations suggest that RA, flight, defensive threat–attack, and escape attempts probably reflect different aspects of anxiety-related reactions, thereby confirming the findings from the factor analysis.

Clinical Relevance of the Defensive Behaviors of the Mice

The factor analysis and the results from the drug experiments lead to the possibility of finding components of defense that are similar to human anxiety reactions.

Risk assessment. Previous reports have suggested that there may be an isomorphism between RA responses in rats and several behaviors often described in GAD patients (D. C. Blanchard et al., 1991) such as apprehensive expectation and vigilance and scanning, involving hyperattentiveness (*Diagnostic and Statistical Manual of Mental Disorders* [*DSM–IV*]; American Psychiatric Association, 1994). With the exception of gepirone, drugs effective against GAD (i.e., BZPs) modulated this particular response. Importantly, anxiolytic drugs that affect RA generally decreased the response in situations where baseline scores were high (i.e., the chase test), whereas they increased RA when control activities were low (i.e., straight alley test). Together, these findings indicate that there is a rather good correspondence in terms of drug effects between the clinical outcome in GAD and the ability to modify RA responses in the MDTB. This strongly suggests that the latter behavior may be considered particularly relevant in modeling some aspects of GAD.

Flight. The observation that PD patients usually report an urgent desire to flee from where the attack is occurring (American Psychiatric Association, 1994) has led several authors to suggest that panic symptoms are due to pathological, spontaneous activation of neuronal mechanisms underlying flight reactions (Deakin & Graeff, 1991; Deakin, Guimaraes, Wang, Hellewell, & Hensman, 1991; Graeff, 1990). In accordance with this suggestion, data from the MDTB clearly demonstrated that panic-modulating agents specifically decrease animals' flight responses. Thus, the clinically effective antipanic agents reduced flight behaviors. Similarly, the putative antipanic compounds befloxatone, PD 135,158, and LY 288513 significantly decreased flight. Furthermore, the anti-GAD agents chlordiazepoxide, diazepam, and gepirone failed to affect this response in a selective manner (i.e., at nonsedative doses). Together, these findings suggest that flight reactions elicited by exposure to a natural predator may serve as an effective experimental model of panic.

Defensive threat and attack behaviors and contextual escape attempts. Although no isomorphism between these defense behaviors and a given symptom in anxiety-related disorders is indicated, the results indicate that these responses are particularly sensitive to modulation by drugs used in the treatment of GAD.

Conclusion

The MDTB studies suggest that this laboratory procedure provides a model capable of responding to and differentiating anxiety-relieving drugs of different classes through specific profiles of effect on different measures. This represents a significant improvement over other animal models for evaluating drugs active against emotional disorders and is consonant with the view that such disorders may represent dysfunction in particular defense systems.

References

American Psychiatric Association. (1994). *Diagnostic and statistical manual of mental disorders* (4th ed.). Washington DC: Author.

Blanchard, D. C., Blanchard, R. J., & Rodgers, R. J. (1991). Risk assessment and animal models of anxiety. In B. Olivier, J. Mos, & J. L. Slangen (Eds.), *Animal models in psychopharmacology* (pp. 117–134). Basel, Switzerland: Birkhauser Verlag AG.

Blanchard, R. J., & Blanchard, D. C., (1984). Affect and aggression: An animal model applied to human behavior. In R. J. Blanchard & D. C. Blanchard (Eds.), *Advances in the study of aggression* (pp. 1–62). Orlando, FL: Academic Press.

Blanchard, R. J., Blanchard, D. C., Rodgers, J., & Weiss, S. M. (1990). The characterization and modelling of antipredator defensive behavior. *Neuroscience and Biobehavioral Reviews, 14*, 463–472.

Blanchard, R. J., Flannelly, K. J., & Blanchard, D. C. (1986). Defensive behavior of laboratory and wild *Rattus norvegicus. Journal of Comparative Psychology, 100*, 101–107.

Blanchard, R. J., Parmigiani, S., Agullana, R., Weiss, S. M., & Blanchard, D. C. (1995). Behaviors of Swiss-Webster and C57/BL/6N sin mice in a fear/defense test battery. *Aggressive Behavior, 21*, 21–28.

Blanchard, R. J., Yudko, E. B., Rodgers, R. J., & Blanchard, D. C. (1993). Defense system psychopharmacology: An ethological approach to the pharmacology of fear and anxiety. *Behavioural Brain Research, 58*, 155–165.

Bradwejn, J., Koszycki, D., Couetoux du Tertre, A., & Bourin, M. (1992). The cholecystokinin hypothesis of panic and anxiety disorders: A review. *Journal of Psychopharmacology, 6*, 345–351.

Burrows, G. D., Judd, F. K., & Norman, T. R. (1993). Long-term drug treatment of panic disorder. *Journal of Psychiatric Research, 27*(Suppl. 1), 111–125.

Deakin, J. F. W., & Graeff, F. G. (1991). 5-HT and mechanisms of defense. *Journal of Psychopharmacology, 5*, 305–315.

Deakin, J. F. W., Guimaraes, F. S., Wang, F., Hellewell, J., & Hensman, R. (1991). 5-HT receptor mechanisms in human anxiety. In M. Briley & S. E. File (Eds.), *New concepts in anxiety* (pp. 74–93). New York: CRC Press.

Graeff, F. G. (1990). Brain defense system and anxiety. In G. D. Burrows, M. Roth, & R. Noyes, Jr. (Eds.), *Handbook of anxiety: Vol. 3. The neurobiology of anxiety* (pp. 307–343). Amsterdam: Elsevier.

Griebel, G., Blanchard, D. C., Agnes, R. S., & Blanchard, R. J. (1995). Differential modulation of antipredator defensive behavior in Swiss-Webster mice following acute or chronic administration of imipramine and fluoxetine. *Psychopharmacology* (Berlin), *120*, 57–66.

Griebel, G., Blanchard, D. C., & Blanchard, R. J. (1996). Evidence that the behaviors in the Mouse Defense Test Battery relate to different emotional states: A factor analytic study. *Physiology and Behavior, 60*, 1255–1260.

Griebel, G., Blanchard, D. C., Jung, A., & Blanchard, R. J. (1995). A model of 'antipredator' defense in Swiss-Webster mice: Effects of benzodiazepine receptor ligands with different intrinsic activities. *Behavioural Pharmacology, 6*, 732–745.

Griebel, G., Blanchard, D. C., Jung, A., Lee, J. C., Masuda, C. K., & Blanchard, R. J. (1995). Further evidence that the Mouse Defense Test Battery is useful for screening anxiolytic and panicolytic drugs: Effects of acute and chronic treatment with alprazolam. *Neuropharmacology, 34*, 1625–1633.

Griebel, G., Blanchard, D. C., Jung, A., Masuda, C. K., & Blanchard, R. J. (1995). 5-HT$_{1A}$ agonists modulate mouse antipredator defensive behavior differently from the 5-HT$_{2A}$ antagonist pirenperone. *Pharmacology, Biochemistry and Behavior, 51*, 235–244.

Griebel, G., Perrault, G., & Sanger, D. J. (1997). Behavioural profiles of the reversible monoamine-oxidase-A inhibitors befloxatone and moclobemide in an experimental model for screening anxiolytic and anti-panic drugs. *Psychopharmacology* (Berlin), *131*, 180–186.

Griebel, G., Sanger, D. J., & Perrault, G. (1996). The Mouse Defense Test Battery: Evaluation of the effects of non-selective and BZ-1 (ω1) selective, benzodiazepine receptor ligands. *Behavioural Pharmacology, 7*, 560–572.

Griebel, G., Sanger, D. J., & Perrault, G. (1997). Genetic differences in the Mouse Defense Test Battery. *Aggressive Behavior, 23*, 19–31.

Johnson, M. R., Lydiard, R. B., & Ballenger, J. C. (1995). Panic disorder: Pathophysiology and drug treatment. *Drugs, 49*, 328–344.

Klein, D. F. (1995). Treatment of panic disorder, agoraphobia, and social phobia. *Clinical Neuropharmacology, 18*, S45–S51.

Lader, M. (1994). Diagnosis and treatment of generalized anxiety disorder. In G. Darcourt, J. Mendlewicz, G. Racagni, & N. Brunello (Eds.), *Current therapeutic approaches to panic and other anxiety disorders* (pp. 113–120). Basel, Switzerland: Karger.

Lister, R. G. (1991). Ethologically based animal models of anxiety disorders. In S. E. File (Ed.), *Psychopharmacology of anxiolytics and antidepressants* (pp. 155–186). New York: Pergamon Press.

Priest, R. G., Gimbrett, R., Roberts, W., & Steinert, J. (1995). Reversible and selective inhibitors of monoamine oxidase A in mental and other disorders. *Acta Psychiatrica Scandinavica, 91*, 40–43.

Roy Byrne, P., Wingerson, D., Cowley, D., & Dager, S. (1993). Psychopharmacologic treatment of panic, generalized anxiety disorder, and social phobia. *Psychiatric Clinics of North America, 16*, 719–735.

Sanger, D. J., Perrault, G., Morel, E., Joly, D., & Zivkovic, B. (1991). Animal models of anxiety and the developments of novel anxiolytic drugs. *Progress in Neuro-Psychopharmacology and Biological Psychiatry, 15*, 205–212.

Treit, D. (1985). Animal models for the study of anti-anxiety agents: A review. *Neuroscience & Biobehavioral Reviews, 9*, 203–222.

Van Megen, H. J., Den Boer, J. A., & Westenberg, H. G. (1994). On the significance of cholecystokinin receptors in panic disorder. *Progress in Neuro-Psychopharmacology and Biological Psychiatry, 18*, 1235–1246.

Westenberg, H. G. M. (1996). Developments in the drug treatment of panic disorder: What is the place of the selective serotonin reuptake inhibitors? *Journal of Affective Disorders, 40*, 85–93.

Westenberg, H. G. M., & Den Boer, J. A. (1993). Serotonin in anxiety related disorders. In P. M. Vanhoutte, P. R. Saxena, R. Paoletti, N. Brunello, & A. S. Jackson (Eds.), *Serotonin: From cell biology to pharmacology and therapeutics* (pp. 249–254). Dordrecht, The Netherlands: Kluwer Academic.

7

Latent Inhibition in Animals as a Model of Acute Schizophrenia: A Reanalysis

Philippe Oberling, Olivier Gosselin, and Ralph R. Miller

Latent Inhibition and Schizophrenia

History

Latent inhibition (LI) is a term that was introduced more than 35 years ago by Lubow and Moore (1959) to describe the retarded acquisition of behavioral control by a stimulus that initially has been presented repeatedly without reinforcement. Simply put, the initial presentation of a conditioned stimulus (CS) by itself has a detrimental effect on the subsequent generation of conditioned responses (CRs) when the CS is paired with an unconditioned stimulus (US); that is, more CS–US trials are necessary to obtain behavioral control by the CS. LI is a remarkably robust phenomenon that has been observed over a wide range of physical stimulus and mammalian species including humans, although the majority of the research on LI has used rats and pigeons as subjects. Furthermore, the LI effect has been obtained with many different test procedures, including a number of classical and instrumental conditioning paradigms (for a recent review, see Lubow, 1989). That prior experience with an event modifies subsequent learning about that event is likely a functional property for any learning mechanism. On these grounds, LI has been the subject of considerable research over the past 30 years. Although initially described as a consequence of habituation, LI has been shown to differ from the phenomenon of habituation with respect to both LI's lesser generalization across contexts and its greater survival over long retention intervals (a

This study was supported by grants from Groupement d'Intérêt Scientifique Sciences de la Cognition (97/C/51) and National Institute of Mental Health (NIMH 33881). We are grateful to Nathalie Fouquet, Chris Frith, and Laure Pain for their helpful comments during the preparation of this chapter.

double dissociation; see Hall, 1991, for a recent review). Many theories of learning have subsequently been used in attempts to account for the LI phenomenon. Among the most prominent theories were those viewing LI as the result of a stimulus-specific attentional decrement (e.g., Lubow, Schnur, & Rifkin, 1976; Mackintosh, 1975; Pearce & Hall, 1980); however, there have been alternative explanations proposed (e.g., Grahame, Barnett, Gunther, & Miller, 1994; Wagner, 1981). To understand the assumed relationship between LI and acute schizophrenia, it must be emphasized that the attentional view of LI has been adopted *uncritically* in clinical research.

Considerable research has been devoted to understanding schizophrenia. Since the initial description of schizophrenia by Bleuler (1911/1966), it has long been recognized that the behaviors of patients with schizophrenia exhibit some patterns that can be described in terms of an attentional dysfunction (see, e.g., Kraepelin, 1919/1971, p. 5, for an initial report). Shortly after Broadbent (1958) published his attentional filter theory, a highly influential article by McGhie and Chapman (1961) summarized a number of clinical manifestations and case reports of schizophrenia and concluded that perception and thinking disturbances in acute schizophrenics were incidental to primary disturbances in the control of directed attention. Without our reviewing the extensive literature that has linked attentional deficits and schizophrenia (for a review, see Gjerde, 1983), it must be noted that historically "many writers regard[ed] a deficit in selective attention as one of the central psychological lesions in schizophrenia" (Anscombe, 1987, p. 24) and that "many theorists . . . view[ed] faulty attention as the fundamental cognitive deficit" of schizophrenia (Mirsky & Duncan, 1986, p. 292). On these grounds, "it is but one step to make the association between latent inhibition and schizophrenia: Both involve some type of attentional process—latent inhibition reflects the normal operation of an attentional process, whereas schizophrenia reflects a dysfunction of an attentional process" (Lubow, 1989, p. 249). As a consequence and largely at the instigation of Lubow and his colleagues, LI soon became a widely used cross-species tool to investigate attentional deficits in both humans (see, e.g., Lubow & Gewirtz, 1995) and nonhuman species (see, e.g., Feldon & Weiner, 1991a).

Human Data

In the framework of LI being a model of schizophrenia—or more precisely stated, a disruption of LI being a model of acute schizophrenia—the first question that has to be answered is, Do patients with acute schizophrenia exhibit a disruption of normal LI? Of the five studies that have directly addressed this issue (i.e., Baruch, Hemsley, & Gray, 1988; N. S. Gray, Hemsley, & Gray, 1992; N. S. Gray, Pilowsky, Gray, & Kerwin, 1995; Lubow, Weiner, Schlossberg, & Baruch, 1987; Swerdlow, Braff, Hartston, Perry, & Geyer, 1996), all used exactly the same, or a very similar, procedure. The most widely cited study reporting a disruption of LI in patients with acute schizophrenia was the one by Baruch et al. In their study, participants listened to a tape recording of nonsense syllables, such as *teff*, in a preexposure phase. For half of the participants (the preexposed group), a white noise was interspersed between the syllables at variable intervals. The tape was then replayed for all participants, with the white noise now being used as a CS that was followed immediately by an increase in a numeral on an illuminated screen (US). This constituted the conditioning phase. Preexposed normal and chronic schizophrenic subjects were slower to learn (i.e., required more trials) to associate this number increment with the CS than were nonpreexposed subjects, which is thought to reflect normal LI processing in both normal and chronic schizophrenic subjects. Baruch et al. reported that patients with acute schizophrenia did not demonstrate normal LI. In the initial phase of an acute psychotic episode, preexposed patients with schizophrenia learned the CS–US association at least as quickly as did nonpreexposed acute schizophrenic patients. This result was replicated by N. S. Gray et al. (1992, 1995) but not by Swerdlow et al. (1996; see also Guterman, Josiassen, Bashore, Johnson, & Lubow, 1996; Lubow et al., 1987, for other failures to observe an LI deficit in patients with schizophrenia). In summary, only half of the above-mentioned studies have detected a deficit of LI in patients with acute schizophrenia. This invites a closer reexamination of the assumed relationship between LI and schizophrenia.

Due primarily to methodological considerations, we feel that it would be tenuous to conclude from the aforementioned studies that patients with acute schizophrenia *exhibit* or *do not exhibit* a deficit in normal LI processing. As a matter of fact, all the studies that have attempted to detect an LI deficit in patients with schizophrenia (i.e., Baruch et al., 1988; N. S. Gray et al., 1992, 1995; Lubow et al., 1987; Swerdlow et al., 1996) have preexposed participants to the CS in the form of a masked stimulus (e.g., the participants are instructed to listen to a series of nonsense syllables, choose one syllable, and count the number of times it is repeated while half of them have been preexposed to the intended CS: a white noise); then, immediately after this initial phase, participants are instructed that *in a new task*, some unspecified sound (actually the white noise) that they will hear will signal an increase in the numeral on a scoreboard. Their job is then to figure out when the numeral is about to increase and to signal immediately before its increase. Such a procedure differs appreciably from what has been called the *LI procedure* in nonhuman species (see, e.g., Lubow, 1973; Lubow & Moore, 1959) in at least three fundamental aspects. First, during the preexposure phase, the white noise is only a background stimulus, not the target stimulus (see Lubow, 1989; Lubow & Gewirtz, 1995, for justifications concerning the use of a masking task). Second, the change in instructions between the preexposure and the conditioning phases is unique to the human studies. Third, during the conditioning phase of the human studies, the participant is explicitly required to make a contingency (or probabilistic) judgment, that is, to determine the extent to which the occurrence of an effect (numerical increment) depends on the occurrence of a given event (for contingency judgment in humans, see

Shanks, 1994; for contingency judgment in rats, see Rescorla, 1968). Such discrepancies between what has been described as the LI procedure in nonhuman species and the procedure used with patients with schizophrenia render quite problematic any conclusion concerning an LI deficit in patients with acute schizophrenia.

Furthermore, in both previously published reports of impaired LI in patients with acute schizophrenia (Baruch et al., 1988; N. S. Gray et al., 1992), slower learning has been observed in the nonpreexposed patients with acute schizophrenia compared with the nonpreexposed normal controls, although the statistical validation of this difference has not been reported. Thus, the intended comparison is quite likely confounded by a difference in baseline performance (see also N. S. Gray et al., 1995). In addition, because compelling evidence has been presented demonstrating that probabilistic judgment is severely impaired in patients with schizophrenia—deluded patients with schizophrenia request uncommonly little information before reaching a decision on a probabilistic inference task (Garety, Hemsley, & Wessely, 1991),—it becomes necessary to determine the following: (a) Do *unmedicated* patients with acute schizophrenia exhibit normal conditioning processes; that is, do they acquire CS–US associations in the same way as do normal participants? (b) if they do, *and only if they do*, do these patients exhibit a deficit in the normal LI effect? and (c) if they do, *and only if they do*, what is the basis of this effect? Is there a total inability to take into account past information, such as the information presented during the preexposure phase, or is there only a partial inability to take into account such information? In other words, if more preexposure was provided during the initial preexposure phase, would it be still impossible to observe LI in patients with acute schizophrenia? A positive answer to this latter question would indicate that this hypothetical deficit of LI in patients with acute schizophrenia results from inadequate preexposure to the CS during the preexposure phase, but with conservation of the processes responsible for normal LI. Clear answers to any of these questions would help clinicians and researchers progress in their comprehension of schizophrenia. In our opinion, this requires experimental procedures that are closer to the one that was initially used to assess LI in nonhuman species, that is, at least without any masking task (see, e.g., Lipp, Siddle, & Vaitl, 1992; Surwit & Poser, 1974; Vidal et al., 1999).

Nonhuman Data

In a survey of the existing data, it is surprising to see the impressive number of studies concerning the disruption of the normal LI that has been reported in nonhuman species, in contrast to the very limited number of studies with patients with schizophrenia. Because many excellent reviews of these issues already exist (e.g., Feldon & Weiner, 1991a; J. A. Gray, Feldon, Rawlins, Hemsley, & Smith, 1991; Lubow, 1989), the purpose of the present chapter is not to review all the available data from nonhuman species, but to use some of the existing data to present a new framework that we believe offers a better understanding of the relationship between LI and acute schizophrenia.

Considerable interest in LI as a putative tool to understand schizophrenia has come from the finding that in nonhuman subjects, LI can be disrupted by treatment with amphetamine (e.g., Solomon et al., 1981; Weiner, Lubow, & Feldon, 1988), a drug that has been shown to induce (e.g., Angrist & Gershon, 1970; Bell, 1973) or exacerbate (e.g., Janowsky, Huey, Storms, & Judd, 1977) schizophrenic symptoms. In addition, LI has been found to be enhanced by the prototypical neuroleptic haloperidol (e.g., Christison, Atwater, Dunn, & Kilts, 1988; Feldon & Weiner, 1991b) in nonhuman animals. Finally, amphetamine-induced disruption of LI has been found to be alleviated by dopaminergic antagonists such as chlorpromazine (Solomon et al., 1981) or haloperidol (e.g., Warburton, Joseph, Feldon, Weiner, & Gray, 1994). In other words, LI has been proven to be a dopamine-sensitive process, a finding convergent with the view that schizophrenia is related to a dysfunction of the dopaminergic system (see, e.g., J. A. Gray et al., 1991).

Recently, however, both amphetamine and haloperidol have been shown to be without an effect on LI *when administered only during the preexposure phase* (Weiner, Feldon, & Katz, 1987; Weiner, Lubow, & Feldon, 1984). Moreover, Weiner et al. (1988) have reported an enhanced degree of conditioned responding in animals receiving injections of amphetamine in the conditioning phase of the experiment, *irrespective of whether they receive amphetamine during preexposure*. J. A. Gray et al. (1995) have found that LI can be disrupted by amphetamine injections, even when they are given after *preexposure*. Finally, three recent articles (Joseph, Peters, & Gray, 1993; Killcross, Dickinson, & Robbins, 1994a; Peters & Joseph, 1993) also have suggested that dopaminergic manipulations on the LI effect have a critical role at conditioning rather than in processing at the time of CS preexposure. It is not possible to determine from these three studies whether amphetamine (or haloperidol) acts by enhancing (decreasing) the salience of the reinforcing stimulus or acts directly on the strength of the CS–US association. Whichever is correct, these studies seriously challenge the view that dopaminergic manipulations affect changes in attention to the CS during preexposure. As a consequence, amphetamine-induced disruption of LI as a model of the attention deficit observed in patients with schizophrenia probably needs a thorough reexamination. This does not necessarily mean that the baby must be thrown out with the bathwater, but at least it urges one to reconsider the relevance of LI disruption with respect to schizophrenia.

In this context, note that LI has been found not to be disrupted by the potent *psychostimulant* phencyclidine (Weiner & Feldon, 1992; see also Robinson, Port, & Stillwell, 1993, for a similar result, but using the glutamatergic antagonist MK-801). To our knowledge, there are no available data concerning LI and ketamine, another potent psychostimulant closely related to phencyclidine. Weiner and Feldon's (1992) result seri-

ously undermines the view that the disruption of LI is a genuine pharmacological model of schizophrenia because phencyclidine not only exacerbates but also produces schizophrenic symptoms (e.g., Domino & Luby,
1973). Nevertheless, it must be acknowledged that LI has been found to
be disrupted after brain depletion of serotonin (Asin, Wirtshafter, & Kent,
1980; Lorden, Rickert, & Berry, 1983; Solomon, Nichols, Kiernan, Kamer,
& Kaplan, 1980; but see Mora et al., 1999), a neurotransmitter that seems
to play a crucial role in schizophrenia.

Neurobiological studies have found that LI is disrupted by lesions of
the hippocampus (e.g., Ackil, Mellgren, Halgren, & Frommer, 1969; Kaye
& Pearce, 1987a, 1987b; McFarland, Kostas, & Drew, 1978; Schmajuk,
Lam, & Christiansen, 1994; Solomon & Moore, 1975; but see Honey &
Good, 1993; Purves, Bonardi, & Hall, 1995), a structure that has been
found to be altered in schizophrenic patients (see, e.g., Kovelman & Scheibel, 1984; Scheibel & Kovelman, 1981). Interestingly, Yee, Feldon, and
Rawlins (1995) have recently shown that the disruptive effect of the subiculum on LI can be prevented by a systemic haloperidol treatment. Moreover, Sotty, Sandner, and Gosselin (1996) have found that the cellular activity (as assessed using c-fos immunochemistry technique) is decreased
in the hippocampus of preexposed rats when compared with nonpreexposed rats, a result that suggests a role of the hippocampus in the LI
effect. However, disruption of LI is not specific to the lesions of the hippocampus because many cognitive processes are altered by hippocampal
lesions (for reviews, see, e.g., Eichenbaum, Otto, & Cohen, 1992; Jarrard,
1995; O'Keefe & Nadel, 1978). In addition, LI does not seem to be a good
predictor of the cerebral structures that are altered in schizophrenia. For
example, lesions of the medial prefrontal cortex do not disrupt LI (Joel,
Weiner, & Feldon, 1997), whereas septal lesions do (e.g., Burton & Toga,
1982; Weiss, Friedman, & McGregor, 1974)—the former structure, but not
the latter one, being thought to be altered in schizophrenia (see, e.g., Robbins, 1990; Weinberger & Lipska, 1995).

Synthesis

In summary, 15 years of intensive research have led to the conclusion that
it is probably overly simplistic to link deficient LI so closely with acute
schizophrenia. This error is not totally surprising considering the absence
of clear comprehension concerning either the LI phenomenon or schizophrenia. From human research, there are insufficient data to date showing
that patients with acute schizophrenia exhibit a true deficit of LI. From
nonhuman research, the drugs that have been shown to mimic schizophrenic symptoms when administered to human participants either do not
affect LI (phencyclidine) or disrupt it (amphetamine) but apparently do so
by acting during the conditioning phase. This latter result suggests that
amphetamine does not specifically mimic the overattentional processing
of one stimulus at the expense of another, a mechanism that is supposedly
the cornerstone of schizophrenia.

Additionally, neurobiological data have offered interesting insight into the neurobiological substrate that subserves normal LI (see, e.g., Weiner, 1990). However, as already mentioned, LI does not seem to be a good predictor of the cerebral structures that are altered in schizophrenia. Surely, these latter neurobiological data have to be considered when evaluating alternatives to the LI-disruption model of schizophrenia. This latter point must be clearly stated to avoid any confusion between the different models of schizophrenia that are currently available and their levels of analysis. An excellent example is provided by the hipocampal lesion model elaborated by Schmajuk (1989) and Schmajuk and Moore (1985, 1988; for a review of the model and its relevance to schizophrenia, see Schmajuk & Tyberg, 1991). On the basis of the initial work of Schmajuk (1987) and Schmajuk and Moore (1988) analyzing how hippocampally lesioned rats mimic cognitive, psychophysiological, and neurophysiological changes found in patients with schizophrenia, Schmajuk (1989; Schmajuk & Moore, 1985, 1988) has developed a real-time version of Pearce and Hall's (1980) attentional model, designated the S-P-H model. To be valid, such a connectionist model must be able to correctly describe most (if not all) the available data that have been experimentally generated on hippocampally lesioned animals that are thought to reflect schizophrenic disturbances. In Schmajuk and Tyberg's (1991, p. 82) review, 17 of the 18 symptoms studied in patients with schizophrenia (among which is the LI deficit) have been observed in hippocampal lesioned animals (among which is the LI deficit), and the S-P-H model correctly describes 12 of them (among which is the LI deficit). In this context, it must be emphasized that the LI-deficit model of schizophrenia focuses on a single deficient cognitive operation (namely, selective attention), whereas the hippocampal models described above try to explain as many deficient operations in schizophrenia as possible. In terms of hierarchy, the consequence is that the LI-deficit model must be seen, if anything, more as a rudimentary model of schizophrenia than as an elaborated one. Rudimentary models have the tremendous advantage of simplicity, but the other side of the coin is that their predictions must be interpreted with caution.

Reanalysis of the Bases for Disruption of Latent Inhibition as a Model of Acute Schizophrenia

The Notion of the Psychopathological Model

In the light of what has already been said, it is appropriate at this time to reassess the validity of the disruption of LI as a model of schizophrenia. McKinney and Bunney (1969) have proposed four criteria for the evaluation of animal models of psychiatric disorders: (a) similarity of inducing conditions, (b) similarity of behavioral states, (c) common underlying neurobiological mechanisms, and (d) reversal by clinically effective treatment techniques. These criteria, albeit largely accepted by the scientific community, represent an instance of perfect achievement for the researchers who are attempting to model psychiatric disorders (for a discussion, see Willner, 1991b). Mainly because it is not always possible to fulfill the four criteria defined by McKinney and Bunney, animal models have been classified in three broad categories according to the kind of validity that they possess: *predictive, face,* or *construct* validity. Predictive validity means that manipulations (generally, therapeutic ones) known to influence the pathological state must have similar effects in the model. Face validity means that there are phenomenological similarities between the model and the disorder modeled. Construct validity means that the model has a sound theoretical rationale linking the model with the bases of the disorder (Willner, 1984, 1991a).

These three perspectives address three broad and different aspects of a model, from which a picture of its overall validity may be assessed. Earlier attempts to develop criteria for validating animal models of human behavior have tended to concentrate largely on the assessment of face validity (e.g., Abramson & Seligman, 1977; McKinney & Bunney, 1969). The identification of the two further categories illustrates two ways in which the literature has developed in recent years. First, there has been a considerable expansion in the literature dealing with the pharmacological exploitation of animal models, much of which contributes to the assessment of predictive validity. Second, there has been significant growth in our understanding of the psychological and neurobiological mechanisms underlying psychopathological processes and in the integration of them into more sophisticated models, that is, models with construct validity: "The exercise of distinguishing different types of validity has practical value: It allows ready identification of areas in which information about a particular model is weak or missing, and ensures that comparisons between different models are made on the basis of comparable data" (Willner, 1991b, p. 3).

Predictive Validity

Despite the fact that LI disruption as a model of attention deficit in acute schizophrenia probably needs to be reconsidered, it is noteworthy that amphetamine-induced disruption of LI has proved to be a very accurate model in predicting the pharmacological efficacy of the antipsychotic agents. As already mentioned, amphetamine-induced disruption of LI has been shown to be reversed by the typical antipsychotics chlorpromazine (Solomon et al., 1981) and haloperidol (Warburton et al., 1994) and by the atypical one, alpha-flupenthixol (Killcross, Dickinson, & Robbins, 1994b). Recently, it has been found that amphetamine-induced disruption of LI was alleviated by the new antipsychotic agents clozapine (Moran, Fischer, Hitchcock, & Moser, 1996), sertindole (Weiner, Kidron, Tarrasch, Arnt, & Feldon, 1994), and olanzapine (Gosselin, Oberling, & Di Scala, 1996). These latter findings suggest that amphetamine-induced disruption of LI is probably a well-suited and cost-effective paradigm for screening new molecules with antipsychotic activity.

In addition to alleviation of amphetamine-induced disruption of LI, a growing literature indicates that many antipsychotic agents potentiate LI (e.g., haloperidol [Christison et al., 1988; Dunn et al., 1993; Feldon & Weiner, 1991b]; sulpiride [Feldon & Weiner, 1991b]; chlorpromazine, fluphenazine, thiothixene, thioridazine, mesoridazine, and metoclopramide [Dunn, Atwater, & Kilts, 1993]; clozapine [Moran et al., 1996; Weiner & Feldon, 1994; but see Dunn et al., 1993]; and sertindole [Weiner et al., 1994]). With regard to schizophrenia, drug-induced potentiation of LI raises interesting issues that deserve mention. If one considers that the LI-deficit model has been promoted *because* amphetamine-induced disruption of LI is thought to mimic schizophrenia-induced disruption of LI, the rationale for any potentiation of LI becomes less clear. That is, if one accepts the view that LI results from a gradual decrease in the attentional processing of the target CS during the preexposure phase, potentiation of LI should result from a larger decrease in the normal attentional processing of this stimulus, that is, from hypoattention. In this respect, any drug that induces sedation might be expected to potentiate LI, irrespective of it having any antipsychotic activity. To date, this statement has not received any support, in that the nonantipsychotic but sedative drugs pentobarbital, chlordiazepoxide, imipramine, and promethazine fail to enhance LI (Dunn et al., 1993), whereas the psychostimulant drug nicotine does enhance LI (Rochford, Sen, & Quirion, 1996; but see Joseph et al., 1993).

In summary, amphetamine-induced disruption of LI appears to be a model with good predictive validity for screening new antipsychotic agents. In particular, blockage of amphetamine-induced disruption of LI appears to screen very accurately for antipsychotic agents, whereas other preparations such as amphetamine-induced discrimination (Arnt, 1996) or amphetamine-induced hyperlocomotion (Gosselin et al., 1996; Sanchez et al., 1991) do not. Conversely, drug-induced potentiation of LI appears to be a tool for which *the theoretical risk* of observing false-positive responses is high.

Face Validity and Construct Validity

As already mentioned, there is insufficient evidence to date that a deficit of normal LI processing occurs in patients with acute schizophrenia (see also Lubow & Gewirtz, 1995, p. 100, for a similar conclusion). As a consequence, we believe that it would be hazardous to look for any face validity (and consequently for any construct validity) in the animal model of LI deficit, a position that can appear provocative, especially when considering the huge amount of data that have been accumulated in nonhuman species that have been interpreted as supporting the model.

Conclusion

The present chapter may appear heretical for researchers who view the disruption of the LI phenomenon as a widely accepted animal model of acute schizophrenia with good predictive, face, and construct validities. However, recall that the model relies on the initial assumption that LI results from a selective attentional decrementation for the target CS. That is, over the preexposure trials, the nonreinforced CS is presumably less and less processed at an attentional level. As a result, the repeated, nonreinforced exposure to the target CS subsequently impairs the CS's ability to enter into new associations, that is, *LI results from an impaired acquisition of CS–US associations* (e.g., Lubow et al., 1976; Mackintosh, 1975; Pearce & Hall, 1980; Wagner, 1981). Recently, however, this position has been seriously challenged by findings that indicate that responding to the latently inhibited CS could be increased by various treatments administered *after* the CS–US pairings. These include testing that is extensively delayed after the CS–US pairings (Kraemer, Hoffmann, & Spear, 1988; Kraemer & Ossenkopp, 1986; Kraemer, Randall, & Carbary, 1991; Kraemer & Roberts, 1984); a "reminder" treatment, which consists of the US administered alone outside the training context (Kasprow, Caterson, Schachtman, & Miller, 1984); and extinction of the training context (Grahame et al., 1994). These results suggest that *LI results from a failure of performance at the time of retrieval of normally acquired CS–US associations*, a position that is well represented by Miller and Schachtman's (1985) and Miller and Matzel's (1988) comparator hypothesis (see also Bouton, 1993; Spear, 1981).

The finding that LI disruption can be identically induced by psychological treatments received after the conditioning phase questions the reality of LI resulting (at least solely) from an attentional deficit (see also Miller & Oberling, 1998; Oberling, Gunther, & Miller, in press; Schmajuk, Lam, & Gray, 1996, for similar conclusions). In this context, we believe that LI disruption can no longer be considered as a model of an attentional deficit. This does not necessarily mean that LI disruption does not capture any critical feature that is displayed by patients with acute schizophrenia. Rather, this suggests that maybe it is time to appeal to other theories of LI for extrapolation to schizophrenia research.

In this regard, Miller and Schachtman's (1985; Miller & Matzel, 1988) comparator hypothesis views normal LI as the result of CS–context associations formed during the preexposure phase that subsequently interfere with the expression of CS–US associations that are acquired in a normal fashion during the conditioning phase (see also Grahame et al., 1994). Thus, the comparator hypothesis predicts that a pathological LI disruption will result from impaired CS–context associations. This is noteworthy because more and more evidence is accumulating that suggests that patients with schizophrenia are unable to correctly process contextual information (see, e.g., Cohen & Servan-Schreiber, 1992; Rizzo, Danion, Van Der Linden, & Grangé, 1996; Rizzo, Danion, Van Der Linden, Grangé, & Rohmer, 1996). Within such a theoretical framework, patients with acute schizophrenia are thought to suffer from an LI disruption because the deficit in contextual information processing weakens CS–context associations.

This viewpoint deserves mention because it would allow us to incorporate the pharmacological data into a new and very different theoretical framework. This viewpoint has numerous consequences because, as mentioned above, drug-induced potentiation of LI appears to be a very selective procedure to screen for antipsychotic agents. Nevertheless, LI disruption viewed as resulting from an attentional deficit renders potentiation of LI highly suspicious because on these grounds any sedative agent would be expected to potentiate LI, a prediction that is clearly incorrect. Conversely, LI disruption resulting from an inability to normally process contextual information would predict that a drug that alleviates contextual deficit, *and only such a drug*, could reinstate (or even potentiate) LI. This would allow us to have a potentially unique theoretical rationale for what an antipsychotic agent must be, that is, a drug that reinstates the normal processing of contextual information. Finally, regarding LI disruption as the consequence of an inability to process contextual information would allow us to reincorporate LI disruption as a model of acute schizophrenia and, with evidence showing that the normal LI deficit can be alleviated by posttraining treatments, start us in the direction of looking for normal encoding of information that is masked in patients with schizophrenia.

Whatever has been said, researchers still need to clearly assess whether patients with acute schizophrenia suffer from impaired LI. Such an assessment needs us to take into account at least two important methodological features that have been neglected in the initial studies. First, experimental preparations for humans that allow us to test for the same processes than the ones described in nonhuman species must be used (see, e.g., Vidal et al., 1999). Second, whatever the difficulties, LI disruption *must be assessed using unmedicated patients with acute schizophrenia*, because any abnormal LI processes might result from the initial effects of drug treatment (antipsychotics in particular), with normalization as the treatment becomes chronic. This point is crucial because the ubiquity of drug treatment in schizophrenia raises major problems for use with patients on any task that is sensitive to dopamine blockade.

References

Abramson, L. Y., & Seligman, M. E. P. (1977). Modelling psychopathology in the laboratory: History and rationale. In J. D. Maser & M. E. P. Seligman (Eds.), *Psychopathology: Animal models* (pp. 1–26). San Francisco: Freeman.

Ackil, J. E., Mellgren, R. L., Halgren, C., & Frommer, G. P. (1969). Effects of CS preexposure on avoidance learning in rats with hippocampal lesions. *Journal of Comparative and Physiological Psychology, 69*, 739–747.

Angrist, B., & Gershon, S. (1970). The phenomenology of experimentally induced amphetamine psychosis: Preliminary observations. *Biological Psychiatry, 2*, 95–107.

Anscombe, R. (1987). The disorder of consciousness in schizophrenia. *Schizophrenia Bulletin, 13*, 241–260.

Arnt, J. (1996). Inhibitory effects on the discriminative stimulus properties of *d*-amphetamine by classical and newer antipsychotics do not correlate with antipsychotic activity: Relation to effects on the reward system? *Psychopharmacology, 124*, 117–125.

Asin, K. E., Wirtshafter, D., & Kent, E. W. (1980). The effect of electrolytic median raphe lesions on two measures of latent inhibition. *Behavioral and Neural Biology, 28*, 408–417.

Baruch, I., Hemsley, D. R., & Gray, J. A. (1988). Differential performance of acute and chronic schizophrenics in a latent inhibition task. *Journal of Nervous and Mental Disease, 176,* 598–606.

Bell, D. S. (1973). The experimental reproduction of amphetamine psychosis. *Archives of General Psychiatry, 29,* 35–40.

Bleuler, E. (1966). *Dementia praecox or the group of schizophrenias* (J. Zinkin, Trans.). New York: International Universities Press. (Original work published 1911)

Bouton, M. E. (1993). Context, time, and memory retrieval in the interference paradigms of Pavlovian learning. *Psychological Bulletin, 114,* 80–99.

Broadbent, D. E. (1958). *Perception and communication.* London: Pergamon Press.

Burton, H. A., & Toga, A. W. (1982). Successive discrimination performance improves with increasing numbers of stimulus preexposure in septal rats. *Behavioral and Neural Biology, 34,* 141–151.

Christison, G. W., Atwater, G. E., Dunn, L. A., & Kilts, C. D. (1988). Haloperidol enhancement of latent inhibition: Relation to therapeutic action? *Biological Psychiatry, 23,* 746–749.

Cohen, J. D., & Servan-Schreiber, D. (1992). Context, cortex and dopamine: A connectionist approach to behavior and biology in schizophrenia. *Psychological Review, 99,* 45–77.

Domino, E., & Luby, E. D. (1973). Abnormal mental states induced by phencyclidine as a model of schizophrenia. In J. E. Cole, A. M. Freedman, & A. J. Friedhoff (Eds.), *Psychopathology and psychopharmacology* (pp. 37–50). Baltimore: Johns Hopkins University Press.

Dunn, L. A., Atwater, G. E., & Kilts, C. D. (1993). Effects of antipsychotic drugs on latent inhibition: Sensitivity and specificity of an animal behavioral model of clinical drug action. *Psychopharmacology, 112,* 315–323.

Eichenbaum, H., Otto, T., & Cohen, N. J. (1992). The hippocampus—What does it do? *Behavioral and Neural Biology, 57,* 2–36.

Feldon, J., & Weiner, I. (1991a). An animal model of attention deficit. In A. Boulton, G. Baker, & M. Martin-Iverson (Eds.), *Neuromethods: Vol. 18: Animal models in psychiatry I* (pp. 313–362). Clifton, NJ: Humana Press.

Feldon, J., & Weiner, I. (1991b). The latent inhibition model of schizophrenic attention disorder: Haloperidol and sulpiride enhance rats' ability to ignore irrelevant stimuli. *Biological Psychiatry, 29,* 635–646.

Garety, P. A., Hemsley, D. R., & Wessely, S. (1991). Reasoning in deluded schizophrenic and paranoid patients: Biases in performance on a probabilistic inference task. *Journal of Nervous and Mental Disease, 179,* 194–201.

Gjerde, P. F. (1983). Attentional capacity dysfunction and arousal in schizophrenia. *Psychological Bulletin, 93,* 57–72.

Gosselin, O., Oberling, P., & Di Scala, G. (1996). Antagonism of amphetamine-induced disruption of latent inhibition by the atypical antipsychotic olanzapine in rats. *Behavioural Pharmacology, 7,* 820–826.

Grahame, N. J., Barnet, R. C., Gunther, L. M., & Miller, R. R. (1994). Latent inhibition as a performance deficit resulting from CS–context associations. *Animal Learning & Behavior, 22,* 395–408.

Gray, J. A., Feldon, J., Rawlins, J. N. P., Hemsley, D. R., & Smith, A. D. (1991). The neuropsychology of schizophrenia. *Behavioral and Brain Sciences, 14,* 1–84.

Gray, J. A., Joseph, M. H., Hemsley, D. R., Young, A. M. J., Warburton, E. C., Boulenguez, P., Grigorian, G. A., Peters, S. L., Rawlins, J. N. P., Tai, C. T., Yee, B. K., Cassaday, H., Weiner, I., Gal, G., Gusak, O., Joel, D., Shadac, E., Shalev, U., Tarrasch, R., & Feldon, J. (1995). The role of mesolimbic dopaminergic and retrohippocampal afferents to the nucleus accumbens in latent inhibition: Implications for schizophrenia. *Behavioural Brain Research, 71,* 19–31.

Gray, N. S., Hemsley, D. R., & Gray, J. A. (1992). Abolition of latent inhibition in acute, but not chronic, schizophrenics. *Neurology, Psychiatry and Brain Research, 1,* 83–89.

Gray, N. S., Pilowsky, L. S., Gray, J. A., & Kerwin, R. W. (1995). Latent inhibition in drug naive schizophrenics: Relationship to duration of illness and dopamine D_2 binding using SPET. *Schizophrenia Research, 17,* 95–107.

Guterman, Y., Josiassen, R. C., Bashore, T. E., Johnson, M., & Lubow, R. E. (1996). Latent inhibition effects reflected in event-related brain potentials in healthy controls and schizophrenics. *Schizophrenia Research, 20,* 315–326.

Hall, G. (1991). *Perceptual and associative learning.* Oxford, England: Clarendon Press.

Honey, R. C., & Good, M. (1993). Selective hippocampal lesions abolish the contextual specificity of latent inhibition and conditioning. *Behavioral Neuroscience, 107,* 23–33.

Janowsky, D. S., Huey, L., Storms, L., & Judd, L. L. (1977). Methylphenidate hydrochloride effects on psychological tests in acute schizophrenic and nonpsychotic patients. *Archives of General Psychiatry, 34,* 189–194.

Jarrard, L. E. (1995). What does the hippocampus really do? *Behavioural Brain Research, 71,* 1–10.

Joel, D., Weiner, I., & Feldon, J. (1997). Electrolytic lesions of the medial prefrontal cortex in rats disrupt performance on an analog of Wisconsin Card Sorting Test but do not disrupt latent inhibition: Implications for animal models of schizophrenia. *Behavioural Brain Research, 85,* 187–201.

Joseph, M. H., Peters, S. L., & Gray, J. A. (1993). Nicotine blocks latent inhibition in rats: Evidence for a critical role of increased functional activity of dopamine in the mesolimbic system at conditioning rather than pre-exposure. *Psychopharmacology, 110,* 187–192.

Kasprow, W. J., Caterson, D., Schachtman, T. R., & Miller, R. R. (1984). Attenuation of latent inhibition by postacquisition reminder. *Quarterly Journal of Experimental Psychology, 36B,* 53–63.

Kaye, H., & Pearce, J. M. (1987a). Hippocampal lesions attenuate latent inhibition and the decline of the orienting response in rats. *Quarterly Journal of Experimental Psychology, 39B,* 107–125.

Kaye, H., & Pearce, J. M. (1987b). Hippocampal lesions attenuate latent inhibition of a CS and of a neutral stimulus. *Psychobiology, 15,* 293–299.

Killcross, A. S., Dickinson, A., & Robbins, T. W. (1994a). Amphetamine-induced disruptions of latent inhibition are reinforcer mediated: Implications for animal models of schizophrenic attentional dysfunction. *Psychopharmacology, 115,* 185–195.

Killcross, A. S., Dickinson, A., & Robbins, T. W. (1994b). Effects of the neuroleptic alpha-flupenthixol on latent inhibition in aversively—and appetitively—motivated paradigms: Evidence for dopamine–reinforcer interaction. *Psychopharmacology, 115,* 196–205.

Kovelman, J. A., & Scheibel, A. B. (1984). A neurobiological correlate of schizophrenia. *Biological Psychiatry, 19,* 601–621.

Kraemer, P. J., Hoffmann, H., & Spear, N. E. (1988). Attenuation of the CS-preexposure effect after a retention interval in preweanling rats. *Animal Learning & Behavior, 16,* 164–168.

Kraemer, P. J., & Ossenkopp, K. P. (1986). The effects of flavor preexposure and test interval on conditioned taste aversions in rats. *Bulletin of the Psychonomic Society, 24,* 219–221.

Kraemer, P. J., Randall, C. K., & Carbary, T. J. (1991). Release from latent inhibition with delayed testing. *Animal Learning & Behavior, 19,* 139–145.

Kraemer, P. J., & Roberts, W. A. (1984). The influence of flavor preexposure and test interval on conditioned taste aversions in the rat. *Learning and Motivation, 15,* 259–278.

Kraepelin, E. (1971). *Dementia praecox and paraphrenia.* Huntington, NY: Krieger. (Original work published 1919)

Lipp, O. V., Siddle, D. A. T., & Vailt, D. (1992). Latent inhibition in humans: Single-cue conditioning revisited. *Journal of Experimental Psychology: Animal Behavior Processes, 18,* 115–125.

Lorden, J. F., Rickert, E. J., & Berry, D. W. (1983). Forebrain monoamines and associative learning: I. Latent inhibition and conditioned inhibition. *Behavioural Brain Research, 9,* 181–199.

Lubow, R. E. (1973). Latent inhibition. *Psychological Bulletin, 79,* 398–407.

Lubow, R. E. (1989). *Latent inhibition and conditioned attention theory.* Cambridge, England: Cambridge University Press.

Lubow, R. E., & Gewirtz, J. C. (1995). Latent inhibition in humans: Data, theory, and implications for schizophrenia. *Psychological Bulletin, 117,* 87–103.

Lubow, R. E., & Moore, A. U. (1959). Latent inhibition: The effect of non-reinforced preexposure to the conditioned stimulus. *Journal of Comparative and Physiological Psychology, 52,* 415–419.

Lubow, R. E., Schnur, P., & Rifkin, B. (1976). Latent inhibition and conditioned attention theory. *Journal of Experimental Psychology: Animal Behavior Processes, 2,* 163–174.

Lubow, R. E., Weiner, I., Schlossberg, A., & Baruch, I. (1987). Latent inhibition and schizophrenia. *Bulletin of the Psychonomic Society, 25,* 464–467.

Mackintosh, N. J. (1975). A theory of attention: Variations in the associability of stimuli with reinforcement. *Psychological Review, 82,* 276–298.

McFarland, D. J., Kostas, J., & Drew, W. G. (1978). Dorsal hippocampal lesions: Effect of preconditioning CS exposure on flavor aversion. *Behavioral Biology, 22,* 398–404.

McGhie, A., & Chapman, J. (1961). Disorders of attention and perception in early schizophrenia. *British Journal of Medical Psychology, 34,* 103–116.

McKinney, W. T., & Bunney, W. E. (1969). Animal model of depression: Review of evidence and implications for research. *Archives of General Psychiatry, 21,* 240–248.

Miller, R. R., & Matzel, L. D. (1988). The comparator hypothesis: A response rule for the expression of association. In G. H. Bower (Ed.), *The psychology of learning and motivation* (Vol. 22, pp. 51–92). Orlando, FL: Academic Press.

Miller, R. R., & Oberling, P. (1998). Analogies between occasion setting and Pavlovian conditioning. In N. A. Schmajuk & P. C. Holland (Eds.), *Occasion setting: Associative learning and cognition in animals* (pp. 3–35). Washington, DC: American Psychological Association.

Miller, R. R., & Schachtman, T. R. (1985). Conditioning context as an associative baseline: Implications for response generation and the nature of conditioned inhibition. In R. R. Miller & N. E. Spear (Eds.), *Information processing in animals: Conditioned inhibition* (pp. 51–88). Hillsdale, NJ: Erlbaum.

Mirsky, A. F., & Duncan, C. C. (1986). Etiology and expression of schizophrenia: Neurobiological and social factors. *Annual Review of Psychology, 37,* 291–319.

Mora, P. D., Fouquet, N., Oberling, P., Gobaille, S. Graeff, F. G., & Sandner, G. (1999). A neurotoxic lesion of serotoninergic neurones using 5,7-dihydroxytryptamine does not disrupt latent inhibition in paradigms sensitive to low doses of amphetamine. *Behavioural Brain Research, 100,* 167–175.

Moran, P. M., Fischer, T. R., Hitchcock, J. M., & Moser, P. C. (1996). Effects of clozapine on latent inhibition in the rat. *Behavioural Pharmacology, 7,* 42–48.

Oberling, P., Gunther, L. M., & Miller R. R. (in press). Latent inhibition and learned irrelevance of occasion setting. *Learning and Motivation.*

O'Keefe, J., & Nadel, L. (1978). *The hippocampus as a cognitive map.* Oxford, England: Oxford University Press.

Pearce, J. M., & Hall, G. (1980). A model of Pavlovian learning: Variations in the effectiveness of conditioned but not unconditioned stimuli. *Psychological Review, 87,* 532–552.

Peters, S. L., & Joseph, M. H. (1993). Haloperidol potentiation of latent inhibition in rats: Evidence for a critical role at conditioning rather than preexposure. *Behavioural Pharmacology, 4,* 183–186.

Purves, D., Bonardi, C., & Hall, G. (1995). Enhancement of latent inhibition in rats with electrolytic lesions of the hippocampus. *Behavioral Neuroscience, 109,* 366–370.

Rescorla, R. A. (1968). Probability of shock in the presence and absence of CS in fear conditioning. *Journal of Comparative and Physiological Psychology, 66,* 1–5.

Rizzo, L., Danion, J. M., Van Der Linden, M., & Grangé, D. (1996). Patients with schizophrenia remember that an event has occurred, but not when. *British Journal of Psychiatry, 168,* 427–431.

Rizzo, L., Danion, J. M., Van Der Linden, Grangé, D., & Rohmer, J. G. (1996). Impairment of memory for spatial context in schizophrenia. *Neuropsychology, 10,* 376–384.

Robbins, T. W. (1990). The case of frontostriatal dysfunction in schizophrenia. *Schizophrenia Bulletin, 16,* 391–402.

Robinson, G. B., Port, R. L., & Stillwell, E. J. (1993). Latent inhibition of the classically conditioned rabbit nictitating membrane response is unaffected by the NMDA antagonist MK801. *Psychobiology, 21,* 120–124.

Rochford, J., Sen, A. P., & Quirion, R. (1996). Effect of nicotine and nicotinic receptor agonists on latent inhibition in the rat. *Journal of Pharmacology and Experimental Therapeutics, 277,* 1267–1275.

Sanchez, C., Arnt, J., Dragsted, N., Hyttel, J., Lembol, H. L., Meier, E., & Skarsfeldt, T. (1991). Neurochemical and in vivo pharmacological profile of sertindole, a limbic-selective neuroleptic compound. *Drug Developmental Research, 22,* 239–250.

Scheibel, A. B., & Kovelman, J. A. (1981). Disorientation of the hippocampal pyramidal cell and its processes in the schizophrenic patients. *Biological Psychiatry, 16,* 101–102.

Schmajuk, N. A. (1987). Animals models for schizophrenia: The hippocampally lesioned animal. *Schizophrenia Bulletin, 32,* 317–327.

Schmajuk, N. A. (1989). The hippocampus and the control of information storage in the brain. In M. Arbib & S. I. Amari (Eds.), *Dynamic interactions in neural networks: Models and data* (pp. 67–102). New York: Springer-Verlag.

Schmajuk, N. A., Lam, Y. W., & Christiansen, B. A. (1994). Latent inhibition of the rat eyeblink response: Effect of hippocampal aspiration lesions. *Physiology and Behavior, 55,* 597–601.

Schmajuk, N. A., Lam, Y. W., & Gray, J. A. (1996). Latent inhibition: A neural network approach. *Journal of Experimental Psychology: Animal Behavior Processes, 22,* 321–349.

Schmajuk, N. A., & Moore, J. W. (1985). Real-time attentional models for classical conditioning and the hippocampus. *Physiological Psychology, 13,* 278–290.

Schmajuk, N. A., & Moore, J. W. (1988). The hippocampus and the classically conditioned nictitating membrane response: A real-time attentional associative model. *Psychobiology, 16,* 20–35.

Schmajuk, N. A., & Tyberg, M. (1991). The hippocampal-lesion model of schizophrenia. In A. Boulton, G. Baker, & M. Martin-Iverson (Eds.), *Neuromethods: Vol. 18. Animal models in psychiatry I* (pp. 67–102). Clifton, NJ: Humana Press.

Shanks, D. R. (1994). Human associative learning. In N.J. Mackintosh (Ed.), *Animal learning and cognition* (pp. 335–374). San Diego, CA: Academic Press.

Solomon, P. R., Crider, A., Winkelman, J. W., Turi, A., Kamer, R. M., & Kaplan, L. J. (1981). Disrupted latent inhibition in the rat with chronic amphetamine or haloperidol-induced supersensitivity: Relationship to schizophrenic attention disorder. *Biological Psychiatry, 16,* 519–538.

Solomon, P. R., & Moore, J. W. (1975). Latent inhibition and stimulus generalisation of the classically conditioned nictitating membrane response in rabbit (*Oryctolagus cunugulus*) following dorsal hippocampal ablation. *Journal of Comparative and Physiological Psychology, 89,* 1192–1203.

Solomon, P. R., Nichols, G. L., Kiernan, J. M., Kamer, R. S., & Kaplan, L. J. (1980). Differential effect of medial and dorsal raphe lesions in the rat: Latent inhibition and septo-hippocampal serotonin levels. *Journal of Comparative and Physiological Psychology, 94,* 145–154.

Sotty, F., Sandner, G., & Gosselin, O. (1996). Latent inhibition in conditioned emotional response: c-fos immunolabelling evidence for brain areas involved in the rat. *Brain Research, 737,* 243–254.

Spear, N. E. (1981). Extending the domain of memory retrieval. In R. R. Miller & N. E. Spear (Eds.), *Information processing in animals: Memory mechanisms* (pp. 341–378). Hillsdale, NJ: Erlbaum.

Surwit, R. S., & Poser, E. G. (1974). Latent inhibition in the conditioned electrodermal response. *Journal of Comparative and Physiological Psychology, 86,* 543–548.

Swerdlow, N. R., Braff, D. L., Hartston, H., Perry, W., & Geyer, M. A. (1996). Latent inhibition in schizophrenia. *Schizophrenia Research, 20,* 91–103.

Vidal, M., Salgado, J. V., Oberling, P., Graeff, F. G., Danion, J. M., & Sandner, G. (1999). *A conditioned response suppression paradigm being sensitive to latent inhibition in humans without a masking task.* Manuscript submitted for publication.

Wagner, A. R. (1981). SOP: A model of automatic memory processing in animal behavior. In R. R. Miller & N. E. Spear (Eds.), *Information processing in animals: Memory mechanisms* (pp. 5–47). Hillsdale, NJ: Erlbaum.

Warburton, E. C., Joseph, M. H., Feldon, J., Weiner, I., & Gray, J. A. (1994). Antagonism of amphetamine-induced disruption of latent inhibition in rats by haloperidol and ondansetron—Implications for a possible antipsychotic action of ondansetron. *Psychopharmacology, 114,* 657–664.

Weinberger, D. R., & Lipska, B. K. (1995). Cortical maldevelopment, anti-psychotic drugs, and schizophrenia: A search for common ground. *Schizophrenia Research, 16,* 87–110.

Weiner, I. (1990). Neural substrates of latent inhibition: The switching model. *Psychological Bulletin, 108,* 442–461.

Weiner, I., & Feldon, J. (1992). Phencyclidine does not disrupt latent inhibition in rats: Implications for animal models of schizophrenia. *Pharmacology, Biochemistry and Behavior, 42,* 625–631.

Weiner, I., & Feldon, J. (1994). The latent inhibition model of schizophrenic attention disorder and of antipsychotic drug action: Comment on Dunn, Atwater and Kilts. *Psychopharmacology, 116,* 379–380.

Weiner, I., Feldon, J., & Katz, Y. (1987). Facilitation of the expression but not the acquisition of latent inhibition by haloperidol in rats. *Pharmacology, Biochemistry and Behavior, 26,* 241–246.

Weiner, I., Kidron, R., Tarrasch, R., Arnt, J., & Feldon, J. (1994). The effects of the new antipsychotic, sertindole, on latent inhibition in rats. *Behavioural Pharmacology, 5,* 119–124.

Weiner, I., Lubow, R. E., & Feldon, J. (1984). Abolition of the expression but not the acquisition of latent inhibition by chronic amphetamine in rats. *Psychopharmacology, 83,* 194–199.

Weiner, I., Lubow, R. E., & Feldon, J. (1988). Disruption of latent inhibition by administration of acute low doses of amphetamine. *Pharmacology, Biochemistry and Behavior, 30,* 871–878.

Weiss, K. R., Friedman, R., & McGregor, S. (1974). Effects of septal lesions on latent inhibition and habituation of the orienting response in rats. *Acta Neurobiologiae Experimentalis, 34,* 491–504.

Willner, P. (1984). The validity of animal models of depression. *Psychopharmacology, 83,* 1–16.

Willner, P. (1991a). Behavioural models in psychopharmacology. In P. Willner (Ed.), *Behavioural models in psychopharmacology: Theoretical, industrial, and clinical perspectives* (pp. 3–18). Cambridge, England: Cambridge University Press.

Willner, P. (1991b). Methods for assessing the validity of animal models of human psychopathology. In A. Boulton, G. Baker, & M. Martin-Iverson (Eds.), *Neuromethods: Vol. 18. Animal models in psychiatry I* (pp. 1–24). Clifton, NJ: Humana Press.

Yee, B. K., Feldon, J., & Rawlins, J. N. P. (1995). Latent inhibition in rats is abolished by NMDA-induced neuronal loss in the retrohippocampal region but this lesion effect can be prevented by systemic haloperidol treatment. *Behavioral Neuroscience, 109,* 227–240.

8

Startle-Response Measures of Information Processing in Animals: Relevance to Schizophrenia

Mark A. Geyer, David L. Braff, and Neal R. Swerdlow

Clinical observations in schizophrenia patients have identified deficiencies in the processing of information, including difficulties in the filtering or gating of sensory stimuli and irrelevant thoughts from intruding into conscious awareness. Indeed, theories describing the group of schizophrenias often conceptualize the common aspect of these disorders as involving deficits in one or more of the multiple mechanisms that enable normal individuals to filter or gate most of the sensory stimuli they receive (Braff & Geyer, 1990; Geyer & Braff, 1987; McGhie & Chapman 1961). Collectively, this class of mechanisms is referred to as *sensorimotor gating*. Theoretically, impairments in gating lead to sensory overload and cognitive fragmentation. The hypothetical construct of sensorimotor gating has been operationalized and explored in both human and animal studies. Our group has developed operational measures of this theoretical construct by taking advantage of the opportunity to study homologous forms of behavioral processes using the startle response. For example, studies have identified startle habituation deficits in schizophrenic patients (e.g., Bolino et al., 1994; Bolino et al., 1992; Braff, Grillon, & Geyer, 1992; Geyer & Braff, 1982) that may reflect failures of sensory filtering that could lead to disorders of cognition. As discussed below, the validity of this gating construct has been assessed most thoroughly using another operational measure that is based on the homologous nature of the startle reflex—namely, the prepulse inhibition (PPI) of startle paradigm.

The startle reflex is a constellation of responses to sudden intense stimuli that has provided a useful approach to studying the neural control of simple behaviors. One major advantage of startle-response paradigms is that homologous behavioral phenomena can be studied in a variety of species (Geyer & Markou, 1995). In humans, the blink-reflex component

This work was supported by grants from the National Institute of Mental Health (MH52885, MH42228, MH01223), the National Institute on Drug Abuse (DA02925), and the U.S. Veterans Affairs VISN 22 Mental Illness Research, Education, and Clinical Center.

of the startle response is measured using electrodes on the relevant muscle; in small animals, the whole-body flinch elicited by startling stimuli is measured, as described elsewhere (Geyer & Swerdlow, 1998). Of importance for the present work is not the reflex phenomenon itself, but the conceptually important forms of behavioral plasticity—including habituation, PPI, and fear potentiation—that are regulated by forebrain circuitry and can be demonstrated using measures of startle. Even these more complex processes exhibit striking similarities across species. One form of startle plasticity is PPI, which is the normal suppression of the startle reflex when the intense startling stimulus is preceded by a weak prestimulus (Graham, 1975; H. S. Hoffman & Searle, 1968; Ison, McAdam, & Hammond, 1973). In PPI, a weak prepulse inhibits a reflex response to a powerful sensory stimulus. In all animals tested, PPI occurs when the prepulse and startling stimuli are in the same or different sensory modalities. It does not appear to be a form of conditioning, because it occurs on the first exposure to the prepulse and pulse stimuli and it does not exhibit habituation over multiple trials. PPI thus appears to reflect the activation of hardwired gating processes that are regulated by forebrain neural circuitry. Virtually all the evidence available supports the belief that PPI is homologous from rodents to humans.

Our first report of deficits in PPI of acoustic startle in schizophrenic patients appeared in 1978 (Braff et al., 1978). Subsequently, the deficit in PPI has been confirmed in studies of medicated but still ill patients with schizophrenia in different countries and by investigators using different methods (Bolino et al., 1994; Braff et al., 1992; Grillon, Ameli, Charney, Krystal, & Braff, 1992; Hamm, Weike, Bauer, Vailt, & Gallhofer, 1995; Weike, Globisch, Hamm, & Bauer, 1996). Deficits in PPI in schizophrenia patients do not simply result from medications or psychotic behavior per se, because schizotypal patients who exhibit behavioral abnormalities but are not receiving antipsychotic medications and are not grossly psychotic also show PPI deficits (Cadenhead, Geyer, & Braff, 1993). Furthermore, there is some evidence that PPI deficits in schizophrenia may be reversed by successful treatment with antipsychotic drugs (Hamm et al., 1995; Kumari, Soni, & Sharma, in press; Weike et al., 1996). Only recently have studies attempted to relate these observed deficits in sensorimotor gating functions to measures of clinical symptoms (Braff, Swerdlow, & Geyer, 1999) or thought disorder. Perry and colleagues have reported significant correlations within groups of schizophrenia patients between deficits in both PPI and visual information processing and thought disorder as assessed by the Rorschach-derived Ego Impairment Index (Perry & Braff, 1994; Perry, Geyer, & Braff, 1999). Further studies in this vein will be important in relating the abnormalities in basic forms of information processing, such as PPI or habituation, to more complex symptoms, treatment outcomes, and quality of life.

Prepulse inhibition deficits are neither unique to nor diagnostic of schizophrenia or any other single form of psychopathology, because they also have been observed in obsessive–compulsive disorder (Swerdlow, Benbow, Zisook, Geyer, & Braff, 1993), Huntington's disease (Swerdlow et al.,

1995), nocturnal enuresis and attention deficit disorder (Ornitz, Hanna, & de Traversay, 1992), and Tourette's syndrome (Castellanos et al., 1996). It is not yet known whether the PPI deficits in these various disorders are identical or related to the same or different underlying substrates. It has been noted, however, that all these disorders are characterized by a loss of gating in sensory, motor, or cognitive domains, have some overlapping symptoms, and also share functional abnormalities within the cortico-striato-pallido-pontine circuitry that modulates PPI (Swerdlow, Caine, Braff, & Geyer, 1992). Thus PPI deficits may reflect some degree of overlap in symptomatology in disorders characterized by disturbances of sensorimotor gating, attentional filtering mechanisms, or related aspects of information processing (see Oberling, Gosselin, & Miller, chap. 7, this volume). With regard to the utility of animal models for exploring this class of information-processing abnormalities, independent of the particular psychiatric disorder in which they may occur, it is most relevant to note that these deficits in sensorimotor gating are the result of abnormalities within a defined brain circuit (see Swerdlow, Caine, et al., 1992, for review).

In view of this evidence of a deficit in startle PPI as a measurable example of the class of sensorimotor gating abnormalities in patients with schizophrenia, extensive studies of the neurobiology and pharmacology of PPI have been conducted in animals. The focus of this review is to summarize the work that has taken advantage of the fact that the cross-species nature of the startle response and PPI enables researchers' use of animal models to investigate behavioral phenomena that are extremely similar to the deficits seen in schizophrenia. Although this line of study is only about a decade old, considerable progress has been made. The chapter begins with a review of studies in which drugs acting on specific neurotransmitter systems and receptors have been used to disrupt PPI in rodents and thereby mimic the abnormality seen in schizophrenia. In general, the drugs used are either *agonists*, which function by mimicking the actions of the natural neurotransmitter at one or more receptors, or *antagonists*, which occupy the relevant receptor or receptors and therefore block the actions of either the experimentally administered agonist or the natural neurotransmitter. The neurotransmitters of relevance here include dopamine (DA), serotonin (5-hydroxytryptamine; 5-HT), and the excitatory amino acid glutamate. After summarizing the drug-induced models of PPI deficits, some nonpharmacological developmental manipulations that also lead to deficits in PPI, such as isolation rearing, are discussed. In addition, because schizophrenia is in part a group of genetic disorders, the review also summarizes recent efforts to apply genetic strategies to the study of PPI deficits in animals. With both drug-induced and developmental models, an important aspect of this work has been the search for improved antipsychotic treatments. In general, schizophrenic patients have been treated for the past 40 years primarily with drugs that act as antagonists at DA receptors, which are called *typical antipsychotics*. These drugs are primarily effective in treating the positive symptoms of schizophrenia, including such phenomena as hallucinations, rather than the negative symptoms, which include the more cognitive disturbances of mood and thought processes. In recent years, it has become clear that some newer drugs, called *atypical antipsychotics*, are effective in patients that did not respond to typical antipsychotics and that these atypical drugs reduce both positive and negative symptoms while having fewer unwanted side effects. Thus, of particular interest in this review is the possibility that a focus on sensorimotor gating deficits might provide animal models that could aid in determining the mechanisms of action of atypical antipsychotics and in identifying novel antipsychotics that have improved therapeutic actions and reduced side effects.

Pharmacology of Prepulse Inhibition in Animals

Dopamine

In rats, PPI is reduced by drugs that facilitate DA function, including the direct DA agonist apomorphine (D. C. Hoffman & Donovan, 1994; Mansbach, Geyer, & Braff, 1988; Swerdlow, Braff, Taaid, & Geyer, 1994; Swerdlow & Geyer, 1993; Swerdlow, Keith, Braff, & Geyer, 1991) and the indirect DA agonists *d*-amphetamine (Mansbach et al., 1988) and cocaine, and these effects are reversed by DA receptor antagonists (Mansbach et al., 1988; Swerdlow & Geyer, 1993; Swerdlow et al., 1991; Swerdlow, Braff, Taaid, & Geyer, 1994). As in patients with schizophrenia (Braff et al., 1992), the apomorphine-induced disruption of PPI is not modality specific, being seen when acoustic prepulses are used to inhibit either acoustic or tactile startle (Geyer, Swerdlow, Mansbach, & Braff, 1990). The D_2 receptor appears to mediate the apomorphine disruption of PPI, because this effect of apomorphine is blocked by the D_2 antagonists haloperidol, raclopride, and spiperone (Mansbach et al., 1988; Swerdlow et al., 1991). Further support for a role of the D_2 receptor, but not the D_1 receptor, in the modulation of PPI is the finding that PPI is disrupted by the D_2 agonist quinpirole, but not the D_1 agonist SKF 38393 (Peng, Mansbach, Braff, & Geyer, 1990; Wan & Swerdlow, 1994). Although evidence (D. C. Hoffman & Donovan 1994; Peng et al., 1990) indicates that D_1 and D_2 receptors may interact in the regulation of PPI, D_1 receptors do not appear to serve as an independent substrate for changes in PPI. The apomorphine-induced disruption of PPI is reversed by the atypical antipsychotic clozapine (Swerdlow & Geyer 1993; Swerdlow et al., 1991), which lacks neuroleptic properties in some behavioral assays, and the putative atypical antipsychotic Seroquel (Swerdlow, Zisook, & Taaid, 1994). Recently, it was reported that some putative D_4 antagonists restore PPI in apomorphine-treated rats, despite the fact that they are inactive in traditional preclinical measures of antipsychotic action (Cassella et al., 1994; Mansbach, Brooks, Sanner, & Zorn, 1998). Thus, converging evidence supports the important involvement of dopaminergic systems, acting via D_2-family receptors, in the control of PPI. These findings in rats parallel the deficits in PPI observed in schizophrenia patients, which are also reported to be corrected by antipsychotics (Hamm et al., 1995).

Several studies suggest that the effects of DA agonists on PPI are mediated by increased DA activity in the nucleus accumbens (NAC). First, low doses of apomorphine that do not decrease PPI in control rats potently disrupt PPI in rats that are surgically altered to have supersensitive DA receptors in the NAC (Swerdlow, Geyer, Braff, & Koob, 1986). Second, the loss of PPI induced by the indirect DA agonist amphetamine is reversed by depletion of DA in the NAC (Swerdlow, Braff, Masten, & Geyer, 1990). Third, PPI is disrupted in rats by infusion of the D_2 agonist quinpirole or DA into the NAC or anteromedial striatum, effects that are reversed by systemic treatment with a D_2 antagonist (Swerdlow, Caine, & Geyer, 1992; Wan, Geyer, & Swerdlow, 1994). Fourth, in vivo microdialysis studies of DA levels in the NAC during startle testing have demonstrated that startling stimuli produce a decrease in DA release in the NAC and that this decrease is blocked by prepulse stimuli (Humby, Wilkinson, Robbins, & Geyer, 1996). Thus, overactivity of NAC DA may be the mechanism underlying the loss of PPI produced by systemic administrations of DA agonists in rats.

Most predictive models for antipsychotic agents, such as the reversal of apomorphine-induced canine vomiting or rodent hyperactivity (Creese, Burt, & Snyder, 1976; Freedman & Giarman 1956), assess the ability of a compound to reverse a behavioral effect of a DA agonist. Many DA receptor antagonists identified in this manner are clinically useful *typical* antipsychotics, which are highly effective in reducing hallucinations and delusions—the positive symptoms of schizophrenia. In contrast, negative or deficit psychotic symptoms—abnormal moods and thought processes—are linked theoretically to reduced forebrain glutamate transmission (Davis, Kahn, Ko, & Davidson, 1991; Javitt & Zukin, 1991). Some evidence indicates that these negative symptoms respond to *atypical* but not typical antipsychotics (Kane, Honigfeld, Singer, & Meltzer, 1987). Unlike the multiplicity of animal models capable of predicting the antidopaminergic properties of typical antipsychotics, no animal model has convincingly demonstrated such predictive validity for identifying agents with atypical antipsychotic properties. The ability of antipsychotics, including the prototypic atypical antipsychotic clozapine, to restore PPI in apomorphine-treated rats strongly correlates with their clinical potency ($r = .99$; Swerdlow, Braff, et al., 1994; Swerdlow & Geyer, 1993). In addition to its sensitivity, the specificity of the PPI model for compounds with antipsychotic efficacy is supported by findings that it predicts no such efficacy for a wide variety of psychoactive drugs that are not antipsychotics (Rigdon & Viik, 1991). Thus, the apomorphine-induced disruption of PPI appears to be sensitive to both typical and atypical antipsychotics but fails to make the important distinction between these two classes of antipsychotics.

Glutamate

In addition to its disruption by DA agonists, PPI also is reduced or eliminated in rats by psychotomimetic noncompetitive glutamate (N-methyl-

D-aspartate; NMDA) antagonists, such as phencyclidine (PCP), dizocilpine, and ketamine (Mansbach & Geyer 1989, 1991). As with the effects
of apomorphine in rats or the abnormalities seen in schizophrenia, both
intramodal and crossmodal PPI are sensitive to noncompetitive NMDA
antagonists (Geyer et al., 1990). In contrast to the effects of DA agonists
on PPI, those of NMDA antagonists are not reversed by typical antipsychotics such as haloperidol (Geyer et al., 1990; Keith, Mansbach, & Geyer,
1991; Swerdlow, Bakshi, & Geyer, 1996) or selective D_1 or D_2 antagonists
(Bakshi, Swerdlow, & Geyer, 1994) but are reversed by the atypical antipsychotics clozapine (Bakshi et al., 1994), olanzapine (Bakshi & Geyer
1995), Seroquel (Swerdlow et al., 1996), and remoxipride (Johansson,
Jackson, & Svensson, 1994). Thus, the PCP disruption of PPI may be a
useful model for identifying compounds with atypical antipsychotic potential. Of particular interest in this regard is the recent report that the
atypical antipsychotic clozapine, unlike typical antipsychotics, appears to
normalize PPI deficits in patients with schizophrenia (Kumari et al., in
press). If confirmed, such results would parallel the effects of antipsychotics seen in the PCP model of PPI deficits in rats. In addition, the
putative novel antipsychotic M100907 (formerly MDL 100,907) is effective
in reversing the effects of NMDA antagonists on PPI (Varty, Bakshi, &
Geyer, 1999). M100907 is a selective antagonist at the 2A subtype of serotonin receptors and is the first drug lacking direct actions at DA receptors to be tested as an antipsychotic in clinical trials in many years. Hence,
the outcome of the ongoing clinical trials with M100907 will test further
the predictive validity of the NMDA model of PPI deficits in schizophrenia.
Such predictive validity may be accompanied by construct validity, because
PCP-induced clinical and glutamatergic effects have been linked to the
characteristics and pathophysiology of deficit-symptom schizophrenia. In
humans, this class of drugs produces symptoms that mimic some features
of schizophrenia (Javitt & Zukin, 1991). Furthermore, ketamine has been
shown to reduce PPI in normal control participants (Karper, Grillon, Charney, & Krystal, 1994), induce psychotic symptoms in normal volunteers
(Malhotra et al., 1996), and exacerbate psychotic symptoms in schizophrenia patients (Lahti, Koffel, LaPorte, & Tamminga, 1995), providing some
validation of the similar animal studies.

Serotonin

PPI in rats is reduced by systemic treatment with serotonin releasers—
including 3, 4-methylenedioxy-N-meth-amphetamine (MDMA), N-ethyl-3,
4-methylenedioxy-amphetamine,   fenfluramine,   and   alpha-ethyltryptamine (Kehne et al., 1992; Kehne, Padich, McCloskey, Taylor, & Schmidt,
1996; Mansbach, Braff, & Geyer, 1989; Martinez & Geyer, 1997)—direct
5-HT_{1A} agonists (Rigdon & Weatherspoon 1992; Sipes & Geyer, 1994,
1995b), and direct agonists for 5-HT_{1B} and 5-HT_2 receptors (Sipes & Geyer,
1994). Similar effects have been reported with MDMA in mice (Dulawa &
Geyer, 1996), although not in human volunteers (Vollenweider, Remens-

berger, Hell, & Geyer, in press). Furthermore, the effects of 5-HT$_{1B}$ agonists on PPI in rats are reproduced by the administration of a 5-HT$_{1D}$ agonist in the guinea pig, suggesting a functional behavioral homology in the roles of these receptors across species (Sipes & Geyer, 1996). Such observations indicate the utility of PPI measures for cross-species comparisons with some but not all drugs. The PPI-disruptive effects of 5-HT releasers are prevented by pretreatment with the 5-HT reuptake inhibitor fluoxetine, which prevents the drug-induced release of 5-HT from presynaptic terminals (Kehne et al., 1992, 1996; Martinez & Geyer, 1997). The PPI-disruptive effects of direct 5-HT$_2$ receptor agonists, including hallucinogens such as 2, 5-dimethoxy-4-iodoamphetamine (DOI), are blocked by pretreatment with nonspecific 5-HT$_2$ antagonists (Sipes & Geyer 1994) or the selective 5-HT$_{2A}$ antagonist M100907 (Padich, McCloskey, & Kehne, 1996), but not by a 5-HT$_{2C}$ antagonist (Sipes & Geyer, 1995a) or the DA blocker haloperidol (Padich et al., 1996). The 5-HT$_{2A}$ antagonist is also effective in blocking the effects of 5-HT releasers on PPI (Padich et al., 1996). In addition, the selectivity of M100907 for the 5-HT$_{2A}$ receptor has facilitated the identification of the ventral pallidum as the region in the brain that mediates the effects of hallucinogens such as DOI on PPI (Sipes & Geyer, 1997). Such findings have contributed to the current investigation of M100907 as putative nondopaminergic antipsychotic in patients with schizophrenia.

Using PPI in Models for Neurodevelopmental Processes Relevant to Schizophrenia

Sensorimotor gating deficits in schizophrenia patients, unlike PPI deficits in drug-treated rats, reflect longitudinal and complex interactions of genetic, developmental, social, and environmental forces. Hence, it is important that startle gating in rats appears to be sensitive to these same forces. In particular, developmental perturbations significantly alter PPI in rats. For example, recent studies (Geyer, Wilkinson, Humby, & Robbins, 1993) indicate that isolation-reared rats exhibit an antipsychotic reversible deficiency in PPI compared with group-reared controls. Isolation rearing involves housing rats in single cages rather than the normal social groups from the time of weaning, through the period of puberty, and into adulthood. After, but not before, puberty, such isolation-reared rats exhibit enduring deficits in PPI that mimic those seen in patients with schizophrenia (Bakshi & Geyer, in press). This developmental time frame is of interest because schizophrenia typically emerges shortly after puberty (Weinberger, 1996). This effect of isolation rearing appears to be developmentally specific, in that similar isolation of adult rats failed to produce the deficit in PPI observed in isolation-reared rats (Wilkinson et al., 1994). Furthermore, the reductions in PPI produced by isolation rearing are reversed by both typical antipsychotics (e.g., haloperidol, raclopride) and atypical antipsychotics (e.g., clozapine, risperidone; Geyer et al., 1993; Varty & Higgins, 1995). Our more recent findings further support the sensitivity of this paradigm to atypical antipsychotics, including olanzapine and Sero-quel (Bakshi, Swerdlow, Braff, & Geyer, 1998). Thus, PPI deficits in isolation-reared rats may be a valuable paradigm that, like the apomor-phine-induced disruption of PPI, is sensitive, but not specific, in its ability to identify compounds with atypical antipsychotic properties.

In another finding of direct relevance to neurodevelopmental theories of schizophrenia (Weinberger, 1996), impaired PPI and enhanced sensitiv-ity to the PPI-disruptive effects of apomorphine have been noted in post-pubescent rats that received neurotoxin lesions of the hippocampus as neonates (Lipska et al., 1995). It will be important to identify the peri-pubertal neural circuit changes that occur in neonatal hippocampal-lesioned rats that are responsible for the development of this supersensi-tive DA-mediated loss of PPI in adulthood. Thus, using strategies that involve either manipulations of the rearing environment or neonatal lim-bic cortical circuitry, PPI studies can potentially be used to examine the contribution of developmental processes to the pathophysiology of senso-rimotor gating deficits in schizophrenia and to identify compounds with potential atypical antipsychotic properties.

Using PPI in Genetic Studies: Strain Analyses and Knockout Strategies

Genetic factors may also be critical determinants of sensorimotor gating in rats, because strain-related differences in the dopaminergic modulation of PPI have been reported (Rigdon, 1990; Swerdlow, Bakshi, & Geyer, 1998). If susceptibility to the gating-disruptive effects of DA agonists is genetically controlled in rats, these studies might offer critical insight into genetic factors mediating the susceptibility to and development of schizo-phrenia in humans, which is partially hereditary. Several new lines of investigation have advanced our understanding of the genetic regulation of PPI. One strategy, applied by Ellenbroek, Geyer, and Cools (1995), used pharmacogenetic selection to produce strains of rats that were either sus-ceptible (APO-SUS) or not susceptible (APO-UNSUS) to the behavioral effects of apomorphine. Male and female rats were identified from each generation who exhibited the most (APO-SUS) or least (APO-UNSUS) gnawing in response to 1.5 mg/kg apomorphine. Within a single genera-tion, APO-SUS rats exhibited significantly less PPI than did APO-UNSUS rats. Rats were also studied that were part of a longstanding breeding program, in which APO-SUS and APO-UNSUS rats were selected for mul-tiple generations. PPI was measured in rats from the 17th and 18th gen-erations of this breeding strategy. Rats descended from the APO-SUS strain exhibited significantly less PPI, compared with the APO-UNSUS rats. Apparently, the physiological substrates that regulate the behavioral sensitivity to apomorphine are associated with substrates that regulate PPI and that are transmitted genetically.

The use of PPI paradigms in mice has received recent attention in part because of the advances in molecular biology that rely on murine

models. In mice, robust PPI is readily demonstrated, as are several pharmacological effects on PPI (Dulawa & Geyer, 1996). Using a classical genetic approach, Bullock et al. (1996) compared PPI among seven mice
strains, and the strains with the highest (C3H/2Ibg) and lowest (DBA/2J/
Ibg) levels of PPI were crossed. A quantitative analysis of inheritance revealed that PPI, but not startle amplitude per se, followed a pattern consistent with dominant transmission. Similar approaches are currently being applied to examine the genetics of PPI in families of patients with
schizophrenia.

Another genetic strategy has recently been applied to understanding
the normal physiological substrates regulating PPI (Dulawa, Hen,
Scearce-Levie, & Geyer, 1997). PPI was compared between wild-type mice
and mice that had been genetically engineered to lack 5-HT_{1B} receptors,
called 5-HT1B *knockouts* (5-HT1BKOs). PPI was significantly reduced in
wild-type mice by the 5-HT1A/1B agonist RU24969, but RU24969 did not
reduce PPI in 5-HT1BKOs. More recently, this strategy has been applied
to the DA system to assess the respective contributions of subtypes of the
D_2-family of DA receptors to the effects of DA agonists on PPI. Strikingly,
knockouts of either the D_3 or the D_4 receptor subtypes had no influence
either on PPI or on the disruption of PPI produced by amphetamine (Ralph
et al., in press). In contrast, the selective knockout of the D_2 receptor subtype abolished the effect of amphetamine while leaving normal PPI intact
(Ralph et al., in press). Such distinctions among these receptor subtypes
had not been made successfully with pharmacological approaches because
the drugs available are not sufficiently selective. These findings with
knockout mice indicate that to the extent that the PPI model is predictive
of the effects of antipsychotics, the D_2 and not the D_3 or D_4 subtypes appear
to be most relevant clinically, even though the latter subtypes are being
explored for the development of antipsychotics. Such experimental findings demonstrate the utility of applying genetic knockout techniques toward understanding the physiological substrates of behaviors and processes such as sensorimotor gating.

Conclusion

The study of sensorimotor gating deficits in schizophrenia and in homologous animal models based on the startle PPI paradigm has already advanced our understanding of possible anatomical, neurochemical, and developmental contributions to information-processing abnormalities in
psychotic disorders. The advantages of focusing on studies of homologous
behaviors that can be quantified in both patients and laboratory animals
in the development of an animal model have facilitated the remarkable
maturation of this model in less than two decades. Although several
groups have reported the utility of PPI as a measure that predicts "typical"
neuroleptic properties, recent studies suggest that only atypical antipsychotics restore PPI in PCP-treated rats. This model is still relatively new,
but findings at least suggest the possibility that the restoration of PPI can

be used as a sensitive measure (with apomorphine) to identify compounds with both typical and atypical antipsychotic properties and as a specific measure (with PCP) to identify only those compounds with atypical antipsychotic properties. Another variant of this model, examining the ability of compounds to restore PPI in isolation-reared rats, appears to be sensitive to both typical and atypical antipsychotic agents. Although the particular behavioral abnormalities being studied in PPI paradigms are not unique to schizophrenia, the narrowed focus of this work on a specific behavior coupled with the effort to establish and use homologous measures in animals has enabled rigorous studies of both pharmacological and neurobiological influences on sensorimotor gating in rodents that have already prompted clinical tests of novel antipsychotic drugs.

References

Bakshi, V. P., & Geyer, M. A. (1995). Antagonism of phencyclidine-induced deficits in prepulse inhibition by the putative atypical antipsychotic olanzapine. *Psychopharmacology, 122*, 198–201.

Bakshi, V. P., & Geyer, M. A. (in press). Ontogeny of isolation rearing-induced deficits in sensorimotor gating in rats. *Physiology and Behavior.*

Bakshi, V. P., Swerdlow, N. R., Braff, D. L., & Geyer, M. A. (1998). Reversal of isolation rearing-induced deficits in prepulse inhibition by Seroquel and olanzapine. *Biological Psychiatry, 43*, 436–445.

Bakshi, V. P., Swerdlow, N. R., & Geyer, M. A. (1994). Clozapine antagonizes phencyclidine-induced deficits in sensorimotor gating of the startle response. *Journal of Pharmacology and Experimental Therapeutics, 271*, 787–794.

Bolino, F., Di Michele, V., Di Cicco, L., Manna, V., Daneluzzo, E., & Cassachia, M. (1994). Sensorimotor gating and habituation evoked by electrocutaneous stimulation in schizophrenia. *Biological Psychiatry, 36*, 670–679.

Bolino, F., Manna, V., Di Cicco, L., Di Michele, V., Daneluzzo, E., Rossi, A., & Casacchia, M. (1992). Startle reflex habituation in functional psychoses: A controlled study. *Neuroscience Letters, 145*, 126–128.

Braff, D. L., & Geyer, M. A. (1990). Sensorimotor gating and schizophrenia: Human and animal model studies. *Archives of General Psychiatry, 47*, 181–188.

Braff, D. L., Grillon,, C., & Geyer, M. (1992). Gating and habituation of the startle reflex in schizophrenic patients. *Archives of General Psychiatry, 49*, 206–215.

Braff, D., Stone, C., Callaway, E., Geyer, M., Glick, I., & Bali, L. (1978). Prestimulus effects on human startle reflex in normals and schizophrenics. *Psychophysiology, 15*, 339–343.

Braff, D. L., Swerdlow, N. R., & Geyer, M. A. (1999). Symptom correlates of prepulse inhibition deficits in male schizophrenic patients. *American Journal of Psychiatry, 156*, 596–602.

Bullock, A. E., Slobe, B. S., & Collins, A. C. (1996). Classical genetic analysis of startle and prepulse inhibition of startle in mice. *Society for Neuroscience Abstracts, 21*, 199.

Cadenhead, K. S., Geyer, M. A., & Braff, D. L. (1993). Impaired startle prepulse inhibition and habituation in schizotypal patients. *American Journal of Psychiatry, 150*, 1862–1867.

Cassella, J., Hoffman, D., Rajachandran, L., Donovan, H., Bankoski, C., Lang, S., Johnson, A., Thurkauf, A., & Hutchison, A. (1994). The behavioral profile of NGD 94-1, a potent and selective dopamine D_4 receptor antagonist [Abstract]. *Proceedings of the American College of Neuropsychopharmacology*, 228.

Castellanos, F. X., Fine, E. J., Kaysen, D. L., Kozuch, P. L., Hamburger, S. D., Rapoport, J. L., & Hallett, M. (1996). Sensorimotor gating in boys with Tourette's syndrome and ADHD: Preliminary results. *Biological Psychiatry, 39*, 33–41.

Creese, I., Burt, D. R., & Snyder, S. H. (1976). Dopamine receptor binding predicts clinical and pharmacological potencies of antischizophrenic drugs. *Science, 192*, 481–483.

Davis, K. L., Kahn, R. S., Ko, G., & Davidson, M. (1991). Dopamine in schizophrenia: A review and reconceptualization. *American Journal of Psychiatry, 148*, 1474–1486.

Dulawa, S. C., & Geyer, M. A. (1996). Psychopharmacology of prepulse inhibition in mice. *Chinese Journal of Physiology, 39*, 139–146.

Dulawa, S. C., Hen, R., Scearce-Levie, K., & Geyer, M. A. (1997). Serotonin 1B receptor modulation of startle reactivity, habituation, and prepulse inhibition, in wild-type and serotonin 1B receptor knockout mice. *Psychopharmacology, 132*, 125–134.

Ellenbroek, B. A., Geyer, M. A., & Cools, M. A. (1995). The behavior of APO-SUS rats in animal models with construct validity for schizophrenia. *Journal of Neuroscience, 15*, 7604–7611.

Freedman, D. X., & Giarman, N. J. (1956). Apomorphine test for tranquilizing drugs: Effect of dibenamine. *Science, 124*, 264.

Geyer, M. A., & Braff, D. L. (1982). Habituation of the blink reflex in normals and schizophrenic patients. *Psychophysiololgy, 19*, 1–6.

Geyer, M. A., & Braff, D. L. (1987). Startle habituation and sensorimotor gating in schizophrenia and related animal models. *Schizophrenia Bulletin, 13*, 643–668.

Geyer, M. A., & Markou, A. (1995). Animal models of psychiatric disorders. In F. E. Bloom & D. J. Kupfer (Eds.), *Psychopharmacology: The fourth generation of progress* (pp. 787–798). New York: Raven Press.

Geyer, M. A., & Swerdlow, N. R. (1998). Measurement of the startle response, prepulse inhibition, and habituation. In J. N. Crawley & P. Skolnick (Eds.), *Current protocols in neuroscience* (pp. 8.7.1–8.7.15). New York: Wiley.

Geyer, M. A., Swerdlow, N. R., Mansbach, R. S., & Braff, D. L. (1990). Startle response models of sensorimotor gating and habituation deficits in schizophrenia. *Brain Research Bulletin, 25*, 485–498.

Geyer, M. A., Wilkinson, L. S., Humby, T., & Robbins, T. W. (1993). Isolation rearing of rats produces a deficit in prepulse inhibition of acoustic startle similar to that in schizophrenia. *Biological Psychiatry, 34*, 361–372.

Graham, F. (1975). The more or less startling effects of weak prestimuli. *Psychophysiology, 12*, 238–248.

Grillon, C., Ameli, R., Charney, D. S., Krystal, J., & Braff, D. L. (1992). Startle gating deficits occur across prepulse intensities in schizophrenic patients. *Biological Psychiatry, 32*, 939–943.

Hamm, A., Weike, A., Bauer, U., Vailt, D., & Gallhofer, B. (1995). Prepulse inhibition in medicated and unmedicated schizophrenics. *Psychophysiology, 33*(Suppl. 1), S65.

Hoffman, D. C., Donovan, H. (1994). D_1 and D_2 dopamine receptor antagonists reverse prepulse inhibition deficits in an animal model of schizophrenia. *Psychopharmacology, 115*, 447–453.

Hoffman, H. S., & Searle, J. L. (1968). Acoustic and temporal factors in the evocation of startle. *Acoustic Society of America Journal, 43*, 269–282.

Humby, T., Wilkinson, L. S., Robbins, T. W., & Geyer, M. A. (1996). Prepulses inhibit startle-induced reductions of extracellular dopamine in the nucleus accumbens of rat. *Journal of Neuroscience, 16*, 2149–2156.

Ison, J. R., McAdam, D. W., & Hammond, G. R. (1973). Latency and amplitude changes in the acoustic startle reflex produced by variations in auditory prestimulation. *Physiology and Behavior, 10*, 1035–1039.

Javitt, D. C., & Zukin, S. R. (1991). Recent advances in the phencyclidine model of schizophrenia. *American Journal of Psychiatry, 148*, 1301–1308.

Johansson, C., Jackson, D. M., & Svensson, L. (1994). The atypical antipsychotic, remoxipride, blocks phencyclidine-induced disruption of prepulse inhibition in the rat. *Psychopharmacology, 116*, 437–442.

Kane, J., Honigfeld, G., Singer, J., & Meltzer, H. (1987) Clozapine for the treatment-resistant schizophrenic: A double-blind comparison with chlorpromazine. *Archives of General Psychiatry, 45*, 789–796.

Karper, L. P., Grillon, C., Charney, D. S., & Krystal, J. H. (1994). The effect of ketamine on pre-pulse inhibition and attention [Abstract]. *Proceedings of the American College of Neuropsychopharmacology*, 124.

Kehne, J. H., McCloskey, T. C., Taylor, V. L., Black, C. K., Fadayel, G. M., & Schmidt, C. T. (1992). Effects of serotonin releasers 3, 4 methylenedioxymethamphetamine (MDMA), 4-chloroamphetamine (PCA) and fenfluramine on acoustic and tactile startle reflexes in rats. *Journal of Pharmacology and Experimental Therapeutics, 260*, 78–89.

Kehne, J. H., Padich, R. A., McCloskey, T. C., Taylor, V. L., & Schmidt, C. J. (1996). 5-HT modulation of auditory and visual sensorimotor gating: I. Effects of 5-HT releasers on sound and light prepulse inhibition in Wistar rats. *Psychopharmacology, 124*, 95–106.

Keith, V. A., Mansbach, R. S., & Geyer, M. A. (1991). Failure of haloperidol to block the effects of phencyclidine and dizocilpine on prepulse inhibition of startle. *Biological Psychiatry, 30*, 557–566.

Kumari, V., Soni, W., & Sharma, T. (in press). Clozapine normalizes information processing deficits in schizophrenia. *American Journal of Psychiatry*.

Lahti, A. C., Koffel, B., LaPorte, D., & Tamminga, C. A. (1995). Subanesthetic doses of ketamine stimulate psychosis in schizophrenia. *Neuropsychopharmacology, 13*, 9–19.

Lipska, B. K., Swerdlow, N. R., Geyer, M. A., Jaskiw, G. E., Braff, D. L., & Weinberger, D. R. (1995). Neonatal excitotoxic hippocampal damage in rats causes post-pubertal changes in prepulse inhibition of startle and its disruption by apomorphine. *Psychopharmacology, 122*, 35–43.

Malhotra, A. K., Pinals, D. A., Weingartner, H., Sirocco, K., Missar, C. D., Pickar, D., & Breirer, A. (1996). NMDA receptor function and human cognition: The effects of ketamine in healthy volunteers. *Neuropsychopharmacology, 14*, 301–307.

Mansbach, R. S., Braff, D. L., & Geyer, M. A. (1989). Prepulse inhibition of the acoustic startle response is disrupted by N-ethyl-3, 4-methylenedioxy-amphetamine (MDEA) in the rat. *European Journal of Pharmacology, 167*, 49–55.

Mansbach, R. S., Brooks, E. W., Sanner, M. A., & Zorn, S. H. (1998). Selective dopamine D4 receptor antagonists reverse apomorphine-induced blockade of prepulse inhibition. *Psychopharmacology, 135*, 194–200.

Mansbach, R. S., & Geyer, M. A. (1989). Effects of phencyclidine and phencyclidine biologs on sensorimotor gating in the rat. *Neuropsychopharmacology, 2*, 299–308.

Mansbach, R. S., & Geyer, M. A. (1991). Parametric determinants in pre-stimulus modification of acoustic startle: Interaction with ketamine. *Psychopharmacology, 105*, 162–168.

Mansbach, R. S., Geyer, M. A., & Braff, D. L. (1988). Dopaminergic stimulation disrupts sensorimotor gating in the rat. *Psychopharmacology, 94*, 507–514.

Martinez, D. L., & Geyer, M. A. (1997). Characterization of the disruptions of prepulse inhibition and habituation of startle induced by alpha-ethyltryptamine. *Neuropsychopharmacology, 16*, 246–255.

McGhie, A., & Chapman, J. (1961). Disorders of attention and perception in early schizophrenia. *British Journal of Medical Psychology, 34*, 102–116.

Ornitz, E. M., Hanna, G. L., & de Traversay, J. (1992). Prestimulation-induced startle modulation in attention-deficit hyperactivity disorder and nocturnal enuresis. *Psychophysiology, 29*, 437–451.

Padich, R. A., McCloskey, T. C., & Kehne, J. H. (1996). 5-HT modulation of auditory and visual sensorimotor gating: II. Effects of the 5-HT2A antagonist MDL 100, 907 on disruption of sound and light prepulse inhibition produced by 5-HT agonists in Wistar rats. *Psychopharmacology, 124*, 107–116.

Peng, R. Y., Mansbach, R. S., Braff, D. L., & Geyer, M. A. (1990). A D_2 dopamine receptor agonist disrupts sensorimotor gating in rats: Implications for dopaminergic abnormalities in schizophrenia. *Neuropsychopharmacology, 3*, 211–218.

Perry, W., & Braff, D. L. (1994). Information-processing deficits and thought disorder in schizophrenia. *American Journal of Psychiatry, 151*, 363–367.

Perry, W., Geyer, M. A., & Braff, D. L. (1999). Sensorimotor gating and thought disturbance measured in close temporal proximity in schizophrenic patients. *Archives of General Psychiatry, 56*, 277–281.

Ralph, R. J., Varty, G. B., Kelly, M. A., Wang, Y.-M., Caron, M. G., Rubinstein, M., Grandy, D. K., Low, M. J., & Geyer, M. A. (in press). The dopamine D_2 but not D_3 or D_4 receptor subtype is essential for the disruption of prepulse inhibition produced by amphetamine in mice. *Journal of Neuroscience.*

Rigdon, G. (1990). Differential effects of apomorphine on prepulse inhibition of acoustic startle reflex in two rat strains. *Psychopharmacology, 102,* 419–421.

Rigdon, G. C., & Viik, K. (1991). Prepulse inhibition as a screening test for potential antipsychotics. *Drug Development Research, 23,* 91–99.

Rigdon, G. C., & Weatherspoon, J. (1992). 5-HT1A receptor agonists block prepulse inhibition of the acoustic startle reflex. *Journal of Pharmacology and Experimental Therapeutics, 263,* 486–493.

Sipes, T. A., & Geyer, M. A. (1994). Multiple serotonin receptor subtypes modulate prepulse inhibition of the startle response in rats. *Neuropsychopharmacology, 33,* 441–448.

Sipes, T. E., & Geyer, M. A. (1995a). DOI disruption of prepulse inhibition of startle in the rat is mediated by 5-HT2A and not by 5-HT2C receptors. *Behavioural Pharmacology, 6,* 839–842.

Sipes, T. E., & Geyer, M. A. (1995b). 8-OH-DPAT disruption of prepulse inhibition in the rat: Localization of site of action with WAY 100, 135. *Psychopharmacology, 117,* 41–48.

Sipes, T. E., & Geyer, M. A. (1996). Functional behavioral homology between rat 5-HT1B and guinea pig 5-HT1D receptors in the modulation of prepulse inhibition of startle. *Psychopharmacology, 125,* 231–237.

Sipes, T. E., & Geyer, M. A. (1997). DOI disrupts prepulse inhibition of startle in rats via 5-HT$_{2A}$ receptors in the ventral pallidum. *Brain Research, 761,* 97–104.

Swerdlow, N. R., Bakshi, V. P., & Geyer, M. A. (1996). Seroquel restores sensorimotor gating in phencyclidine (PCP)-treated rats. *Journal of Pharmacology and Experimental Therapeutics, 279,* 1290–1299.

Swerdlow, N. R., Bakshi, V. P., & Geyer, M. A. (1998). Discrepant findings of clozapine effects on prepulse inhibition of startle: Is it the route or the rat? *Neuropsychopharmacology, 18,* 50–56.

Swerdlow, N. R., Benbow, C. H., Zisook, S., Geyer, M. A., & Braff, D. L. (1993). A preliminary assessment of sensorimotor gating in patients with obsessive compulsive disorder (OCD). *Biological Psychiatry, 33,* 298–301.

Swerdlow, N. R., Braff, D. L., Masten, V. L., & Geyer, M. A. (1990). Schizophrenic-like sensorimotor gating abnormalities in rats following dopamine infusion into the nucleus accumbens. *Psychopharmacology, 101,* 414–420.

Swerdlow, N. R., Braff, D. L., Taaid, N., & Geyer, M. A. (1994). Assessing the validity of an animal model of sensorimotor gating deficits in schizophrenic patients. *Archives of General Psychiatry, 51,* 139–154.

Swerdlow, N. R., Caine, S. B., Braff, D. L., & Geyer, M. A. (1992). Neural substrates of sensorimotor gating of the startle reflex: A review of recent findings and their implications. *Journal of Psychopharmacology, 6,* 176–190.

Swerdlow, N. R., Caine, B. C., & Geyer, M. A. (1992). Regionally selective effects of intracerebral dopamine infusion on sensorimotor gating of the startle reflex in rats. *Psychopharmacology, 108,* 189–195.

Swerdlow, N. R., & Geyer, M. A. (1993). Clozapine and haloperidol in an animal model of sensorimotor gating deficits in schizophrenia. *Pharmacology, Biochemistry and Behavior, 44,* 741–744.

Swerdlow, N. R., Geyer, M., Braff, D. L., & Koob, G. F. (1986). Central dopamine hyperactivity in rats mimics abnormal acoustic startle in schizophrenics. *Biological Psychiatry, 21,* 23–33.

Swerdlow, N. R., Keith, V. A., Braff, D. L., & Geyer, M. A. (1991). The effects of spiperone, raclopride, SCH 23390 and clozapine on apomorphine-inhibition of sensorimotor gating of the startle response in the rat. *Journal of Pharmacology and Experimental Therapeutics, 256,* 530–536.

Swerdlow, N. R., Paulsen, J., Braff, D. L., Butters, N., Geyer, M. A., & Swenson, M. R. (1995). Impaired prepulse inhibition of acoustic and tactile startle in patients with Huntington's disease. *Journal of Neurology, Neurosurgery, and Psychiatry, 58,* 192–200.

Swerdlow, N. R., Zisook, D., & Taaid, N. (1994). Seroquel (ICI 204, 636) restores prepulse inhibition of acoustic startle in apomorphine-treated rats: Similarities to clozapine. *Psychopharmacology, 114*, 675–678.

Varty, G. B., Bakshi, V. P., & Geyer, M. A. (1999). M100907, a serotonin 5-HT$_{2A}$ receptor antagonist and putative antipsychotic, blocks dizocilpine-induced prepulse inhibition deficits in Sprague-Dawley and Wistar rats. *Neuropsychopharmacology, 20*, 11–321.

Varty, G. B., & Higgins, G. A. (1995). Examination of drug-induced and isolation-induced disruptions of prepulse inhibition as models to screen antipsychotic drugs. *Psychopharmacology, 122*, 15–26.

Vollenweider, F. X., Remensberger, S., Hell, D., & Geyer, M. A. (in press). Opposite effects of 3,4-methylenedioxymethamphetamine (MDMA) on sensorimotor gating in rats versus healthy humans. *Psychopharmacology*.

Wan, F. J., Geyer, M. A., & Swerdlow, N. R. (1994). Accumbens D$_2$ substrates of sensorimotor gating: Assessing anatomical localization. *Pharmacology, Biochemistry, and Behavior, 49*, 155–163.

Wan, F. J., Swerdlow, N. R. (1994). Intra-accumbens infusion of quinpirole impairs sensorimotor gating of acoustic startle in rats. *Psychopharmacology, 113*, 103–109.

Weike, A., Globisch, J., Hamm, A., & Bauer, U. (1996). Prepulse inhibition and habituation of skin conductance responses in schizophrenics: Neuroleptic drug effects. *Psychophysiology, 33*(Suppl. 1), S88.

Weinberger, D. R. (1996). Schizophrenia as a neurodevelopmental disorder: A review of the concept. In S. R. Hirsch & D. R. Weinberger (Eds.), *Schizophrenia* London: Blackwood Press.

Wilkinson, L. S., Killcross, S. S., Humby, T., Hall, F. S., Geyer, M. A., & Robbins, T. W. (1994). Social isolation in the rat produces developmentally specific deficits in prepulse inhibition of the acoustic startle response without disrupting latent inhibition. *Neuropsychopharmacology, 10*, 61–72.

Part III

Development

9

Sensory and Integrative Development in the Human Fetus and Perinate: The Usefulness of Animal Models

Benoist Schaal, Jean-Pierre Lecanuet, and
Carolyn Granier-Deferre

Animal models have long been used to gain a better understanding of multiple levels of organization, function, and development in the human fetus and newborn (e.g., Gottlieb, 1973; Kuo, 1967; Schneirla, 1965). The possible payoff of this research strategy in neural and behavioral development has been eloquently advocated by a pioneer embryologist, Leonard Carmichael (1970):

> We must emphasize that the first responses of the human fetus and the more and more complex patterns of behavior during prenatal and early postnatal life can be best understood when considered in a general biological setting. The comparison of behavior of the human fetus before birth with other mammalian fetuses is more illuminating in understanding what the young human organism can do than is a comparison of the behavior of the adult human being with the behavior of any other adult mammal. . . . A proper understanding of the complementary roles of maturation and learning in the development of human prenatal and postnatal behavioral capacity can thus be illuminated by comparing early prenatal and neonatal human behavior changes with the fetal and early postnatal behavior of a variety of other mammals. (p. 447)

How and when should animal models be used to investigate the reciprocal roles of genes, structures, and functions in human pre- and perinatal integrative development? Reliance on animal models has offered means to validate hypotheses that for ethical or practical reasons cannot be fully assessed in humans; the selection of an animal model is a com-

We would like to express our gratitude to R. Hudson and two anonymous reviewers for their comments and suggestions and to A. Y. Jacquet, T. Lubart, and P. Michaux for their help with the English version.

promise between the assumed comparability (*homology* principle) of the model with the modeled process or situation and the model's practical advantages (e.g., availability, financial feasibility, ease of control and breeding, reduction of biological complexity, and shortness of life span). Another way of exploiting animal models has been to generalize hypotheses derived from animal investigations to human research. In this framework, reliance on the homology principle has not been a prerequisite because the choice of the nonhuman species under scrutiny has not been a priori driven by human issues. Although the latter research line has sometimes been misleading, it has generally produced large advances in empirical research in humans and at the same time has generated cautiousness in animal-to-human extrapolations. In perinatal development, the discovery of previously unsuspected motor, sensory, and cognitive abilities in sometimes phylogenetically distant species have suggested comparable possibilities in the human fetus (e.g., in ovo auditory imprinting in birds and in utero auditory priming in humans). In addition to the generalization of research ideas, experiments on animal fetuses have brought about new concepts and methods the application of which to human issues has proved to be heuristic. Some of these concepts and methods are described below.

This chapter emphasizes two areas in both animal and human models of fetal development that have received the most attention to date: the development of chemical reception and hearing. Sensory stimulations in utero and how they affect fetal and neonatal detection and integration abilities are examined. Note that these two sensory modalities have not benefited from an equal share of investigation in both human and nonhuman species. Whereas chemosensation has been explored more in animal than in human perinates, the reverse has been true for audition. This unbalanced research attention is noticeable in studies dealing with the earliest stages of sensory and cognitive development, and the main reasons for it are to be sought in anthropomorphic adult-based preconceptions of sensory competences in animal and human infants. Nevertheless, current knowledge of both sensory modalities has profited from a great deal of conceptual feedback and continuous exchange of empirical research between animal and human models. In the studies presented below, indications of the rationale for choosing the animal models and, whenever possible, the limits of generalizations that can be made from animal data to the human are given.

Animal Models of Fetal Sensory Ecology

It is now almost a truism to state that the development of an organism results from the interplay of the environment with genetic, neural, and behavioral activity. The environmental imprint has indeed been well documented in sensory and perceptual development of higher vertebrates, especially in species-specific response development (e.g., Gottlieb, 1991). Such experience-sensitive processes of early development, which consequences can be stable over long periods of life, have been thoroughly studied in neonates of various species. An increasing amount of research suggests that such processes can be traced back to the fetal period (e.g., Hall & Oppenheim, 1987; Previc, 1991; Smotherman & Robinson, 1995). It is thus a first important step to characterize the qualitative and quantitative stimulating potency of fetal ecology in both sensory modalities.

Fetal Chemosensory Ecology

The presence of odor-active compounds in utero has received little attention to date in human and animal species. Nevertheless, there are now data showing that normal olfactory function is closely dependent on the trophic action of exogenous input in both adult (Laing & Panhuber, 1980) and young (Brunjes & Frazier, 1986; Wilson & Sullivan, 1994) animals. The stimulative power of the prenatal environment might similarly activate fetal chemosensory processes. Thus one may wonder whether odorous compounds are normally present in the prenatal environment and how permeable this environment is to external influences.

Odorant compounds in amniotic fluid. Easy sampling of amniotic fluid (AF) in the pregnant ewe has allowed the development of chemoanalytic methods that have been used for human AF. The analysis of the volatile substance from the ewes' AF has provided a chromatographic profile dominated by volatile esters, aromatic ketones, and acids (Schaal, Orgeur, & Rognon, 1995). Some of these compounds have been identified and described as having odor properties, indicating that the amniotic pool is rich in diverse putative stimuli. The transposition of the same methods to human AF has resulted in similar conclusions (Schaal, Orgeur, & Rognon, 1995), namely, that human AF is replete with low-concentration odorivector compounds that may taint the fetal environment with a given odor background.

Maternal influences on the amniotic odor environment. Although many clinicians had come to the conclusion that the aromas ingested by pregnant women are transported to the fetal compartment (Hauser, Chitayat, Berns, Braver, & Muhlhauser, 1985), a maternal influence over the fetal chemical environment has only very recently been experimentally confirmed. The pregnant ewe was used as a model essentially for practical reasons, mainly, the ease of chronic implantation of catheters into the amniotic compartment in conscious fetuses, allowing sampling of acceptable AF volumes for chemical analyses. Ewes fed daily with cumin seeds during the last 2 weeks of gestation were examined for the transfer of selected aromas of cumin at different levels of the conceptus (Schaal, Orgeur, Desage, & Brazier, 1994). At term, different fluids were sampled in cesarean-sectioned ewes (i.e., maternal veinous plasma, fetal plasma from both umbilical and jugular veins, and AF). Compared with control ewes, cumin-treated ewes evidenced detectable plasma levels of cumin aroma markers (six volatiles representative of cumin odor; cf. Desage, Schaal, Orgeur, Soubiran, & Brazier, 1995). These markers could also be detected up- and downstream of the fetal brain (in the umbilical and jugular blood), but not in the AF. It is thus clear that odorous constituents of the mother's diet are transferred into the fetal circulation at levels detectable by gas chromatography. The nondetection of the cumin aroma in the AF could be a consequence of either fetal metabolization, its reexportation to the maternal compartment, or the inadequacy of the analytic method. A study using direct injections of cumin aromas into the pregnant ewes' circulation (to bypass the gastrointestinal step) resulted in traces of cumin aroma markers in AF, indicating that the detection method was adequate. Thus, the transplacental transfer of the cumin aromas is very low in sheep. However, despite this apparently low mother-to-fetus transfer of dietary odorants in the ewe, odor preference experiments with prenatally exposed lambs indicate that the transferred fraction can have sensory and behavioral significance (Schaal, Orgeur, & Arnould, 1995). Considering placental structure and physiology, rodent or lagomorph species (e.g., rabbits) might be more appropriate models of human transplacental aroma traffic. Indeed, it has been shown that hemochorial placentas (characterized by three tissue layers separating maternal and fetal blood) are very permeable to any solutes near term, in contrast with the apparently less permeable sheep epitheliochorial (comprising six-tissue layers between mother and fetus) placenta (e.g., Flexner & Gellhorn, 1942).

To our knowledge, no chemical verification of the transfer of odor-active compounds has been reported in the human fetal compartment, but an experiment of our group indicates that near-term pregnant women ingesting gel capsules filled with cumin produce AF that bear traces of cumin aroma markers (Schaal, Desage, Cohen, Defaux, & Brazier, 1999). Furthermore, AF aromatic profiles from pregnant women consuming odorous condiments could be differentiated from those of control women by adult noses (Hauser et al., 1985; Mennella, Johnson, & Beauchamp, 1995), and parents could discriminate the odor of the AF of their own infant from the odor of the AF of an unrelated infant (Schaal & Marlier, 1998).

Fetal Sound Ecology

In the beginning of the nineteenth century, Bichat (cited in Carmichael, 1970) concluded from his observations that the fetal guinea pig is isolated from external stimulations and that the human fetus probably also develops in an almost silent environment. In contrast, the first acoustical recordings made on pregnant women all described the uterus as an extremely noisy environment (Henschall, 1972; Walker, Grimwade, & Wood, 1971), dominated by maternal cardiovascular sounds of such pressure levels that they would mask most external sounds, except for very loud low-frequency ones emitted in the mother's vicinity (train or airplane noises). These acoustic measures indicated sound pressure levels (SPLs) averaging 90 dB (SPL), and even reaching 96 dB (SPL) during wave R of the electrocardiogram (Walker et al., 1971). It is surprising that few researchers questioned such deafening sound values in utero. The idea that the human fetus is exposed to such an overwhelming sound, in conjunction with data on in ovo imprinting in birds, inspired many subsequent studies (presented in the next two sections). Recordings from pregnant ewes and goats, obtained with hydrophones implanted close to the fetal neck, showed that this once classical view was wrong, however, and that when the ewe remains silent and stands still, the womb is a rather silent environment with a background noise pressure level comparable to that of the external noise (Armitage, Baldwin, & Vince, 1980).

The acoustical structure of the human intrauterine environment, explored initially with microphones inserted either close to the uterus (Bench, 1968; Murooka, Koie, & Suda, 1976; Walker et al., 1971) or inside the uterus, after amniotomy, during labor, or just after delivery (Henshall, 1972; Johansson, Wedenberg, & Westin, 1964; Walker et al., 1971) led to questionable results. Cervix opening, fluid loss, contractions, and increased maternal cardiovascular activity clearly modify the intrauterine acoustical features. The best situation to obtain precise in vivo information about the fetal acoustical environment before birth is thus to perform recordings in animal models within the closed uterus. The sheep and the goat appear to model adequately the situation of the woman because the conceptus (fetus and the embryonic annexes) has similar dimensions; in addition, recordings can be made during a large time window (several weeks before and during delivery) in freely moving animals.

Intrauterine background noise. Sheep and human recordings gather the same sources of intrauterine background noise originating from physiological (e.g., gastrointestinal, cardiovascular, or respiratory) and behavioral (motor, vocal) activities. Its frequency band ranges from a few Hz to about 500–700 Hz but can reach 1000 Hz when the ewe moves or eats (Gerhardt, 1989; Vince, Billing, Baldwin, Toner, & Weller, 1985). Maximum SPL (80 dB in the sheep) was found at frequencies below 100 Hz. However, when control recordings were realized on dead ewes, highest SPLs were traced back to artifactual infrasounds generated by building-related low-frequency noises. Above 100 Hz, the SPLs averaged no more than 50–60 dB (Gerhardt & Abrams, 1987; Gerhardt, Abrams, & Oliver, 1990; Vince et al., 1985), the average level of external background noise.

At odds with the initial human analyses, maternal heart sounds could only rarely be recorded in the pregnant ewe, but they could be detected on 25% to 50% of the recording during birth (Vince et al., 1985). Their auditory pressure was then 64–89 dB at very low frequencies. Recent studies suggested that the discrepancy found between sheep and human data was not only due to the fact that human recordings were done during labor, but that SPL of vascular sounds vary within the uterus. First, Querleu, Renard, and Versyp (1981; Querleu, Renard, Versyp, Paris-Delrue, & Crépin, 1988) showed that pressure levels ranged from 28 to 65 dB, with the lowest value obtained far from the placenta. The maternal heartbeat was found to emerge only 25 dB above the background noise. These authors suggested that noise from the placenta probably has a greater masking effect than cardiac noise. Moreover, Benzaquen, Gagnon, Hunse, and Foreman (1990), performing recordings at the fetal neck level, were able to record maternal cardiovascular sounds in only 2 out of 10 mothers. In this location, far from the placenta, Gagnon, Benzaquen, and Hunse (1992) measured less than 40 dB above 200 Hz.

Attenuation of external sounds. Initial human studies concluded that the higher the frequency of the external sound, the higher its attenuation in the uterus (Querleu et al., 1981; Walker et al., 1971). For more than a decade, it was thus believed that only low-frequency noises could reach the fetal ear. However, ovine investigations, allowing to study the whole human audible frequency range, yielded a U-shaped relationship between sound frequency and its attenuation. These results can be summarized as follows (Lecanuet et al., 1998; Peters, Abrams, Gerhardt, & Griffiths, 1993): (a) Low-frequency (<300 Hz) pressure levels are generally similar in and ex utero; (b) in utero SPL loss is moderate between 400 and 1000 Hz and averages 6,5 dB/octave between 1000 and 4000–8000 Hz (depending on the sound-source distance and the depth of the hydrophone inside the abdomen), thus peaking at 20 dB; in all studies, attenuation never exceeded 30–35 dB (SPL) up to 10 kHz; and (c) at higher frequencies, the pressure levels in utero increase and may be even higher than ex utero. These SPL increases correspond to series of pressure peaks of resonance probably due to the presence of standing waves (Lecanuet et al., 1998). In utero SPL of external experimental sounds varies systematically as a function of the distance of the transducer to the sound source. This relationship has been extensively examined in the pregnant ewe, showing that sound attenuation starts at lower frequencies when the source is more distant from the intra-abdominal hydrophone (Gerhardt et al., 1990; Lecanuet et al., 1998).

Signal-to-noise relationship. Recent human and ovine in utero recordings show that external sounds have to reach 60 dB to be clearly recognizable to human listeners. The transmission of external stimuli and maternal vocalizations indicates that (a) human speech (Querleu et al., 1988), as well as sheep bleatings (ranging between a few Hz to 2400 Hz), emerges from the maternal background noise (Vince et al., 1985); (b) human speech has well-preserved prosodic characteristics; and (c) the content of human speech is partially intelligible—some phonemes (up to 30%) and words can be recognized by adults when the recordings are performed far from the placenta (Querleu et al., 1988). This was confirmed when human voices were recorded in the pregnant ewe by Vince et al. (1985), Gerhardt (1989), and Griffiths, Brown, Gerhardt, Abrams, and Morris (1994). The latter study showed that phonemes emitted by a female voice had a mean intelligibility score of 34%, whereas it reached 55% for a male voice. Human studies performed with a hydrophone placed near the fetal head all show nevertheless a better transmission of the maternal voice compared with male and female external voices (Benzaquen et al., 1990; Querleu et al., 1988).

Animal Models of Fetal Sensory Detection

The study of neurosensory and behavioral activity in utero is central to issues relating to cellular and structural neural organization and to functional development. Animal studies have now firmly established that minimal but influential function occurs in utero, long before complete maturation of the corresponding receptor system. This has been verified in both chemosensory and auditory modalities through global or acute manipulations of the prenatal environment.

Olfactory Activation in Utero

Neonatal response-based experiments in the rat, rabbit, and sheep demonstrate that the aromas carried in the mother's diet are detected by the fetal olfactory system (Bilko, Altbäcker, & Hudson, 1994; Hepper, 1988a; Schaal, Orgeur, & Arnould, 1995), but thus far, there is no direct demonstration of nasal chemoreception in the human fetus in utero. Many influential authors have claimed that the olfactory system could not function in fetal conditions because proper (airborne) odor stimuli and pulsatile nasal currents do not exist before birth (e.g., Feldman, 1920; Gueubelle, 1984; Humphrey, 1978). However, indirect evidence in the human and direct experimental animal data support the possibility of nasal chemoreception in the human fetus. First, the chemoreceptor systems in the near-term human fetal nose are morphologically and functionally similar to those of the neonate (Schaal, Orgeur, & Rognon, 1995). Second, the chemosensory responses of premature infants, as early as the 7th to 8th gestational month, suggest that olfactory activation is possible in a fetus of equivalent gestational age. The direct, causal investigation of olfactory responsiveness will be extremely difficult to test in the human fetus for ethical and practical reasons. The main methodological difficulty resides in the fetal inaccessibility to the application of molecular stimuli, especially to temporally defined stimuli, which are necessary to rigorously probe odor detection performance. Moreover, if such chemostimuli could be administered to the fetus through maternal circulation, their transfer rate kinetics would be too imprecise and subject to high individual variations. Thus, animal models are required to test fetal activation by odor stimuli administered in close contact with nasal (or oral) chemoreceptors.

Odor detection in utero. Evidence of in utero nasal chemoreception is provided by experiments on both rodents (Coppola & Millar, 1997; Molina, Chotro, & Domingez, 1995; Smotherman, Robinson, Ronca, Alberts, & Hepper, 1989) and sheep (Schaal et al., 1991). These models were chosen because (a) the studied structures are homologous to those of the human,

(b) chemoreceptive maturation is advanced during the last period of a long gestation, and (c) for the sheep model, chronically instrumented conscious fetuses can be prepared easily. Intranasal infusions of distinct odor qualities to near-term ovine fetuses induced contrasting heart rate patterns. Dramatic autonomic change followed infusions of 2-methyl-2-thiazoline (a foul odor highly repulsive to adult sheep) which elicited reliable heart rate decrements. Citral infusions (bearing a lemon odor) induced a weak accelerative effect. The potential effect of the *pressure* stimulation associated with the fluid injections was ruled out with the use of control stimuli (.09% saline) that did not trigger heart rate changes. Similar results were obtained in rat and mouse fetuses that were odor infused through the mouth. Animal research has thus shown that the chemoreceptors of sheep and rodent fetuses can detect the presence of odorants experimentally infused into their nose or mouth and that they respond differently to qualitatively distinct stimuli. Rat fetuses also display the same behavioral reaction when presented with odorants in either water or gas, demonstrating that fetal chemosensors are functional in their age-adequate liquid environment as well as in the age-inadequate gaseous medium (Smotherman & Robinson, 1990). The fact that fetal chemoreceptors are able to respond to waterborne as well as to airborne odorants lends credence to the idea that nearly born human premature infant studies may be a good way to approach the dynamics of chemosensory function in fetuses of the same gestational age. However, parallel animal investigations are necessary to thoroughly understand stimulus–response relationships by systematically varying the psychophysical and effective properties of the stimuli.

Chemosensory discrimination in utero. Differential treatment of odor qualities has been assessed in premature human infants born at 31–37 gestational weeks (Pihet, Mellier, Bullinger, & Schaal, 1997). Whether such discriminative capacities are already present in the fetus of corresponding age is difficult to test directly. Again, animal experiments have provided the empirical basis that suggests that the human fetal chemoreceptors are sufficiently developed for flavor discrimination. Schaal et al.'s (1991) previously mentioned experiment demonstrated differential responsiveness in the sheep fetus to odorants administered nasally. Recent work with the same model revealed discriminative taste responses earlier in gestation. Robinson, Wong, Robertson, Nathanielsz, and Smotherman (1995) made electromyographic recordings from facial, lingual, esophageal, cephalic, and segmental muscle activity and heart rate variations when fetuses were administered different kinds of flavors through a catheter sutured on their tongue. The most interesting results derived from infusions of homo- and heterospecific milks: Whereas sheep's colostrum consistently induced a reduction in facial, lingual, and esophageal activity, mature sheep's milk evoked an activation of these muscles accompanied with a slowing down of heart rate; in contrast, cow's milk did not reliably affect any of these behavioral and autonomic variables. Thus, the fetal sheep reacts in a special way to chemical cues carried in homospecific milk, and even more to milk obtained from conspecific females soon after bearing their young. Whether fetal chemosensory systems are genetically or environmentally tuned to detect specific compounds in the age-adequate fluid encountered after birth (colostrum) is an open issue. The developmental neural mechanisms involved in this hypothetical sensitization or preparation process implies (a) that amniotic and postamniotic environments share the same odorants and (b) that the amniotic chemical ecology might channel the detection ability and the reinforcing value of these odorants. Both of these issues are examined in the **Animal Models of Fetal Sensory Integration and Postnatal Consequences** section.

Auditory Activation in Utero

Human prenatal hearing has been extensively studied using involuntary reactivity. Analyses of cardiac and motor responses to airborne auditory stimulations have shown that near-term fetuses are reactive to various pure tones and bandwidths, as well as to complex sounds (speech and musical sequences). Ranges of the stimulations studied have been limited to frequencies from around 100 Hz to around 5000 Hz. Fetal heart rate decelerations are mostly evoked with low-level stimuli between 85 and 100 dB (SPL) ex utero, and startling responses (heart rate accelerations and immediate eyeblinks, limb, or body movements) are mostly evoked with stimuli delivered at or above 105 dB (SPL). Human near-term fetuses are also able to make some acoustic discriminations (cf. Lecanuet, Granier-Deferre, & Busnel, 1995, for review).

The simple presentation of controlled sounds (compared with the more invasive presentation of chemostimuli) to the human fetus as well as the availability of its responses (through ultrasonographic techniques) has stimulated direct investigation of the human. Nevertheless, animal models have been necessary to complete the understanding of in utero hearing. The fetal guinea pig (first cochlear potentials [CP]: 48–53 days of a 68-day-long gestation), the fetal sheep (first CP: 109 days of a 145-day-long gestation), and, to a lesser extent, the fetal cat (first CP: 1–2 days before term: gestation duration: 52–65 days) were chosen for the characterization of the neuroanatomical correlates of auditory processing inside the womb. They have been especially useful for examination of the course of functional development from before the onset of hearing to birth and also for examination of an old controversial issue in the human, that is, whether the cochlea can be activated by high frequencies (higher than 5000 Hz) in utero.

Electrophysiological and autoradiographic studies. The guinea pig has been used for decades to model human normal and abnormal hearing physiology. This species has a wide frequency range of hearing (from 80 Hz to 50 kHz) and follows an anatomical development comparable to that of the human. The functional development of the guinea pig's auditory system has been studied in different experimental preparations using (a) prematurely delivered fetuses with the ear canal cleared from any fluids

(Romand, 1971; Sedlacek, 1976); (b) fetuses left attached to the mother but immersed in a physiological solution (Chodynicki, 1968; Rawdon-Smith, Carmichael, & Willman, 1938); and (c) chronically implanted fetuses inside the uterus (Scibetta & Rosen, 1969). Both electrophysiological and autoradiographic techniques have revealed that the whole auditory tract is activated in utero in response to exogenous acoustic stimulations (Horner, Servières, & Granier-Deferre, 1987). Beginning in the mid-1980s, the fetal lamb became the most widely used model for human fetal audition. The ovine functional auditory development has been studied in chronically implanted fetuses inside the closed uterus (Woods & Plessinger, 1989). Stimulations have been delivered either through earphones fixed nearest to the fetal auditory meatus or through a sound generator placed on the maternal abdomen. Analyses of the fetal cochlear potentials and the brainstem and cortical auditory-evoked responses in various animal models (guinea pig, sheep, and cat) indicate similar characteristics and developmental course in and ex utero in prematurely delivered fetuses and in species in which audition starts after birth.

It seems impossible to measure absolute auditory thresholds in the human fetus. An interesting indirect approach, which might help to estimate them, was performed by researchers in the fetal lamb. They defined the acoustic isolation of the fetal cochlea by comparing the external SPL of one-third-octave bandwidths necessary to elicit cochlear microphonic potentials of same amplitude before and after delivery. Acoustic isolation was highly variable across individuals and related to the frequency of the bandwidth (e.g., 6–17 dB at 125 Hz, 25–52 dB at 1000 Hz, and 27–56 dB at 2000 Hz).

Autoradiographic methods have permitted the visualization of the in utero metabolic activation of the fetal brain through local variations in the uptake of radiolabeled 2-deoxyglucose (2-DG). Airborne pure tones induced a marked increase in 2-DG uptake in the brainstem of the guinea pig, and vibro-acoustic stimulation induced a marked increase in 2-DG uptake in the whole auditory tract, including the cortex, in the fetal sheep (Abrams, Hutchinson, Gerhardt, Evans, & Pendergast, 1987; Abrams, Hutchinson, McTiernann, & Merwin, 1987). Further, in the guinea pig, the presence of frequency-specific auditory labeling in the cochlear nucleus and in the inferior colliculus revealed the tone-dependent organization of the auditory structures in utero (Horner et al., 1987; cf. Granier-Deferre & Abrams, 1989). The application of this same method on the guinea pig permitted assessment of the possibility that the fetus hears the music pregnant women listen to through earphones. The transmission of very loud sounds to the fetus via the mother's skull and spine could indeed not be totally excluded. No 2-DG labeling was noted in the auditory structures of fetuses from pregnant guinea pigs exposed to high-pitched frequencies through earphones (Horner et al., 1987).

Even though much is now known about prenatal hearing, the reliance on animal models is still necessary to resolve questions that remain open, such as the functional status of the middle ear in the fluid medium, fetal auditory psychophysics, and the possible coactivation of the vestibular and somesthesic systems with broadband or low-frequency band noises. The issue of a possible auditory activation by the vestibular system early in development is of particular interest. Vibro-acoustic stimulations indeed evoke brainstem auditory responses earlier in fetal sheep than do acoustic stimuli (Woods & Plessinger, 1989), and they reliably elicit startle responses in the human fetus at 26 to 28 weeks of gestation (2–3 weeks before pure tones or narrowband noises of above 500 Hz; Lecanuet et al., 1995). However, when considering the qualitative characteristics of human prenatal hearing, animal models have clear limitations; for example, it is not possible to study the impact of maternal background noise, which probably activates constantly the fetal ear, on the perception of low-level external sounds,[1] or its consequences as a function of fetal head location within the uterus (could the famous "cocktail party" effect be present for recurrent external sound stimulations?); likewise, they will be of little help in untangling major issues related to the perception of complex sounds such as speech or music (how distinctly are the different acoustic units integrated?). Such questions might be better answered through the comparative study of behavioral and autonomic responses in the human fetus and perinate.

Animal Models of Fetal Sensory Integration and Postnatal Consequences

The data presented above support that both sensory systems under scrutiny have ample opportunity to be prenatally activated, from as early as midgestation in the human fetus. To learn how and to what extent chemosensory and auditory functional development is shaped in utero will require further animal–human interactive studies. Current findings clearly support that the integrative activity of the brain is at least partially tuned by fetal experience. The data also support the conception of pre- and perinatal development in terms of patterned ontogenetic adaptations (Hall & Oppenheim, 1987), that is, physiological and behavioral specializations eliciting adaptive responses to specific challenges encountered in and ex utero. This conception has been particularly well delineated in studies on the transition to extrauterine life, the success of which may largely depend on in utero learned associations (e.g., Ronca & Alberts, 1995; Teicher & Blass, 1977).

Prenatal Integration of Chemosensory Information and Postnatal Consequences

Prenatal odor acquisition. It has now been established from different empirical sources, mainly in the rat, that the animal fetal brain is able to

---

[1]Selective perception of a familiar sound in a high-level background noise that normally should mask it (e.g., recognition of own name uttered during a noisy cocktail party).

detect, encode, and store chemosensory information and that prenatal acquisitions influence neonatal behavior (Molina et al., 1995; Pedersen & Blass, 1992; Schaal & Orgeur, 1992; Smotherman, 1982). The fetal rat is able to extract essential characteristics (i.e., intensity, quality, and familiarity) of chemical stimulations artificially introduced in utero. Postnatal behavioral consequences of these intra-amniotic odor manipulations demonstrate the impact of prenatal flavor exposure. Although these processes have not yet been extensively investigated in other species, this conclusion may be generalized to the rabbit (Bilko, Altbäcker, & Hudson, 1994) and the sheep (Schaal, Orgeur, & Arnould, 1995). Neonatal selective responses to prenatal experiences also have been shown in the absence of any chemical manipulation of the AF. Newborn rats and lambs are generally attracted to the odor of conspecific AF (Teicher & Blass, 1977) and even more to the odor of their own AF when presented simultaneously with the AF collected from another mother (Hepper, 1987; Schaal, Orgeur, & Arnould, 1995). AF odor is thus sufficiently individually discriminable (even in ewes fed the same diet during gestation) to induce selective responding in neonates in favor of their own AF. Comparable results recently have been obtained in the human: 2-day-old neonates displayed longer duration head turns to AF odor than to a control stimulus (Schaal, Marlier, & Soussignan, 1995). In addition, when presented with the odor of their familiar AF versus an unfamiliar AF, 3-day-old infants oriented longer to the former (Marlier, Schaal, & Soussignan, 1998; Schaal, Marlier, & Soussignan, 1998). Like the other mammalian models studied so far, human AF possesses idiosyncratic odor qualities that are discriminable to the neonate. Therefore, some form of olfactory acquisition may occur prenatally in the human species.

Mechanisms of prenatal odor acquisition. It is still unclear if nonspecific encoding of quantitative features (odor-intensity-based responses) or a more specific, odor-quality-based encoding, or both, underlie the processes involved in prenatal odor learning. As mentioned above, the fetal rat seems responsive to both sources of discriminative cues. Controlled manipulations of the fetal chemo-environment provide further insight into quality-specific effects. For example, rabbit pups exposed to juniper flavor during gestation exhibit an attraction to the odor of juniper and, at the same time, a slight enhancement of the electric potential (electro-olfactogram; EOG) of their olfactory mucous membrane (Semke, Distel, Hudson, 1995). A similar EOG increase is induced by repeated odor exposure in adult mice and rats (Wang, Wysocki, & Gold, 1993; Youngentob & Kent, 1995). The level of analysis limits the location of this plasticity mechanism to the olfactory mucosa. How this peripheral plasticity is regulated in the fetus remains unclear, but several lines of research suggest the possibility of stimulus-induced mechanisms involving either the proliferation of specific olfactory receptor proteins on the cilia of existing neuroreceptors, the selection of specific neuroreceptors, or the adjustment of given neuron populations by stimulus-controlled apoptosis (Najbauer & Leon, 1995). However, nonassociative or associative exposure to odors in utero could also affect synaptic organization and function at higher brain levels, as has been elegantly demonstrated in the olfactory bulb of the neonatal rat (Wilson & Sullivan, 1994).

Oral chemosensation also provides evidence of environmentally induced functional changes at the periphery of the system. Reduction of environmental sodium (through dietary restriction in the pregnant female) is followed by a reduction in peripheral taste responses in the young rat (Hill & Przekop, 1988). This effect was observed only if sodium restriction occurred during a prenatal sensitive period (on or before Embryonic Day 8), and it did not affect the responsiveness to other taste stimuli. In addition, taste response alterations continued into adulthood, even after sodium enrichment in the postnatal environment (Hill & Vogt, 1989). Another study used an extracellular dehydration technique to alter the prenatal electrolyte balance (Nicolaïdis, Galaverna, & Metzler, 1990). When exposed as adults to a two-choice test between pure water and salted water, offspring born to dehydrated women displayed a greater salt preference than did control offspring. The mechanisms responsible for this effect are yet unknown: They do not seem to reflect the peripheral action of sodium but may be related to maternal hormonal–metabolic changes. A comparable electrolyte imbalance was suggested to be associated with vomiting during human pregnancy, and a similar enhancement of salt appetite was accordingly predicted in the offspring (Nicolaïdis et al., 1990). A correlation between adult salt preference and the intensity of their mother's vomiting was assessed in a sample of college students (Crystal & Bernstein, 1995). Descendants of mothers who evidenced moderate to severe vomiting during pregnancy reported a higher level of salt use and manifested a greater preference for salty foods than descendants of mothers reporting no or mild vomiting. This is a rare instance showing that gestational events can influence lifelong taste preference in humans and that conclusions derived from animal research can be successfully generalized to the human.

Various chemosensory learning processes have been examined in utero (Smotherman & Robinson, 1995): (a) *habituation*, a response decrement to repeated exposure to the same stimulus; (b) *mere exposure* learning (or familiarization or sensitization) induced in the absence of any obvious reinforcement; and (c) associative learning resulting from the pairing of a stimulus with a positive or negative reinforcer. These various learning processes generally have been indexed through changes in attentional (arousing or soothing effects) or hedonic responses measured either in the fetus or in the neonate. Using a bioassay consisting in the facial wiping response elicited by stimulation applied around the mouth, Robinson and Smotherman (1995) have begun to examine the neurochemical systems involved in fetal learning in the rat. Opioid agonists induce a reduction in this facial wiping response that is reversible with opioid antagonists, indicating that endogenous opioid systems are mature in the rat fetus. Certain stimuli (e.g., oral infusion of bovine light cream resembling rat milk) are also effective elicitors of opioid activity in that they attenuate facial wiping in the same way as opioid agonists. Among the other stimuli

screened, such as saline, sucrose, lactose, lipids, dimethyl-disulfide
(DMDS, which is present in the pups' saliva) and human infant formulas,
only DMDS activated the opioid systems. The opioid activity of bovine
cream and DMDS was apparent from the initial postnatal exposure, indicating that it was apparently effective without any previous chemosensory experience with them. Milk can further prompt classical conditioning
of opioid response in the fetus. Fetuses can indeed exhibit reduced skin
reactivity (in terms of decreased facial wiping response) in response to
perioral touch or sucrose after three touch (conditioned stimulus [CS])–
milk (unconditioned stimulus [US]) or sucrose (CS)–milk (US) pairings.
The presentation of the CS alone did not modify the response criterion;
only the CS reexposure after CS–US association led to successful conditioning. The conditioned response (reduced facial wiping) to the CS was
abolished after opioid activity blockade, indicating that CS–milk associations are mediated by opioid systems (Robinson et al., 1993; Smotherman
& Robinson, 1995). Clearly, milk is only available in the postnatal niche.
But milk and amniotic fluid share many odor compounds, and this transnatal chemosensory continuity might enhance the conditionability of the
neonate to odors encountered in utero (Marlier et al., 1998). If opioidergic
circuits of the fetal brain are responsive to milk flavor, one may wonder
whether reinforcing situations involving such mechanisms do naturally
exist in utero. Some opportunities for in utero chemosensory associations
have been suggested and sometimes explored in animal models. First, the
contingency between metabolite flow and aroma flow after a pregnant female's ingestion may be one context of associative learning. Aromas and
sweet-tasting metabolites may, for example, be associated in a recurrent
and cumulative way that potentially associates chemosensory activation,
arousal, increased inhalation of AF, and opioid release. Second, stressful
situations applied to the mother have been shown to simultaneously produce alterations in placental physiology and elicit enhanced fetal micturition (Zimmer, Chao, Guy, Marks, & Fifer, 1993), a process that may associate acute changes in AF composition, in fetal arousal, and in maternal
vocal and motor activity. Third, variations of fetal oxygenation (due to cord
compression) have been shown to support fetal learning in the rat: Oxy-
gen-deficiency episodes associated with an odor in utero induce avoidance
to that odor in the neonate, whereas reoxygenation favors the development
of appetitive responses (Hepper, 1991). Numerous subtle processes occurring in the natural fetal environment could thus provide sources of positive
or negative reinforcement of prenatal contingent chemosensory stimuli.

Prenatal Integration of Auditory Information and Postnatal Consequences

Auditory deprivation and overexposure effects. Animal studies performed on species in which the auditory function starts before (chicks),
near (cat), or after (mouse, rat, gerbil) birth have shown that the auditory
input is necessary to the maintenance of normal sound integration at the

brainstem level. Bilateral auditory deprivation starting before or during the period of appearance of cochlear potentials causes anatomical alterations similar to those induced by bilateral destruction of the cochlea: (a) reduced neuronal amount and size along the brainstem auditory relays; (b) enhanced electrophysiological auditory thresholds or delay in the development of auditory sensitivity, and (c) reduced discrimination ability of complex rhythmic structures (Moore, 1985). Deprivation of one ear causes neuronal and behavioral alterations affecting mostly binaural structures and function, for example, spatial localization (Clements & Kelly, 1978; Knudsen, Knudsen, & Esterly, 1982). Conversely, prolonged exposure to selectively enriched sound environments, which do not induce any acoustic trauma, stimulates local dendritic growth (Smith, Gray, & Rubel, 1983); modifies the reactivity of central acoustic units (Clopton & Winfield, 1976; Sanes & Constantine-Paton, 1983); and seems to facilitate selective discriminative auditory tasks (Clopton, 1986). From these data, it can be hypothesized that sounds reaching the human fetal ear might also contribute to normal development of auditory structures and functions in utero (cf. Granier-Deferre & Lecanuet, 1987, for review).

Measurement of exogenous sound attenuation in the womb has shown that the fetal cochlea is not fully protected against acoustical trauma provoked by sustained exposure to very loud noises. Animal investigations first underlined the deleterious effects of such exposure. Douek, Dodson, Bannister, Ashcroft, and Humphries (1976) and Cook et al. (1982) provided evidence of auditory trauma in guinea pigs born to females exposed during gestation respectively to the noise of incubators (of the type used at that time for premature neonates, contributing to their hearing loss) and of weaving machines. In the postnatal rat, Lenoir and Pujol (1980) showed that loud noises, which have no effect on the adult cochlea, induce irreversible damages if administered at the functional onset period of cochlear development (18–35 weeks of human gestation). Animal studies thus point to the necessity of human investigations. Some epidemiological reports on this point have shown that children of mothers exposed 8 hr/day to weaving machines (average level: 100 dB [SPL]) suffer significant hearing loss (Daniel & Laciak, 1982; Lalande, Hétu, & Lambert, 1986).

Prenatal auditory acquisitions. After the first human intra-abdominal recordings suggesting that the maternal heartbeat was the dominant source of prenatal sound stimuli, the consequences of sustained exposure to natural sounds (maternal cardiovascular noises in the 1970s and speech stimuli in the 1980s) were extensively studied in the human neonate. Most of this research was directly inspired by data on auditory imprinting in animals. In the 1970s, the necessity of in ovo exposure to conspecific calls for adequate posthatching recognition of them was demonstrated in many avian species. This was shown for the recognition of general features of the conspecific call (Gottlieb, 1973), of the individual signature of vocalizations (Guyomarch, 1974), or of artificial stimuli (Green & Adkins, 1975; Lien, 1976).

It was then hypothesized that human prenatal exposure to certain aspects of the maternal sound environment might promote various forms of learning (i.e., habituation, nonassociative sensitization, and associative learning). Behavioral evidence of such prenatal (or perinatal) acquisitions was evidenced in 2- to 4-day-old neonates. Familiar stimuli or classes of stimuli might, more or less specifically, lose their startling properties after repeated exposure during fetal life, soothe the crying newborn, and elicit differential motivated responses in choice tests (e.g., differential head orientation or nonnutritive sucking).

Habituation to startling stimuli. Short-term cardiac and motor habituation to repeated acoustic stimulations has been demonstrated in both human and animal models (review in Lecanuet & Schaal, 1996). More interesting are long-term habituations to startling or stressful noises. Human and guinea pig neonates are significantly less disturbed by a startling sound if they have been repeatedly exposed to it before birth. For example, the longer the prenatal exposure of human neonates—living in the Osaka, Japan, airport neighborhood—to airplane noises, the better the quality of their sleep compared with babies whose mothers had lived in this area for shorter times during pregnancy (Ando & Hattori, 1977). Long-term habituation was also demonstrated in the fetal guinea pig exposed to the vocalization of a bantam hen, an aversive stimulation for this species (Vince, 1979).

Soothing and orienting effects. Two classes of sound stimuli have been studied for their soothing properties on the neonate: maternal heartbeat and other intrauterine sounds and musical sequences. The initial work of Salk (1960, 1962) on the soothing effect of mother's heartbeat sound on the neonate was followed by numerous investigations that led to contradictory outcomes (cf. review in Lecanuet, Granier-Deferre, & Busnel, 1989). These inconsistencies were to be sought in differences in experimental design, type of stimuli used, dependent variables, and their timing (short-term or long-term effects). Murooka et al. (1976), comparing various stimuli, concluded that any noise having an acoustical structure similar to that of the intrauterine background noise had a short-term pacifying effect. Further, the sensitivity and reinforcing value of cardiovascular sounds was confirmed with a nonnutritive-sucking-choice procedure in 3-day-old babies (DeCasper & Sigafoos, 1983). Finally, infants reduced motor activation and crying and showed attentional orienting response to musical sequences that their mothers were exposed to regularly during pregnancy (newly born neonates: Feijoo, 1981; 4- to 5-day-olds: Hepper, 1988b).

Auditory preferences. Preferences for various types of stimuli encountered in the perinatal environments have been described in very young neonates (2–4 days old). The very precocial appearance of these selective responses in the neonate has been taken as partial evidence of fetal auditory training.

Parental voices. Early neonatal preference for the mother's voice over another female's voice was first evidenced by DeCasper and Fifer (1980). This preference was confirmed with *low-pass filtered*[2] (Spence & DeCasper, 1987) and cardiovascular sounds mixed with versions modeling the intra-uterine mother's voice (Fifer & Moon, 1989; Moon & Fifer, 1990). In contrast, neonates do not prefer their father's voice to another male voice, an absence of preference that probably reflects more limited prenatal exposure with the father's voice than with the mother's voice (DeCasper & Prescott, 1984). The long-lasting prenatal familiarization with the maternal voice may also explain why newborns discriminate normally intoned speech from "motherese"-intoned speech (i.e., with exaggerated contours) only for the maternal voice (Hepper, Scott, & Shahidullah, 1993).

Speech sequences. Two- to 4-day-old neonates suck more when hearing a story their mother had read out loudly during the last 6 weeks before birth as compared with a story they have never been exposed to (DeCasper & Spence, 1986). The fact that the infants do not differentiate the speech sequence read by the mother and the same sequence read by another woman has been interpreted as evidence of prenatal acquisition of some acoustic features of the story (e.g., prosodic characteristics). Similar results in the neonate have been obtained with sung utterances (i.e., lullabies; Satt, 1984). DeCasper, Lecanuet, Busnel, Granier-Deferre, and Maugeais (1994) have generalized this conclusion to near-term fetuses.

Musical sequences. Newborns whose mothers had been singing a "lalala"-type melody during pregnancy preferred this melody to an unfamiliar melody containing the same segmental information (viz., the syllable "la") and the same notes, but with a different temporal order, relative number, and duration (Panneton, 1985). Likewise, newborns exposed from the 34th gestational week onward to a sequence of either classical music or jazz preferred the prenatally experienced music sequence (Woodward, 1992).

Maternal language. Two-day-old newborns born to either Spanish- or English-speaking women preferred their mother's language to the unfamiliar one (Moon, Cooper, & Fifer, 1993). In these tests, the stimulus speech sequence was uttered by the same nonfamiliar female speaker, so that the preference for the native language was not confounded with a preference for the mother's voice. In all these studies, neonates had some postnatal exposure to the maternal language before they were tested; these data may thus reflect either auditory acquisition occurring prenatally or postnatally only, or the additive effect of prenatal familiarization with postnatal exposure to a specific language. One study suggests that the former mechanism, prenatal learning, may dominate in maternal language perception. Four-day-old offspring of either French- or Russian-speaking mothers were shown to discriminate sequences of these two different languages when both

---

[2]Sounds from which all frequency components above a certain cutoff frequency were removed, leaving only the low-frequency sounds.

of them were spoken by a nonfamiliar bilingual woman (Mehler et al., 1988; Mehler, Lambertz, Jusczyk, & Amiel-Tison, 1986). The neonates still expressed discrimination of low-pass filtered versions of the two language sequences, indicating that the prosody of the spoken sentences might carry the discriminant cue. Finally, neonates born to mothers speaking neither French nor Russian were unable to discriminate between those two languages, as if the absence of previous exposure to the prosodic cues of these languages rendered impossible their differentiation.

Many studies conducted during the last 25 years have demonstrated that newborns process speech stimuli in a similar way as do adults (review in Aslin, Pisoni, & Jusczyk, 1983). This usually has been seen as a consequence of an inherited human capacity to process linguistic sounds (Chomsky, 1975) rather than as the effect of a prenatal exposure to speech sounds. Human prenatal exposure to a variety of sounds, including speech, may contribute to the maintenance, tuning, and specification of general auditory abilities necessary for the neonate to process sounds that will be relevant postnatally, as was advocated 20 years ago by Gottlieb (1973, 1991) on the basis of the data he accumulated on the processing of specific sounds by chicks before and after hatching.

Conclusion

It is thus clear from the data surveyed above that the current understanding of the sensory and integrative development of the human fetus would not have been achieved without the reliance on animal models. They have served as heuristic sources and as means to validate new and unexpected hypotheses raised by human studies. It must however also be underlined that animal-to-human extrapolations sometimes have led to misleading hypotheses and empirical effort (recall, e.g., the hypothesis of the sonic insulation of the fetus in utero). Whenever possible, animal data should thus be directly tested in the human fetus. In the future, descriptive investigations with animal models are still essential to complete our knowledge on (a) normal and deviant fetal and perinatal sensory ecologies, (b) fetal sensory, behavioral, and cognitive integration of the environment, and (c) the functional significance of fetal acquisitions in terms of adaptative specializations for both the prenatal and postnatal environments. Experimental studies, conducted in parallel with the descriptive approaches, should be pursued to explore the processes and developmental contexts that promote normative development. As Lewkowicz and Lickliter (1994) have noted, "One way to push forward the experimental exploration of early sensory organization and to create new insights into underlying mechanisms will be through the choice of appropriate animal models" (p. 405).

References

Abrams, R. M., Hutchison, A. A., Gerhardt, K. J., Evans, S. L., & Pendergast, J. (1987). Local cerebral glucose utilization in fetal sheep exposed to noise. *American Journal of Obstetrics and Gynecology, 157,* 456–460.

Abrams, R. M., Hutchinson, A. A., McTiernann, M. J., & Merwin, G. E. (1987). Effects of cochlear ablation on local cerebral glucose utilization in fetal sheep. *American Journal of Obstetrics and Gynecology, 157*, 1438–1442.

Ando, Y., & Hattori, H. (1977). Effects of noise on sleep of babies. *Journal of the Acoustical Society of America*, 62, 199–204.

Armitage, S. E., Baldwin, B. A., & Vince, M. A. (1980). The fetal sound environment of sheep. *Science, 208*, 1173–1174.

Aslin, R. N., Pisoni, D. B., & Jusczyk, P. (1983). Auditory development and speech perception in infancy. In M. M. Haith & J. J. Campos (Eds.), *Handbook of child psychology: Vol. II. Infancy and developmental psychobiology* (pp. 527–687). New York: Wiley.

Bench, R. J. (1968). Sound transmission to the human fetus through the maternal abdominal wall. *Journal of Genetic Psychology, 113*, 1172–1174.

Benzaquen, S., Gagnon, R., Hunse, C., & Foreman, J. (1990). The intrauterine sound environment of the human fetus during labor. *American Journal of Obstetrics and Gynecology, 163*, 484–490.

Bilko, A., Altbäcker, V., & Hudson, R., (1994). Transmission of food preference in the rabbit: The means of information transfer. *Physiology and Behavior, 56*, 907–912.

Brunjes, P. C., & Frazier, L. L. (1986). Maturation and plasticity in the olfactory system of vertebrates. *Brain Research Reviews, 11*, 1–45.

Carmichael, L. (1970). The onset and early development of behavior. In P. H. Mussen (Ed.), *Carmichael's manual of child psychology* (3rd ed., Vol. 1, pp. 447–563). New York: Wiley.

Chodynicki, S. (1968). Embryogenesis of the auditory part of the inner ear in the guinea pig. *Acta Theriologica, 13*, 219–260.

Chomsky, N. (1975). *Reflections on language.* New York: Pantheon Books.

Clements, M., & Kelly, J. B. (1978). Auditory spatial responses of young guinea pigs (*Cavia porcellus*) during and after ear blocking. *Journal of Comparative Physiological Psychology, 92*, 34–44.

Clopton, B. M. (1986). Neural correlates of development and plasticity in the auditory, somatosensory and olfactory systems. In W. T. Greenough & J. M. Juraska (Eds.), *Developmental neuropsychobiology* (pp. 220–256). New York: Academic Press.

Clopton, B. M., & Winfield, J. A. (1976). Effect of early exposure to patterned sound on unit activity in rat inferior colliculus. *Journal of Neurophysiology, 39*, 1081–1089.

Cook, R. O., Konishi, T., Salt, A. N., Hamm, C. W., Lebetkin, E. H., & Koo, J. (1982). Brainstem evoked responses of guinea-pigs exposed to high noise levels in utero. *Developmental Psychobiology, 15*, 95–104.

Coppola, D. M., & Millar, L. C. (1997). Olfaction in utero: Behavioral studies of the mouse fetus. *Behavioral Processes, 39*, 53–68.

Crystal, S. R., & Bernstein, I. M. (1995). Morning sickness: Impact on offspring salt preference. *Appetite, 25*, 231–240.

Daniel, P., & Laciak, W. (1982). Observations cliniques et expériences concernant l'état de l'appareil cochléo-vestibulaire des sujets exposés au bruit durant la vie foetale [Clinical observations and experiments on cochlea-vestibular status in subjects exposed to noise during fetal life]. *Revue de Laryngologie, 103*, 313–318.

DeCasper, A. J., & Fifer, W. P. (1980). Of human bonding: Newborns prefer their mother's voice. *Science, 208*, 1174–1176.

DeCasper, A. J., Lecanuet, J. P., Busnel, M.-C., Granier-Deferre, J. P., & Maugeais, R. (1994). Fetal reaction to recurrent maternal speech. *Infant Behavior and Development, 17*, 159–164.

DeCasper, A. J., & Prescott, P. A. (1984). Human newborns' perception of male voices: Preference, discrimination, and reinforcing value. *Developmental Psychobiology, 17*, 481–491.

DeCasper A. J., & Sigafoos, A. D. (1983). The intrauterine heartbeat: A potent reinforcer for newborns. *Infant Behavior and Development, 6*, 19–25.

DeCasper, A. J., & Spence, M. J. (1986). Prenatal maternal speech influences newborn's perception of speech sounds. *Infant Behavior and Development, 9*, 133–150.

Desage, M., Schaal, B., Orgeur, P., Soubiran, J., & Brazier, J. L. (1995). Gas chromatographic-mass spectrometric method to characterize the transfer of dietary odorous compounds into plasma and milk. *Journal of Chromatography, B. Biomedical Applications, 678*. 204–210.

Douek, E., Dodson, H. C., Bannister, L. H., Ashcroft, P., & Humphries, K. N. (1976). Effects of incubator noise on the cochlea of the newborn. *Lancet, 20*, 1110–1115.

Feijoo, J. (1981). Le foetus, Pierre et le Loup [The fetus, Peter and the wolf]. In E. Herbinet & M.-C. Busnel (Eds.), *L'Aube des sens: Cahiers du nouveau-né* (pp. 192–209). Paris: Stock.

Feldman, W. M. (1920). *Principles of ante-natal and post-natal child physiology*. New York: Longmans-Green.

Fifer, W. P., & Moon, C. (1989). Psychobiology of newborn auditory preferences. *Seminars in Perinatology, 13*, 430–433.

Flexner, L. B., & Gellhorn, A. (1942). The comparative physiology of placental transfer. *American Journal of Obstetrics and Gynecology, 43*, 965–974.

Gagnon, R., Benzaquen, S., & Hunse, C. (1992). The fetal sound environment during vibroacoustic stimulation in labor: Effect on fetal heart rate response. *Obstetrics and Gynecology, 79*, 950–955.

Gerhardt, K. J. (1989). Characteristics of the fetal sheep sound environment. *Seminars in Perinatology, 13*, 362–370.

Gerhardt, K. J., & Abrams, R. M. (1987). The sound environment of the fetal sheep in utero. *Federation Proceedings, 46*, 356–358.

Gerhardt, K. J., Abrams, R. M., & Oliver, C. C. (1990). Sound environment of the fetal sheep. *American Journal of Obstetrics and Gynecology, 162*, 282–287.

Gottlieb, G. (Ed.). (1973). *Behavioral embryology*. New York: Academic Press.

Gottlieb, G. (1991). Experiential canalization of behavioral development: Theory. *Developmental Psychology, 27*, 4–13.

Granier-Deferre, C., & Abrams, R. M. (1989). Effects of sound on fetal cerebral glucose utilization. *Seminars in Perinatology, 13*, 371–379.

Granier-Deferre, C., & Lecanuet, J.-P. (1987). Influence de stimulations auditives précoces sur la maturation anatomique et fonctionnelle du système auditif [The influence of early sound stimulations on structural and functional maturation of the auditory systems]. *Progrès en Néonatologie, 7*, 236–249.

Green, J. A., & Adkins, E. K. (1975). The effect of prenatal auditory stimulation on early vocalization and approach behavior in the Japanese quail (*Coturnix Coturnix Japonica*). *Behaviour, 2*, 145–155.

Griffiths, S. J., Brown, W. S., Jr., Gerhardt, K. J., Abrams, R. M., & Morris, R. J. (1994). The perception of speech sounds recorded within the uterus of a pregnant sheep. *Journal of the Acoustical Society of America, 96*, 2055–2063.

Gueubelle, F. (1984). Perception of environmental conditions by fetus in utero. *Progress in Reproductive Biology and Medicine, 11*, 110–119.

Guyomarch, J.-C. (1974). L'empreinte auditive prénatale chez le poussin domestique [Prenatal auditory imprinting in the domestic chick]. *Revue du Comportement Animal, 8*, 3–6.

Hall, W. G., & Oppenheim, R. W. (1987). Developmental psychology: Prenatal, perinatal and early postnatal aspects of behavioral development. *Annual Review of Psychology, 38*, 91–128.

Hauser, G. J., Chitayat, D., Berns, L., Braver, D., & Muhlhauser, B. (1985). Peculiar odours in newborns and maternal prenatal ingestion of spicy foods. *European Journal of Pediatrics, 144*, 403.

Henschall, W. R. (1972). Intrauterine sound levels. *Journal of Obstetrics and Gynecology, 112*, 577.

Hepper, P. G. (1987). The amniotic fluid: An important priming role in kin recognition. *Animal Behavior, 35*, 1343–1346.

Hepper, P. G. (1988a). Adaptive fetal learning: Prenatal exposure to garlic affects postnatal preferences. *Animal Behavior, 36*, 935–936.

Hepper, P. G. (1988b). Fetal "soap" addiction. *Lancet, 1*, 1147–1148.

Hepper, P. G. (1991). Transient hypoxic episodes: A mechanism to support associative fetal learning. *Animal Behavior, 41*, 477–480.

Hepper, P. G., Scott, D., & Shahidullah, S. (1993). Newborn and fetal response to maternal voice. *Journal of Reproductive and Infant Psychology, 11*, 147–153.

Hill, D. L., & Przekop, P. R. (1988). Influences of dietary sodium on functional taste receptor development: A sensitive period. *Science, 241*, 1826–1828.

Hill, D. L., & Vogt, M. B. (1989). Behavioral taste responses in rates "recovered" from sodium deprivation instituted during early development. *Chemical Senses, 14*, 710.

Horner, K., Servières, J., & Granier-Deferre, C. (1987). Deoxyglucose demonstration of in utero hearing in the guinea-pig fetus. *Hearing Research, 26*, 327–333.

Hudson, R. (1985). Do newborn rabbits learn the odor stimuli releasing nipple-search behavior? *Developmental Psychobiology, 18*, 575–585.

Humphrey, T. (1978). Functions of the nervous system during prenatal life. In U. Stawe (Ed.), *Perinatal physiology* (pp. 651–683). New York: Plenum.

Johansson, B., Wedenberg, E., & Westin, B. (1964). Measurement of tone response by the human fetus: A preliminary report. *Acta Otolaryngologica, 57*, 188–192.

Knudsen, E. I., Knudsen, P. F., & Esterly, S. D. (1982). Early auditory experience modifies sound localization in barn owls. *Nature, 295*, 238–240.

Kuo, Z. Y. (1967). *The dynamics of behavior development*. New York: Random House.

Laing, D. G., & Panhuber, H. (1980). Olfactory sensitivity of rats reared in an odorous or deodorized environment. *Physiology and Behavior, 25*, 555–558.

Lalande, N. M., Hétu, R., & Lambert, J. (1986). Is occupational noise exposure during pregnancy a risk factor of damage to the auditory system of the fetus? *American Journal of Industrial Medicine, 10*, 427–435.

Lecanuet, J.-P., Gautheron, B., Locatelli, A., Schall, B., Jacquet, A.-Y., & Busnel, M. C. (1998). What sounds reach fetuses: Biological and nonbiological modeling of the transmission of pure tone. *Developmental Psychobiology, 33*, 203–219.

Lecanuet, J.-P., Granier-Deferre, C., & Busnel, M.-C. (1989). Sensorialité foetale: Ontogenèse des systèmes sensoriels, conséquences de leur fonctionnement foetal [Fetal sensoriality: Ontogeny of sensory systems, consequences of their prenatal functioning]. In J. P. Relier, J. Laugier, & B. L. Salle (Eds.), *Médecine périnatale, médecine-sciences* (pp. 201–225). Paris: Flammarion.

Lecanuet, J.-P., Granier-Deferre, C., & Busnel, M.-C. (1995). Human fetal auditory perception. In J. P. Lecanuet, W. P. Fifer, N. A. Krasnegor, & W. P. Smotherman (Eds.), *Fetal development: A psychobiological perspective* (pp. 239–262). Hillsdale, NJ: Erlbaum.

Lecanuet, J. P., & Schaal, B. (1996). Fetal sensory competences. *European Journal of Obstetrics and Gynecology, 68*, 1–23.

Lenoir, M., & Pujol, R. (1980). Sensitive period to acoustic trauma in the rat pup cochlea: Histological findings. *Acta Otolaryngologica, 89*, 317–322.

Lewkowicz, D. J., & Lickliter, R. (1994). *The development of intersensory perception: Comparative perspectives*. Hillsdale, NJ: Erlbaum.

Lien, J. (1976). Auditory stimulation of coturnix embryo (*Coturnix Coturnix Japonica*): A precursor of language acquisition in young infants. *Cognition, 29*, 143–178.

Marlier, L., Schaal, B., & Soussignan, R. (1998). Neonatal responsiveness to the odors of amniotic fluid and milk: A test of transnatal chemosensory continuity. *Child Development, 64*, 611–623.

Mehler, J., Jusczyk, P., Lambertz, G., Halsted, N., Bertoncini, J., & Amiel-Tison, C. (1988). A precursor of language acquisition in young infants. *Cognition, 29*, 143–178.

Mehler, J., Lambertz, G., Jusczyk, P., & Amiel-Tison, C. (1986). Discrimination de la langue maternelle par le nouveau-né [Discrimination of maternal language in the newborn]. *Compte-Rendus de l'Académie des Sciences, Paris, 303*, 637–640.

Mennella, J., Johnson, A., & Beauchamp, G. K. (1995). Garlic ingestion by pregnant women alters the odor of amniotic fluid. *Chemical Senses, 20*, 207–209.

Molina, J. C., Chotro, M. G., & Domingez, H. D. (1995). Fetal alcohol learning resulting from alcohol contamination of the prenatal environment. In J. P. Lecanuet, W. P. Fifer, N. E. Krasnegor, & W. P. Smotherman (Eds.), *Fetal development: A psychobiological perspective* (pp. 419–438). Hillsdale, NJ: Erlbaum.

Moon, C., Cooper, R. P., & Fifer, W. P. (1993). Two-day-olds prefer their native language. *Infant Behavior and Development, 16,* 495–500.

Moon, C., & Fifer, W. P. (1990). Newborns prefer a prenatal version of mother's voice. *Infant Behavior and Development, 13,* 530 (International Conference on Infant Studies issue).

Moore, D. R. (1985). Postnatal development of the mammalian central auditory system and the neural consequence of auditory deprivation. *Acta-Otolaryngologica* (Stockholm), *421* (Suppl.), 19–38.

Murooka, H., Koie, Y., & Suda, D. (1976). Analyse des sons intrautérins et de leurs effets tranquillisants sur le nouveau-né [Analysis of intrauterine sounds and their soothing effects on the newborn]. *Journal de Gynécologie Obstétrique et de Biologie de la Reproduction, 5,* 367–376.

Najbauer, J., & Leon, M. (1995). Olfactory experience modulates apoptosis in the developing olfactory bulb. *Brain Research, 674,* 245–251.

Nicolaïdis, S., Galaverna, O., & Metzler, C. H. (1990). Extracellular dehydration during pregnancy increases salt appetite of offspring. *American Journal of Physiology, 258,* R281–R283.

Panneton, R. K. (1985). *Prenatal auditory experience with melodies: Effects on postnatal auditory preferences in human newborns.* Unpublished doctoral dissertation, University of North Carolina at Greensboro.

Pedersen, P. A., & Blass, E. M. (1992). Prenatal and postnatal determinants of the 1st suckling episode in albino rats. *Developmental Psychobiology, 15,* 349–355.

Peters, A. J. M., Abrams, R. M., Gerhardt, K. J., & Griffiths, S. K. (1993). Transmission of airborne sounds from 50–20,000 Hz into the abdomen of sheep. *Journal of Low Frequency Noise and Vibration, 12,* 16–24.

Pihet, S., Mellier, D., Bullinger, A., & Schaal, B. (1997). Réponses comportementales aux odeurs chez le nouveau-né prématuré [Behavioral responses to odors in the premature infant]. *Enfance, 1,* 33–46.

Previc, F. H. (1991). A general theory concerning the prenatal origins of cerebral lateralization in humans. *Psychological Review, 98,* 299–334.

Querleu, D., Renard, X., & Versyp, F. (1981). Les perceptions auditives du foetus humain [Auditory perceptions in the human fetus]. *Médecine et Hygiène, 39,* 2101–2110.

Querleu, D., Renard, X., Versyp, F., Paris-Delrue, L., & Crépin, G. (1988). Fetal hearing. *European Journal of Obstetrics and Reproductive Biology, 29,* 191–212.

Rawdon-Smith, A. F., Carmichael, L., & Willman, B. (1938). Electrical responses from the cochlea of the fetal guinea-pig. *Journal of Experimental Psychology, 23,* 531–535.

Robinson, S. R., Arnold, H. M., Spear, N. E., & Smotherman, W. P. (1993). Experience with milk and an artificial nipple promotes conditioned opioid activity in the rat fetus. *Developmental Psychobiology, 26,* 375–387.

Robinson, S. R., & Smotherman, W. P. (1995). Habituation and classical conditioning in the rat fetus: Opioid involvements. In J. P. Lecanuet, W. P. Fifer, N. E. Krasnegor, & W. P. Smotherman (Eds.), *Fetal development: A psychobiological perspective.* (pp. 295–314). Hillsdale, NJ: Erlbaum.

Robinson, S. R., Wong, C. H., Robertson, S. S., Nathanielsz, P. W., & Smotherman, W. P. (1995). Behavioral responses of the chronically instrumented sheep fetus to chemosensory stimuli presented in utero. *Behavioral Neuroscience, 109,* 551–562.

Romand, R. (1971). Maturation des potentiels cochléaires dans la période périnatale chez le chat et le cobaye [Maturation of cochlear potentials in the perinatal cat and guinea pig]. *Journal of Physiology* (Paris), *63,* 763–782.

Ronca, A. I., & Alberts, J. R. (1995). Maternal contributions to fetal experience: Transition from prenatal to postnatal life. In J. P. Lecanuet, W. P. Fifer, N. E. Krasnegor, & W. P. Smotherman (Eds.), *Fetal development: A psychobiological perspective* (pp. 331–350). Hillsdale, NJ: Erlbaum.

Salk, L. (1960). The effects of the normal heartbeat sound on the behavior of newborn infants. Implications for mental health. *World Mental Health, 12,* 1–8.

Salk, L. (1962). Mother's heartbeat as an imprinting stimulus. *Annals of the New York*

Academy of Science, 24, 753–763.

Sanes, D. H., & Constantine-Paton, M. (1983). Altered activity patterns during development reduce normal neural tuning. *Science, 221,* 1183–1185.

Satt, B. J. (1984). *An investigation into the acoustical induction of intra-uterine learning.* Unpublished doctoral dissertation, California School of Professional Psychology, Los Angeles.

Schaal, B., Desage, M., Cohen, H., Defaux, O., & Brazier, J. L. (1999). *Mothers-to-fetus transfer of food aromas: Chemical evidence.* Manuscript in preparation.

Schaal, B., & Marlier, L. (1998). Maternal and paternal perception of individual odor signatures in human amniotic fluid. *Biology of the Neonate, 74,* 266–273.

Schaal, B., Marlier, L., & Soussignan, R. (1995). Neonatal responsiveness to the odour of amniotic fluid. *Biology of the Neonate, 67,* 397–406.

Schaal, B., Marlier, L., & Soussignan, R. (1998). Olfactory function in the human fetus: Evidence from selective neonatal responsiveness to the odor of amniotic fluid. *Behavioral Neuroscience, 112,* 1438–1449.

Schaal, B., & Orgeur, P. (1992). Olfaction in utero: Can the rodent model be generalized? *Quarterly Journal of Experimental Psychology: B. Comparative and Physiological Psychology, 44B,* 245–278.

Schaal, B., Orgeur, P., & Arnould, C. (1995). Chemosensory preferences in newborn lambs: Prenatal and perinatal determinants. *Behaviour, 132,* 352–365.

Schaal, B., Orgeur, P., Desage, M., & Brazier, J. L. (1994). Transfer of the aromas of the pregnant and lactating mother's diet to fetal and neonatal environments in the sheep. *Chemical Senses, 20,* 93–94.

Schaal, B., Orgeur, P., Lecanuet, J. P., Poindron, P., Locatelli, A., & Granier-Deferre, C. (1991). Chemoréception nasale in utero: Expériences préliminaires chez le foetus ovin [Nasal chemoreception in utero: First experiments in the ovine fetus]. *Compte-Rendus de l'Académie des Sciences, Paris, 313* (Série III), 319–325.

Schaal, B., Orgeur, P., & Rognon, C. (1995). Odor sensing in the human fetus: Anatomical, functional and chemo-ecological bases. In J. P. Lecanuet, N. A. Krasnegor, W. A. Fifer, & W. Smotherman (Eds.), *Prenatal development: A psychobiological perspective* (pp. 205–237) Hillsdale, NJ: Erlbaum.

Schneirla, T. C. (1965). Aspects of stimulation and organization in approach/withdrawal processes underlying vertebrate behavioral development. *Advances in the Study of Behavior, 1,* 1–74.

Scibetta, J. J., & Rosen, M. G. (1969). Response evoked by sound in the fetal guinea-pig. *Obstetrics and Gynecology, 33,* 830–836.

Sedlacek, J. (1976). Fetal and neonatal development of evoked responses in guinea-pig auditory cortex. *Journal of Physiologica Bohemoslovaca, 25,* 13–21.

Semke, E., Distel, H., & Hudson, R. (1995). Specific enhancement of olfactory receptor sensitivity associated with fetal learning of food odors in the rabbit. *Naturwissenschaften, 82,* 148–149.

Smith, Z. D. J., Gray, L., & Rubel, E. W. (1983). Afferent influences on brain stem auditory nuclei of the chicken: Nucleus laminaris dendritic length following monaural acoustic deprivation. *Journal of Comparative Neurology, 220,* 199–205.

Smotherman, W. P. (1982). Odor aversion learning by the rat fetus. *Physiology and Behavior, 29,* 769–771.

Smotherman, W. P., & Robinson, S. R. (1990). Rat fetuses respond to chemical stimuli in gas phase. *Physiology and Behavior, 47,* 863–868.

Smotherman, W. P., & Robinson, S. R. (1995). Classical conditioning of opioid activity in the fetal rat. *Behavioral Neuroscience, 108,* 951–961.

Smotherman, W. P., Robinson, S. R., Ronca, A. E., Alberts, J. R., & Hepper, P. G. (1989). Heart rate response of the rat fetus and neonate to a chemosensory stimulus. *Physiology and Behavior, 50,* 47–52.

Spence, M. J., & DeCasper, A. J. (1987). Prenatal experience with low frequency maternal voice sounds influences neonatal perception of maternal voice samples. *Infant Behavior and Development, 10,* 133–142.

Teicher, M. H., & Blass, E. M. (1977, November). First suckling response in the newborn albino rat: The roles of olfaction and amniotic fluid. *Science, 198,* 635–636.

Vince, M. A. (1979). Postnatal consequences of prenatal sound stimulation in the guinea-pig. *Animal Behavior, 27,* 908–918.

Vince, M. A., Billing, A. E., Baldwin, B. A., Toner, J. N., & Weller, C. (1985). Maternal vocalizations and other sounds in the fetal lamb's sound environment. *Early Human Development, 11,* 164–170.

Walker, D. W., Grimwade, J. C., & Wood, C. (1971). Intrauterine noise: A component of the fetal environment. *American Journal of Obstetrics and Gynecology, 109,* 91–95.

Wang, H., Wysocki, C. J., & Gold, G. (1993). Induction of olfactory receptor sensitivity in mice. *Science, 260,* 998–1000.

Wilson, D. A., & Sullivan, R. M. (1994). Neurobiology of associative learning in the neonate: Early olfactory learning. *Behavioral and Neural Biology, 61,* 1–18.

Woods, J. R., & Plessinger, M. A. (1989). Fetal sensory sequencing: Application of evoked potentials in perinatal physiology. *Seminars in Perinatology, 13,* 380–392.

Woodward, S. C. (1992). *The transmission of music into the human uterus and the response to music of the human fetus and neonate.* Unpublished doctoral dissertation, University of Cape Town, Cape Town, South Africa.

Youngentob, S. L., & Kent, P. F. (1995). Enhancement of odorant-induced mucosal activity patterns in rats trained on an odorant identification task. *Brain Research, 670,* 82–88.

Zimmer, E. Z., Chao, C. R., Guy, G. P., Marks, F., & Fifer, W. P. (1993). Vibroacoustic stimulation evokes human fetal micturition. *Obstetrics and Gynecology, 31,* 178–180.

10

What Has the Psychology of Human Perception Learned From Animal Studies?

Claude Bonnet and Christian Wehrhahn

Sensory systems enable animals and humans to perceive stimuli in their surroundings and to decide whether to respond to them. Evolution has provided each species with a sensory system appropriate for processing the relevant part of the signals present in their surroundings. Comparison of the behavior of different animal species, including humans, allows generalizations across different individuals and across species with respect to the sensory modalities used. In fact, such a comparative approach relies on Darwin's idea of continuity among animal species, including humans (Vauclair, 1996). It stresses the particular interest of such comparisons not only for structural and physiological studies but also for behavioral and presumably cognitive studies (see Dennett, 1983).

We believe that any perceptual theory should take into account the biological constraints of the underlying mechanisms as the only way to bridge the gap between perception and physiological function of neuronal structures. For example, visual motion has been found to be the most widely distributed aspect extracted from the surroundings in numerous animals, vertebrates as well as invertebrates. The so-called Reichardt detector or correlation model (Hassenstein & Reichardt, 1953; Reichardt, 1957) of visual motion was initially elaborated for invertebrates and has been generalized and modified to apply to higher vertebrates including humans.

This chapter examines how visual scientists focusing on human perception have gained ideas and knowledge from three types of animal studies: (a) behavioral studies, which are too frequently neglected, because they may provide suggestive views on functional aspects of vision related to the behavioral space and capacities of each species; (b) single-cell recording, which is certainly the field that has suggested most of the inter-

We thank H. Mittelstaedt for his constructive remarks and J. Liter for suggesting numerous improvements of the English. This chapter was written while Christian Wehrhahn was on a stay in the University of Strasbourg with the financial support of the Centre National de la Recherche Scientifique.

pretations in the functioning of perception; and (c) lesion studies, which act at a more global level, tentatively bridging the gap between structures and functions, as they have behavioral counterparts.

A Neglected Approach: Comparative Aspects of Vision in Behavioral Studies

In many animals, the sense of motion has developed so sufficiently as to allow them to actively generate specific patterns of movements, to provide them with additional information about their surroundings. For example, in humans, *microsaccades* (i.e., very small jumps of the eyes with an amplitude of some arcmin) which occur spontaneously about three times per second, are generated. By measuring these eye movements and feeding them back on a TV monitor, a stabilized retinal image can be generated. Any low-contrast pattern shown on the monitor will vanish shortly. Among other things, the microsaccades serve to prevent this process. Microsaccades also serve to suppress the perception of a blind spot in one's vision— the patch on a person's retina through which the ganglion cells connect the eye to the brain. A similar phenomenon has been observed in the flight behavior of houseflies. The housefly instantly turns to a vertical black line displayed anywhere in their field of vision. Stabilizing the image of such an object on its retina leads the housefly to no discernible response toward the object (Wehrhahn, 1980). Although we do not know what the housefly sees, we may conclude from the absence of its otherwise spontaneous turning response that it does not see the line.

In their article, von Holst and Mittelstaedt (1950) proposed that any active movement generated by an animal was actually coded by some (then unknown) neural mechanism that provided the visual system with the information on what to expect from this movement. One effect of this is that when a person looks around and moves his or her head and eyes, he or she perceives the visual scene as stable in spite of large movement on the retina. In contrast, if the motion is passively generated, for example, if the eye is moved gently with the finger, one readily perceives a motion of the scene. Again it was shown with a very simple experiment by Mittelstaedt (1949) that this mechanism also exists in the drone fly. The head of a fly is connected to its thorax by a very flexible neck, which can be turned easily by 180° and fixed in this position relative to the body by means of a tiny bridge of beeswax, gently melted during the gluing procedure. When a fly with its head so inverted turns even a tiny bit, its visual system then expects a motion in a direction opposite to what it is actually seeing. This leads to a turn in the opposite direction, which in its respective way is again producing an expectation, instantaneously leading to completely chaotic behavior. This is alleviated only when the wax bridge is removed and the fly is allowed to regain its normal head posture.

However, although different species may share the same visual mechanisms, their behavior may appear to be very different. Comparing visually based behavioral capacities among species may be misleading if one

does not take into account the specific characteristics of each visual system
and the behavioral constraints in which the animal is embedded. Regarding the latter, it is clear that a flying predator does not require the same
visual information to survive as its terrestial prey. We do not touch on the
question of which determines which, but we will rely on the general idea
that the specific biological and behavioral functions that have evolved in
a species are adequate for the survival needs of this species, although they
clearly imply limitations. For example, phylogenetic evolution has led
some animals to develop very specific senses, such as the location of prey
observed in snakes through the perception of the ultrared radiation emitted by warm-blooded animals or the perception of the orientation of the
magnetic field of the earth found in honeybees.

Comparing sensitivity performance among species can sometimes lead
to unfounded conclusions. Although most cat lovers praise the visual sensitivity of their pet, compared with their own, on the basis of their experience, vision scientists would disillusion them. In absolute values, the
cat's keenness of perception is much lower than man's. In contrast to the
rod-free fovea found in humans, the area centralis of the cat has about 10
times more rods than cones. The ratio of the number of cones to the number of ganglion cells is about 5:1 in the area centralis of the cat, whereas
it is around 1:3 in the human fovea (for a review, see Boycott & Wässle,
1991). Proportionally, the decline of visual acuity with the eccentricity of
the image of the visual stimulus on the retina is comparable in cats and
in humans. The upper limit of the cat's contrast sensitivity function (CSF)
has been estimated to be 20 cpd (cycles per degree) at best, whereas, in
comparable photopic conditions, that of humans is around 50–60 cpd. Both
CSFs cover about 6 octaves of spatial frequencies, so that the optimum of
the cat's CSF is about 1 log unit (or 3 octaves) below that of humans. Now
consider a third species: the falcon. The upper limit of its CSF is about
150 cpd with an optimum at a spatial frequency that is barely visible to
humans. Would one say that the falcon has a much higher acuity than
primates? In absolute value, this is certainly true.

Now imagine that these three predators have the same prey, a small
gray mouse presented on a gray background. De Valois and De Valois
(1990) have suggested that one considers, not the absolute value of contrast sensitivity, but the spatial frequency content of the retinal images
that are useful for each species, taking into account their height above the
ground. In other words, the question becomes, At what greatest distance
could they still detect their common prey? In reprocessing these examples,
we come to estimates such as 0.5 m for the cat, 5 m for the human, and
50 m for the falcon. These distances are more consistent with the successful prey-catching behavior of our three predators!

Another example of rough considerations about different organisms
that may lead to incorrect conclusions is that of *stereoscopic vision*. Stereoscopic vision or *stereopsis* is one mechanism of depth perception based
on the central fusion of binocular images. It was long believed that
binocular stereopsis existed only in mammals with frontal eyes. However, some nonmammals also have frontal eyes, for example, the falcon

and the toad. Although falcons were proved to have stereopsis, the toad, although it has binocular vision, does not have binocular stereopsis (see Fox, 1981). Many animals with lateral vision also have some binocular vision and even stereopsis. For example, pigeons may have a spatially restricted binocular stereopsis involved in their pecking behavior (Nalbach, Wolf-Oberhollenzer, & Kirschfeld, 1990). Again, it is seen that phylogenetic evolution has provided different solutions, which are adaptive and provide survival advantages. An extreme case is binocular stereopsis in the praying mantis, a relatively large carnivorous insect that catches small insects with its long, extended forelegs.

The Neuron Receptive Field Epopee

Even results of the most simple experiments concerning the sensitivity to light can be understood only when the biophysical processes occurring in the optical apparatus of the eye and in the photoreceptors are known. Even more so, the cognitive abilities of our visual system can be related to brain function only when the basic functions of the respective visual pathways have been characterized through electrophysiological experiments. For ethical reasons, these procedures cannot be carried out in humans. Scientists, therefore, have turned to animals to analyze neural function. Ethical and practical considerations have favored the use of species such as frog, rabbit, or fish to study basic neurobiological functions of the retina. However, these studies are far from sufficient to understand higher processes of vision in the human brain. The visual system of cats had long been studied under the assumption of a strong structural similarity to that of humans. Clearly, monkeys are more directly comparable to humans.

The eye is the most important sensory organ in humans. Its optical apparatus projects the environment on the retina. A fine set of light sensors, the rods and the cones, transforms the luminance in each point of the retina into an electrical signal. The rods are used to see in the dark and are most sensitive to green light. The red-, green-, and blue-sensitive cones are used for seeing in daylight. The first steps in the neuronal processing of light signals already take place in the retina. The electrical signals of the cones are transmitted via a network of interneurons to the ganglion cells. These form the optic nerve, which is about 10 cm long and connects the eyes and the brain. Whereas the magnitude of the signal of a cone is proportional to the light intensity, the ganglion cells carry a different signal. It contains information about the difference of the intensities in adjacent parts of the retina. Thus, the ganglion cells provide a signal about the contrast at a certain place in the retina. This is achieved by inhibitory and excitatory interactions within the network of the retina. Together with the adaptation to the average intensity of the surrounding, this is the most important task of the retina. In humans, all signals coming from the eyes pass through the 1 million fibers in the optic nerve. These signals are action potentials, lasting about 1 ms each. If we assume that one action potential per ganglion cell per second is transmitted through the optic nerve, and we would like to store this information, we would require for a period of 20 min roughly 1 gigabyte, the capacity of the hard disk of an average PC. This enormous amount of data is handled by our central nervous system apparently without any effort.

Vision is created through the interaction of eye and brain. A simple example of the result of such an interaction is the perception of motion. The signals processed for conscious perception of motion are not explicitly found at the level of the retina. Eighty percent of the axons leaving the retina end up in the lateral geniculate nucleus, the first relay station in the brain where these signals are transmitted to other cells, which in turn connect to the primary visual cortex, also called the first visual area (V1). This is situated at the occipital pole of the brain. It is here where one can expect the first neuronal circuits concerned with the perception of motion. Researchers know from many physiological experiments, however, that the retina provides important preprocessing of data.

Hartline and Graham (1932) were the first to succeed in recording electrical activity from single axons in the optic nerve of a horseshoe crab *(Limulus)*, indicating that vision is achieved by processing electrical signals in the central nervous system. From there, our knowledge of brain functions changed completely. Moreover, this experiment triggered a long series of physiological discoveries, which has not yet ended. Despite the fact that the *Limulus* has a compound eye, a structure rather different from the eyes of mammals, the authors demonstrated a logarithmic relation between the frequency of the action potentials and the intensity of the light. Such a compression process was thereafter found in other species, particularly in mammals, as well as other sensory modalities.

The idea of a compression process has been generalized to relating the function of receptors to that of visual neurons in the form of a spatial compression. It gives rise to the basic concept, or at least the most influential one, in visual neuroscience, that of receptive field (RF). Ganglion cells are not connected in a one-to-one fashion to receptors, but each ganglion cell receives information from a set of neighboring receptors that form its receptive field (in the classical sense). In fact, each visual cell is characterized by a receptive field, which is the area of the retina and of the corresponding visual space in which a stimulation should be presented to modulate the cell response. Receptive fields of neurons were discovered in the ganglion cells of the cat by Kuffler (1953). They had concentric receptive fields consisting either of an on-center and off-surround or an off-center and on-surround. In the first case, when shining a light in the central part of the receptive field, an increase in the rate of firing is observed. In the second case, an increase in the rate of firing occurs when the light is turned off. Hartline, Wagner, and Ratliff (1956) demonstrated, in the *Limulus* eye, the existence of lateral inhibition between neighboring photoreceptors and suggested that it could be the basis for contour enhancement.

What the Frog's Eye Tells Us About Man's Brain

Barlow (1953) and Lettvin, Maturana, McCulloch, and Pitts (1959) initiated a wealth of experiments on the frog's ganglion cells. These studies became very influential in the theoretical thinking of many visual scientists. Among the five types of ganglion cells that were described, two types of receptive field properties may deserve special attention. Convex-edge detectors have relatively small RFs (2°–5°) and respond best to moving small dark spots. These neurons were called "bug detectors" because it was shown that the prey-catching behavior of frogs and toads was triggered by lures of similar size, speed, and contrast characteristics to those giving the best response of these neurons (see Ingle, 1971). Dimming detectors have large RFs (15° or more) and respond best to large, dark objects or shadows moving rapidly through the RF. In the same vein as above, they were interpreted as "predator detectors."

The idea that certain lures directly trigger certain behaviors has been very influential in this field (e.g., Ingle, 1971). Consequently, the fact that some neurons respond to a restricted subset of stimulus dimensions in their receptive fields encouraged some to speculate about their functional role in perception. The implication of that approach was that "these cells may provide as full a representation of the world as the frog needs" (Lennie, Trevarthen, Van Essen, & Wässle, 1990, p. 110). Barlow (1953) developed this point of view in an article and later expanded it into a neuronal theory for perception (Barlow, 1972). In the same vein, Steinman-Gilinsky (1984) proposed that identification of objects would result from the activation of specialized neurons, which she called *cognon*.

The main idea that emerged from this approach was that of a hierarchical processing of information within the visual system. Another view of the results obtained in the frog (Lettvin et al., 1959), in the pigeon (Maturana & Frenk, 1963), or in the rabbit (Levick, 1967) suggested that, ignoring some peculiarities of each of these species, their visual neurons appeared to be selective to a restricted set of local features in the environment: overall illumination, contrast, motion and its direction, size, and orientation of edges.

Hierarchical Neural Model of Visual Perception

In the mid-1950s, Torsten Wiesel and David Hubel began recording from the more central parts of the visual pathway of the cat and later in the monkey. They found that cells in the primary visual cortex of higher mammals very often cannot be driven by switching on or switching off a dot of light but need to be stimulated by more complex stimuli to yield measurable responses. Recording from the striate cortex (V1) of the cat, they described cells that, aside from those found in layer 4, had more or less rectangular RFs (see Hubel, 1987). They were best activated by bright or dark bars or by luminous edges crossing their RF and appeared to be selective to the orientation of these contours. The maximum firing rate was obtained when the orientation of the contour coincided with the long axis of the RF. Three classes of these cortical neurons were described. The *simple* cells exhibit parallel and separated on and off zones. The *complex* cells are on and off in every part of their RF. The *hypercomplex* cells have an inhibitory zone at one or at both ends of their RF. They have also been called *corner detector* or later *end-stopped* cells. For Hubel and Wiesel, these three classes of neurons were hierarchically organized, and their organization was fundamental in understanding the processing of visual form.

Studies of the cat's visual system also provide more detailed knowledge about earlier levels of processing. Ganglion cells all have circular RFs with concentric and antagonistic zones. They have been classified by Enroth-Cugell and Robson (1966) as two functional types: the *X-sustained* and *Y-transient* ganglion cells. Cleland and Levick (1974) and Stone and Fukuda (1974) later described the *W* cells, with, in particular, their direction-selective properties. The importance of the latter seems restricted with respect to primates. In terms of behavioral functionality, the retinal neurons of the cat (and of the mokey) are activated by more abstract stimuli in the sense that they are further away from objects of the animal world. No mouse detector was found in the cat's retina!

A briskly expanding image may suggest a danger of collision and provokes an appropriate avoidance behavior. One of the long-lasting questions has been whether such a behavior is based on a type of mental reconstruction of a three-dimensional motion from the two-dimensional retinal image or if the visual system is wired to directly analyze such a motion. Schiff (1965), using a shadow-caster device, has shown that different species (fiddler crabs, frogs, chickens, cats, monkeys, and humans) have an avoidance behavior under such conditions. The question is not entirely solved concerning newborn infants before 3 weeks of age, as some maturational component may be involved. But the question of basic neural mechanisms involved in the processing of an approaching object has been clarified by the demonstration that many cells in the medial superior temporal area (V5A) in both anesthetized and alert monkeys respond specifically to such a stimulus (Graziano, Andersen, & Snowden, 1994; Tanaka & Saito, 1989). These cells have large RFs (20°), and more of them are selective for expansion than for contraction. They may be involved in the visually guided behavior for the avoidance of obstacles using information about time-to-collision (Lee, 1976).

The basic knowledge of the *epigenesis* (i.e., environmental influences during development) of the visual neurons was mainly obtained from studies of kittens and later confirmed in the monkey. Schematically, the debate was to know whether the selective properties of striate cells such as orientation or binocular selectivity were due to a genetic implementation or due to visual experience. A long series of experiments was run in kittens raised in darkness, or deprived from visual stimuli of a specific orientation during their early experience. Several conclusions emerged from these studies (see review in Fregnac & Imbert, 1978). First, at birth, most of the visual cells present some orientation selectivity. The proportion of orientation-selective cells increases during normal development. Second, sensory deprivation only affects the normal specification of visual neurons when it happens during a critical period. If normal visual experience reappears before the end of that period, recovery is possible. Moreover, recovery occurs only if the animal is allowed to move actively. A similar scheme concerns binocular vision. All these observations point to the conclusion that the basic characteristics of the visual system are genetically based, but they become fully active only if the animal (or the human) has a normal visual experience during some early critical period of development. Implications for the reduction of long-lasting effects of early *ambly-opia* (i.e., lazy eye) in humans have changed many practices in pediatric ophthalmology.

Trigger-Feature Analysis or Cooperative Interactions Within Cell Assemblies?

In a simplified (and somewhat casual) manner, the current theoretical concepts used to describe visual processing can be attributed to two seemingly contradictory classes: bottom-up and top-down models. One example of the former is to consider early vision as several analytical processes coding local features of the stimulus. The RF size imposes the idea that such an analysis is local. Top-down models, on the other hand, reinforced also by phenomenal considerations of the Gestalt theory, stress more global mechanisms based on cognitive processes that are represented through distributed activities within a neural network of more or less unspecific neurons. However, these networks require some preprocessing of the visual input signals.

Clearly, single-cell studies have advanced the idea that each neuron has a local function in processing specific features of the stimulus, as if they work independently of each other. This is more a result of the single-cell recording technique than a basic assumption. However, the idea that each neuron can be considered as a *module* (i.e., functional structure that processes specific information independently from other structures) in Fodor's sense (i.e., cognitively encapsulated) was clearly expressed by Barlow (1972) and made popular the idea of a "grandmother detector" or a "yellow volkswagen detector."

This view of a purely hierarchical mode of functioning seems too extreme to many vision scientists. Changes in the functional properties of orientation-selective neurons are observed when a region just outside of the classical RF is stimulated. Blakemore and Tobin (1972) hypothesized lateral inhibition between neighboring columns of orientation, and it was demonstrated later in V1 and V5 that long-range interactions on an even larger scale substantially determine the functional properties of orientation-selective neurons (Allman, Miezin, & McGuinness, 1985; Gilbert, 1998; Gilbert & Wiesel, 1990).

On the basis of Hebb's (1949) suggestions, cooperative activities in neural networks have been modeled. Hebb proposed that synaptic contacts between nerve cells would be strengthened through repeated use and that this was the neural basis of memory and learning. Recent psychophysical experiments indicate substantial judgmental influences in perceptual learning. Physiological experiments in awake monkeys show that depending on the instructions that are given, the same set of neurons (recorded from with many electrodes simultaneously) will show activity patterns differing in their temporal structure for the same stimulus (Ahissar et al., 1992). Thus, processes like dynamical linking could be responsible for switching between different states of one and the same set of neurons.

In conclusion, both bottom-up as well as top-down processes seem to contribute to even simple aspects of perception. Determining the precise nature of each of these processes will be possible only through a succession of sophisticated physiological and psychophysical (Thorpe, Fize, & Marlot, 1996) experiments.

Modularity in Action: Lesion Studies in Different Species

In this section, we argue that lesion experiments play a very specific role in the functional characterization of anatomically or functionally separable parts of the central nervous system, because they allow—if carried out carefully—conclusions of the sort that a specific part of the brain is indispensable for a specific function. We have to emphasize here that great care has to be taken in drawing such conclusions (see, e.g., Mittelstaedt, 1997).

The first arguments favoring a relative specialization of cortical areas came from lesion studies. Changeux (1983) mentioned the fact that in Egyptian times, some associations had already been made between the localization of an accidental lesion in human and behavioral deficits. Traditionally, Broca (1861) is credited for having discovered the area controlling speaking. Many other areas have been discovered since, and their precise functional characterization has been made through physiological experiments in rhesus monkeys (Zeki, 1993).

Before considering lesions in primates, we first look at the effects of lesions in the responses to moving stimuli in flies. Insects such as flies were first used as a model system because of their very clear and stereotyped response to moving stimuli. Another important feature that is specific to insects is their stereotyped anatomy, especially in their central nervous system. The most striking aspect of this for our present concern is that in the central nervous system of each specimen of the same species, neurons can be found whose anatomical structure and physiological response are basically identical. Thus, a specific neuron can be studied in many animals and characterized quantitatively with a precision that is impossible in vertebrate brains. Visually guided behavior was studied in free as well as in restrained flies. The behavioral responses to moving stimuli were measured quantitatively and compared with the response of neurons in the optic lobes (Wehrhahn, 1985). It was found that, very similar to primates, there exists a special motion center. It is situated in one of the optic lobes of each eye and is composed of around 60 giant nerve cells arranged in four layers. Each of these layers contains cells that are specifically activated by motion in one of the four cardinal directions: up, down, left, or right (Hausen, 1993).

Flies of a somewhat larger species (e.g., the blow fly) were tested for their response to horizontal motion. Microsurgical lesions were applied. The axons of a group of giant neurons, the horizontal cells that selectively respond to horizontal motion in one direction, were cut. After they recovered from the operation, the response to horizontal motion of these flies was tested again. When these tests were finished, the flies were sacrificed, and the exact position of the lesion was identified by staining the brain and reconstructing the respective ganglion. It was shown that in all flies with successful lesions to their horizontal cell axons, the reponse to motion in a particular direction was completely abolished, whereas the responses to motion in the other direction was unaffected (Hausen & Wehrhahn, 1983, 1990). These experiments therefore proved that the horizontal cells play an indispensable role in the perception of at least some aspects of horizontal motion in flies when they were flying.

Experimentally induced lesions have been invaluable for the understanding of the function of different areas in the central nervous system of primates. A particularly well studied aspect of vision in primates is again the perception of motion. The middle temporal area (MT or V5) of the human brain is especially active when subjects perceive a visual stimulus in motion. It is situated laterally and ventrally in the occipital lobe of the brain (Zeki et al., 1991). In macaque monkeys, MT and V1 are heavily interconnected with one another, and there is reason to suppose from activation studies that the same is also true in the human brain. Anatomy and physiology of V1 and MT in the monkey have been studied in great detail. V1 seems to be the main input region into higher brain areas supposedly mediating and at the same time preprocessing the signals processed further for conscious vision.

A conspicuous feature of the striate cortex (V1) is layer 4B, which consists of heavily *myelinated nerve fibers* (i.e., those fibers having a fatty insulation around their axon that improves their speed of conduction). With appropriate staining in a section perpendicular to the surface of the brain, these fibers will appear dark. Hence, it was long before anyone attempted single-cell recording from this area. The neurons actually found in layer 4B of the striate cortex during single-cell recording predominantly respond to motion stimuli. Study of a patient blinded by loss of area V1 showed that activity in MT is sufficient to mediate limited but nevertheless conscious perception of visual motion (Barbur, Watson, Frackowiak, & Zeki, 1993). This supports the view that extrastriate areas of the visual cortex are capable of contributing directly to visual perception without the absolute necessity of preprocessing by V1 (Stoerig & Cowey, 1997; Zeki, 1993).

Small reversible lesions of the cortex can be achieved by injection with a neurotoxin (here ibotenic acid) into the desired region through a micropipette. When recording from area medium temporale (MT) of an awake monkey, this can be done in a region with neurons whose receptive field is known. Thus, performance of the monkey can be analyzed quantitatively through behavioral tests immediately before and after the injection as well as later, when the effects of the injection have subsided (Dürsteler, Wurtz, & Newsome, 1987; Newsome & Pare, 1988; Newsome, Wurtz, Dürsteler, & Mikami, 1985). These studies showed that a monkey treated with ibotenic acid in a particular region of MT was blind to motion in the respective part of its field of view, and only there, as long as the neurotoxin was active. Thus, in contrast to area V1, area MT does play an indispensable role in at least some aspects of motion perception (Maunsell & van Essen, 1983).

Zihl, von Cramon, and Mai (1991) described a patient with large bilateral lesions in the occipital lobe outside the striate cortex, who had been diagnosed with *akinetopsia* (visual motion blindness). The most striking perceptual consequence of those lesions was a very abnormal sensation of motion. The patient referred to moving scenes or objects as "restless" or "unstationary" or undergoing episodic shifts in location. This patient had no field defects and relatively normal acuity, three-dimensional and color vision, as well as visual space perception and visual identification of shapes, objects, or faces. Using positron emission topography and magnetic resonance imaging (MRI), Shipp, de Jong, Zihl, Frackowiak, and Zeki (1994) were able to show that areas V1 and MT were inactive when the patient viewed even strong motion stimuli on a monitor screen. It was shown further that the patient had some residual vision, which was ascribed to having an intact V3 area and, possibly, neural reorganization after the lesion.

Thus, on the basis of anatomical and physiological studies in intact monkeys (Zeki, 1974, 1991) as well as experimental lesion studies in these animals, it is possible not only to understand even complex consequences of *ischemic lesions* (i.e., a lesion that blocks locally the blood circulation) in humans but also to identify certain areas in the brain indispensable for certain functions. This is an important step in developing strategies for rehabilitation and also lays the ground for future clinical work with the goal of better therapeutic treatments.

Conclusion

Behavioral, electrophysiological, and lesion studies carried out in animals in a comparative perspective have clearly improved our understanding of the structures and functions of the components of the brain involved in visual perception. Although it is reasonable to expect that the benefit of animal studies with respect to an understanding of human perception depends on the phylogenetic proximity between species, even behavioral and physiological experiments in flies, an insect species very far from mammals, have revealed general principles of neural function in vision common to all species. However, to transpose knowledge from animal studies to humans requires us to look carefully at the effect of the genetic, behavioral, and environmental constraints in which the animal has evolved.

References

Ahissar, E., Vaadia, E., Ahissar, M., Bergman, H., Arieli, A., & Abeles, M. (1992, September 4). Dependence of cortical plasticity on correlated activity of single neurons and on behavioral context. *Science, 257,* 1412–1415.

Allman, J. M., Miezin, F., & McGuinness, E. (1985). Stimulus specific responses from beyond the classical receptive field: Neurophysiological mechanisms for local–global comparisons in visual neurons. *Annual Review of Neurosciences, 8,* 407–430.

Barbur, J. L., Watson, D. J. G., Frackowiak, R. S. J., & Zeki, S. M. (1993). Conscious visual perception without V1. *Brain, 116,* 1293–1302.

Barlow, H. B. (1953). Summation and inhibition in the frog's retina. *Journal of Physiology, 119,* 69–88.

Barlow, H. B. (1972). Single units and sensation: A neuron doctrine for perceptual psychology? *Perception, 1,* 371–394.

Blakemore, C., & Tobin, E. A. (1972). Lateral inhibition between orientation detectors in the cat's visual cortex. *Experimental Brain Research, 15,* 439–440.

Boycott, B. B., & Wässle, H. (1991). Functional architecture of the mammalian retina. *Physiological Reviews, 71,* 447–480.

Broca, P. (1861). Remarques sur le siège de la faculté du langage articulé, suivies d'une observation d'aphénie (perte de la parole) [Remarks on the site of articulated language faculty, followed with one observation of aphenia (loosing of speech)]. *Bulletin de la Société d'Anthropologie, 6,* 330–357.

Changeux, J.-P. (1983). *L'homme neuronal* [The neuronal man]. Paris: Fayard.

Cleland, B. G., & Levick, W. R. (1974). Brisk and sluggish concentrically organized ganglion cells in the cat's retina. *Journal of Psychology, 240,* 421–456.

Dennett, D. C. (1983). Intentional systems in cognitive ethology: The 'panglossian paradigm' defended. *Behavioral and Brain Sciences, 6,* 343–390.

De Valois, R. L., & De Valois, K. (1990). *Spatial vision.* New York: Oxford University Press.

Dürsteler, M. R., Wurtz, R. H., & Newsome, W. T. (1987). Directional pursuit deficits following lesions of the foveal representation within the superior temporal sulcus of the macaque monkey. *Journal of Neurophysiology, 57,* 1262–1287.

Enroth-Cugell, C., & Robson, J. G. (1966). The contrast sensitivity of retinal ganglion cells of the cat. *Journal of Physiology, 187,* 517–552.

Fox, R. (1981). Stereopsis in animals and human infants. In R. N. Aslin, J. R. Alberts, & M. R. Petersen (Eds.), *Development in perception* (pp. 335–381). New York: Academic Press.

Fregnac, Y., & Imbert, M. (1978). Early development of visual cortical cells in normal and dark reared kittens: Relationship between orientation selectivity and ocular dominance. *Journal of Physiology, 278,* 27–44.

Gilbert, C. D. (1998). Adult cortical dynamics. *Psychological Review, 78,* 467–485.

Gilbert, C. D., & Wiesel, T. N. (1990). The influence of contextual stimuli on the orientation selectivity of cells in primary visual cortex of the cat. *Vision Research, 30,* 1689–1701.

Graziano, M. S. A., Andersen, R. A., & Snowden, R. J. (1994). Tuning of MST neurons to spiral motions. *Journal of Neurosciences, 14,* 54–67.

Hartline, H. K., & Graham, C. H. (1932). Nerve impulse from single receptors in the eye. *Journal of Cellular and Comparative Physiology, 1,* 277–295.

Hartline, H. K., Wagner, H. G., & Ratliff, F. (1956). Inhibition in the eye of *Limulus. Journal of General Physiology, 39,* 651–673.

Hassenstein, B., & Reichardt, W. (1953). Der Schluss von Reiz-Reaktions-Funktionen auf Systemstrukturen [Influence of system structure from signal–response functions]. *Zeitschrift für Naturforschung, 8b,* 518–524.

Hausen, K. (1993). The decoding of retinal image flow in insect vision. In F. A. Miles & J. Wallman (Eds.), *Visual motion and its role in the stabilization of gaze* (pp. 203–235). Amsterdam: Elsevier.

Hausen, K., & Wehrhahn, C. (1983). Microsurgical lesion of horizontal cells changes optomotor yaw responses in the blow fly *Calliphora erythrocephala. Proceedings of the Royal Society of London, Series B, 219,* 211–216.

Hausen, K., & Wehrhahn, C. (1990). Neural circuits mediating visual flight control in flies: II. Separation of two control systems by microsurgical brain lesions. *Journal of Neurosciences, 10,* 351–360.

Hebb, D. (1949). *The organization of behavior: A neuropsychological theory.* New York: Wiley.

Hubel, D. H. (1987). *Eye, brain, and vision.* New York: Scientific American Library.

Ingle, D. J. (1971). Prey-catching behavior of anurans towards moving and stationary objects. *Vision Research* (Suppl. 3), 447–456.

Kuffler, S. W. (1953). Discharge patterns and functional organization of the mammalian retina. *Journal of Neurophysiology, 16,* 37–68.

Lee, D. N. (1976). A theory of visual control of braking based on information about time-to-collision. *Perception, 5,* 437–459.

Lennie, P., Trevarthen, C., Van Essen, D. C., & Wässle, H. (1990). Parallel processing of visual information. In L. Spillmann & J. S. Werner (Eds.), *Visual perception: The neurophysiological foundations* (pp. 103–128). New York: Academic Press.

Lettvin, J. Y., Maturana, H. R., McCulloch, W. S., & Pitts, W. H. (1959). What the frog's eye tells the frog's brain. *Proceedings of the Institute of Radio Engineers, 47,* 1940–1951.

Levick, W. R. (1967). Receptive fields and trigger features of ganglion cells in the visual streak of the rabbit's retina. *Journal of Physiology, 188,* 285–307.

Maturana, H. R., & Frenk, S. (1963). Directional movement and horizontal edge detectors in the pigeon retina. *Science, 142,* 977–979.

Maunsell, J. H. R., & Van Essen, D. C. (1983). Functional properties of neurons in the middle temporal visual area of the macaque monkey: I. Selectivity for stimulus direction, speed, and orientation. *Journal of Neurophysiology, 49,* 1127–1147.

Mittelstaedt, H. (1949). Telotaxis und Optomotorik von Eristalis bei Augeninversion [Target orientation and optomotor behavior in Eristalis with eye inversion]. *Naturwissenschaften, 34,* 90–93.

Mittelstaedt, H. (1997). Interaction of eye-, head-, and trunk-bound information in spatial perception and control. *Journal of Vestibular Research, 7,* 283–302.

Nalbach, H. O., Wolf-Oberhollenzer, F., & Kirschfeld, K. (1990). The pigeon's eye viewed through an ophthalmoscopic microscope: Orientation of retinal landmarks and significance of eye movements. *Vision Research, 30,* 529–540.

Newsome, W. T., & Pare, E. B. (1988). A selective impairment of motion perception following lesions of the middle temporal visual area (MT). *Journal of Neurosciences, 8,* 2201–2211.

Newsome, W. T., Wurtz, R. H., Dürsteler, M. R., & Mikami, A. (1985). Deficits in visual motion processing following ibotenic acid lesions of the middle temporal visual area of the macaque monkey. *Journal of Neurosciences, 5,* 825–840.

Reichardt, W. (1957). Autokorrelationsauswertung als Funktionsprinzip des Zentralnervensystems (bei der optischen Wahrnehmung eines Insekts) [Autocorrelation mechanisms as a functional principle of the central nervous system (in insect vision)]. *Zeitschrift für Naturforschung, 12b,* 448–457.

Schiff, W. (1965). The perception of impending collision: A study of visually directed avoidant behavior. *Psychological Monographs, 79* (Whole No. 604).

Shipp, S., de Jong, B. M., Zihl, J., Frackowiak, R. S. J., & Zeki, S. M. (1994). The brain activity related to residual motion vision in a patient with bilateral lesions of V5. *Brain, 117,* 1023–1038.

Steinman-Gilinsky, A. (1984). *Mind and brain: Principles of neuropsychology.* New York: Praeger.

Stone, J., & Fukuda, Y. (1974). Properties of cat retinal ganglion cells: A comparison of W-cells with X- and Y-cells. *Journal of Neurophysiology, 37,* 722–748.

Stoerig, P., & Cowey, C. (1997). Blindsight in man and monkey. *Brain, 120,* 535–559.

Tanaka, K., & Saito, H.-A. (1989). Analysis of motion of the visual field by direction, expansion/contraction, and rotation cells clustered in the dorsal part of the medial superior temporal area of the macaque monkey. *Journal of Neurosciences, 62,* 626–641.

Thorpe, S., Fize, D., & Marlot, C. (1996). Speed of processing in the human visual system. *Nature, 381,* 520–522.

Vauclair, J. (1996). *Animal cognition: An introduction to modern comparative psychology.* Cambridge, MA: Harvard University Press.

Von Holst, E., & Mittelstaedt, H. (1950). Das Reafferenzprinzip [The reafference principle]. *Naturwissenschaften, 20,* 646.

Wehrhahn, C. (1980). Visual fixation and tracking in flies. In L. A. Segel (Ed.), *Mathematical models in molecular and cellular biology* (pp. 568–603). Cambridge, England: Cambridge University Press.

Wehrhahn, C. (1985). Visual guidance of flies during flight. In G. A. Kerkut & L. I. Gilbert (Eds.), *Comprehensive insect physiology, biochemistry and pharmacology: Vol. 6. Nervous systems: Sensory* (pp. 673–684). Oxford, England: Pergamon Press.

Zeki, S. M. (1974). Functional organization of a visual area in the posterior bank of the superior temporal sulcus in the rhesus monkey. *Journal of Physiology, 236,* 549–473.

Zeki, S. M. (1991). Cerebral akinetopsia (visual motion blindness): A review. *Brain, 114,* 811–824.

Zeki, S. M. (1993). *A vision of the brain.* Oxford, England: Basil Blackwell.

Zeki, S. M., Watson, J. D. G., Lueck, C. J., Friston, K. J., Kennard, C., & Frackowiak, R. S. J. (1991). A direct demonstration of functional specialization in human visual cortex. *Journal of Neurosciences, 11,* 641–649.

Zihl, J., Von Cramon, D., & Mai, N. (1991). Selective disturbance of movement vision after bilateral posterior brain damage: Further evidence and follow up observations. *Brain, 114,* 2235–2252.

11

An Animal Model for a Physiological Interpretation of Human Bisexuality

Claude Aron

Defining Bisexuality

To represent world structure and material things, astrophysicians have long used theoretical models, which have been constantly modified in accordance with the development of knowledge in nuclear physics. Similarly, integrative physiology, whose aim is to explain the structural complexity of living beings, also resorts to experimental models, which are necessarily adapted to the advances in this field of research.

Although Richard von Krafft-Ebing (1931) coined the term *bisexuality* as early as 1886, this form of sexuality has long been a misunderstood phenomenon, which was erroneously related to homosexuality by researchers. At the present time, physiologists know that a noticeable proportion of people have sexual interactions with both males and females rather than exclusively male–male or female–female sexual interactions (Zinik, 1985).

Bisexuality is not specifically a human trait. Sexual contacts between animals of the same sex have long been observed. This has been reported for females, namely in cows (Pearl & Surface, 1915), in monkeys (Hamilton, 1914), in does (Hammond & Marshall, 1925), and in sows (McKenzie, 1926), which spontaneously mounted other females, and also for male rats (Stone, 1924), which adopted the *lordosis* posture when mounted by other males. (Lordosis, which involves raising the head, showing a concave arch of the spine, and deviating the tail on one side, thus exposing the genital region, is normally shown by a sexually receptive female when mounted by a male.) Subsequently, other animals swelled the number of species that were observed to spontaneously display bisexual behavior (see, for reviews, Aron, 1996; Beach, 1968; Goy & Roy, 1991).

It is necessary to define bisexuality in nonhuman species behaviorally because physiologists know nothing of the emotional processes involved in sexual interactions between partners of the same sex in animals. However, we are aware of the fact that bisexual males (Chabli, Schaeffer, & Aron, 1991; Van de Poll & Van Dis, 1977) and bisexual females (Beach, 1968; Goy & Roy, 1991) are vigorous copulators. This means that males and females in some species possess a neuromuscular organization compatible with the display of bisexuality. A male rat may then behave like a female rat while adopting a lordosis posture when mounted by a male congener. The term *heterotypical* behavior has been used to designate this kind of behavior because it does not conform to that of the genetic sex, in contrast to *homotypical* behavior, which refers to the genetic expectation of the male or female typical behavior. A female rat may be considered hetero-typical when she mounts other females with pelvic thrusting, as does a male mounting a female, but homotypical when she displays lordosis re-sponses to a male mounts.

This chapter has two objectives. The first is to review the main find-ings that have led us to some tentative interpretation of the neuroendo-crine mechanisms of bisexuality in laboratory rats. Until the pioneer work of Dörner, Döcke, and Moustafa (1968) and Davis and Barfield (1979), these mechanisms were underinvestigated in the female sex. Therefore data related to the male are emphasized in the next section. The second objective is to address the question of whether animal experimentation would provide a better understanding of bisexuality in human beings.

Mechanisms of Bisexuality in Laboratory Rats

Assessment of Heterotypical Sexual Behavior

Hormonal manipulations are necessary to study the neuroendocrine mech-anisms of lordosis in the male rat because there are obvious strain differ-ences in the display of spontaneous lordosis in male rats. Södersten and Larsson (1974) observed frequent spontaneous lordosis response by males of a Danish strain of rats, whereas Södersten, De Jong, Vreeburg, and Baum (1974) reported that a Dutch strain of rats did not display bisexu-ality. In my laboratory, spontaneous bisexuality of males of a Wistar strain of rats was rather infrequent (Chabli et al., 1991; Schaeffer, Roos, & Aron, 1990).

In most of the experiments that are reported below, I used rats cas-trated as adults from two strains (W1 and W2) of Wistar rats bred in my colony. Lordosis behavior was induced by injecting these rats subcutane-ously with a synthetic estrogen, estradiol benzoate with or without a sub-sequent dose of progesterone. Experiments were conducted also with go-nadally intact rats given or not given hormonal treatments. The rats were kept under natural rhythm of lighting from 1987, when controlled lighting began (lights from 2:00 a.m. until 4:00 p.m.). Free access to commercial laboratory food and to tap water was allowed, except for a group that was placed on a 23-hr-food-deprivation cycle when I conducted tests for *anos-mia* (loss or impairment of sense of smell).

Lordosis behavior in the male rat was tested for 10 min at the begin-ning of the dark period of either natural or controlled lighting cycles, by placing experimental animals with adult males designated as stimulus males and selected for showing vigorous mounting behavior of receptive females and other males. Two parameters were used for the estimation of the lordosis behavior: (a) The *lordosis score*—the proportion of animals displaying lordosis responses to male mounts—served as a measurement of willingness to display heterotypical sexual behavior and (b) the *lordosis quotient*, which was computed by dividing the number of lordosis responses by the number of mounts and multiplying by 100, served as a measure of sexual performance.

We implanted testosterone in ovariectomized female rats and tested them for mounting behavior with receptive females. These latter females sought sexual contact and displayed lordosis when mounted. Any testosterone-treated female that mounted a stimulus female with pelvic thrusting was considered as displaying heterotypical behavior.

Dimorphic Sexual Organization of the Rat

During prenatal development in male rats, the testes produce androgen (Csernus, 1986; Resko, Feder, & Goy, 1968) with two peaks of testosterone secretion, the first just before delivery (Weisz & Ward, 1980) and the second immediately after birth (Corbier, Kerdelhue, Picon, & Roffi, 1978; Gogan, Slama, Bizzini-Koutznetzova, Dray & Kordon, 1981; Roffi, Chami, Corbier, & Edwards, 1987). Testosterone is responsible for the processes of masculinization that take place during the prenatal period (Gladue & Clemens, 1980). These include changes in the structure of the genitalia and brain. The perinatal testosterone surges also cause *defeminization*, an inhibition of responsiveness to estrogen and progesterone (Whalen & Edwards, 1967). Defeminization occurs during both the prenatal and the postnatal periods (Whalen & Olsen, 1981; Whalen, Gladue, & Olsen, 1986).

The medial preoptic area of the brain (MPOA) has been found to be a target for testosterone. For example, Gorski, Gordon, Shryne, and Southam (1978) found that one part of the MPOA, called *sexual dimorphic nucleus* (SDN), is larger in males than in females and that hormonal manipulations that prevent the conversion of testosterone into estrogen by aromatase could modify its development shortly after birth (George & Ojeda, 1982; Weisz, Brown, & Ward, 1982).

According to Vom Saal and Bronson (1978), intrauterine position of female mice fetuses between male fetuses could influence the adult mating behavior, a female between two males receiving the most testosterone. In contrast, Baum, Woutersen, and Slob (1991) did not find evidence in the rat that androgens passed from male to female fetuses. This corroborates previous data from Weisz and Ward (1980) suggesting that testosterone of endogenous origin could influence brain sexual differentiation in some female rats. Thus, the females that display spontaneous mounting behavior in some strains of rat could have been prenatally exposed to the action of androgens.

Impermanence of Organization of Sexual Behavior

Over the past three decades, strong evidence has been provided that the defeminizing effects of androgens during a critical perinatal period are not permanent in the male rat. In those rats that do not spontaneously display lordosis behavior, the possibility of inducing lordosis behavior with estrogens has been demonstrated in males castrated as adults (Aren-Engelbrektsson, Larsson, Södersten, & Wilhelmsson, 1970; Chabli, Schaeffer, Samama, & Aron, 1985; Davidson, 1969) and in noncastrated males (Chabli, Schaeffer, & Aron, 1989; Schaeffer, Roos, & Aron, 1990). In contrast, there has been no agreement concerning the effects of progesterone on lordosis behavior in estrogen-primed male rats. Progesterone of either exogenous origin (Chabli et al., 1985; Olster & Blaustein, 1988; Södersten, 1976; Van de Poll & Van Dis, 1977) or adrenocortical endogenous origin (Chabli et al., 1989; Schaeffer, Chabli, & Aron, 1986) has been shown to be capable of potentiating the effects of estrogen. However, Davidson and Levine (1969), Clemens and Gladue (1978), Moreines, McEwen, and Pfaff, (1986), and McEwen (1988) did not observe any facilitatory effects of progesterone.

The results from my laboratory have suggested that some imbalance between the doses of estrogen and progesterone may account for the negative effects of progesterone reported by some laboratories. Strain differences in hormonal sensitivity must also be taken into consideration. Long-Evans male rats have appeared more responsive to estrogen treatment than do Sprague-Dawley males (Whalen et al., 1986). Similarly, W2 male rats in my colony have displayed more frequent lordosis responses than W1 males after estrogen treatment. In any case, it may be assumed that despite previous processes of behavioral organization, a neural substrate for lordosis remains sensitive to activation by ovarian hormones in adult male rats. We therefore have explored the mechanisms subserving bisexuality in the rat.

The Brain as a Source of Bisexuality

The question might be asked whether the ventromedial nucleus (VMN) of the hypothalamus, which is known to govern lordosis behavior in the female rat (Carrer, Asch, & Aron, 1973; Kennedy, 1964; Kennedy & Mitra, 1963), is also involved in the control of lordosis behavior in the male rat. This was first suggested by Davis and Barfield (1979), who showed activation of lordosis behavior after estrogen implantation into the mediobasal region of the hypothalamus in the male rat. Yet, the possibility remains that lordosis was displayed in the male in the absence of this nucleus. To answer this question (Chateau, Chabli, & Aron, 1987), lesions were placed into the VMN of male rats castrated in adulthood. Lordosis testing was performed after treatment with doses of estrogen and progesterone capable of inducing lordosis behavior in 50% of control rats. VMN lesions completely suppressed the display of lordosis compared with sham-operated animals. The VMN may then be considered as a target for ovarian hormones in the activation of lordosis behavior in both sexes.

An elegant study by Masco and Carrer (1980) showed that the amygdala was involved in the display of lordosis by the female rat. They observed that amygdaloid lesions placed into the corticomedial nucleus (CMN) rendered female rats less receptive, whereas amygdaloid lesions placed into the laterobasal nucleus (LBN) had opposite effects. This encouraged me to research with D. Chateau whether such lesions would also affect lordosis behavior in the male. The time of castration and the schedule of hormonal treatment were the same as in the experiments described above. In accordance with Masco and Carrer's findings, we (Chateau & Aron, 1988) observed that CMN lesions severely impaired the display of lordosis in the male rat. Further experiments (Chateau & Aron, 1989) using discrete lesions placed into different regions of the CMN and of the LBN provided evidence that the willingness to display lordosis was dependent on the posterior part of the CMN. A sharp decrease in the occurrence of lordosis resulted from such lesions. By contrast, lesions of the anterior part of the CMN did not affect the proportion of animals displaying lordosis but increased lordosis quotient values. As to the CMN, the LBN represents a common substrate for the modulation of lordosis in both sexes in the rat. However, its major influence is inhibitory in nature because male rats bearing lesions placed into the posterior part of the LBN showed more frequent lordosis responses and higher lordosis quotient values than did controls.

Compared with the small number of male animals that have been shown to display spontaneous lordosis behavior, mounting behavior by female animals is a fairly widespread phenomenon. One should have then expected that the mechanisms of bisexuality would be examined in the female when the MPOA was identified as the neural structure governing copulatory behavior in the male rat. In 1956, Soulairac and Soulairac observed that MPOA lesions suppressed mounting behavior in the male rat. Heimer and Larsson (1966–1967) confirmed these data, and Van Dis and Larsson (1970) reported that mounting behavior in the male rat resulted from the activation of MPOA by testosterone. In a similar vein, Dörner et al. (1968) showed that testosterone implantation in the preoptic area elicited mounting behavior in the female rat. It is surprising that no attempts have been made to determine whether MPOA lesions suppress mounting behavior in females as they do in males. In reality, there is rather little information about the neural mechanisms regulating bisexual behavior in the female. Oboh, Paredes, and Baum (1995), however, have recently shown that mounting behavior is associated with increments in the Fos-immunoreactive neurons in the MPOA. Because Fos is a protein secreted by neurons that are active, these data suggest an involvement of the MPOA in mounting in females as well as in males.

The septum also plays a major role in the control of lordosis behavior. Nance, Shryne, and Gorski (1974, 1975) reported that lesions encompassing the lateral and ventral portions of the septal region facilitated lordosis behavior in castrated female and male rats given estrogen and progesterone. These observations suggested a septal inhibitory function in both sexes. They were confirmed by Kondo, Shinoda, Yamanouchi, and Arai (1990) in male rats and by Kondo, Koizumi, Arai, Kakeyama, and Yamanouchi (1993) in female rats. Kondo et al. (1990) showed that inputs from the lateral septum stimulate a lordosis inhibitory center located in the dorsal preoptic area (DPOA) in the male rat.

Olfactory Control of Heterotypical Behavior

Schaeffer and Aron (1981) and Schaeffer, Al Satli, Kelche, and Aron (1982) showed that the number of male rats castrated as adults and given estrogen and progesterone that displayed lordosis in response to male mounts was higher in animals exposed to urine from other male rats than in animals not exposed to urine. Subsequent experiments (Chabli et al., 1985) indicated that progesterone was necessary for the olfactory signals to exert their facilitating effects in estrogen-treated rats. The willingness to display lordosis appeared to be dependent on the accessory olfactory system (Schaeffer, Roos, & Aron, 1986). Complete destruction of the accessory olfactory bulbs in hormonally treated males significantly increased the number of rats showing lordosis. The main olfactory system also play a role. Rats made anosmic by the intranasal application of zinc sulfate showed increased lordosis quotient, although the proportion of rats showing lordosis was not increased (Chateau & Aron, 1990). As a whole, the data indicate that the accessory olfactory bulb inhibits the display of lordosis and that the olfactory cues from other males release this inhibition.

The olfactory environment also influences heterotypical behavior in the female rat. Boehm and Aron (1988, 1990) and Boehm, Lazarus, and Aron (1991) reported facilitating effects of olfactory cues emitted by estrous female urine on mounting behavior in castrated female rats given testosterone. The effect of female urine may be considered specific because urine from ovariectomized rats remained without effect. Olfactory bulb removal and intranasal zinc sulfate application sharply impaired the display of mounting behavior in testosterone-treated females. The main olfactory system may then be assumed to modulate mounting behavior by the female rat. Whether the accessory olfactory system is also involved remains an open question.

Bisexuality in the Rat: Fantasy or Reality?

It is frustrating that we do not yet have a clear understanding of the mechanisms of bisexuality in non-hormonally-manipulated rats. Perhaps this lack of information is due to the very rare occurrence of spontaneous lordosis by males of most strains of rats. Frequent display of lordosis by males in a Danish Wistar strain, as reported by Södersten et al. (1974), may be considered an exception because these authors did not observe any lordosis response in a Dutch Wistar strain. For my part, I used a W1 strain of rats, in which less than 5% of males displayed spontaneous lordosis behavior. It is worth mentioning that Thornton, Wallen, and Goy (1987) reported similar strain differences in the capacity to display lordosis responses in the guinea pig.

Must we then consider that castrated male rats primed with estrogen, with or without progesterone, represent an artificial model, one deprived of ecological and physiological significance? I do not believe so. Even if few males display spontaneous lordosis behavior, it is important to determine the mechanisms that subserve this behavior and also to ask why some males are incapable to expressing their bisexuality.

Organizational Processes

In the language of students of the processes by which male animals become different structurally and behaviorally from females, two terms have evolved: *organization* and *activation*. As mentioned earlier, hormones present during early development cause structural changes in both males and females. These differentiating effects of hormones are called organizational effects. In many species, such as rats, mice, guinea pigs, cats, and dogs, gonadal hormones must be present for these animals to mate. If the testes or ovaries are removed, mating ceases but can be restored by giving synthetic hormones. This restoration process is called activation.

Given this background, we ask, Are some males more defeminized than others during the perinatal period? On the one hand, observations from Götz and Dörner (1980) provided a support for the notion that impairment of testosterone secretion during fetal life accounts for the display of lordosis by male rats. Androgen deficiency during prenatal life was then regarded as the causal factor of the high incidence of lordosis in estrogen-treated male rats that had been exposed to prenatal stress (Dörner, Götz, & Döcke, 1983). On the other hand, Whalen et al. (1986) showed that prenatal treatment with a drug that prevented the conversion of testosterone to estrogen rendered adult Long-Evans male rats more sensitive to estrogen than Sprague-Dawley males. However, how impairment of organizational processes as such are capable of inducing heterotypical behavior in non-hormonally-treated males remains an open question.

The Nature of Hormonal Control

Because activational processes are required for the expression of sexual behavior, it might also be asked which hormonal conditions are compatible with the display of heterotypical behavior in males that spontaneously show lordosis responses to mounts by other males. In keeping with observations made in the rat (Södersten et al., 1974) and in the guinea pig (Thornton et al., 1987), we have not been able to demonstrate differences (Schaeffer, Chabli, & Aron 1990) in plasma testosterone and estradiol values among male rats that display or fail to display spontaneous lordosis behavior. The absence of lordosis responses in male rats should then result from a lack of neural sensitivity to circulating estrogens (Schaeffer, Chabli, & Aron 1990; Södersten et al., 1974).

However, the possibility cannot be ruled out that progesterone is involved in the regulation of spontaneous bisexuality. Progesterone of exogenous origin (Chabli et al., 1985) or of endogenous origin (Schaeffer, Chabli, & Aron, 1986) has been shown to be capable of potentiating the effects of estrogen in castrated male rats. Moreover, Schaeffer, Chabli, and Aron (1990) observed higher levels of plasma progesterone in male rats that display spontaneous lordosis behavior than in those that fail to do so. Nevertheless, new insights are needed because progesterone facilitatory effects on lordosis behavior in castrated males have been shown to be strictly dependent on an interaction between the hormonal and sensory signals at the level of the mediobasal hypothalamus. Samama and Aron (1989) provided evidence that progesterone increased both the number and the rate of occupancy of estradiol receptors and that olfactory signals from the male potentiated this action.

Olfaction and Hormone Action

The finding that olfactory signals enhanced estrogen-receptor binding prompted Schaeffer, Roos, and Aron (1990) to investigate the olfactory mechanisms regulating the display of lordosis behavior in non-hormonally-manipulated noncastrated rats. Male Wistar rats, that showed a very low capacity to respond with lordosis when mounted, were insensitive to an exposure to male urine or to accessory olfactory bulb removal. Unexpectedly, estrogen or estrogen and progesterone treatment did not render gonadally intact rats sensitive to the effects of accessory olfactory bulb removal by contrast with exposure to male urine, which was capable of facilitating lordosis behavior in male rats given estrogen and progesterone. These discrepancies between the results observed in castrated and noncastrated rats may be explained by the existence of structures located in the MPOA, the lateral septum, and the accessory olfactory bulb (Saito & Moltz, 1986) that facilitate mounting behavior but that inhibit lordosis behavior in the male rat. MPOA lesions (Hennessey, Wallen, & Edwards, 1986), septal lesions (Kondo et al., 1990), and accessory olfactory bulb lesions (Schaeffer, Roos, & Aron, 1986) have all been shown to facilitate lordosis behavior in estrogen- and progesterone-treated castrated male rats. One must then suppose that the inhibitory system is more efficient in noncastrated animals, which are exposed to the action of endogenous testosterone, than in castrated animals. The preoptic and septal systems quite likely remain active in accessory-olfactory-bulb lesioned, gonadally intact animals. By contrast, it may be that the olfactory signals exert their action on both the accessory olfactory bulb and other inhibitory structures. This is a possible explanation that accounts for the efficiency of these signals on the display of lordosis in noncastrated rats.

Masculine Sexual Activity and Lordosis Behavior

In all the experiments conducted with castrated or noncastrated animals, we used sexually inexperienced male rats. However, Van de Poll and Van Dis (1977) reported that sexually experienced animals were more sensitive to the feminine effects of estrogen or estrogen and progesterone than were sexually naive animals. The question can be asked whether sexual experience might influence the display of lordosis behavior in gonadally intact males deprived of hormonal support. Sexually inexperienced W1 male rats were then tested (Chabli et al., 1991) four times at 5-day intervals for lordosis with vigorous stimulus males immediately after testing masculine behavior with a highly receptive female. A small number of rats displayed lordosis during the first test, but more and more rats showed this behavior from the first to the fourth test. A second group was tested only once for both masculine and feminine behavior as above and afterward three times at 5-day intervals for lordosis behavior in the absence of any previous testing for masculine sexual activity. A few rats displayed lordosis during the first test. The rats that did not show lordosis behavior during the first test did not display lordosis in the following tests. No relationship existed between the degree of masculine activity—intromission without ejaculation or ejaculation—and the occurrence of lordosis. None of the rats that remained sexually inactive during the next tests displayed any lordosis activity when presented to stimulus males.

The above results led to the assumption that the difference between the Danish and the W1 strains certainly was not due to some inability of the males of the W1 strain to spontaneously display lordosis behavior. The results also show that successive presentation of inexperienced male rats to highly receptive females is a prerequisite for some males of the W1 strain to acquire the ability to display lordosis behavior. The main question that emerges from these observations concerns the mechanisms whereby mounting activity rendered sexually inexperienced male rats capable of displaying lordosis behavior. The possibility of a reflexlike release of luteinizing hormone from the pituitary gland and the subsequent rise in testosterone in males that displayed mounting has to be taken into consideration (Macrides, Bartke, & Dalterio, 1975). Such a rise of testosterone has been previously observed in mice (Macrides et al., 1975) and rats (Purvis & Haynes, 1974). As suggested by Södersten et al. (1974), the differences in the occurrence of lordosis by male rats could be due to differences in the capacity to transform testosterone into estrogen, and a substrate for increased conversion might be present in the hypothalamus of the sexually active males exposed to olfactory cues emitted by stimulus males.

We are far from a complete understanding of the physiological mechanisms of bisexuality in the male rat. Notwithstanding, the present results show that gonadally intact animals may constitute a useful tool for further progress in this field of research.

Relationship Between Physiology and Behavior in Humans

We can make conjectures regarding the mechanisms of human bisexuality only from what is known in the male rat because knowledge about the neuroendocrine regulation of mounting behavior in the female is presently underresearched.

Three essential questions deserve attention. Is human sexual behavior organized by virtue of mechanisms of defeminization and of masculinization, as it is in animals? Is there any reason to think that activation of central nervous structures by sex hormones is responsible for the expression of sexual behavior in humans? What is the role of genetic factors, as opposed to educational and cultural factors, in the determination of human sexual orientation?

Organizational Processes

Testis interstitial tissue develops from the 8th week of pregnancy onward in the human (Siiteri & Wilson, 1974). It produces androgens until the 21st week. A peak of secretion occurs between the 11th and the 17th week, and a decline in androgen secretion is observed from the 17th to the 21st week (Reyes, Boroditsky, Winter, & Fairman, 1974). However, Naftolin, Ryan, and Petro (1972) showed that the hypothalamic median eminence of the human fetus was capable of converting androgens into estradiol between the 10th and 21st week. Therefore, it is likely that sexual behavior organization occurs in the human the same as in the rat.

Other observations provide support to this assumption. Dörner, Schenck, Schmiedel, and Ahrens (1983) and Ellis, Ames, Peckham, and Burke (1988) have claimed that stressful events during pregnancy could result in a high incidence of gay male sexual orientation in the human as it has been previously observed in the rat. Ehrhardt et al. (1985) have reported that girls born from mothers given diethylstilbestrol during pregnancy frequently became lesbians. These data suggest that gay or lesbian sexual orientation may result from impairment of organizational processes during fetal life.

Many problems remain to be clarified, however. Swaab and Fliers (1985) have observed that the sexually dimorphic nucleus (SDN) of the hypothalamus only develops in the human preoptic area at the age of 4 years and starts to regress at 50 years of age. Swaab and Hofman (1988) reported that the cell number of the SDN increases at the same rate in boys and girls until 2 to 4 years of age, after which a sex difference occurs because of a decrease in cell number in girls. Unexpectedly, Allen, Hines, Shryne, and Gorski (1989) did not find in the human the SDN that Gorski et al. (1978) had identified in the rat. However, according to Swaab, Gooren, and Hofman (1992), Allen et al. did not establish a sex difference in the SDN because they used a biased age sample. In spite of the fact that there is no agreement on the localization of the structure involved in sexual behavior organization, one cannot rule out the possibility that activational mechanisms are involved in the expression of human sexuality.

Activational and Neuroendocrine Mechanisms

Until the 1960s (see Money, 1961, for review), the role played by hormones in sexual desire and sexual activity was far from clarified in both men and women. Presently we have no reason to think that human sexuality does not depend on hormonal control (see Aron, 1984, for review). Nevertheless, studies in male and female homosexuals did not demonstrate differences in plasma testosterone or estradiol concentrations compared with male and female heterosexuals (see Downey, Ehrhardt, Schiffman, Dyrenfurth, & Becker, 1987; Gladue, 1988; Vague & Favier, 1977, for reviews). These observations are in keeping with experimental observations in the rat. The question then has arisen of whether neuroanatomical differences in gay males and heterosexual males might be involved in the mediation of effects of hormones on the brain.

In 1988, Swaab and Hofman reported that the SDN and POA did not differ in heterosexual and gay men. This led them to find out elsewhere in the brain an eventual dimorphism in gay males. They observed such a dimorphism in the hypothalamic suprachiasmatic nucleus (SCN). The size of the SCN and its content in vasopressin cells appeared to be increased in gay men (see Swaab et al., 1992, for review). Later, LeVay (1991) reported that one of the interstitial nuclei of the anterior hypothalamus (INAH), named INAH3, was less developed in gay than in heterosexual men and that its size was comparable to that observed in heterosexual women. Finally, Allen and Gorski (1992) established that the anterior commissure was more developed in gay men than in either heterosexual men or women.

The main criticism about these neuroanatomical observations consists in the absence of any experimental evidence in the rat as in the human that the dimorphic structures just described are involved in the control of sexuality. There is no information in the rat about the physiological significance of the INAH3. What is the significance of the increase in the number of SCN vasopressin cells in gay men? The SCN is involved in the rhythm of male copulatory activity in the rat (Södersten, Hansen & Srebo, 1981). But this does not mean that it plays any major role in the determinism of sexual behavior. Obviously we know nothing about the physiological significance of the dimorphism of the anterior commisure in gay men.

Problems of Data Interpretation

It may be asked why the neuroanatomical studies concerning the control of gay sexual orientation have been focused on the anterior hypothalamic–preoptic region of the brain. The VMN is known to govern the display of lordosis behavior in the male rat. Indeed, the POA is also involved in this control, but in an inhibitory manner. Although MPOA stimulates mounting behavior, it inhibits lordosis behavior in the male rat. Similarly, the DPOA exerts inhibitory effects on the display of lordosis in the male. From a strictly physiological point of view, one might have expected the MPOA to be underdeveloped in gay men with a feminine gender role behavior. Is the lack of development of the INAH3 responsible for the release of the inhibitory function exerted by the DPOA in the male rat? Yet, we have no experimental reason to assign the role of the DPOA to the INAH3. Rather, one should take into consideration the possibility that the VMN might play a role in the control of sexual behavior in gay men with feminine gender identity. The main question that may then be addressed is whether common physiological mechanisms underlie the expression of sexuality in virile and gay nonvirile men. This problem remains a matter of speculation.

Genetic Evidence

In animals, there is only indirect evidence for a genetic control of bisexuality. There are obvious strain differences in the display of lordosis by intact rat and guinea pig males. Within a strain, the males may also differ in their ability to display hormone-induced lordosis behavior.

    In humans, the display of gay or lesbian sexual orientation appears to be more concordant in monozygotic twins (52%) than in dizygotic twins (22%) or adoptive brothers (11%) raised in a same parental environment (Bailey & Pillard, 1991). Whitam, Diamond, and Martin (1993) confirmed these observations, noting concordant sexual orientation in 65% of monozygotic twins versus 35% in dizygotic twins. Of course, genetic factors are involved in the determination of sexual orientation. However, the absence of concordance noted in a noticeable number of monozygotic twins indicates that other factors are implicated. Note that monozygotic twins did not show any concordance when raised in different familial environments.

    Hamer, Hu, Magnuson, Hu, and Pattatuci's (1993) observations also suggest the existence of genetic determination of sexual orientation in humans. In a genetic analysis of 40 pairs of gay brothers, genetic markers on the X chromosome were typed for each pair of brothers. For markers at the Xq28, 33 pairs inherited the same alleles from their mother, whereas 7 pairs of brothers were discordant for their maternal alleles. It then remains to explain these genetic discordances. Indeed Hu et al. (1995) replicated their data on a second sample of gay brothers. Nevertheless, it is not likely that a single gene is responsible for the determinism of gay sexual orientation. Hypothetical genes would have to be cloned and their sites of expression determined in either the hypothalamic or the limbic system to specify the mechanisms involved in the genetic control of sexual orientation.

Conclusion

Since the 1920s, the animal model has been a useful and essential tool for the study of reproduction. However, until new techniques that are ethically acceptable are discovered, physiologists must recognize their ignorance about brain activation by hormones in humans. In contrast, there is evidence in favor of analogy between the hormonal mechanisms governing sexual behaviors in animals and in humans. For example, testosterone has been shown to activate sexual receptivity in the female rat during the diestrous period of estrous cycle (Aron & Asch, 1963). In women, a peak of testosterone coincides with a peak of sexual arousal at midcycle (Persky, Lief, Strauss, Miller, & O'Brien, 1978). In healthy men (Stoleru, Ennaji, Cournot, & Spira, 1993) as in male rats and mice, sexual arousal may induce a surge of both luteinizing hormone and testosterone (Macrides et al., 1975; Purvis & Haynes, 1974). These data suggest an involvement in humans of the brain structures that mediate the effects of hormones on sexual behavior in rats.

The situation is different when gay men are compared with sexually heterotypical rats. Those male rats that display spontaneous lordosis behavior vigorously mount congeners of the same sex. On the contrary, both masculine and feminine gender identities in human males are compatible with male–male sexual behavior. A counterpart statement applies to lesbianism. Consequently, we are far from an understanding of the physiological events that subserve homosexuality in the human. Recently, Zhou, Hofman, Gooren, and Swaab (1995) observed that in male-to-female transsexuals, the central section of the bed nucleus of the stria terminalis was less developed than in heterosexual participants. Perhaps we can expect that further studies will provide reliable information concerning the hypothalamic and the limbic structures that may be involved in the physiological regulation of sexual orientation in both humans and animals.

In any case, we must not consider a rodent to be a reliable model for psychological studies of bisexuality. It is likely that sexuality in animals is under more rigid hormonal control than in humans. There is strong evidence that the influence of sensory environment on sexual orientation is strictly dependent on the hormonal state of a male rat. By contrast, in humans, sexual orientation is mainly subordinated to the influence of educational and social environment. No one may disregard the important role of parental influence in the determination of gender and sexual identity in both sexes. Explanations based on simple physiological cause–effect mechanisms do not account for the complexity of human sexuality in both sexes. Indeed, the weight of cultural influences may be the determining factor. However, we have no reason, in the absence of any other evidence, to underestimate the biological background of human sexuality.

References

Allen, L. S., & Gorski, R. A. (1992). Sexual orientation and the size of the anterior commissure in the human brain. *Proceeding of the National Academy of Sciences, USA, 89,* 7199–7202.

Allen, L. S., Hines, M., Shryne, J., & Gorski, R. A. (1989). Two sexually dimorphic cell groups in the human brain. *Journal of Neuroscience, 9,* 497–506.

Aren-Engelbrektsson, B., Larsson, K., Södersten, P., & Wilhelmsson, M. (1970). The female lordosis pattern induced in male rats by estrogen. *Hormones and Behavior, 1,* 181–188.

Aron, C. (1984). La neurobiologie du comportment sexuel des mammifères [Neurobiology of sexual behavior in mammals]. In J. Delacour (Ed.), *Neurobiologie des comportements* (pp. 57–108). Paris: Hermann.

Aron, C. (1996). La Bisexualité et l'ordre de la nature [Bisexuality and the order of nature]. Paris: Odile Jacob.

Aron, C., & Asch, G. (1963). Action exercée par la testostérone, au cours même du cycle oestral, sur le comportement sexuel et sur l'activité ovarienne de la ratte [Effects of testosterone during estrous cycle on sexual behavior and ovarian activity in the female rat]. *Comptes Rendus de la Société de Biologie, 157,* 645–648.

Bailey, J. M., & Pillard, R. C. (1991). A genetic study of male sexual orientation. *Archives of General Psychiatry, 48,* 1089–1096.

Baum, M. J., Woutersen, P. J. A., & Slob, A. K. (1991). Sex difference in whole-body androgen contents in rats on fetal days 18 and 19 without evidence that androgen passes from males to females. *Biology of Reproduction, 44,* 747–751.

Beach, F. A. (1968). Factors involved in the control of mounting behavior in female mammals. In M. Diamond (Ed.), *Perspectives in reproduction and sexual behavior* (pp. 83–131). Bloomington: Indiana University Press.

Boehm, N., & Aron, C. (1988). Facilitatory effects of olfactory cues emitted by estrous females on mounting behavior in the female rat. *Physiology and Behavior, 43,* 669–671.

Boehm, N., & Aron, C. (1990). Inhibitory effects of centrally and peripherally induced anosmia on mounting behavior in the female rat. *Physiology and Behavior, 48,* 367–370.

Boehm, N., Lazarus, C., & Aron, C. (1991). Interactions of testosterone with the olfactory system in the display of mounting behavior in the female rat. *Physiology and Behavior, 50,* 1001–1006.

Carrer, H., Asch, G., & Aron, C. (1973). New facts concerning the role played by the ventromedial nucleus in the control of estrous cycle duration and sexual receptivity in the rat. *Neuroendocrinology, 13,* 129–139.

Chabli, A., Schaeffer, C., & Aron, C. (1989). Lordosis inhibiting effects of the endogenous progesterone in the male rat primed with estrogen. *Physiology and Behavior, 45,* 1007–1010.

Chabli, A., Schaeffer, C., & Aron, C. (1991). Bisexual behavior in the male rat: Influence of masculine sexual activity on the display of lordosis behavior. *Hormones and Behavior, 25,* 560–571.

Chabli, A., Schaeffer, C., Samama, B., & Aron, C. (1985). Hormonal control of the perception of the olfactory signals which facilitate lordosis behavior in the male rat. *Physiology and Behavior, 35,* 729–734.

Chateau, D., & Aron, C. (1988). Heterotypic sexual behavior in male rats after lesions in different amygdaloid nuclei. *Hormones and Behavior, 22,* 379–388.

Chateau, D., & Aron, C. (1989). Lordosis behavior in male rats after lesions in different regions of the corticomedial amygdaloid nucleus. *Hormones and Behavior, 23,* 448–455.

Chateau, D., & Aron, C. (1990). Peripheral anosmia and display of lordosis behavior in the male rat. *Behavioural Processes, 22,* 33–40.

Chateau, D., Chabli, A., & Aron, C. (1987). Effects of ventromedial nucleus lesions on the display of lordosis behavior in the male rat: Interactions with facilitory effects of male urine. *Physiology and Behavior, 39,* 341–345.

Clemens, L. G., & Gladue, B. A. (1978). Feminine sexual behavior in rats enhanced by prenatal inhibition of androgen aromatization. *Hormones and Behavior, 11,* 190–201.

Corbier, P., Kerdelhue, B., Picon, R., & Roffi, J. (1978). Changes in testicular weight and serum gonadotrophin and testosterone levels before, during and after birth in the perinatal rat. *Endocrinology, 103,* 1985–1991.

Csernus, V. (1986). Production of sexual steroids in rats during pre- and early postnatal life. *Experimental and Clinical Endocrinology, 88,* 1–5.

Davidson, J. M. (1969). Effects of estrogen on the sexual behavior of male rats. *Endocrinology, 84,* 228–233.

Davidson, J. M., & Levine, S. (1969). Progesterone and heterotypic sexual behavior in male rats. *Journal of Endocrinology, 44,* 129–130.

Davis, P. G., & Barfield, R. J. (1979). Activation of feminine behavior in castrated male rats by intrahypothalamic implants of estradiol benzoate. *Neuroendocrinology, 28,* 228–233.

Dörner, G., Döcke, F., & Moustafa, S. (1968). Differential localization of a male and female hypothalamic mating center. *Journal of Reproduction and Fertility*, *17*, 583–586.

Dörner, G., Götz, F., & Döcke, F. (1983). Prevention of demasculinization and feminization of the brain in prenatally stressed male rats by perinatal androgen treatment. *Experimental and Clinical Endocrinology*, *81*, 88–90.

Dörner, G., Schenck, B., Schmiedel, B., & Ahrens, L. (1983). Stressful events in prenatal life of bi- and homosexual men. *Experimental and Clinical Endocrinology*, *81*, 83–87.

Downey, J., Ehrhardt, A. A., Schiffman, M., Dyrenfurth, I., & Becker, J. (1987). Sex hormones in lesbian and heterosexual women. *Hormones and Behavior*, *21*, 347–357.

Ehrhardt, A. A., Meyer-Bahlburg, H. F. L., Rosen, L. R., Feldman, J. F., Veridiano, Z. P., Zimmerman, I., & McEwen, B. (1985). Sexual orientation after prenatal exposure to exogenous estrogen. *Archives of Sexual Behavior*, *14*, 57–77.

Ellis, L., Ames, A., Peckham, W., & Burke, D. (1988). Sexual orientation of human offspring may be altered by severe maternal stress during pregnancy. *Journal of Sex Research*, *25*, 152–157.

George, F. W., & Ojeda, S. R. (1982). Changes in the aromatase activity in the rat brain during embryonic neonatal and infantile development. *Endocrinology*, *111*, 522–529.

Gladue, B. A. (1988). Hormones in relationship to homosexual/bisexual/heterosexual gender orientation. In J. M. A. Sitsen (Ed.), *Handbook of sexology: Vol. 6. The pharmacology and endocrinology of sexual function* (pp. 388–409). Amsterdam: Elsevier.

Gladue, B. A., & Clemens, L. G. (1980). Masculinization diminished by disruption of prenatal estrogen biosynthesis in male rats. *Physiology and Behavior*, *25*, 589–593.

Gogan, F., Slama, A., Bizzini-Koutznetzova, B., Dray, F., & Kordon, C. (1981). Importance of perinatal testosterone in sexual differentiation in the male rat. *Journal of Endocrinology*, *91*, 75–79.

Gorski, R. A., Gordon, J. H., Shryne, J. E., & Southam, A. M. (1978). Evidence for a morphological sex difference within the medial preoptic area of the rat brain. *Brain Research*, *148*, 333–346.

Götz, F., & Dörner, G. (1980). Homosexual behavior in prenatally stressed male rats after castration and estrogen treatment in adulthood. *Endocrinology*, *76*, 115–117.

Goy, R. W., & Roy, M. (1991). Heterotypical sexual behavior in female mammals. In M. Haug, P. Brain, & C. Aron (Eds.), *Heterotypical behavior in man and animals* (pp. 71–97). London: Chapman & Hall.

Hamer, D. H., Hu, S., Magnuson, V. L., Hu, N., & Pattatuci, A. M. L. (1993, July). A linkage between DNA markers on the X-chromosome and male sexual orientation. *Science*, *261*, 321–327.

Hamilton, G. V. (1914). A study of sexual tendencies in monkeys and baboons. *Animal Behaviour*, *4*, 295–318.

Hammond, J., & Marshall, F. H. (1925). *Reproduction in the rabbit*. London: Olivier & Boyd.

Heimer, L., & Larsson, K. (1966–1967). Impairment of mating behavior in male rats following lesions in the preoptic–anterior hypothalamic continuum. *Brain Research*, *3*, 248–263.

Hennessey, A. C., Wallen, K., & Edwards, D. A. (1986). Preoptic lesions increase the display of lordosis behavior by male rats. *Brain Research*, *370*, 21–28.

Hu, S., Pattatucci, A. M. L., Patterson, C., Li, L., Fulker, D. W., Cherny, S. S., Kruglyak, L., & Hamer, D. H. (1995). Linkage between sexual orientation and chromosome Xq28 in males but not in females. *Nature Genetics*, *11*, 248–256.

Kennedy, G. C. (1964). Hypothalamic control of the endocrine and behavioural changes associated with oestrus in the rat. *Journal of Physiology*, *172*, 383–392.

Kennedy, G. C., & Mitra, J. (1963). Hypothalamic control of energy balance and the reproductive cycle in the rat. *Journal of Physiology*, *166*, 395–407.

Kondo, Y., Koizumi, T., Arai, Y., Kakeyama, M., & Yamanouchi, K. (1993). Functional relationships between mesencephalic central gray and septum in regulating lordosis in female rats: Effects of central lesions. *Brain Research Bulletin*, *36*, 635–638.

Kondo, Y., Shinoda, A., Yamanouchi, K., & Arai, Y. (1990). Role of septum and preoptic area in regulating masculine and feminine behavior in male rats. *Hormones and Behavior*, *24*, 421–434.

Krafft-Ebing, R. V. (1931). *Psychopathia sexualis* [Sexual psychopathy] (16th & 17th eds.; R. Lobstein, Trans.). Paris: Payot.

LeVay, S. (1991, August 30). A difference in hypothalamic structure between heterosexual and homosexual men. *Science, 253,* 1034–1037.

Macrides, F., Bartke, A., & Dalterio, S. (1975). Strange female increases plasma testosterone levels in male mice. *Science, 189,* 1104–1106.

Masco, D. H., & Carrer, H. F. (1980). Sexual receptivity in female rats after lesion or stimulation in different amygdaloid nuclei. *Physiology and Behavior, 24,* 1073–1080.

McEwen, B. S. (1988). Genomic regulation of sexual behavior. *Journal of Steroid Biochemistry, 30,* 179–183.

McKenzie, E. F. (1926). The normal oestrous cycle in the sow. *Missouri University Experimental Station Research Bulletin, 86,* 1–48.

Money, J. (1961). Sex hormones and other variables in human erotism. In W. C. Young & G. W. Corner (Eds.), *Sex and internal secretions* (Vol. 2, pp. 1383–1400). Baltimore: Williams & Wilkins.

Moreines, J., McEwen, B., & Pfaff, D. (1986). Sex differences in response to discrete estradiol injections. *Hormones and Behavior, 20,* 445–451.

Naftolin, F., Ryan, K. J., & Petro, Z. (1972). Aromatization of androstenedione by anterior hypothalamus of adult male and female rats. *Endocrinology, 90,* 295–298.

Nance, D. M., Shryne, J., & Gorski, R. A. (1974). Septal lesions: Effects on lordosis behavior and pattern of gonadotrophin release. *Hormones and Behavior, 5,* 73–81.

Nance, D. M., Shryne, J., & Gorski, R. A. (1975). Facilitation of female sexual behavior in male rats by septal lesions: An interaction with estrogen. *Hormones and Behavior, 6,* 289–299.

Oboh, A. M., Paredes, R. G., & Baum, M. J. (1995). A sex comparison of increments in Fos immunoreactivity in forebrain neurons of gonadectomized, testosterone-treated rats after mounting an estrous female. *Neurobiology of Learning and Memory, 63,* 66–73.

Olster, D. H., & Blaustein, J. D. (1988). Progesterone facilitation of lordosis in male and female Sprague-Dawley rats following priming with estradiol pulses. *Hormones and Behavior, 22,* 294–304.

Pearl, R., & Surface, F. M. (1915). On the assumption of male secondary sex characters by a cow with cystic degeneration of the ovaries. *Maine Agricultural Experimental Station Bulletin, 237,* 65–80.

Persky, H., Lief, H. I., Strauss, D., Miller, W. R., & O'Brien, C. P. (1978). Plasma testosterone level and sexual behavior of couples. *Archives of Sexual Behavior, 7,* 157–173.

Purvis, K., & Haynes, J. A. (1974). Short term effects of copulation, human chorionic injection and non-tactile association with a female on testosterone levels in the male rat. *Journal of Endocrinology, 60,* 429–439.

Resko, J. A., Feder, H. H., & Goy, R. W. (1968). Androgen concentration in plasma and testis of developing rats. *Journal of Endocrinology, 40,* 485–491.

Reyes, F. I., Boroditsky, R. S., Winter, J. S. D., & Fairman, C. (1974). Studies on human sexual development: II. Fetal and maternal serum gonadotropin and sex steroid concentration. *Journal of Clinical Endocrinology and Metabolism, 38,* 612–617.

Roffi, J., Chami, F., Corbier, P., & Edwards, D. A. (1987). Testicular hormones during the first few hours after birth and the tendency of adult male rats to mount receptive females. *Physiology and Behavior, 39,* 625–628.

Saito, T. R., & Moltz, H. (1986). Copulatory behavior of sexually naive and sexually experienced male rats following removal of the vomeronasal organ. *Physiology and Behavior, 37,* 507–510.

Samama, B., & Aron, C. (1989). Changes in estrogen receptors in the mediobasal hypothalamus mediate the facilitatory effects exerted by the male's olfactory cues and progesterone on the feminine behavior in the male rat. *Journal of Steroid Biochemistry, 32,* 525–529.

Schaeffer, C., & Aron, C. (1981). Studies on feminine sexual behavior in the male rat: Influence of olfactory stimuli. *Hormones and Behavior, 15,* 377–385.

Schaeffer, C., Al Satli, M., Kelche, C., & Aron, C. (1982). Olfactory environment and lordosis behavior in the female and male rat. In W. Breipohl (Ed.), *Olfaction and endocrine regulation* (pp. 115–126). London: IRL Press.

Schaeffer, C., Chabli, A., & Aron, C. (1986). Endogenous progesterone and lordosis behavior in male rats given estrogen alone. *Journal of Steroid Biochemistry*, 25, 99–102.

Schaeffer, C., Chabli, A., & Aron, C. (1990). Lordosis behavior in gonadally intact male rats: Correlation with blood progesterone concentration but not with blood testosterone and 17β-estradiol values. *Biology of Behavior*, 15, 53–61.

Schaeffer, C., Roos, J., & Aron, C. (1986). Accessory olfactory bulb lesions and lordosis behavior in the male rat feminized with ovarian hormones. *Hormones and Behavior*, 20, 118–127.

Schaeffer, C., Roos, J., & Aron, C. (1990). Lordosis behavior in intact male rats: Effects of hormonal treatment and/or manipulation of the olfactory system. *Hormones and Behavior*, 24, 50–61.

Siiteri, P. K., & Wilson, J. D. (1974). Testosterone formation and metabolism during male sexual differentiation in the human embryo. *Journal of Clinical Endocrinology and Metabolism*, 38, 113–125.

Södersten, P. (1976). Lordosis behavior in male, female and androgenized female rats. *Journal of Endocrinology*, 70, 409–420.

Södersten, P., De Jong, F. H., Vreeburg, J. T. M., & Baum, M. J. (1974). Lordosis behavior in intact male rats: Absence of correlation with mounting behavior or testicular secretion of estradiol-17β and testosterone. *Physiology and Behavior*, 13, 803–808.

Södersten, P., Hansen, S., & Srebo, B. (1981). Suprachiasmatic lesions disrupt the daily rhythmicity on the sexual behavior of normal male rats and of male rats treated neonatally with antiestrogens. *Journal of Endocrinology*, 88, 125–130.

Södersten, P., & Larsson, K. (1974). Lordosis behavior in castrated male rats treated with estradiol benzoate or testosterone propionate in combination with an estrogen antagonist MER-25, and in intact male rats. *Hormones and Behavior*, 5, 13–18.

Soulairac, A., & Soulairac, M. L. (1956). Effets de lésions hypothalamiques sur le comportement sexuel et le tractus génital du rat [Effects of hypothalamic lesions on sexual behavior and genital tract in the rat]. *Annales d'Endocrinologie*, 17, 731–745.

Stoleru, S. G., Ennaji, A., Cournot, A., & Spira, A. (1993). LH pulsatile secretion and testosterone blood levels are influenced by sexual arousal in human males. *Psychoneuroendocrinology*, 18, 205–215.

Stone, C. P. (1924). A note on "feminine" behavior in adult male rats. *American Journal of Physiology*, 68, 39–41.

Swaab, D. F., & Fliers, E. (1985, May). A sexually dimorphic nucleus in the human brain. *Science*, 228, 1112–1115.

Swaab, D. F., Gooren, L. J. G., & Hofman, M. A. (1992). The human hypothalamus in relation to gender and sexual orientation. In D. F. Swaab, M. A. Hofman, M. Mirmiran, R. Ravid, & F. W. Van Leeuven (Eds.), *Progress in Brain Research: Vol. 93. The human hypothalamus in health and disease* (205–219). Amsterdam: Elsevier Science.

Swaab, D. F., & Hofman, M. A. (1988). Sexual differentiation of the human hypothalamus: Ontogeny of the sexually dimorphic nucleus of the preoptic area. *Developmental Brain Research*, 44, 314–318.

Thornton, J., Wallen, K., & Goy, R. W. (1987). Lordosis behavior in males of two inbred strains of guinea pig. *Physiology and Behavior*, 40, 703–709.

Vague, J., & Favier, G. (1977). Hormones sexuelles et homosexualité [Sexual hormones and homosexuality]. In *Hormones et sexualité: Problèmes actuels en endocrinologie et nutrition* (Vol. 21, pp. 197–217). Paris: Expansion Scientifique Française.

Van de Poll, N. E., & Van Dis, H. (1977). Hormone induced lordosis and its relation to masculine sexual activity in male rats. *Hormones and Behavior*, 8, 1–7.

Van Dis, H., & Larsson, K. (1970). Seminal discharge following intracranial electrical stimulation. *Brain Research*, 23, 381–386.

Vom Saal, F. S., & Bronson, F. H. (1978). In utero proximity of female mouse fetuses to males: Effect on reproductive performance during later life. *Biology of Reproduction*, 19, 842–853.

Weisz, J., Brown, B. L., & Ward, I. L. (1982). Maternal stress decreases steroid aromatase activity in brains of male and female rat fetuses. *Neuroendocrinology*, 35, 374–379.

Weisz, J., & Ward, I. L. (1980). Plasma testosterone and progesterone titers in pregnant rats, their male and female fetuses and neonatal offspring. *Endocrinology, 109,* 306–316.

Whalen, R. E., & Edwards, D. A. (1967). Hormonal determinants of the development of masculine and feminine behavior in male and female rats. *Anatomical Record, 157,* 173–180.

Whalen, R. E., Gladue, B. A., & Olsen, K. L. (1986). Lordotic behavior in male rats: Genetic and hormonal regulation of sexual differentiation. *Hormones and Behavior, 20,* 73–82.

Whalen, R. E., & Olsen, K. L. (1981). Role of aromatization in sexual differentiation: Effects of prenatal ATD treatment and neonatal castration. *Hormones and Behavior, 15,* 107–122.

Whitam, F. L., Diamond, M., & Martin, J. (1993). Homosexual orientation in twins: A report on 61 pairs and 3 triplet sets. *Archives of Sexual Behavior, 22,* 187–206.

Zhou, J. N., Hofman, M. A., Gooren, L. J. G., & Swaab, D. F. (1995). A sex difference in the human brain and its relation to transsexuality. *Nature, 378,* 68–70.

Zinik, G. (1985). Identity conflict or adaptative flexibility? Bisexuality reconsidered. *Journal of Homosexuality, 1,* 7–19.

12

Self-Recognition in Nonhuman Primates: Past and Future Challenges

James R. Anderson and Gordon G. Gallup, Jr.

In the present chapter, we give an overview of the known facts regarding self-recognition in primates, addressing the issue of how some nonhuman and most human primates come to understand that a reflection, televised image, or photograph can be a representation of themselves. We present what appears to us to be the most parsimonious explanation of the data and then go on to examine some of the challenges that have arisen in the context of emerging theory regarding the uneven phylogenetic distribution of the capacity for self-recognition. The challenges have taken various forms: new data, methodological objections, and particular philosophical stances. It will be seen that with some refinements, the hypothesis advanced by Gallup (1970, 1982) regarding the phylogenetic distribution of the capacity for self-recognition in primates has proved to be robust. Self-recognition research in nonhuman primates has given rise to new concepts and methods in the comparative and developmental study of self-awareness. Indeed, in terms of methodology, it can be argued that work with nonhuman primates has been superior to comparable work with human infants and toddlers.

Chimpanzees and the Revelation of Self-Recognition

Although the original article on self-recognition in chimpanzees (Gallup, 1970) is widely cited, some of the criticisms that have been leveled against it and its implications stem from an inadequate appreciation of the procedures described therein. For this reason, we review the different phases of that experiment. In Phase 1, four individually housed chimpanzees were each presented with a large mirror outside their cage. The mirror remained in place for 10 days, during which time behavioral sampling focused on looking toward the mirror, social responses directed toward it, and mirror-mediated, self-directed responses. At the end of phase 1, the mirror was removed, and the chimpanzee was anesthetized and painted with a bright, odorless mark on one eyebrow ridge and the opposite ear.

Phase 2 started after the chimpanzee had fully recovered from the anesthetic: In the absence of the mirror, the chimpanzee was observed, and any spontaneous investigation of the marks on its head were recorded. Only after this control period did Phase 3 start: The mirror was reintroduced, and observations again focused on mirror-influenced behaviors, including touches directed toward the marks.

The main results were as follows: During Phase 1, on initial exposure to the mirror, chimpanzees typically reacted with interest (looking toward the mirror) and apparently social responses (e.g., vocalizations and threats). With increasing exposure to the reflection, however, these two categories of response steadily declined while a new type of behavior emerged, namely, using the reflection to visually and tactually inspect otherwise invisible parts of the body, such as inside the mouth or behind the ears. During Phase 2 (chimpanzee marked and mirror removed), very low frequencies of spontaneous mark-directed responses were recorded. During Phase 3 (chimpanzee marked and mirror reintroduced), there was a resumption of interest in the mirror accompanied by a striking increase in the number of mark-directed responses. Further, the chimpanzees not only used the mirror to guide their hands toward the marks on their head but also looked or sniffed at their fingers after touching the marks. Thus, the two-part mark test provided objective, confirmatory evidence for what was suggested by the chimpanzees' earlier spontaneous bouts of self-exploration in front of the mirror, namely, the ability to correctly identify the source of image in the mirror, that is, self-recognition.

When Phase 1 of the same procedure was carried out with individuals of two Old World monkey species, rhesus and stumptailed macaques, the early pattern of results was broadly similar to that obtained with the chimpanzees: strong but declining visual interest associated with frequent bouts of social responding, as if the reflection was perceived as an unfamiliar conspecific. In contrast to the chimpanzees, however, none of the monkeys showed any instances of mirror-mediated inspection of normally unseen body parts. During Phase 2 (subject marked, mirror absent) low frequencies of mark-directed touching in the absence of the mirror were recorded, but again unlike the chimpanzees, in Phase 3, the monkeys continued to behave as if they were unaware of the marks on their own head in the renewed presence of the mirror. They did show a resumption of interest in the reflection during Phase 3, but this was accompanied by an increase in social responses, not self-directed ones, as if the marked head of the animal in the mirror increased the social salience of the situation. Thus, whereas chimpanzees had shown evidence of self-recognition, monkeys failed to show any signs that they self-recognized. Gallup (1970) advanced the hypothesis that the capacity for self-recognition might be restricted to humans and the great apes.

Self-Recognition in Primates: Extensions and Exclusions

Several subsequent studies have confirmed the capacity for self-recognition in chimpanzees and have increased our understanding of the phenomenon by presenting evidence that self-recognition depends on adequate social experience (Gallup, McClure, Hill, & Bundy, 1971); the development of self-recognition in infant chimpanzees is broadly similar to that seen in infant humans, although the earliest signs of self-recognition may occur later (Lin, Bard, & Anderson, 1992; Povinelli, Rulf, Landau, & Bierschwale, 1993); some chimpanzees show a rapid onset of mirror-mediated self-directed behaviors (i.e., after less than 1 hr of exposure, Povinelli et al., 1993); the ability to self-recognize is maintained over test–retest intervals of at least 1 year (Calhoun & Thompson, 1988); self-recognizing chimpanzees show rapid adaptation to distorting mirrors (Kitchen, Denton, & Brent, 1996); not all apparently normal chimpanzees show evidence of self-recognition in a mirror (Swartz & Evans, 1991); prime and postprime adult chimpanzees appear less likely to show self-recognition than adolescents and young adults (Povinelli et al., 1993).

In accordance with Gallup's (1970) hypothesis that self-recognition would be found in other members of the great ape family, the occurrence of spontaneous, mirror-mediated self-exploration in orangutans followed by mark-test verification was reported by Lethmate and Dücker (1973) and Suarez and Gallup (1981). A longitudinal study of an enculturated (i.e., human-reared and sign-language trained) orangutan documented progressive changes in reactions to the reflection and the first of several positive responses on the mark test at 25 months of age (Miles, 1994). Recently, evidence has been presented for mirror self-recognition in bonobos (sometimes called *pygmy chimpanzees*). Westergaard and Hyatt (1994; see also Hyatt and Hopkins, 1994) described mirror use to aid inspection of otherwise invisible body parts in 4 bonobos of a group of 9, and Walraven, van Elsacker, and Verheyen (1995) reported similar behaviors in 4 bonobos of a group of 7 tested over a 10-day period. So far, there are no published results of formal mark tests carried out with this species.

Among the great apes, the gorilla has given the most inconsistent picture regarding self-recognition. Whereas some attempts to demonstrate self-recognition have failed to produce any positive evidence (Ledbetter & Basen, 1982; Suarez & Gallup, 1981; Swartz & Evans, 1994), some researchers have reported convincing evidence in other gorillas. For example, Patterson and Cohn (1994) reported that an enculturated gorilla started to show mirror-mediated self-directed behavior after the age of 3 years and that the same individual passed a variant of the mark test at 19 years, that is, touching the target area of her forehead an average of once per control session (forehead wiped with a clean, damp cloth) compared with 47 times during the experimental session (forehead wiped with makeup). Swartz and Evans (1994) alluded to a positive mark test in another human-reared, non-language-trained gorilla. Law and Lock (1994) reported live video-mediated self-inspection in 1 gorilla, whereas Parker (1994) described some less controlled instances of zoo-housed gorillas looking at their reflection and wiping marks off their faces, as well as several other forms of contingency testing suggestive of self-recognition. However, Eddy, Gallup, and Povinelli (1996) have shown that contingent facial and body movements alone in front of a mirror are not adequate indicators of self-recognition. Theoretical and methodological aspects of the enigmatic gorilla self-recognition literature are further discussed elsewhere (Gallup, 1997; Mitchell, 1993; Povinelli, 1994; Swartz & Evans, 1994).

In contrast to the great apes, in which at least some individuals of all four species have shown clear mirror self-recognition, all other nonhuman primates tested for their reactions to mirrors have failed to show any convincing signs that they self-recognize. This is despite numerous original approaches involving explicit manipulations to facilitate the emergence of self-recognition, if the basic capacity is indeed present. Anderson (1984b) and Gallup (1987) have described early failed attempts to produce evidence of mirror self-recognition in monkeys. The most significant of these studies are summarized in Exhibit 12.1, which also includes more recent efforts.

Monkeys and the "Monkey in the Mirror"

An impressive arsenal of innovative techniques has been used by researchers in the quest to demonstrate self-recognition in monkeys, but so far they all have failed to provide acceptable evidence. Instead, reports of monkeys' reactions toward mirrors usually emphasize the social character of the behaviors that are displayed. Such reactions are typically instantaneous and of variable intensity and persistence depending on individual and species characteristics (see Anderson, 1984b; Gallup, 1968, 1975). Persistence is well documented: Although mirror-elicited social responses typically wane with prolonged exposure (e.g., Anderson & Bayart, 1985; Gallup, 1970, 1977), the robustness of the reflection-as-conspecific effect is evident from resumptions of mirror-directed social displaying during the mark test (Anderson, 1983b; Bayart & Anderson, 1985; Gallup, 1970, 1977) and in response to a temporal or locational change in mirror presence (Gallup & Suarez, 1991; Suarez & Gallup, 1986b). Evidence for reliable species differences in social responsiveness toward reflections is less systematic but includes the finding that less visually capable species such as prosimians show relatively weak and short-lived social responses to their reflection (Fornasieri, Roeder, & Anderson, 1991) and a report of marked differences between individual members of a dozen species of primates in response to a single 30-min mirror exposure (Inoue-Nakamura, 1997). Several authors have reported individual differences in the mirror-image reactions of monkeys and have suggested links with factors such as age, sex, dominance, and early rearing history (Anderson, 1983a, 1983b; Collinge, 1989; Gallup & McClure, 1971; Gallup, Wallnau, & Suarez, 1980; Hall, 1962; Riviello, Visalberghi, & Blasetti, 1992). It has been suggested that group-housed macaques respond to their image as if it were a conspecific of equal status (Neel, 1996), but more systematic data are required.

Monkeys have excellent individual-recognition abilities, and they are highly sensitive to slight changes in the behavior of conspecifics (Anderson, 1998; Cheney & Seyfarth, 1990). Therefore it is not surprising that

Exhibit 12.1. Failed Attempts to Facilitate Mirror Self-Recognition in Monkeys

Manipulation	Justification	References
Early mirror exposure (from birth or shortly thereafter)	Capitalize on early learning abilities	Gallup, Wallnau, and Suarez (1980) Anderson (1983b)
Extended mirror exposure	Maximize familiarity with the reflection	Gallup (1977) Anderson (1983b) Platt and Thompson (1985)
Sequential marking	Increase awareness of marks, progressing to critical target area	Anderson (1984b) R. L. Thompson and Boatwright-Horowitz (1994)
Physical access to mirror	Maximize visual access and allow tactile exploration	Anderson (1983b) Eglash and Snowdon (1983) Platt and Thompson (1985)
Multiple fixed mirrors	Create array of reflections	Anderson (1983b)
Portable mirrors	Increase manipulation of and control over reflections	Anderson and Roeder (1989)
Paired or group exposure	Make use of social recognition abilities	Gallup et al. (1980) Anderson (1983a) Eglash and Snowdon (1983) Platt and Thompson (1985) Anderson and Roeder (1989) Riviello, Visalberghi, and Blasetti (1992)
Modeling and shaping	Train response sequences necessary for mark-directed responding	Benhar, Carlton, and Samuel (1975) Anderson (1984b) Mitchell and Anderson (1993) R. L. Thompson and Boatwright-Horowitz (1994)
Reinforcement of mirror-mediated responding	Enhance awareness of mirror–environment correspondence	Anderson (1986) Itakura (1987) Marchal and Anderson (1993)
Increase mark saliency	Increase attentiveness to critical marks	Benhar, Carlton, and Samuel (1975) Gallup, Wallnau, and Suarez (1980) Suarez and Gallup (1981) Anderson (1983a) Hauser, Kralik, Botto-Mahan, Garrett, and Oser (1995)
Angled mirrors	Avoid aversive eye contact with reflection	Anderson and Roeder (1989)

Exhibit 12.2.   Social Phenomena Elicited by Mirror-Image Simulation in Monkeys

Effect	Description	References
Overt social responses	Threats, appeasement gestures, sexual displays, play, and so on	Gallup (1968, 1975) Anderson (1984b, 1994)
Spontaneous recovery of social responses after mirror removal–relocation	Temporary resumption in social responding to the reflection	Suarez and Gallup (1986b) Gallup and Suarez (1991)
Visual reinforcement	Performance of operant responses for mirror-image stimulation	Gallup (1966) Benhar, Carlton, and Samuel (1975)
Attenuation of isolation syndrome by mirror rearing	Reduced tendency to display abnormal behaviors	Anderson and Chamove (1986)
Attenuation of separation-induced agitation	Reduced locomotion and vocalization scores	Anderson (1983a)
Social facilitation	Increased drinking in presence of mirror	Anderson and Bayart (1985) Straumann and Anderson (1991)

their reactions in the unusual social situation presented by a mirror are not identical to those displayed to a live conspecific (see Anderson, 1983a, 1983b; cf. R. L. Thompson & Boatwright-Horowitz, 1994). Some sort of social response on initial exposure to a mirror appears to be more or less universal in visually capable primates, which, along with a variety of other mirror-induced social phenomena (see Exhibit 12.2), reinforces the conclusion that overall, the monkey in the mirror is perceived as a "strange conspecific" (Anderson, 1994).

The Hypothesis of a Qualitative Cognitive Difference

Since the original finding of self-recognition in chimpanzees and failure to find it in macaques (Gallup, 1970), converging lines of evidence have served to shape and reinforce the hypothesis (Gallup, 1982, 1985; Povinelli, 1993; see also Anderson, 1996) that there may be a fundamental difference in cognition between those hominoid primates (humans and the great apes) that have the capacity for self-recognition and those primates that do not (prosimians and monkeys). The reasoning is as follows: The ability to correctly interpret the source of the reflection as oneself—to become the object of one's own attention—requires a cognitive category of "self" (Gallup, 1975, 1977, 1982). Great apes and humans show evidence of this capacity when they recognize themselves in a mirror, a televised image, or a photograph. The repeated failure of monkeys to do likewise (although systematic data are restricted to mirror studies) can be attributed to a lack of the requisite cognitive category of "self."

Challenges

The picture outlined above, of a restricted phylogenetic distribution of self-recognition and its implications for the evolution of cognition, has not gone unchallenged. Indeed, over the years, each new attempt to find self-recognition in monkeys (see Exhibit 12.1) has constituted a challenge, bringing new methodological approaches or innovative techniques to bear on the issue. Some researchers have proposed alternatives to the phylogenetic discontinuity hypothesis of self-recognition, on the basis of empirical or conceptual grounds. The view has even been expressed that mirror-mediated self-recognition is unimportant as far as self-concept is concerned. The most significant of these challenges are reviewed and evaluated below.

Self-Recognition as a Simple Learned Response

Epstein, Lanza, and Skinner (1981) suggested that self-recognition in chimpanzees (and humans) could be explained entirely on the basis of reinforcement and set out to train pigeons to peck at a dot on their bodies that could only be seen in a mirror. The ultimate aim was to replace the cognitive explanation of self-recognition with one based on reinforcement contingencies. Using operant conditioning procedures, Epstein et al. trained 3 pigeons to peck at blue dots placed on their bodies and to turn around to peck at dots that appeared briefly on one of two walls of the experimental chamber, which were ostensibly first detected in the mirror in the front wall. Once an acceptable approximation to this response was obtained, the experimenters fitted each pigeon with a collar, to prevent a direct view of its chest, although it could see the reflected chest in the mirror. It was reported that the pigeons made head movements and pecked in the direction of a blue dot stuck onto the chest only when the mirror was present. Epstein et al. equated the pigeons' performance with that of chimpanzees passing the mark test and argued against the need for self-concept as a causal mechanism.

There are numerous problems with this attempted operant-conditioning-based simulation and explanation of self-recognition. First, from an empirical perspective, Epstein et al.'s (1981) description of the birds' behavior does not make it clear whether the birds in fact pecked toward the dot or if they were merely searching in space in response to the presence of a discriminative cue, that is, the mirror (Gallup, 1984); it is also possible that head bobbing and pecking while facing the mirror might reflect extinction-induced aggression toward the reflection rather than use of the mirror for self-inspection (Gallup, 1982; Gallup & Suarez, 1986). R. K. R. Thompson and Contie (1994) described two failures to replicate the findings reported by Epstein et al., including a particularly painstaking reconstruction of the experimental setup specified by those authors. Despite the careful step-by-step conditioning procedure, none of the 6 pigeons tested in the second attempt showed any body dot-directed responses when wearing the collar, either in the presence or the absence of the mirror. Further experiments revealed that some but not all of the pigeons appeared to have learned something about the contingency between reflected dots on the walls of the experimental chamber and their true locations, but R. K. R. Thompson and Contie emphasized that they found no evidence for mirror-mediated self-directed behaviors of the type reported by Epstein et al. (1981), and they concluded that pigeons lack the necessary perceptual skills for self-recognition.

Other flaws in Epstein et al.'s (1981) attempt to explain self-recognition in terms of reinforcement contingencies were pointed out by Gallup (1982, 1987) and by Davis (1989). The original attempt to train pigeons to peck at dots on their bodies in the presence of a mirror was misguided because it amounted to trying to teach the birds to perform the criterion response. The elaborate series of experimental procedures required to obtain the reported approximation to mirror-mediated dot inspection was in stark contrast to the spontaneous emergence of mirror-mediated self-inspection observed in chimpanzees. The two types of behavior, were the pigeon version shown to be reliable, were surely based on different psychological mechanisms.

Self-Recognition as Gradated Phenomenon

Some authors view self-recognition as a sort of continuum along which (presumably) all organisms can be placed and that although monkeys might not be capable of mirror-mediated mark-directed behavior in the mark test, they do show precursors or earlier stages of self-recognition. This position, which appears to originate from (a) a Piagetian stage-theory approach to the development of self-recognition in human infants (Bertenthal & Fischer, 1978) and (b) a commitment to evolutionary continuity, was taken by Eglash and Snowdon (1983) and by Boccia (1994). In their study of mirror-image responses in pygmy marmosets, a tiny South American callitrichid, Eglash and Snowdon (1983) hung a mirror or a board in the home cage (the animals were housed in pairs) and recorded a variety of social and exploratory behaviors. They did not administer a mark test because they considered it inappropriate owing to a lack of self-grooming in this species. On the basis of their observations of diminishing social responses to the mirror, some "look–hide–look" sequences, and marmosets looking at their own image while moving, Eglash and Snowdon implied that pygmy marmosets self-recognized.

Such a conclusion is clearly unwarranted. Habituation to mirror images is widespread among animals, quite likely reflecting the fact that the

strange conspecific (Anderson, 1994) is becoming less unfamiliar or threatening with time. Furthermore, as pointed out by Gallup (1987), because
observation sessions were limited to 20 min each day, the continued occurrence of "one to two" mirror-directed threats each day by the pygmy
marmosets in fact represents a persistent tendency to treat the reflection
as a conspecific. The look-and-hide sequences, also anthropomorphically
called "playing peekaboo" by Eglash and Snowdon (1983), are uninform-
ative with regard to the marmosets' understanding of the mirror image.
Human children usually play peekaboo with other children, not with their
own image, so, in fact, if this is indeed what the marmosets were doing
(and there is no evidence that they were in fact playing), this observation
would suggest that the reflection is perceived as a social stimulus rather
than as a reflection of the marmoset itself (Gallup, 1987). It is even conceivable that the marmosets were responding to the reflection of the
cagemate; the lack of detail in the original report precludes confirmation
or rejection of this possibility.

A final flaw in Eglash and Snowdon's (1983) conclusion comes from
their interpretation of the marmosets' visually following their own movements while looking in the mirror. The authors equate this behavior with
"reality testing" reported in human infants. They correctly point out that
self-recognition involves the viewer understanding that the source of mim-
icked movements in the mirror is itself, but it clearly does not follow that
repeating one's movements while looking at the mirror signifies self-
recognition. Instead, the marmosets may well have been merely experimenting with the unusual contingencies afforded by the mirror, without
any recognition whatsoever of the identity of the reflected image.

Boccia (1994) adopted the most explicit stage approach to mirror self-
recognition in nonhuman primates in her study of subadult and adult female pigtail macaques' responses to mirrors. Although group-reared in the
presence of mirrors, the monkeys were tested individually in a chamber
with a mirror covering one wall. Subjects were said to pass a test designed
to assess a specific stage of self-recognition if they simply touched the
mirror (mirror task); looked into the mirror and then up toward a light-
weight ball, which was fixed to a rod, which was itself attached to a vest
worn by the subject, so that the ball was above the subject's head (the ball
was attached to the rod while the subject was anesthetized; hat task); or
turned around to look at a toy that dropped from the ceiling but was first
seen in the mirror (toy task). No reliability data were presented, but according to Table 23.2 in Boccia (1994), 14, 13, and 12 monkeys out of 14
passed the mirror, hat, and toy tasks, respectively, and these data are used
to argue for a "gradual or developmental emergence [of] this capacity" (i.e.,
self-recognition; p. 358).

We do not agree with Boccia's (1994) gradual emergence view of self-
recognition. That self-recognition is the product of developmental processes involving an interaction of maturational and experiential factors is
not disputed (Anderson, 1984a; Gallup, 1979; Lewis & Brooks-Gunn,
1979), but it is not clear how touching the surface of a mirror on one wall
of an otherwise featureless test chamber can tell us about at what stage

of self-recognition an individual might be. The finding that monkeys will turn to look at and even attempt to reach for an object first seen in a mirror, that is, that they learn to understand mirror space, was established in the literature before Boccia's study (Anderson, 1986; Brown, McDowell, & Robinson, 1965). As also pointed out by earlier authors, this response must be ruled out as evidence for self-recognition because the performance could result from simple contingency learning. Describing such behaviors as requiring "coordination of own [reaching/body] movements with mirror image" (Boccia, 1994, p. 352) does not help to establish whether the viewing individual has any understanding that the reflection is a representation of its own body, and the vague notion of precursors of self-recognition, or proposing that monkeys show "incipient" self-recognition (Boccia, 1994, p. 358) or "protorecognition" is not particularly helpful for furthering the understanding of how these primates perceive their reflection. Although some may eschew an all-or-none approach to the question of self-recognition, in a final anaysis, we must decide whether an organism is capable of it.

Motivational Factors

A recent challenge to the many published failures to find self-recognition in monkeys accuses early attempts of not paying sufficient attention to whether the monkeys either see the critical mark or are motivated enough to attempt to remove it once it has been detected with the mirror (Hauser, Kralik, Botto-Mahan, Garrett, & Oser, 1995). This accusation is unfounded (Anderson & Gallup, 1997). As long ago as 1975, Benhar, Carlton, and Samuel set out to increase the salience of the reflection for a baboon by dyeing the subject's hair blonde and then by shaving its head. The baboon reacted intensely on seeing the reflection, but only with a mixture of social responses and flight, not with any self-directed behavior. In an explicit effort to ensure that monkeys would pay attention to novel marks on their bodies, Gallup et al. (1980) introduced the use of directly visible marks, whereby the subject was marked not only on the head but also on a part of the body that could easily be seen without a mirror (e.g., the abdomen or a wrist). Using this procedure, it has been possible to rule out motivational factors as an explanation for failures to pass the mark-test criterion for self-recogniton, because subjects typically do show interest in the visible marks (Boccia, 1994; Gallup et al., 1980; Suarez & Gallup, 1981). This point may be especially relevant with regard to failures to find self-recognition in gorillas. After habituation to the reflection, in the basic version of the mark test, gorillas may show little or no increase in looking at the reflection (Ledbetter & Basen, 1982; Suarez & Gallup, 1981; Swartz & Evans, 1994), which contrasts with the mark-test increase in mirror-directed looking typically reported in monkeys, even though these primates do not self-recognize. Thus, attentional or motivational factors might have been a valid criticism of some of the failures to find self-recognition in gorillas, but positive responding to directly visible marks by gorillas weakens this argument (Gallup, 1987; Suarez & Gallup, 1981).

Another way of focusing the subject's attention on marks on the body is the sequentrking procedure described by Anderson (1984b). New marks were added to a juvenile stump-tailed macaque's body each day, without anesthesia. The subject typically attempted to remove all directly visible marks but made no attempt to touch the only mark that was visible only in the mirror, on the head. A similar procedure was attempted in vain by R. L. Thompson and Boatwright-Horowitz (1994). One more way of increasing salience of the critical mark was introduced by Anderson (1983b). For several days before the mark test, subjects (stump-tailed macaques) were wiped on the head with a damp cloth just before being placed into the test cage containing the mirror. In this way, they were allowed to get used to seeing no mark on the head of the mirror image after the wiping procedure. On the test day, however, the subjects were wiped again, but this time they were marked with a cloth impregnated with dye. The macaques showed an immediate increase in interest and social behaviors directed to the mirror image during the mark test but no signs of self-recognition. Variants of this procedure have been used by other researchers (Patterson & Cohn, 1994; Swartz & Evans, 1994). Most monkeys and apes have good visual abilities, and they are highly responsive to marks and other unusual changes that they see on their own or on other individuals' bodies. Thus, in direct contrast to Hauser et al.'s (1995) assertion, the literature contains no shortage of self-recognition studies that have taken appropriate steps to invalidate potential criticisms based on attentional or motivational factors.

Does the Mark Test Have Inherent Flaws?

Heyes (1994) has suggested that increased mark-directed responding by great apes during mark tests might reflect a general increase in face-touching behavior because of the longer recovery period since anesthesia, which allows marking of the subject without its knowing, compared with the control period, which usually starts after the subject is awake but before the mirror phase. Heyes further has suggested that species differences in mark-directed responding may be accounted for by corresponding differences in the probability of spontaneous touches directed toward the face and head region.

These criticisms can be refuted on several grounds (Gallup et al., 1995). First, Povinelli et al. (1997; see also Gallup et al., 1995) have presented data to show that increased touching of the head in a self-recognizing chimpanzee is specific to the marked regions; it is not generalized head touching, as Heyes (1994) implies. Also, there is ample evidence for mirror self-recognition in great apes from studies that do not involve anesthetizing the subjects (Calhoun & Thompson, 1988; Lin et al., 1992; Miles, 1994; Patterson & Cohn, 1994; Swartz & Evans, 1994). Second, the original self-recognition experiment by Gallup (1970) included several chimpanzees that had no prior experience of mirrors. Unlike mirror-experienced chimpanzees, mirror-naive chimpanzees that were also anesthetized and marked showed no mirror-mediated mark-directed responses, so a simple recovery-from-anesthesia explanation again appears untenable. Also, mark-responding chimpanzees usually display a cluster of such responses when the mirror is reintroduced, before rapidly losing interest in it, which is in contrast to the monotonic increase that would be expected from Heyes's suggestion of a progressive recovery from anesthesia. Finally, there is little evidence to support Heyes's suggestion that monkeys touch their heads or faces less frequently than chimpanzees; in fact, the contrary has been shown (Suarez & Gallup, 1986a). Thus, rather than containing inherent flaws, the mark test when well conducted represents a powerful technique for verifying whether an individual self-recognizes.

Mirrors and Aversive Eye Contact

In many species of monkeys, staring at another individual may signify aggression. It has been suggested (Gallup et al., 1980; Hauser et al., 1995; Premack, 1983) that gaze aversion could be a confounding factor in mirror studies with monkeys. For example, the monkeys could become so focused on the aggression-related qualities of the reflection that they are unable to make the transition from social responding to self-recognition, or they may avoid making eye contact with the image and as a result never receive sufficient experience with the image to learn that their behavior is the source of the behavior depicted in the mirror. However, this seems an unlikely explanation for monkeys' failure to self-recognize. Many monkeys stare at their own reflection while displaying affiliative or playful facial expressions, or else while calm and showing no particular facial expression, especially after prolonged exposure. R. L. Thompson and Boatwright-Horowitz (1994) have been able to increase the duration of eye-directed looks in a mirror by making access to water contingent on the behavior in two water-deprived pigtail macaques. One other study has explicitly addressed the issue of gaze aversion by presenting the monkeys with angled mirrors—that is, two mirrors positioned in such a way that the viewing monkey is unable to engage the reflection in eye contact; it sees itself only side-on (Anderson & Roeder, 1989). The capuchin monkeys in this study showed fewer mirror-directed social responses in the angled-mirrors condition than in the more usual face-on condition, but even this reduction in the social salience of the reflection failed to lead to any signs of self-recognition. In summary, the "aggressive stare-out" hypothesis of monkeys' failure to arrive at mirror self-recognition can be rejected.

Positive Mark Tests in Monkeys?

Three studies claim to have found evidence for self-recognition in monkeys based on a positive mark test. Because these claims contradict the vast majority of efforts that have failed to find evidence of self-recognition and therefore imply inadequacies in previous attempts, they require scrutiny.

R. L. Thompson and Boatwright-Horowitz (1994) have reported that after recovery from anesthesia, their two individually tested pigtail macaques were videotaped in a control (no-mirror) condition for at least 10 min before the mirror was reintroduced for 1 hr. Their champion monkey first glanced toward the mirror after 10 min, then turned away. Six minutes later, she looked at the mirror again, displayed a jaw-thrust facial expression toward it, touched her marked brow with the knuckles and the back of the left hand, looked at her hand, then jaw thrusted again and turned away. The entire sequence lasted 3–4 s. No other mark-directed responses occurred. What happened during the remaining major part of the test is not described. In their evaluation, R. L. Thompson and Boatwright-Horowitz stated that the "response topography was there" (p. 345) and that this single episode consituted "a positive mark test" (p. 343). However, by the authors' own admission, attempted replications were "ambiguous at best" (p. 345) and "disappointing" (p. 345). There are other problems with this account. Although it is stated that no mark-directed responses occurred during the control condition, unfortunately, no information is presented regarding the subject's head touching in general. If the monkey also touched other parts of its head, even infrequently, the brief sequence described may well be of no particular importance. Further, the extreme brevity of the behavior contrasts with the focused attempts to inspect and remove the mark typical of great apes who show self-recognition, yet like other macaques, pigtails are assiduous when it comes to self- and social grooming (Rosenblum, Kaufman, & Stynes, 1966).

Another positive mark test was claimed for another female pigtail macaque (the only 1 of 15 tested) by Boccia (1994). After recovery from anesthesia, each monkey received a 30-min mirror-present period, preceded by a 30-min control period with no mirror. The monkey in question "looked in the mirror, swiped her hand across her face in the vicinity of the mark, and then looked at her hand" (p. 354). It is stated that this behavior occurred four times, but from the descriptions given in Table 23.3, there was considerable variability in what was accepted as a positive response. The monkey was marked on the left brow and right ear, but the swipes were made to the brow, the bridge of the nose, the side of the face, and the bridge of the nose. Three of these behaviors were followed by the monkey licking and grooming (once) the hand and once by her looking at her hand. It is also important to note that when these ostensible mark-directed behaviors occurred, the monkey was not monitoring its own reflection in the mirror, nor was it even oriented toward the mirror (see Gallup, 1994). No attempt at replication appears to have been made, there is no information regarding the monkey's general tendency to lick or groom its hand, and there is no mention of responses to the mark on the subject's wrist, which could be related to the hand-directed responses described. The author acknowledges the differences between chimpanzees' careful monitoring of the reflection while investigating the marks and the crude swipes she observed in her study and proposes "incipient recognition" or "proto-recognition" instead of "full self-recognition" (p. 358). However, it is unclear how our understanding of self-recognition in primates is advanced by the introduction of such terms.

Ostensibly the strongest claim for mirror-mediated mark-directed responding has been made by Hauser et al. (1995), who tested cotton-top tamarins. These authors erroneously concluded that previous attempts to find self-recognition in monkeys had neglected mark salience in the mark test (see above and Anderson & Gallup, 1997), so they dyed the crest of white hair on the tamarins' heads a different color. A total of 13 mark-directed responses were reported in 5 tamarins. Unfortunately, Hauser et al. give no information on interobserver reliability for these responses, their incidence during a control period in the absence of the mirror, responses to other parts of the tamarins' bodies that were washed as a precaution, intrasubject reliability of the mark-directed responses (because testing stopped when any mark-directed response was noted), or the actual form of the responses. Ironically, although Hauser et al.'s article contains the strongest claim for self-recognition in monkeys, it is conceptually and methodologically the weakest and presents no convincing data or arguments for self-recognition in the subjects studied (see Anderson & Gallup, 1997, for a fuller critique).

Beyond the Mark Test

It is interesting that the three most explicit claims for self-recognition by monkeys have been based on (unconvincing) responses on the mark test. However, Gallup (e.g., 1982, 1987) has repeatedly pointed out that the mark test of self-recognition is best seen as an objective means of verifying self-recognition, which is already evident in great apes' spontaneous use of the mirror to inspect parts of their body that cannot otherwise be seen. Instances of mirror-mediated self-inspection of this type are usually prolonged and clearly goal oriented, such as when a chimpanzee carefully picks at its teeth while monitoring the reflection. No similar behaviors have been observed in monkeys. Hauser et al. (1995) have described two acts by cotton-top tamarins that they suggest belong to this category of behavior. One involves a female rolling sideways and looking at her back in the mirror, and the other involves a female looking through her legs with her head upside down and then looking directly at her rear and tail. But similar behaviors occur in nonmirror contexts in tamarins, for example, during play. Further, it cannot be concluded that these brief acts are mirror mediated just because they occur in a close temporal relation to looking at the mirror, which may be the most salient visual stimulus in the monkeys' otherwise relatively barren environment.

Recently, it has been suggested that monkeys' ability to use spatially displaced visual feedback about their own movements to control a cursor by means of a joystick might provide an alternative approach to self-recognition, or at least its precursors (Heyes, 1994; Vauclair, 1996). Jorgensen, Suomi, and Hopkins (1995) compared capuchin monkeys, chimpanzees, and humans on the ability to bring a cursor into contact with a target on a screen and on their understanding of which of two cursors they controlled with the joystick. On an easier version of the task in which the decoy (i.e., computer-controlled) cursor behaved relatively simply, there were broad similarities in the three species' performances. However, when the decoy cursor was programmed to become increasingly more efficient at catching up with the target, the capuchin monkeys' performance deteriorated considerably more than that of the other two species, suggesting greater difficulty in differentiating cursor movements initiated by the subject and those initiated by the computer. Although it is clear that some form of kinesthetic–visual matching with the mirror image is necessary for the development of self-recognition (Mitchell, 1993) and that the joystick paradigm involves some form of contingency learning, it is not clear how the joystick paradigm can provide an adequate alternative for answering the question of whether an individual recognizes itself. Indeed, the joystick task used by Jorgensen et al. (1995) provides evidence for an underdeveloped sense of self as agent in capuchin monkeys compared with chimpanzees and humans.

Self-Recognition Is Not Self-Awareness

A final challenge to comparative self-recognition research seeks to diminish the value of the entire endeavor, by equating mirror self-recognition with the simple ability to avoid colliding into objects (Heyes, 1994) or by appealing to the fact that human self-awareness extends beyond physical self–nonself differentiation to encompass a wide range of psychological dimensions such as emotion, ambition, imagination, and the concept of mortality (Heyes, 1994). Both criticisms are invalid. First, the necessity for distinguishing between a sensory self, necessary for navigation in the environment and for avoiding injury, and a representational self, which makes self-recognition possible, is widely recognized (Gallup, 1985; Lewis, 1994; Mitchell, 1993; Neisser, 1988). Chimpanzees and monkeys both perceive their own reflections, but their responses to them are quite different. Thus, to conclude that for self-recognition to emerge, "all that the animal needs to know about itself is that its body is distinct from the rest of the world" (p. 915), as does Heyes (1994), is to miss the point.

It is true that human self-awareness is a multifaceted concept (Mitchell, 1993, 1994) and that chimpanzees or any other nonhuman primates are unlikely to possess exactly the same kinds of self-awareness as humans. No one has said that they do. But in contrast to Heyes (1994), it does not follow that self-recognition is not explainable in terms of self-concept. The study of self-concept in nonhuman primates is in its infancy, and it is quite possible that mirror studies will contribute to this domain in novel ways. For example, social psychologists have shown that mirror-induced objective self-awareness in humans (Duval & Wicklund, 1972) can affect a number of psychological processes—including performance on psychomotor tasks, use of personal pronouns, self-evaluative and self-presentative responses—all effects that are explained in terms of the self-concept. We do not yet know whether mirrors can induce similar effects in great apes, but given what is already known about self-recognition and social cognitive abilities in these primates, it is clearly premature to claim before the evidence is in that mirror self-recognition in great apes is not related to self-concept (Anderson, 1993).

Conclusion

Nonhuman primates have provided a fruitful model for theories and testable hypotheses about the ontogenetic and phylogenetic development of the concept of self. The finding that the capacity for visual self-recognition may be limited to humans and members of the great ape species has allowed the construction of a framework in which the comparative study of social cognition can be systematically approached (Gallup, 1982, 1985). Two major implications of this theory—that some aspects of mind can be operationalized and studied objectively and that self-concept and mind may be shared only by humans and some nonhuman primates—are resulting in increased efforts to understand how these phenomena come about and how they can be best conceptualized and investigated. The way forward will surely involve increased experimental rigor and reliable empirical findings; there will be little room for weakly supported assertions and criticisms based on faith rather than good data.

References

Anderson, J. R. (1983a). Mirror-image stimulation and short separations in stumptail monkeys. *Animal Learning & Behavior, 11,* 138–143.

Anderson, J. R. (1983b). Responses to mirror image stimulation and assessment of self-recognition in mirror- and peer-reared stumptail macaques. *Quarterly Journal of Experimental Psychology, 35B,* 201–212.

Anderson, J. R. (1984a). The development of self-recognition: A review. *Developmental Psychobiology, 17,* 35–49.

Anderson, J. R. (1984b). Monkeys with mirrors: Some questions for primate psychology. *International Journal of Primatology, 5,* 81–98.

Anderson, J. R. (1986). Mirror-mediated finding of hidden food by monkeys (*Macaca tonkeana* and *M. fascicularis*). *Journal of Comparative Psychology, 100,* 237–242.

Anderson, J. R. (1993). To see ourselves as others see us: A response to Mitchell. *New Ideas in Psychology, 11,* 339–346.

Anderson, J. R. (1994). The monkey in the mirror: A strange conspecific. In S. T. Parker, R. W. Mitchell, & M. L. Boccia (Eds.), *Self-awareness in animals and humans: Developmental perspectives* (pp. 315–329). New York: Cambridge University Press.

Anderson, J. R. (1996). Chimpanzees and capuchin monkeys: Comparative cognition. In A. E. Russon, K. A. Bard, & S. T. Parker (Eds.), *Reaching into thought: The minds of the great apes* (pp. 23–56). Cambridge, England: Cambridge University Press.

Anderson, J. R. (1998). Social stimuli and social rewards in primate learning and cognition. *Behavioural Processes, 42,* 159–175.

Anderson, J. R., & Bayart, F. (1985). Les effets du miroir sur le comportement de macaques: Habituation, évitement et facilitation sociale [The effects of a mirror on the behavior of macaques: Habituation, avoidance, and social facilitation]. *Biology of Behaviour, 10,* 159–167.

Anderson, J. R., & Chamove, A. S. (1986). Infant stumptailed macaques reared with mirrors or peers: Social responsiveness, attachment, and adjustment. *Primates, 27*, 63–82.

Anderson, J. R., & Gallup, G. G., Jr. (1997). Self-recognition in *Saguinus*? A critical essay. *Animal Behaviour, 54*, 1563–1567.

Anderson, J. R., & Roeder, J.-J. (1989). Responses of capuchin monkeys (*Cebus apella*) to different conditions of mirror-image stimulation. *Primates, 30*, 581–587.

Bayart, F., & Anderson, J. R. (1985). Mirror-image reactions in a tool-using, adult male *Macaca tonkeana. Behavioural Processes, 10,* 219–227.

Benhar, E. E., Carlton, P. L., & Samuel, D. (1975). A search for mirror-image reinforcement and self-recognition in the baboon. In S. Kondo, M. Kawai, & A. Ehard (Eds.), *Contemporary primatology* (pp. 202–208). Tokyo: Japan Science Press.

Bertenthal, B. I., & Fischer, K. W. (1978). Development of self-recognition in the infant. *Developmental Psychology, 14*, 44–50.

Boccia, M. L. (1994). Mirror behavior in macaques. In S. T. Parker, R. W. Mitchell, & M. L. Boccia (Eds.), *Self-awareness in animals and humans: Developmental perspectives* (pp. 350–360). New York: Cambridge University Press.

Brown, W. L., McDowell, A. A., & Robinson, E. M. (1965). Discrimination learning of mirrored cues by rhesus monkeys. *Journal of Genetic Psychology, 106*, 123–128.

Calhoun, S., & Thompson, R. L. (1988). Long-term retention of self-recognition by chimpanzees. *American Journal of Primatology, 15*, 361–365.

Cheney, D. L., & Seyfarth, R. M. (1990). *How monkeys see the world*. Chicago: University of Chicago Press.

Collinge, N. E. (1989). Mirror reactions in a zoo colony of *Cebus* monkeys. *Zoo Biology, 8*, 89–98.

Davis, L. H. (1989). Self-consciousness in chimps and pigeons. *Philosophical Psychology, 2*, 249–259.

Duval, S., & Wicklund, R. A. (1972). *A theory of objective self-awareness*. New York: Academic Press.

Eddy, T. J., Gallup, G. G., Jr., & Povinelli, D. J. (1996). Age differences in the ability of chimpanzees to distinguish mirror-images of self from video images of others. *Journal of Comparative Psychology, 110*, 38–44.

Eglash, A. R., & Snowdon, C. T. (1983). Mirror-image responses in pygmy marmosets (*Cebuella pygmaea*). *American Journal of Primatology, 5*, 211–219.

Epstein, R., Lanza, R. P., & Skinner, B. F. (1981). "Self-awareness" in the pigeon. *Science, 212*, 695–696.

Fornasieri, I., Roeder, J.-J., & Anderson, J. R. (1991). Les réactions au miroir chez trois espèces de lémuriens (*Lemur fulvus, L. macaco, L. catta*) [Reactions to a mirror in three species of lemurs (*Lemur fulvus, L. macaco, L. catta*)]. *Comptes Rendus de l'Académie de Sciences de Paris, 312*, 349–354.

Gallup, G. G., Jr. (1966). Mirror-image reinforcement in monkeys. *Psychonomic Science, 5*, 39–40.

Gallup, G. G., Jr. (1968). Mirror-image stimulation. *Psychological Bulletin, 70*, 782–793.

Gallup, G. G., Jr. (1970). Chimpanzees: Self-recognition. *Science, 167*, 86–87.

Gallup, G. G., Jr. (1975). Towards an operational definition of self-awareness. In R. H. Tuttle (Ed.), *Socioecology and psychology of primates* (pp. 309–341). The Hague, The Netherlands: Mouton.

Gallup, G. G., Jr. (1977). Absence of self-recognition in a monkey (*Macaca fascicularis*) following prolonged exposure to a mirror. *Developmental Psychobiology, 10*, 281–284.

Gallup, G. G., Jr. (1979). Self-recognition in chimpanzees and man: A developmental and comparative perspective. In M. Lewis & L. A. Rosenblum (Eds.), *The child and its family* (pp. 107–126). New York: Plenum.

Gallup, G. G., Jr. (1982). Self-awareness and the emergence of mind in primates. *American Journal of Primatology, 2*, 237–248.

Gallup, G. G., Jr. (1984). Will reinforcement subsume cognition? *Contemporary Psychology, 29*, 593–594.

Gallup, G. G., Jr. (1985). Do minds exist in species other than our own? *Neuroscience and Biobehavioral Reviews, 9*, 631–641.

Gallup, G. G., Jr. (1987). Self-awareness. In G. Mitchell & J. Erwin (Eds.), *Comparative primate biology: Vol. 2B. Behavior, cognition, and motivation* (pp. 3–16). New York: Alan R. Liss.

Gallup, G. G., Jr. (1994). Self-recognition: Research strategies and experimental design. In S. T. Parker, R. W. Mitchell, & M. L. Boccia (Eds.), *Self-awareness in animals and humans: Developmental perspectives* (pp. 35–50). New York: Cambridge University Press.

Gallup, G. G., Jr. (1997). On the rise and fall of self-conception in primates. In G. Snodgrass & R. Thompson (Eds.), *Annals of the New York Academy of Sciences: Vol. 818. The self across psychology: Self-recognition, self-awareness, and the self-concept* (pp. 73–82). New York Academy of Sciences.

Gallup, G. G., Jr., & McClure, M. K. (1971). Preference for mirror-image stimulation in differentially reared rhesus monkeys. *Journal of Comparative and Physiological Psychology, 75,* 403–407.

Gallup, G. G., Jr., McClure, M. K., Hill, S. D., & Bundy, R. A. (1971). Capacity for self-recogntion in differentially reared chimpanzees. *Psychological Record, 21,* 69–74.

Gallup, G. G., Jr., Povinelli, D. J., Suarez, S. D., Anderson, J. R., Lethmate, J., & Menzel, E. W., Jr. (1995). Further reflections on self-recognition in primates. *Animal Behaviour, 50,* 1525–1532.

Gallup, G. G., Jr., & Suarez, S. D. (1986). Self-awareness and the emergence of mind in humans and other primates. In J. Suls & A. G. Greenwald (Eds.), *Psychological perspectives on the self* (pp. 3–26). Hillsdale, NJ: Erlbaum.

Gallup, G. G., Jr., & Suarez, S. D. (1991). Social responding to mirrors in rhesus monkeys (*Macaca mulatta*): Effects of temporary mirror removal. *Journal of Comparative Psychology, 105,* 376–379.

Gallup, G. G., Jr., Wallnau, L. B., & Suarez, S. D. (1980). Failure to find self-recognition in mother–infant and infant–infant rhesus monkey pairs. *Folia Primatologica, 33,* 210–219.

Hall, K. R. L. (1962). Behaviour of monkeys towards mirror images. *Nature, 196,* 1258–1261.

Hauser, M. D., Kralik, J., Botto-Mahan, C., Garrett, M., & Oser, J. (1995). Self-recognition in primates: Phylogeny and the salience of species-typical features. *Proceedings of the National Academy of Sciences, USA, 92,* 10811–10814.

Heyes, C. M. (1994). Reflections on self-recognition in primates. *Animal Behaviour, 47,* 909–919.

Hyatt, C. W., & Hopkins, W. D. (1994). Self-awareness in bonobos and chimpanzees: A comparative approach. In S. T. Parker, R. W. Mitchell, & M. L. Boccia (Eds.), *Self-awareness in animals and humans: Developmental perspectives* (pp. 248–253). New York: Cambridge University Press.

Inoue-Nakamura, N. (1997). Mirror self-recognition in primates: A phylogenetic approach. *Japanese Psychological Research, 39,* 266–275.

Itakura, S. (1987). Mirror-guided behavior in Japanese monkeys (*Macaca fuscata fuscata*). *Primates, 28,* 149–161.

Jorgensen, M. J., Suomi, S. J., & Hopkins, W. D. (1995). Using a computerized testing system to investigate the preconceptual self in nonhuman primates. In P. Rochat (Ed.), *The self in infancy: Theory and research* (pp. 243–256). Amsterdam: Elsevier.

Kitchen, A., Denton, D., & Brent, L. (1996). Self-recognition and abstraction abilities in the common chimpanzee studied with distorting mirrors. *Proceedings of the National Academy of Sciences, USA, 93,* 7405–7408.

Law, L. E., & Lock, A. J. (1994). Do gorillas recognize themselves on television? In S. T. Parker, R. W. Mitchell, & M. L. Boccia (Eds.), *Self-awareness in animals and humans: Developmental perspectives* (pp. 308–312). New York: Cambridge University Press.

Ledbetter, D. H., & Basen, J. (1982). Failure to demonstrate self-recognition in gorillas. *American Journal of Primatology, 2,* 307–310.

Lethmate, J., & Dücker, G. (1973). Untersuchungen zum Selbsterkennen im Spiegel bei Orang-utans und einigen anderen Affenarten [Experiments on self-recognition in a mirror in orangutans, chimpanzees, gibbons and several monkey species]. *Zeitschrift für Tierpsychologie, 33,* 248–269.

Lewis, M. (1994). Myself and me. In S. T. Parker, R. W. Mitchell, & M. L. Boccia (Eds.), *Self-awareness in animals and humans: Developmental perspectives* (pp. 20–34). New York: Cambridge University Press.

Lewis, M., & Brooks-Gunn, J. (1979). *Social cognition and the acquisition of self.* New York: Plenum.

Lin, A. C., Bard, K. A., & Anderson, J. R. (1992). Development of self-recognition in chimpanzees (*Pan troglodytes*). *Journal of Comparative Psychology, 106,* 120–127.

Marchal, P., & Anderson, J. R. (1993). Mirror-image responses in capuchin monkeys (*Cebus capucinus*): Social responses and use of reflected environmental information. *Folia Primatologica, 61,* 165–173.

Miles, H. L. W. (1994). Me Chantek: The development of self-awareness in a signing orangutan. In S. T. Parker, R. W. Mitchell, & M. L. Boccia (Eds.), *Self-awareness in animals and humans: Developmental perspectives* (pp. 254–272). New York: Cambridge University Press.

Mitchell, R. W. (1993). Mental models of mirror-self-recognition: Two theories. *New Ideas in Psychology, 11,* 295–325.

Mitchell, R. W. (1994). Multiplicities of self. In S. T. Parker, R. W. Mitchell, & M. L. Boccia (Eds.), *Self-awareness in animals and humans: Developmental perspectives* (pp. 81–107). New York: Cambridge University Press.

Mitchell, R. W., & Anderson, J. R. (1993). Discriminative learning of scratching, but failure to obtain imitation and self-recognition in a long-tailed macaque. *Primates, 34,* 301–309.

Neel, M.-A. (1996). Mirrors, monkeys, and group dynamics. *Primates, 37,* 411–421.

Neisser, U. (1988). Five kinds of self-knowledge. *Philosophical Psychology, 1,* 35-59.

Parker, S. T. (1994). Incipient mirror self-recognition in zoo gorillas and chimpanzees. In S. T. Parker, R. W. Mitchell, & M. L. Boccia (Eds.), *Self-awareness in animals and humans: Developmental perspectives* (pp. 301–307). New York: Cambridge University Press.

Patterson, F. G. P., & Cohn, R. H. (1994). Self-recognition and self-awareness in lowland gorillas. In S. T. Parker, R. W. Mitchell, & M. L. Boccia (Eds.), *Self-awareness in animals and humans: Developmental perspectives* (pp. 273–290). New York: Cambridge University Press.

Platt, M. M., & Thompson, R. L. (1985). Mirror responses in a Japanese macaque troop (*Arashiyama West*). *Primates, 26,* 300–314.

Povinelli, D. J. (1993). Reconstructing the evolution of mind. *American Psychologist, 48,* 493–509.

Povinelli, D. J. (1994). How to create self-recognizing gorillas (but don't try it on macaques). In S. T. Parker, R. W. Mitchell, & M. L. Boccia (Eds.), *Self-awareness in animals and humans: Developmental perspectives* (pp. 291–300). New York: Cambridge University Press.

Povinelli, D. J., Gallup, G. G., Jr., Eddy, T. J., Bierschwale, D. T., Engstrom, M. C., Perilloux, H. K., & Toxopeus, I. B. (1997). Chimpanzees recognize themselves in mirrors. *Animal Behaviour, 53,* 1083–1088.

Povinelli, D. J., Rulf, A. B., Landau, K. R., & Bierschwale, D. T. (1993). Self-recognition in chimpanzees (*Pan troglodytes*): Distribution, ontogeny, and patterns of emergence. *Journal of Comparative Psychology, 107,* 347–372.

Premack, D. (1983). Animal cognition. *Annual Review of Psychology, 34,* 351–362.

Riviello, M. C., Visalberghi, E., & Blasetti, A. (1992). Individual differences in responses toward a mirror by captive tufted capuchin monkeys (*Cebus apella*). *Hystrix, 4,* 35–44.

Rosenblum, L. A., Kaufman, I. C., & Stynes, A. J. (1966). Some characteristics of adult social and autogrooming patterns in two species of macaque. *Folia Primatologica, 4,* 438–451.

Straumann, C., & Anderson, J. R. (1991). Mirror-induced social facilitation in stumptailed macaques (*Macaca arctoides*). *American Journal of Primatology, 25,* 125–132.

Suarez, S. D., & Gallup, G. G., Jr. (1981). Self-recognition in chimpanzees and orangutans, but not gorillas. *Journal of Human Evolution, 10,* 157–188.

Suarez, S. D., & Gallup, G. G., Jr. (1986a). Face touching in primates: A closer look. *Neuropsychologia, 24,* 597–600.

Suarez, S. D., & Gallup, G. G., Jr. (1986b). Social responding to mirrors in rhesus macaques (*Macaca mulatta*): Effects of changing mirror location. *American Journal of Primatology*, *11*, 239–244.

Swartz, K. B., & Evans, S. (1991). Not all chimpanzees (*Pan troglodytes*) show self-recognition. *Primates*, *32*, 483–496.

Swartz, K. B., & Evans, S. (1994). Social and cognitive factors in chimpanzee and gorilla mirror behavior and self-recognition. In S. T. Parker, R. W. Mitchell, & M. L. Boccia (Eds.), *Self-awareness in animals and humans: Developmental perspectives* (pp. 189–206). New York: Cambridge University Press.

Thompson, R. K. R., & Contie, C. L. (1994). Further reflections on mirror usage by pigeons: Lessons from Winnie-the-Pooh and Pinocchio too. In S. T. Parker, R. W. Mitchell, & M. L. Boccia (Eds.), *Self-awareness in animals and humans: Developmental perspectives* (pp. 392–409). New York: Cambridge University Press.

Thompson, R. L., & Boatwright-Horowitz, S. L. (1994). The question of mirror-mediated self-recognition in apes and monkeys: Some new results and reservations. In S. T. Parker, R. W. Mitchell, & M. L. Boccia (Eds.), *Self-awareness in animals and humans: Developmental perspectives* (pp. 330–349). New York: Cambridge University Press.

Vauclair, J. (1996). *Animal cognition: An introduction to modern comparative psychology.* Cambridge, MA: Harvard University Press.

Walraven, V., van Elsacker, L., & Verheyen, R. (1995). Reactions of a group of pygmy chimpanzees (*Pan paniscus*) to their mirror-images: Evidence of self-recognition. *Primates*, *36*, 145–150.

Westergaard, G. C., & Hyatt, C. W. (1994). The responses of bonobos (*Pan paniscus*) to their mirror images: Evidence of self-recognition. *Human Evolution*, *9*, 273–279.

Part IV ――――――――――――――――――

Cognition

13

Animal Models of Medial Temporal Lobe Amnesia: The Myth of the Hippocampus

Christopher A. Duva, Tom J. Kornecook, and John P. J. Pinel

In the past decade, there have been major advances in our understanding of the role of the medial temporal lobes (MTLs) in memory. In particular, some of the difficulties in drawing conclusions from human neuropsychological patients about the anatomical substrates of memory have been circumvented through the use of animal models of *MTL amnesia*, and the relative contributions of the various MTL structures to memory have begun to be clarified.

The most significant advance arising from the study of animal models of MTL amnesia is the replacement of the universal assumption of hippocampal preeminence with a less hippocampalcentric view. The purpose of this chapter is twofold: first, to describe the emergence of the new view of the relative contributions of various MTL structures to object-recognition memory and, second, to describe the critical role played in this emergence by the comparative study of animal models of MTL amnesia.

This chapter comprises five sections. The first section summarizes the clinical observations that have led to the widely held view that the MTL amnesic syndrome is specifically a consequence of bilateral damage to the hippocampus. The second describes the development of the monkey and rat models of MTL object-recognition amnesia. The third summarizes the early research with the monkey model, which supported the view that damage to the hippocampus, and perhaps the amygdala, was responsible for the object-recognition deficits produced by MTL lesions. The fourth describes recent studies of the monkey and rat models, which indicate that the rhinal cortex—not the hippocampus or amygdala—is the major MTL object-recognition structure. Finally, the fifth section discusses the critical role played by the comparative study of animal models in the discoveries described in the preceding sections.

Medial Temporal Lobe Amnesia and the Hippocampus: Evidence From Neuropsychological Patients

A relationship between MTL pathology and memory impairment was first reported in 1890 (Bechterev, 1900); however, intensive investigation of MTL amnesia did not begin until 1957, the year that the case of H.M. was first reported (Scoville & Milner, 1957). H.M. underwent a bilateral medial temporal lobectomy as a treatment for an otherwise intractable case of epilepsy. Recent magnetic resonance imaging (MRI) data have shown that this procedure resulted in the removal of the anterior portion of H.M.'s hippocampus, his amygdala, and a substantial amount of his medial temporal cortex (Corkin, Amaral, Johnson, & Hyman, 1994). The operation was successful in alleviating H.M.'s epilepsy, but it left him with severe anterograde amnesia (almost totally incapable of forming new memories) and mild retrograde amnesia (with difficulty recalling information acquired in the several years immediately before his surgery). H.M.'s remote memories (e.g., memories from his childhood), however, were left intact, and his linguistic skills, perception, attention, motivation, personality, and intelligence quotient remained relatively normal.

H.M.'s anterograde amnesic symptoms were specific. Severely affected were conscious memories, such as memories of names, faces, words, events, or objects (e.g., Milner, 1966; Milner, Corkin, & Teuber, 1968; Scoville & Milner, 1957); relatively unaffected were his ability to learn and retain a variety of sensorimotor and priming tasks (e.g., Corkin, 1965; Milner et al., 1968). Remarkably, he could retain these tasks even though he had no conscious awareness of having learned them. For example, in one sensorimotor task, reverse mirror drawing, H.M. learned to trace a pattern while viewing his hand through a series of mirrors; days later, he retained this ability although he had no conscious memory of performing the task before. Similarly, in one priming task, the incomplete-picture test, H.M. was shown a series of line drawings of familiar objects; days later, his retention was shown by his improved ability to identify fragmented versions of the same drawings although he had no conscious memory of previously seeing the drawings.

H.M.'s normal ability to hold information in short-term storage, along with the specificity of the anterograde effects of his MTL lesions, suggested that the hippocampus consolidates only some types of memory; that is, it is involved in the hypothetical transfer of specific types of memory from short-term to long-term storage (Brooks & Baddeley, 1976; Cohen, 1984; Cohen & Squire, 1980; Nadel, 1992; O'Keefe & Nadel, 1978). The labels *explicit* and *implicit* (Graf & Schacter, 1985) have been most frequently used to refer to the types of memory that are impaired or not impaired, respectively, after MTL damage. The presence of anterograde and, to lesser extent, retrograde deficits for explicit memory (conscious memory) in conjunction with relatively intact implicit memory (memory demonstrated by improved performance in the absence of conscious memory) is the hallmark of the MTL amnesic syndrome.

On the basis of their work with H.M. and several other neuropsychological patients, Scoville and Milner (Milner, 1966; Scoville & Milner, 1957) suggested that the MTL amnesic syndrome was the result of bilateral damage to the hippocampal region: to the hippocampus (i.e., the dentate gyrus and Ammon's horn) and its adjacent cortex. Three pieces of evidence were central to this conclusion. First, the severity of the MTL amnesia was positively correlated with the extent of hippocampal region excision. Second, significant memory impairments were not observed in patients after selective excision of other MTL structures, such as the uncus or amygdala. Third, unilateral temporal lobectomy resulted in severe MTL amnesia only if there was some type of damage to the contralateral hippocampal region (Penfield & Milner, 1958).

More recent neuropsychological evidence linking hippocampal damage with MTL amnesia comes from patients who have survived an ischemic episode. Cerebral ischemia, the cessation or interruption of oxygen to the brain (see Schmidt-Kastner & Freund, 1991), can occur as a result of various kinds of trauma (Berlyne & Strachan, 1968; Muramato, Kuru, Sugishita, & Toyokura, 1979), but it is most commonly caused by cardiopulmonary arrest (McNeill, Tidmarsh, & Rostall, 1965). Survivors of ischemic episodes often display memory impairment similar to H.M.'s and neuropathology that is most apparent in the hippocampus (Adams, Bierly, Connor & Triep, 1966; Brierly & Graham, 1984; Volpe, Herscovitch, Raichle, Gazzaniga, & Hirst, 1983; Volpe & Hirst, 1983; Volpe, Holtzman, & Hirst, 1986).

The most well-documented case of ischemia-induced amnesia is that of R.B. (Zola-Morgan, Squire, & Amaral, 1986). R.B. was rendered amnesic in 1978 by an ischemic episode that occurred during coronary bypass surgery. Like H.M., he displayed severe anterograde amnesia against a background of otherwise normal cognitive function. After his death 4 years later, R.B.'s brain was subjected to a histological analysis, which revealed radical cell loss in the mediolateral and rostrocaudal extent of the CA1 subfield of the hippocampus. The remainder of the brain displayed only patchy and inconsistent cell loss, which Zola-Morgan et al. (1986) concluded was unlikely to have produced the memory deficit.

The case of R.B. is widely cited in support of the view that hippocampal lesions alone can result in significant amnesic symptoms. However, the possibility that neuropathology not revealed by conventional histological techniques contributed to the memory impairment cannot be ruled out in this and other cases of ischemia-induced amnesia. Indeed, the recent use of more sensitive histological methods, such as silver impregnation, has revealed ischemia-induced extrahippocampal neuropathology in brain regions known to be important for memory (Nunn & Jarrard, 1994). It is also possible that ischemia-induced amnesia is mediated by less apparent functional changes occurring outside the hippocampus, such as changes in neuronal morphology or metabolic responsiveness. In support of this, various metabolic and electrophysiological abnormalities have been observed in neocortical sites in rats after ischemia (Dietrich, Ginsberg, & Bustro, 1986; Peruche, Klaasens, & Krieglstein, 1995).

In conclusion, much of the human neuropsychological evidence implicating hippocampal damage in MTL amnesia comes from a few case reports, most notably those of H.M. and R.B. Although this evidence is suggestive, it is far from conclusive; indeed, in their original report of H.M., Scoville and Milner (1957) concluded that damage to the entire hippocampal region, including the adjacent cortex, was the cause of the syndrome. Nevertheless, the idea that damage to the hippocampus per se is sufficient to produce full-blown MTL amnesia became widely accepted.

Development of Animal Models of Medial Temporal Lobe Amnesia

Human neuropsychological patients rarely have brain damage restricted to a single structure, and they virtually never have complete bilateral lesions of a particular structure that spare surrounding structures. Consequently, attempts based on the study of human patients to prove that bilateral damage to any specific MTL structure causes MTL amnesia can, at best, be only suggestive. The only way to identify the specific anatomical locus of MTL amnesia is to make discrete bilateral lesions of candidate structures and to evaluate their effects on memory. Because ethical considerations prohibit such studies in humans, reports of MTL amnesia in human patients stimulated numerous attempts to develop animal models of the disorder.

Early attempts to develop an animal model of human MTL amnesia focused primarily on assessing the effects of hippocampal lesions on the performance of the various memory tasks that were popular in the stimulus–response (S-R) era. These efforts met with little success (Correll & Scoville, 1965; Douglas, 1967; Isaacson, Douglas, & Moore, 1961; Kimble 1963; Orbach, Milner, & Rasmussen, 1960). Hippocampal lesions in monkeys and rats were found to impair performance on some spatial memory tasks, but their effects on nonspatial memory tasks were slight (see O'Keefe & Nadel, 1978), especially when compared with the profound anterograde memory deficits seen in human amnesics.

Several explanations were offered to account for the fact that bilateral hippocampal lesions had such mild effects on the performance of memory tasks in rats and monkeys when bilateral medial temporal lobectomy had such severe effects in humans (Gaffan, 1974; Horel, 1978; Iversen, 1976). However, in retrospect, it is clear that one major reason why these early attempts to develop an animal model of MTL amnesia failed was that the memory tasks that were used did not involve the type of memory that is impaired in human MTL amnesia: The rat and monkey memory tests of the S-R era were largely tests of implicit rather than explicit memory. Also contributing to these early failures was the narrow focus on the hippocampus. Although Milner (1966) had concluded that damage to the hippocampal region was responsible for H.M.'s amnesia, early investigators virtually ignored the possible contribution of damage to structures other than the hippocampus. This, as you will soon learn, proved to be a crucial oversight.

Monkey Models of Medial Temporal Lobe Amnesia

Mishkin (1978) developed the first animal model of MTL amnesia in the monkey (*Macaca mulatta*) using a modified version of a visual object-recognition memory test originally devised by Gaffan (1974). On each trial of the test, the monkey is presented with an unfamiliar object (the *sample* object) over the center well of a three-well food tray. The objects are ordinary, everyday items, such as soft drink cans, small toys, plastic containers, and household objects of various sizes, shapes, colors, and textures. During this first phase of the trial, the monkeys push the sample object aside to obtain food, which is concealed beneath it. Next, an opaque screen is lowered in front of the monkey while the now-familiar sample and an unfamiliar object are positioned over the two side wells. After a retention delay, the screen is raised, and the monkey's task is to remember the sample, so that it can select the other object to obtain the food hidden beneath it. Different objects are used on each trial.

Learning the *nonmatching* rule (i.e., learning to choose the unfamiliar object instead of the sample object) typically takes monkeys a few hundred trials at the shortest delays of about 10 s. Then, once the monkeys are performing at 90% correct or better, the interval between the presentation of the sample object and the choice phase is increased, typically to delays ranging from 30 s to 40 min, with a slight monotonic decline in the accuracy of performance. The fact that the monkeys performing this task must hold a representation of an object in memory for several minutes suggests that it may tap the same kind of memory that is impaired in MTL amnesia (i.e., explicit memory). This task is now referred to as the *nonrecurring-items delayed nonmatching-to-sample* (DNMS) task and is a central component of the monkey model of human MTL amnesia.

Mishkin (1978) found that monkeys with large bilateral lesions of the MTL could perform the DNMS task when short delays (i.e., 10 s) were interposed between the presentation of the sample object and the choice phase but were impaired at longer delays. The fact that the monkeys could perform normally at short delays suggested that their deficit at longer delays reflected a memory impairment—not perceptual, motor, motivational, or attentional problems. Mishkin's was the first demonstration that a lesion that approximated the one that H.M. had received could produce a comparable object-recognition deficit in a nonhuman species. However, only lesions that included the hippocampus, amygdala, and their adjacent cortical areas resulted in a significant memory deficit: Hippocampectomy alone or amygdalectomy alone had only slight effects. There appeared to be a synergistic effect when the hippocampus and amygdala were lesioned in combination: The resultant memory deficit was greater than would be expected by summing the effects of the two lesions. Mishkin, therefore, concluded that conjoint damage to the hippocampus and amygdala was necessary to produce the MTL amnesic syndrome in monkeys and, by extension, in humans.

Since Mishkin's (1978) initial experimental studies of the effects of MTL lesions and DNMS, other tests designed to assess both explicit and implicit memory in monkeys have been developed. Monkeys with large MTL lesions have been found to perform poorly on other tests of object-recognition memory, such as delayed retention of object discrimination, concurrent object discrimination, and delayed response with and without distraction (Zola-Morgan & Squire, 1985), whereas their ability to learn and perform various sensorimotor tasks has been unaffected (Zola-Morgan & Squire, 1984).

Human MTL amnesics have been shown to perform poorly on many of the very same tasks, including DNMS, that have been used to assess explicit memory in monkeys (Squire, Zola-Morgan, & Chen, 1988). The remarkble similarity between the behavioral deficits following MTL lesions in monkeys and humans is strong evidence that MTL-lesioned monkeys tested on object-recognition tasks are viable models of human MTL amnesia (Squire, 1992; Squire & Zola-Morgan, 1985).

Rat Models of Medial Temporal Lobe Amnesia

Several rat models of MTL amnesia recently have been developed, all of which use a modified version of the DNMS paradigm (Aggleton, 1985; Rothblat & Hayes, 1987). The task devised by Mumby, Pinel, and Wood (1990) is the most similar to the monkey DNMS task. Rats are first presented with a sample object over a baited food well at one end of an elevated runway. The rat runs to the object from a central compartment and displaces it to obtain the food. The sample is then removed and placed at the opposite end of the runway over an empty food well, which is hidden from the rat's view by a guillotine door. Next to the sample is positioned as unfamiliar object. The door is raised after the prescribed delay, and the rat runs to the objects and displaces the unfamiliar object, whereupon food is delivered to the food well beneath it.

Rats typically learn this task to criterion (85% correct) at delays of about 5 s in 200 to 400 trials. Once the nonmatching rule has been learned, delays of 15 s to 10 min can be interposed between the presentation of the sample and novel objects to test memory retention. Retention declines as the delays are increased but is still well above chance at 10 min. Indeed, the performance of rats on the DNMS task is comparable to the performance of monkeys at delays of 2 min or less.

A test battery similar to the test battery that is used to assess object-recognition deficits in monkeys with MTL lesions has been developed for rats (Mumby, Pinel, Kornecook, Shen, & Redila, 1995). In addition to DNMS, this test battery includes object discrimination; object discrimination reversal; concurrent object discrimination; DNMS with lists of three, five, and seven objects; and temporal-order recognition tasks—all conducted in the same Mumby box apparatus.

Medial Temporal Lobe Structures and Object-Recognition Memory: Hippocampus and Amygdala?

Since the monkey and rat models of MTL amnesia were developed, they have been the focus of intensive research. Most of this research has focused on the question of which particular MTL structures must be damaged to produce MTL amnesia. This research occurred in two phases: The first focused on assessing the effects of combined hippocampal and amygdaloid lesions; the second focused on comparing the effects of hippocampal lesions with rhinal cortical lesions. This section discusses the first of these two phases. It, like the section that follows, focuses on experiments in which monkeys or rats have received lesions to one or more MTL structures and then had their memory assessed with one or more object-recognition tasks, usually the DNMS task.

Much of the initial work that followed the development of the monkey model of MTL amnesia focused on Mishkin's initial results and the resulting *combined-lesion* hypothesis, the idea that MTL amnesia requires bilateral damage to both the hippocampus and amygdala (Mishkin, 1978). Several early studies seemed to support the hypothesis by showing that conjoint hippocampal–amygdaloid lesions produced a substantially more severe object-recognition deficit than did lesions to either structure alone (Murray & Mishkin, 1984; Saunders, Murray, & Mishkin, 1984; Zola-Morgan & Squire, 1984, 1985). There was a general consensus that hippocampal damage was critical for the development of full-blown MTL amnesia in the monkey model; the finding that amygdaloid damage also seemed to be critical was reasonable because the amygdala has many connections with the hippocampus and with other brain areas believed to be important for memory, areas such as the mediodorsal nucleus of the thalamus and the prefrontal cortex (Murray, 1992).

Be that as it may, evidence soon began to accumulate that contradicted the combined-lesion hypothesis. For example, lesions of the hippocampus and its underlying cortex that completely spared the amygdala were shown to significantly impair object-recognition memory (Mahut, Zola-Morgan, & Moss, 1982; Zola-Morgan & Squire, 1986), although not quite as severely as the combined lesion.

The possible contribution of cortical damage to the memory impairments resulting from combined hippocampal–amygdaloid lesions also began to be considered at this time: Zola-Morgan, Squire, and Amaral (1989) emphasized that amygdaloid damage was not the only component of the combined lesion that distinguished it from a hippocampectomy. The anterior–ventral surgical approach used during amygdaloid *aspiration* (or withdrawal) requires removal of the underlying and adjacent cortical tissue, that is, removal of the rhinal cortex and parts of the piriform and periamygdaloid cortices. Damage to these areas rather than to the amygdala per se could have been the reason that the combined lesion produced a more severe memory deficit than hippocampectomy alone in some experiments. In support of this interpretation, Zola-Morgan, Squire, and Amaral (1989) found that hippocampectomy produced in combination with a circumscribed electrolytic lesion of the amygdala did not produce a more severe DNMS impairment than hippocampectomy alone. In a related experiment by Zola-Morgan, Squire, Clower, and Rempel (1993), monkeys received a hippocampectomy in which the cortical aspect of the lesion was extended forward to include the cortex underlying the amygdala (i.e., to include the anterior entorhinal cortex and the perirhinal cortex) while leaving the amygdala itself intact. These monkeys were found to be nearly as impaired on DNMS as monkeys that had received a combined aspiration lesion of the hippocampus, amygdala, and underlying cortex. These two studies were the first to demonstrate the importance of the rhinal cortex to object-recognition memory in monkeys. Murray (1992) reexamined the extent of the cortical damage sustained in monkeys with combined lesions from an earlier study (Murray & Mishkin, 1984) and found that the monkeys with amygdalar aspiration lesions had sustained substantial damage to the perirhinal cortex.

On the basis of the above findings, the combined lesion hypothesis is now considered to be incorrect. In retrospect, it is clear that much of the early confusion surrounding this hypothesis stemmed from the fact that researchers paid little attention to the cortical areas adjacent to the amygdala. It is now generally accepted that the amygdala does not play a significant role in object-recognition memory (Mishkin & Murray, 1994; Murray, 1992; 1996; Squire, 1992) and that damage to the rhinal cortex, as a result of the aspiration procedure commonly used to ablate the amygdala, was largely, if not totally, responsible for the object-recognition deficit previously attributed to amygdalar damage.

Medial Temporal Lobe Structures and Object-Recognition Memory: Hippocampus or Rhinal Cortex

Recent studies of both the monkey and rat models of MTL amnesia have demonstrated that the role of the hippocampus in object-recognition memory, much like the role of the amygdala, has been grossly overestimated. These experiments strongly suggest that the rhinal cortex is the key MTL structure in object-recognition memory.

Monkey Studies

Contrary to early reports (Mishkin, 1978; Murray & Mishkin, 1984; Saunders et al., 1984), some investigators have found that bilateral aspiration of the hippocampus does produce significant object-recognition deficits in monkeys (e.g., Mahut et al., 1982; Zola-Morgan & Squire, 1986); naive hippocampectomized monkeys took longer to learn the DNMS task, and once they learned it, they were impaired at delays ranging from 15 s to 10 min. One possible explanation for the differences in the findings of various experiments was that the monkeys had received different degrees of preoperative training experience (Zola-Morgan & Squire, 1986). In general, memory impairments after hippocampal lesions were most severe when the monkeys had recieved no preoperative training (Mahut et al., 1982; Zola-Morgan & Squire, 1986), only mild when preoperative training was brief (Mishkin, 1978), and absent when there was extensive preoperative training (Murray & Mishkin, 1984). The fact that significant deficits occurred only when there was no pretraining suggests that the deficits may not have been pure object-recognition deficits.

As with the combined hippocampal–amygdalar lesion, aspiration lesions of the hippocampus necessarily damage underlying cortical tissue. This damage occurs primarily to the posterior rhinal cortex (i.e., to the perirhinal cortex) and to the parahippocampal gyrus. The contribution that this damage makes to the behavioral deficits observed after hippocampectomy has been appreciated only recently.

Unlike previous studies that sought to determine the relative contributions of amygdalar and hippocampal damage to MTL amnesia, current research has focused on trying to dissociate the object-recognition deficits resulting from hippocampal damage and those resulting from damage to the adjacent medial temporal cortical areas. This has proved difficult because it is technically challenging to reliably produce circumscribed hippocampal lesions in monkeys: Conventional aspiration lesions require removal of substantial amounts of underlying cortex, and accurate stereotaxic lesions are difficult because the size and shape of the monkey hippocampus vary considerably from monkey to monkey (Alvarez-Royo, Clower, Zola-Morgan, & Squire, 1991). Consequently, to make circumscribed hippocampal lesions in monkeys, researchers have begun to use MRI scanning to locate the monkey hippocampus before attempting either radio-frequency or neurotoxic lesions.

In one such study, neurotoxin infusion was used to produce combined lesions of the monkey hippocampus and amygdala while leaving the adjacent cortex intact (O'Boyle, Murray, & Mishkin, 1993). These selective lesions produced no impairment on the DNMS at any delays up to 3.5 min, the longest delay at which the monkeys were tested.

In another study in which the monkey hippocampus was lesioned without substantially damaging the adjacent cortex, radio-frequency lesions in monkeys produced damage to between 38% and 75% of the hippocampus. These circumscribed hippocampal lesions produced no deficits in the monkeys' ability to learn the DNMS task (Alvarez, Zola-Morgan, & Squire, 1995). Then, when the monkeys were tested at delays of 8 s, 15 s, 60 s, 10 min, and 40 min, there were impairments at only the two longest delays. Furthermore, on two other tests of object-recognition memory, there were no impairments. The DNMS deficit at the 10-min and 40-min delays led Alvarez et al. (1995) to conclude that the hippocampus is essential for object-recognition memory. This interpretation has generated considerable controversy (Murray, 1996; Murray & Mishkin, 1996; Nadel, 1992) because during the two long delays, the monkeys were removed from the test apparatus and returned to their home cages, a procedure that could have contributed to the observed impairment. In addition, Murray (1996) has suggested that the lesions in the Alvarez et al. (1995) study may have inadvertently damaged the fibers connecting the fornix with the rhinal cortex and that this damage may also have contributed to the observed impairment.

In a third study of the effects of circumscribed hippocampal lesions in monkeys on DNMS, monkeys with neurotoxic hippocampal lesions were left in the test apparatus during all the intervals. These monkeys displayed no DNMS impairments at any of the delays at which they were tested, even at the 10-min and 40-min delays (Murray & Mishkin, 1996).

Because circumscribed hippocampal lesions in monkeys produce little, if any, deficit in DNMS, the severe deficits after hippocampal aspiration, which requires the removal of substantial amounts of underlying cortex, suggest that the cortical damage is critical. Studies in which only the cortex adjacent to the hippocampus has been ablated have supported this conclusion. Zola-Morgan, Squire, Amaral, and Suzuki (1989) ablated the perirhinal and parahippocampal cortices in naive monkeys and found a severe impairment in their ability to learn the DNMS task; some were unable to reach criterion even after 1,500 trials. When tested at delays, the monkeys with cortical lesions performed significantly worse than control monkeys but were not quite as impaired as monkeys with combined lesions of the cortex and hippocampus.

Similarly, Meunier, Bachevalier, Mishkin, and Murray (1993) found that rhinal cortex lesions in monkeys with preoperative training impaired both the ability to relearn the DNMS task and performance at all retention delays at which the monkeys were tested (from 15 s to 2 min). They also found a dissociation between the behavioral effects of entorhinal and perirhinal cortex lesions. Their findings suggest that the perirhinal cortex is disproportionately involved in the learning or maintenance of the DNMS rule, whereas both the entorhinal and perirhinal areas contribute to retention of memories for objects.

In conclusion, recent studies of the monkey model of MTL amnesia indicate that the hippocampus plays only a minor role, if any, in object-recognition memory. In contrast, damage to the rhinal cortex is sufficient to produce severe impairments of object-recognition memory (Mishkin & Murray, 1994; Murray, 1996).

Rat Studies

Until recently, the major obstacle to drawing firm conclusions about the role of the hippocampus in object-recognition memory has been the inability to produce circumscribed hippocampal lesions in monkeys. Studies with rats provided an alternative approach to dissociating the amnesic effects of hippocampal lesions and cortical damage: In rats, the hippocampus is accessible to aspiration beneath the parietal cortex and can be readily ablated without damaging the rhinal cortex. Although the rat model of MTL amnesia was developed more than a decade after the monkey model, important developments in its study have occurred quickly because of the greater ease and lower cost of working with rats than monkeys and because of the foundation laid by the earlier monkey studies.

Hippocampectomy, amygdalectomy, or a combined lesion has little, if any, effect on DNMS performance in preoperatively trained rats. Rothblat and Kromer (1991) found that hippocampectomy produced no deficits at the two delays at which their rats were tested (i.e., 10 and 30 s). Mumby, Wood, and Pinel (1992) found DNMS impairments at only their longest delay (i.e., 10 min) after hippocampectomy, amygdalectomy, or a combined lesion.

Even in rats without preoperative training, hippocampal or amygdalar lesions produce little, if any, impairment in object-recognition memory. Rats with aspiration (Aggleton, Hunt, & Rawlins, 1986) or neurotoxic (Glenn & Mumby, 1996) lesions of the hippocampus learned the DNMS task in the same number of trials as controls and displayed no impairment at any of their delays (ranging from 0 to 120 s). In another study, Mumby et al. (1995) assessed the effects of hippocampal aspiration on the performance of rats that had received no pretraining on a battery of object-recognition tasks. Hippocampectomized rats learned the DNMS task as quickly as controls and were impaired at only the longest DNMS retention delay of 2 min; they required more trials to learn the object discrimination and concurrent object discrimination tasks than controls; but they displayed no deficits on discrimination reversal, DNMS with lists, or temporal order recognition tests.

In contrast to the mild object-recognition deficits produced in rats by hippocampal lesions, profound deficits have been observed after rhinal cortical damage. In the previously mentioned Mumby et al. (1992) study of hippocampal and amygdalar lesions, several rats received inadvertent damage to the rhinal cortex as a result of hippocampectomy and were severely impaired on the DNMS task. Similarly, Aggleton, Blindt, and Rawlins (1989) found severe DNMS impairments in rats after combined hippocampal–amygdaloid lesions that produced inadvertent cortical damage. Mumby and Pinel (1994) found that rats with aspiration lesions limited to the rhinal cortex performed normally at short delays (i.e., 4 s) but were impaired at delays from 15 s to 5 min. Kornecook, Lui, Duva, Anzarut, and Pinel (1995) found that rhinal cortex lesions produced DNMS deficits at retention intervals greater than 30 s in pretrained rats but did not affect their ability to reattain criterion or perform at shorter delays; impairments on object-discrimination and concurrent object-discrimination tasks also were reported, whereas discrimination reversal was unaffected. Otto and Eichenbaum (1992) showed that the recognition deficits after rhinal cortical lesions were not limited to visual stimuli: Rats with rhinal cortical lesions were able to learn an odor-guided DNMS task at short delays but were impaired when the delay was greater than 15 s.

The results obtained with rats are remarkably similar to those found with monkeys: In different experiments, hippocampectomy alone has resulted in only a mild impairment of object recognition or no impairment at all. In the majority of cases, hippocampectomized rats have learned the nonmatching rule at a rate equivalent to controls and have performed normally at short delays. It is only with the use of long delays that a deficit sometimes appears. Adding an amygdalectomy does not exacerbate the effects of a hippocampal lesion. Also, as in monkeys, hippocampectomy in rats does not produce a widespread deficit in other tests of object-recognition memory. Out of six tests of object-recognition memory, damage to the hippocampus has resulted in a significant impairment on only two tasks: object discrimination and concurrent object discrimination. On the other hand, rhinal cortical lesions have resulted in profound delay-dependent DNMS impairments as well as deficits on most other object-memory tasks. Taken in combination, these results support a limited role for the hippocampus in object-recognition memory and provide further evidence for the preeminence of the rhinal cortex.

Animal Models of Ischemia-Induced Amnesia

One line of evidence often cited in support of a significant role for the hippocampus in object-recognition memory comes from animal models of cerebral-ischemia-induced amnesia. Monkeys and rats subjected to forebrain ischemia display DNMS impairments and observable neuropathology confined primarily to the CA1 subfield of the hippocampus (Bachevalier & Mishkin, 1989; Wood, Mumby, Pinel, & Phillips, 1993; Zola-Morgan, Squire, Rempel, Clower, & Amaral, 1992). Paradoxically, this deficit is usually far more severe than the mild deficit sometimes found after complete bilateral hippocampectomy.

How can ischemia-induced damage apparently limited to the hippocampus produce a profound DNMS deficit when complete destruction of both hippocampi produces only a slight deficit, if any? Bachevalier and Mishkin (1989) have suggested two possibilities. First, a partially damaged hippocampus may result in the functional disorganization of extrahippocampal circuitry: Although the hippocampus itself may not be critical for object-recognition memory, a partially damaged, malfunctioning hippocampus may have a disruptive effect on other structures that are involved in object-recognition memory. Second, in addition to the CA1 cell loss that is apparent after ischemia, neuropathology that is undetectable with conventional histological techniques may be occurring in brain regions critical for object-recognition memory, and this damage, not the hippocampal damage, may be responsible for the ischemia-induced object-recognition deficit.

These hypotheses have not been addressed in the monkey model, but research with the rat model has indicated that ischemia-induced DNMS impairments are likely the result of extrahippocampal neuropathology, not the disruptive effect on other structures of a damaged hippocampus. Mumby et al. (1996) has reasoned that if the disruptive effect of a damaged hippocampus were responsible for the poor DNMS performance of ischemic rats, then ablating a hippocampus that was damaged by ischemia would attenuate this impairment. However, this did not occur. The DNMS performance of ischemic rats did not improve following hippocampectomy, thus supporting the alternative hypothesis: unidentified extrahippocampal neuropathology. Mumby et al. (1996)

then proceeded to provide more direct evidence for this alternative hypothesis.

Mumby et al. (1996) hypothesized that unidentified extrahippocampal damage was responsible for the object-recognition deficits produced by forebrain ischemia and that this damage was produced by hippocampal activity in the postischemia period. They supported this hypothesis with a startling finding: Bilateral hippocampectomy before or immediately after ischemia virtually eliminates the development of subsequent DNMS impairments. The finding that bilateral hippocampectomy actually improves the object-recognition memory of ischemic subjects is arguably the strongest single piece of evidence that the hippocampus is not critically involved in object-recognition memory (see Mumby, chap. 14, this volume).

Further evidence against the hypothesis that ischemia-produced object-recognition deficits result from the disruptive effects of a partially damaged hippocampus was provided by Duva et al. (1997) using the rat model. They produced partial bilateral hippocampal lesions with the neurotoxin N-methyl-D-aspartate. Although these lesions damaged much of the same area as did ischemia (i.e., the dorsal CA1), the lesioned rats displayed no deficits in learning or performing the DNMS task, with or without preoperative training.

The findings in rats, then, provide a potential way to reconcile the results of the ischemia studies with the results of the ablation studies. Ischemia-induced DNMS impairments in rats appear to be caused by extrahippocampal neuropathology that is in some way mediated by the postischemic hippocampus. The location of this damage is still unknown, but several recent studies have shown that ischemia-induced neuropathology can be detected in extrahippocampal brain regions thought to be important for memory if more sensitive assays (e.g., silver impregnation) are used (Crain, Westerkam, Harrison, & Nadler, 1988; Freund, Buzsaki, Leon, & Somogyi, 1990; Nunn & Jarrard, 1994). It is now necessary to determine if damage to these extrahippocampal areas has a disruptive effect on object-recognition memory and if the damage is produced by events occurring in the postischemic hippocampus.

Conclusion: Role of Animal Models in the Recent Advances in the Understanding of Object-Recognition Memory

In the last decade, it has become increasingly apparent that the rhinal cortex, not the hippocampus, is the major MTL structure in object-recognition memory. Indeed, evidence for this point of view now seems almost unequivocal. The experimental study of animal models of the object-recognition deficits produced by bilateral MTL damage has played a critical role in these recent developments. Because the lesion method cannot be used to conduct experiments in human patients, questions of the causal relation between lesions to various MTL structures and ensuing memory deficits could not be directly addressed by research in human patients; only uncontrolled case studies and correlational studies were possible in humans.

The successful application of animal models to the study of the object-recognition deficits produced by MTL lesions illustrates several points about the use of animal models. The following are five of them.

First, the effective use of animal models typically involves a productive interplay with research on human patients. Often research on human patients identifies phenomena of interest and suggests productive hypotheses but is stopped from making further progress by the inability to conduct experiments. But this interaction is not a one-way street: Progress made with animal models often suggests new productive avenues of research to researchers working with humans. For example, the rhinal cortex has become an obligatory area of focus for the postmortem analysis of the brains of humans with memory disorders.

Second, in developing animal models of behavioral disorders, it is important to devise tests that tap the specific behavioral effects observed in humans. Initial progress in developing animal models of MTL amnesia was slow because the first efforts to develop a model focused on tests of implicit rather that explicit memory. The ability to test both human and nonhuman subjects on virtually identical tests of object-recognition memory has been a major strength of comparative research on MTL amnesia.

Third, it is a major advantage in studying a phenomenon to have models in two nonhuman species. There is always concern about the generalizability of findings to humans from experiments done on another species, but the concern is substantially less when there is convergence from the findings of two or more species, particularly when they are not closely related. Research on animal models of human MTL amnesia has been particularly convincing because of the high degree of concordance between the results of research on the monkey and rat models.

Fourth, although there seems to be an implicit assumption that primate animal models of human phenomena are generally the best, they are not superior in every way. For example, because the cost of monkey models is prohibitive for many researchers and a major impediment for even those who can afford to use them, they are not conducive to the conduct of experiments that involve either subject attrition or large numbers of subjects. In research on animal models of MTL amnesia, progress has resulted from the productive interplay between research on monkeys and rats.

Fifth, the best animal models are not always those that are most isomorphic with the human condition: In some cases, a key difference is a major advantage. For example, one advantage of the rat model of MTL amnesia over the monkey model is that the rat hippocampus is located more dorsally in rats than it is in primates. As a result, it is much easier in rats than it is in humans or monkeys to destroy the hippocampus without damaging the rhinal cortex.

References

Adams, J. H., Bierly, J. B., Connor, R. C. T., & Triep, C. (1966). The effects of systemic hypotension upon the human brain. *Brain, 89,* 135–154.

Aggleton, J. P. (1985). One-trial object recognition by rats. *Quarterly Journal of Experimental Psychology, 37,* 279–294.

Aggleton, J. P., Blindt, H. S., & Rawlins, J. N. P. (1989). Effects of amygdaloid and amygdaloid–hippocampal lesions on object recognition memory and spatial working memory in rats. *Behavioral Neuroscience, 103,* 962–974.

Aggleton, J. P., Hunt, P. R., & Rawlins, J. N. P. (1986). The effects of hippocampal lesions upon spatial and non-spatial tests of working memory. *Behavioural Brain Research, 19,* 133–146.

Alvarez, P., Zola-Morgan, S., & Squire, L. R. (1995). Damage limited to the hippocampal region produces long-lasting memory impairments in monkeys. *Journal of Neuroscience, 15,* 3796–3807.

Alvarez-Royo, P., Clower, R. P., Zola-Morgan, S., & Squire, L. R. (1991). Stereotaxic lesions of the hippocampus in the monkey: Determination of the surgical coordinates and analysis of lesions using magnetic resonance imaging. *Journal of Neuroscience Methods, 38,* 223–232.

Bachevalier, J., & Mishkin, M. (1989). Mnemonic and neuropathological effects of occluding the posterior cerebral artery in *Macaca mulatta. Neuropsychologia, 27,* 83–105.

Bechterev, V. M. (1900). Demonstration eines Gehirns mit zerstörung der vorderen und inneren teile der Hirnrinde beider schläfenlappen [Demonstration of a brain with destruction of anterior and interior sections of the cerebral cortex of both temporal lobes]. *J. Neurologisches Zentpalblatt, 19,* 900–991.

Berlyne, N., & Strachan, M. (1968). Neuropsychiatric sequelae of attempted hanging. *British Journal of Psychiatry, 114,* 411–422.

Brierly, J. B., & Graham, D. L. (1984). Hypoxia and vascular disorders of the central nervous system. In J. H. Adams, J. Corsellis, & L. W. Duchen (Eds.), *Greenfield's neuropathology* (pp. 125–208). New York: Wiley.

Brooks, D. N., & Baddeley, A. D. (1976). What can amnesic patients learn? *Neuropsychologia, 14,* 111–122.

Cohen, N. J. (1984). Preserved learning capacity in amnesia: Evidence for multiple memory systems. In L. R. Squire & N. Butters (Eds.), *The neuropsychology of memory* (pp. 83–103). New York: Guilford Press.

Cohen, N. J., & Squire, L. R. (1980). Preserved learning and retention of pattern analyzing skills in amnesia: Dissociation of knowing how and knowing what. *Science, 210,* 207–210.

Corkin, S. (1965). Tactually guided maze-learning in man: Effects of unilateral cortical excisions and bilateral hippocampal lesions. *Neuropsychologia, 3,* 339–351.

Corkin, S., Amaral, D. G., Johnson, A., & Hyman, B. T. (1994). H.M.'s MRI scan shows sparing of the posterior half of the hippocampus and parahippocampal gyrus. *Society for Neuroscience Abstracts, 20,* 1289.

Correll, R. E., & Scoville, W. B. (1965). Performance on delayed match following lesions of medial temporal lobe structures. *Journal of Comparative and Physiological Psychology, 60,* 360–367.

Crain, B. J., Westerkam, W. D., Harrison, A. H., & Nadler, J. V. (1988). Selective neuronal death after transient forebrain ischemia in the Mongolian gerbil: A silver impregnation study. *Neuroscience, 27,* 387–402.

Dietrich, W. D., Ginsberg, M. D., & Bustro, R. (1986). Effect of transient cerebral ischemia on metabolic activation of a somatosensory circuit. *Journal of Cerebral Blood Flow and Metabolism, 6,* 405–413.

Douglas, R. J. (1967). The hippocampus and behavior. *Psychological Bulletin, 67,* 416–442.

Duva, C. A., Floresco, S. B., Lao., T. L., Wunderlich, G. R., Pinel, J. P. J., & Phillips, A. G. (1997). Disruption of spatial but not object-recognition memory by excitotoxic lesions of the dorsal hippocampus in rats. *Behavioral Neuroscience, 111,* 1184–1196.

Freund, T. F., Buzsaki, G., Leon, A., & Somogyi, P. (1990). Hippocampal cell death following ischemia: Effects of brain temperature and anesthesia. *Experimental Neurology, 108,* 251–260.

Gaffan, D. (1974). Recognition impaired and association intact in the memory of monkeys after transection of the fornix. *Journal of Comparative and Physiological Psychology, 86,* 1100–1109.

Glenn, M. J., & Mumby, D. G. (1996). Place- and object-recognition deficits following lesions of the hippocampus or perirhinal cortex in rats: A double dissociation. *Society for Neuroscience Abstracts, 22,* 1120.

Graf, P., & Schacter, D. L. (1985). Implicit and explicit memory for new associations in normal and amnesic subjects. *Journal of Experimental Psychology: Learning, Memory, and Cognition, 11,* 501–508.

Horel, J. A. (1978). A critique of the hippocampal memory hypothesis. *Brain, 101,* 403–445.

Isaacson, R. L., Douglas, R. J., & Moore, R. Y. (1961). The effect of radical hippocampal ablation on acquisition of avoidance response. *Journal of Comparative and Physiological Psychology, 54,* 625–635.

Iversen, S. (1976). Do hippocampal lesions produce amnesia in animals? In C. C. Pfeiffer & J. R. Smythies (Eds.), *International review of neurobiology* (Vol. 19, pp. 1–49). New York: Academic Press.

Kimble, D. P. (1963). The effects of bilateral hippocampal lesions in rats. *Journal of Comparative and Physiological Psychology, 56,* 273–283.

Kornecook, T. J., Lui, M., Duva, C. A., Anzarut, A., & Pinel, J. P. J. (1995). Effects of perirhinal or rhinal cortex lesions on object-memory tasks in the rat. *Society for Neuroscience Abstracts, 21,* 1935.

Mahut, H., Zola-Morgan, S., & Moss, M. (1982). Hippocampal resections impair associative learning and recognition memory in the monkey. *Journal of Neuroscience, 2,* 1214–1229.

McNeill, D. L., Tidmarsh, D., & Rostall, M. L. (1965). A case of amnesic syndrome following cardiac arrest. *British Journal of Psychiatry, 11,* 697–699.

Meunier, M., Bachevalier, J., Mishkin, M., & Murray, E. A. (1993). Effects on visual recognition of combined and separate ablations of the entorhinal and perirhinal cortex in rhesus monkeys. *Journal of Neuroscience, 13,* 5418–5432.

Milner, B. (1966). Amnesia following operations on the temporal lobes. In C. W. M. Whitty & O. L. Zangwill (Eds.), *Amnesia* (pp. 109–123). London: Butterworth.

Milner, B., Corkin, S., & Teuber, H. L. (1968). Further analysis of the hippocampal amnesic syndrome: 14-year follow-up study of H.M. *Neuropsychologia, 6,* 215–234.

Mishkin, M. (1978). Memory in monkeys severely impaired by combined but not by separate removal of amygdala and hippocampus. *Nature, 273,* 297–298.

Mishkin, M., & Murray, E. A. (1994). Stimulus recognition. *Current Opinion in Neurobiology, 4,* 200–206.

Mumby, D. G., & Pinel, J. P. J. (1994). Rhinal cortex lesions and object recognition in rats. *Behavioral Neuroscience, 108,* 11–18.

Mumby, D. G., Pinel, J. P. J., Kornecook, T. J., Shen, M. J., & Redila, V. A. (1995). Memory deficits following lesions of the hippocampus or amygdala in rats: Assessment by an object-memory test battery. *Psychobiology, 23,* 26–36.

Mumby, D. G., Pinel, J. P. J., & Wood, E. R. (1990). Nonrecurring-items delayed nonmatching-to-sample in rats: A new paradigm for testing nonspatial working memory. *Psychobiology, 18,* 321–326.

Mumby, D. G., Wood, E. R., Duva, C. A., Kornecook, T. J., Pinel, J. P. J., & Phillips, A. G. (1996). Ischemia-induced object-recognition deficits in rats are attenuated by hippocampal ablation before or soon after ischemia. *Behavioral Neuroscience, 110,* 266–281.

Mumby, D. G., Wood, E. R., & Pinel, J. P. J. (1992). Object-recognition memory is only mildly impaired in rats with lesions of the hippocampus and amygdala. *Psychobiology, 20,* 18–27.

Muramoto, O., Kuru, Y., Sugishita, M., & Toyokura, Y. (1979). Pure memory loss with hippocampal lesions. *Archives of Neurology, 36,* 54–56.

Murray, E. A. (1992). Medial temporal lobe structures contributing to recognition memory:

The amygdaloid complex versus the rhinal cortex. In J. P. Aggleton (Ed.), *The amygdala: Neurobiological aspects of emotion, memory, and mental dysfunction* (pp. 453–470). New York: Wiley-Liss.

Murray, E. A. (1996). What have ablation studies told us about the neural substrates of stimulus memory? *Seminars in the Neurosciences, 8,* 13–22.

Murray, E. A., & Mishkin, M. (1984). Severe tactual as well as visual memory deficits follow combined removal of the amygdala and hippocampus in monkeys. *Journal of Neuroscience, 4,* 2565–2580.

Murray, E. A., & Mishkin, M. (1996). 40-minute visual recognition memory in rhesus monkeys with hippocampal lesions. *Society for Neuroscience Abstracts, 22,* 281.

Nadel, L. (1992). Multiple memory systems: What and why? *Journal of Cognitive Neuroscience, 4,* 179–187.

Nunn, J. A., & Jarrard, L. E. (1994). Silver impregnation reveals neuronal damage in the cingulate cortex following 4 VO ischaemia in the rat. *NeuroReport, 5,* 2363–2366.

O'Boyle, J. R., Murray, E. A., & Mishkin, M. (1993). Effects of excitotoxic amygdalo–hippocampal lesions on visual recognition in rhesus monkeys. *Society for Neuroscience Abstracts, 19,* 438.

O'Keefe, J., & Nadel, L. (1978). *The hippocampus as a cognitive map.* London: Oxford University Press.

Orbach, J., Milner, B., & Rasmussen, T. (1960). Learning and retention on monkeys after amygdala–hippocampal resection. *Archives of Neurology, 3,* 230–251.

Otto, T., & Eichenbaum, H. (1992). Complimentary roles of the orbital prefrontal cortex and the perirhinal–entorhinal cortices in an odor-guided delayed-nonmatching-to-sample task. *Behavioral Neuroscience, 106,* 762–775.

Penfield, W., & Milner, B. (1958). Memory deficit produced by bilateral lesions in the hippocampal zone. *Archives of Neurology and Psychiatry, 79,* 475–497.

Peruche, B., Klaasens, H., & Krieglstein, J. (1995). Quantitative analysis of the electrocorticogram after forebrain ischemia in the rat. *Pharmacology, 50,* 229–237.

Rothblat, L. A., & Hayes, L. L. (1987). Short-term object recognition in the rat: Nonmatching with trial-unique stimuli. *Behavioral Neuroscience, 101,* 587–590.

Rothblat, L. A., & Kromer, L. F. (1991). Object-recognition memory in the rat: The role of the hippocampus. *Behavioral Brain Research, 42,* 25–32.

Saunders, R. C., Murray, E. A., & Mishkin, M. (1984). Further evidence that amygdala and hippocampus contribute equally to recognition memory. *Neuropsychologia, 22,* 785–796.

Schmidt-Kastner, R., & Freund, T. F. (1991). Selective vulnerability of the hippocampus in brain ischemia. *Neuroscience, 40,* 599–636.

Scoville, W. B., & Milner, B. (1957). Loss of recent memory after bilateral hippocampal lesions. *Journal of Neurology, Neurosurgery, and Psychiatry, 20,* 11–21.

Squire, L. R. (1992). Memory and the hippocampus: A synthesis from findings with rats, monkeys, and humans. *Psychological Review, 99,* 195–231.

Squire, L. R., & Zola-Morgan, S. (1985). The neuropsychology of memory: New links between humans and experimental animals. In D. Olton, S. Corkin, & E. Gamzu (Eds.), *Conference on memory dysfunctions* (pp. 137–149). New York: New York Academy of Sciences Press.

Squire, L. R., Zola-Morgan, S., & Chen, K. (1988). Human amnesia and animal models of amnesia: Performance of amnesiac patients on tests designed for the monkey. *Behavioral Neuroscience, 11,* 210–221.

Volpe, B. T., Herscovitch, P., Raichle, M. E., Gazzaniga, M. S., & Hirst, W. (1983). Cerebral blood flow and metabolism in human amnesia. *Journal of Cerebral Blood Flow and Metabolism, 3,* 5–6.

Volpe, B. T., & Hirst, W. (1983). The characterization of the amnesic syndrome after hypoxic ischemic injury. *Archives of Neurology, 40,* 436–440.

Volpe, B. T., Holtzman, J. D., & Hirst, W. (1986). Further characterization of patients with amnesia after global hypoxic ischemic injury: Preserved recognition memory. *Neurology, 36,* 408–411.

Wood, E. R., Mumby, D. G., Pinel, J. P. J., & Phillips, A. G. (1993). Impaired object recognition memory in rats following ischemia-induced damage to the hippocampus. *Behavioral Neuroscience, 107,* 51–62.

Zola-Morgan, S., & Squire, L. R. (1984). Preserved learning in monkeys with medial temporal lesions: Sparing of motor and cognitive skills. *Journal of Neuroscience, 4,* 1072–1085.

Zola-Morgan, S., & Squire, L. R. (1985). Medial temporal lesions in monkeys impair memory on a variety of tasks sensitive to human amnesia. *Behavioral Neuroscience, 99,* 22–34.

Zola-Morgan, S., & Squire, L. R. (1986). Memory impairments in monkeys following lesions limited to the hippocampus. *Behavioral Neuroscience, 100,* 155–160.

Zola-Morgan, S., Squire, L. R., & Amaral, D. G. (1986). Human amnesia and the medial temporal region: Enduring memory impairments following bilateral lesions limited to the field CA1 of the hippocampus. *Journal of Neuroscience, 6,* 2950–2967.

Zola-Morgan, S., Squire, L. R., & Amaral, D. G. (1989). Lesions of the amygdala that spare the adjacent cortical regions do not impair memory or exacerbate the impairment following lesions of the hippocampal formation. *Journal of Neuroscience, 9,* 1922–1936.

Zola-Morgan, S., Squire, L. R., Amaral, D. G., & Suzuki, W. A. (1989). Lesions of the perirhinal and parahippocampal cortex that spare the amygdala and hippocampal formation produce severe memory impairment. *Journal of Neuroscience, 9,* 4355–4370.

Zola-Morgan, S., Squire, L. R., Clower, R. P., & Rempel, N. L. (1993). Damage to the perirhinal cortex exacerbates memory impairment following lesions to the hippocampus. *Journal of Neuroscience, 13,* 251–265.

Zola-Morgan, S., Squire, L. R., Rempel, N. L., Clower, R. P., & Amaral, D. G. (1992). Enduring memory impairment in monkeys after ischemic damage to the hippocampus. *Journal of Neuroscience, 12,* 2582–2596.

14

Animal Models of Global Amnesia: What Can They Tell Us About Memory?

Dave G. Mumby

Animal models of amnesia play a pivotal role in the study of brain–memory relations, providing links among comparative neuroanatomy, observations of both normal and disordered memory in humans, and theories of memory that originate mostly from studies in rats. This chapter considers some of the unique contributions that animal models of amnesia make to the study of memory and also some of the limitations of these models. It examines how the questions that guide research with animal models of amnesia have changed in recent years, reflecting the growing prevalence of cognitive neuroscience approaches to the study of memory and developments in our understanding of both normal memory and human amnesia.

This chapter has three main sections. The first section considers different types of animal models, the central features of global amnesia, and the development of animal models of amnesia. The second section considers some of the contributions that animal models of amnesia make to our understanding of various amnesic syndromes. The focus is on three general issues: the critical brain damage in amnesia, the types of memory that are affected, and etiological factors. The third section considers how animal models of amnesia have contributed to our understanding of normal memory in two general areas: multiple memory systems and consolidation of long-term memory. I make no attempt to provide a comprehensive review of any one issue. Instead, my objective is to highlight a few concerns that have implications for the ways in which we use animal models of amnesia to study memory.

Animal Models of Amnesia

When Is an Animal Model a Model of Amnesia?

There are at least two types of animal models that address questions about memory systems and functions. The first type of model purports to be isomorphic with an amnesic syndrome in humans, reproducing its core symptoms and associated brain damage. The main purpose of isomorphic models is to establish the necessary and sufficient conditions to produce the clinical syndrome, thus providing a starting point for more detailed studies. Some models reproduce only certain components of the amnesic syndrome, for example, retrograde amnesia or deficits in delayed recall. Their purpose is to link specific symptoms to specific aspects of the neuropathology in a complex human disorder.

The second type of model makes no expressed attempt to reproduce any aspect of amnesia but regards nonhuman animals as appropriate model systems for studying the functional anatomy of memory. Lesion experiments represent just one of several approaches that use this type of animal model. The behavioral effects of a lesion may emulate certain features of amnesia, but the primary goal is to understand normal memory, and any relevance to amnesia is only secondary. In the present article, therefore, I do not consider this type of animal model to be a model of amnesia.

Global Amnesia in Humans

Global amnesia occurs after bilateral damage to either one of two brain areas: the medial diencephalon or the medial temporal lobe. Common causes include chronic alcohol abuse, tumors, traumatic head injury, transient cerebral ischemia, and temporal lobe surgery. Different amnesic groups share several characteristics, and their differences are viewed by some as reflecting different cognitive deficits superimposed on a core amnesic syndrome that is common to all of them.

Amnesia is characterized by an impaired ability to form new long-term memories for certain kinds of information (*anterograde* amnesia), with variable loss of memory for information or events experienced before the onset of amnesia (*retrograde* amnesia). The memory impairment is selective, occurring in the absence of other cognitive or intellectual impairments, and this distinguishes amnesia from other disorders, such as Parkinson's, Huntington's, and Alzheimer's diseases, that include memory impairment within a constellation of other symptoms. Some memory abilities are spared in amnesia, including short-term memory, perceptual and motor skill learning, priming, and some forms of classical conditioning.

Early Models of Amnesia in Animals

Attempts to model amnesia in monkeys began soon after the initial descriptions of the amnesic patient H.M., who suffered a devastating and selective memory impairment after bilateral removal of medial portions of his temporal lobes (Scoville & Milner, 1957). Early attempts to model H.M.'s amnesia were disappointing. Monkeys with lesions similar to H.M.'s performed normally on visual discrimination tasks and delayed-response tasks (Mishkin, 1954; Orbach, Milner, & Rasmussen, 1960) and on delayed matching-to-sample (DMS) tasks (Correll & Scoville, 1965; Drachman & Ommaya, 1964), which led some investigators to conclude that different neural systems mediate memory in humans and nonhumans. Others questioned the adequacy of the tasks that had been used. Unfortunately, during the 1960s, amnesia was not well understood, and it was not clear which type of memory tasks would be suitable for modeling it. It is now believed that visual discrimination learning in animals depends on a type of memory ability that is spared in amnesia. Moreover, the longest retention delay used in the aforementioned delay tasks—12 s (Drachman & Ommaya, 1964)—is well within the intact short-term memory range of amnesic patients. Thus, the monkeys with medial temporal lesions in these early studies may have experienced amnesia that simply went undetected.

Although these early attempts to model amnesia in animals are often characterized as failures, they did tell us some things about amnesia. They later confirmed, in retrospect, evidence from amnesic patients that lesions of the temporal lobes or diencephalon have little effect on short-term memory or on certain kinds of long-term memory. They also indicated that a model of amnesia cannot involve just any memory task, it requires tasks that depend critically on memory abilities that are impaired in amnesia.

A major turning point was Mishkin's (1978) finding that monkeys with bilateral removal of the hippocampus and amygdala were impaired on a test of object recognition: the trial-unique delayed nonmatching-to-sample (DNMS) task. On each DNMS trial, a sample object is briefly presented, and then after a retention delay, during which it is hidden from view, the sample is presented again along with a novel object. Different objects are used on each trial, and the correct response is always to select the novel object. The DMS task is virtually identical, except that the correct response is to select the sample on the choice part of the trial. Accurate performance of DNMS or DMS tasks, therefore, requires the ability to recognize the sample after the retention delay has expired. Several studies have confirmed that monkeys with medial temporal lesions or midline diencephalic lesions are impaired on DNMS or DMS tasks if the retention delay is longer than a few seconds (reviewed by Duva, Kornecook, and Pinel, chap. 13, this volume). Because the effective lesions are similar to those associated with amnesia in humans and because the tasks require recognition memory, which is impaired in amnesia, these findings constitute an animal model of amnesia.

Recognition is only one of many memory abilities that are impaired in amnesia, and some memory abilities are unaffected. Therefore, the performance of monkeys with medial temporal lesions on additional memory tasks may be expected to model more features of global amnesia than a delay-dependent DNMS deficit alone. Accordingly, a small battery of tests has been used to provide a broader characterization of memory abilities in the monkey models. For example, monkeys with medial temporal or diencephalic lesions are impaired at learning several object discriminations concurrently and on DNMS or DMS tasks, but they are unimpaired at learning difficult pattern discriminations and motor skills (Squire,

1992). An advantage of these tasks is that nearly identical versions can be administered to humans, and when they are, patients with amnesia display a similar pattern of spared and impaired performance to that of monkeys with large medial temporal or midline diencephalic lesions (e.g., Aggleton, Nicol, Huston, & Fairbairn, 1988; Aggleton, Shaw, & Gaffan, 1992; Holdstock, Shaw, & Aggleton, 1995; Squire, Zola-Morgan, & Chen, 1988). Some of these tasks have been adapted for use in rats (Mumby, Pinel, Kornecook, Shen, & Redila, 1995; Mumby, Pinel, & Wood, 1990; Rothblat & Hayes, 1987), providing a potential for the development of rat models that parallel the successful monkey models of amnesia.

What Can Animal Models Tell Us About Amnesia?

The Minimal Brain Lesion for Amnesia

It has been known for decades that bilateral damage to midline diencephalic or medial temporal areas can produce amnesia, yet there remains uncertainty about the role of damage to specific structures within these areas. It is difficult to determine the critical damage in patients with amnesia because most of them have damage to several structures. For example, medial temporal lobe amnesia is associated with variable bilateral damage to the hippocampus, amygdala, the cortical areas overlying these structures, and temporal lobe white matter. Things are further complicated by the requirement of having to wait until death occurs naturally or by accident before the patient's brain can be examined in detail. The physical appearance and functional consequences of a lesion can gradually evolve after the initial damage, due to regrowth or reorganization. Animal models are critical for determining the minimal lesion required to produce amnesia because they allow control over the location and extent of a surgical lesion and detailed examination of the brain near the time of memory assessment.

Asking what structures must be damaged to produce amnesia first requires some agreement about what features of amnesia should be modeled. There are several dimensions to the memory impairment in amnesia. Should we expect our animal models to represent all of them? Or is it sufficient to assume that reproducing a single core symptom indicates the presence of global amnesia? Most investigators seem to have chosen the latter strategy. By far, the majority of studies of amnesia in nonhumans have used either the DNMS or the DMS task, and deficits on these tasks are often interpreted as indicating global amnesia. I return to this issue again later, but for now, the important point is that the search for the minimal lesion that will produce amnesia has, more or less, involved a search for the minimal lesion that will produce DNMS or DMS deficits.

Following Mishkin's (1978) report that bilateral removal of the hippocampus and amygdala produced severe DNMS deficits, whereas bilateral removal of either structure alone produced only mild deficits, several other studies seemed to support this claim (see reviews by Duva et al., this volume, and by Murray, 1996). There were, however, alternative interpretations. For instance, Horel (1978) hypothesized that amnesia was caused by damage to the temporal stem: a fiber pathway that links the temporal cortex with the amygdala and the frontal cortex. The temporal stem is damaged in monkeys and humans with amygdalo-hippocampal lesions, and Cirillo, Horel, and George (1989) observed severe DMS deficits in monkeys with anterior-temporal-stem lesions that spared the amygdala and hippocampus (cf. Zola-Morgan, Squire, & Mishkin, 1982). The rhinal cortex (entorhinal and perirhinal cortex), as well as the parahippocampal gyrus, was also damaged in H.M. and is damaged in monkeys with amygdalo-hippocampal lesions. It is now clear that rhinal cortex lesions impair DNMS performance in monkeys (Meunier, Bachevalier, Mishkin, & Murray, 1993) and rats (Mumby & Pinel, 1994) and that lesions of the hippocampus and amygdala that spare the rhinal cortex have negligible effects on DNMS performance (Mumby, Wood, & Pinel, 1992; O'Boyle, Murray, & Mishkin, 1995). These findings suggest that the contribution to amnesia of hippocampal and amygdalar damage has been overestimated, and many investigators are currently focusing instead on the rhinal cortex.

Why did it take almost 20 years to realize the importance of the rhinal cortex? The reasons underscore two major shortcomings of monkey models: Few investigators have access to them, and the research is expensive for those who do. As a result, the appropriate surgical controls for the amygdalar and hippocampal lesions were not done until more than a decade after Mishkin's (1978) study. This helped to sustain the hypothesis that medial temporal lobe amnesia was caused by combined damage to the hippocampus and amygdala. Still, despite slow progress at times, we have clearly learned a great deal about the damage underlying temporal lobe amnesia through the study of animal models.

Animal models have also been used to determine the critical damage in diencephalic amnesia. The most common form of diencephalic amnesia is Korsakoff's amnesia, which is associated with damage in two regions: the mammillary bodies and the midline thalamus (Victor, Adams, & Collins, 1971). Lesions in the mediodorsal region of the thalamus produce DNMS deficits in monkeys (Aggleton & Mishkin, 1983) and rats (Mumby, Pinel, & Dastur, 1993), but lesions of the mammillary bodies do not (Aggleton & Mishkin, 1985). These findings from lesion experiments in monkeys and rats are consistent with the hypothesis that the critical lesion in diencephalic amnesia is in the mediodorsal region of the thalamus. Nevertheless, even if we assume that surgical lesions of the thalamus reproduce the critical brain damage of Korsakoff's amnesia, we must be cautious in assuming that the functional consequences of the lesions are the same. Korsakoff's disease has an insidious course, which may allow for neural reorganization as the neuropathology progresses over months or years. The functional consequences may be quite different from those of discrete surgical lesions in the same critical areas. Moreover, the amnesic syndrome may reflect interactions among the functional consequences of damage in several areas, including some that are not affected by a surgical lesion. Patients with Korsakoff's disease have frontal lobe pathology that may contribute to some of their symptoms (Janowsky, Shimamura, Kritchevsky, & Squire, 1989).

Lost and Spared Memory Abilities in Amnesia

The presence of some normal memory abilities in amnesia suggests that there are at least two kinds of long-term memory, and attempts to describe the critical differences between the spared and impaired abilities have been based mostly on studies in normal humans and patients with amnesia. One descriptive scheme distinguishes between *explicit* memory, which involves conscious recollection of information, and *implicit* memory, which involves the expression of stored information in the absence of conscious recollection. Patients with amnesia are impaired on tasks that require explicit memory, but not on tasks that only require implicit memory (Graf & Schacter, 1985). Another scheme contrasts *declarative* memory, which is said to be impaired in amnesia, and *procedural* memory, which is said to be spared. Information in declarative memory consists of previously experienced perceptions, thoughts, or facts, which for the most part can be described verbally by the individual who possesses them (Squire, 1992). Procedural memories, on the other hand, are inherent in the quality of learned actions, such as motor or perceptual skills.

There are obvious difficulties in applying the concept of declarative memory to animals. Animals cannot describe what they remember, so we cannot confirm or disconfirm their use of declarative memory. An interesting solution has been to elaborate the definition of declarative memory so that it includes defining features that can be operationalized in memory tasks for nonhuman animals. During the past 10 years, descriptions of declarative memory have begun to include the capacity for the *flexible* use of stored representations of previous experiences. The idea is that declarative memory includes information about the relations that exist between separate items, and this allows remembered information to be expressed in a variety of ways. Memory tasks that require the flexible use of stored information can be devised for animals. The finding that rats with fornix lesions fail such tasks has been viewed as evidence that the hippocampus is critical for declarative memory (Eichenbaum, Matthews, & Cohen, 1989).

What about the explicit–implicit memory distinction? We have no way of knowing if an animal experiences anything like the conscious recollection of a past event. Can the existence of explicit memory ever be confirmed in animals? Perhaps not entirely, but a general strategy for asking whether a memory task for animals involves processes that are similar to explicit memory is to examine the effects of certain task manipulations that are known to have different effects on explicit and implicit remembering in humans. For example, distraction during the retention interval disrupts the performance of humans on explicit-memory tests but not implicit-memory tests (Graf & Schacter, 1985). DNMS performance in rats

(Mumby, 1992) and monkeys (Zola-Morgan & Squire, 1985) is disrupted when the subjects must perform a distraction task during the retention interval. Does this mean that the DNMS task requires explicit memory in rats and monkeys? The effect of distraction by itself might not be very convincing, but the evidence could become more compelling if enough manipulations were found to have similar effects on explicit memory in humans and DNMS performance in animals.

The important point is that current theories about the types of memory affected in amnesia are difficult to evaluate in animal models, and attempts to do so have at times relied on circular arguments (e.g., Squire, 1992). For example, it has been argued that DNMS is a declarative memory task for animals, for the following reasons: (a) Recognition tasks for humans involve declarative memory. (b) Medial temporal damage impairs recognition memory in humans. (c) Medial temporal damage also impairs DNMS performance in monkeys and rats. (d) Therefore, monkeys use declarative memory to solve the DNMS task. This conclusion may be wrong, even if the first three premises are true.

Etiological Factors in Amnesia

An animal model has etiological validity if its neuropathology is produced by processes similar to those underlying the human condition. For example, amnesia can occur in humans after ischemic stroke, and ischemia-induced DNMS deficits in monkeys and rats are assumed to be etiologically valid models of the recognition deficits in this amnesic group (Squire, 1992). The primary etiological factor in Korsakoff's amnesia is thiamine deficiency, and daily administration of the thiamine antagonist pyrithiamine produces diencephalic lesions and learning and memory deficits in a variety of species. Pyrithiamine-induced thiamine deficiency (PTD) in rats is used to model the etiology, diencephalic neuropathology, and memory deficits of Korsakoff's amnesia. PTD in rats impairs performance on DNMS tasks (Mumby, Mana, et al., 1995), on tests of spatial memory (Mair, Anderson, Langlais, & McEntee, 1988), and on certain olfactory- and auditory-based learning tasks (Mair, Knoth, Rabchenuk, & Langlais, 1991). The diencephalic lesions consistently involve intralaminar and mediodorsal thalamic nuclei and, more variably, the posterior thalamic nuclei and medial mammillary bodies. There can also be widespread damage to cortical areas and white matter (Langlais & Savage, 1994), similar to that which is seen in patients with Korsakoff's disease (Harper, Kril, & Halloway, 1985). Thiamine deficiency also causes diencephalic lesions and memory impairment in monkeys (Witt & Goldman-Rakic, 1983).

Animal models with etiological validity may be more homologous with human amnesia than models that involve surgical lesions, but they still have unique limitations. For instance, they can be misleading when used to make inferences about the minimal lesion in amnesia. For example, it has been argued that the hippocampus is the critical site of damage in ischemia-induced amnesia because memory deficits are frequently observed in ischemic subjects whose damage appears to be mostly confined to the hippocampus (Squire, 1992). The findings do confirm that ischemia causes memory impairment, but they actually tell us very little about what damage is critical. Even a meticulous examination involving several histological methods can still overlook important pathology.

Perhaps the best use for models with etiological validity is for studying the processes that produce the neuropathology in complex disorders, such as ischemia or thiamine deficiency, where an initial metabolic disruption puts into motion several pathogenic sequelae, which interact in complex ways to determine the final outcome. It has been suggested that the pattern of brain damage and cognitive impairment after ischemia or PTD results from pathological processes that occur in two stages: There is *primary* damage to selectively vulnerable brain areas, such as the thalamus in the case of PTD or the hippocampus in the case of ischemia, and there is the potential for *secondary* brain damage, which results not directly from the thiamine deficiency or ischemia, but from pathogenic processes that are caused by the primary damage (Mumby et al., 1996). Possible mechanisms for the mediation of secondary damage include seizures or edema, both of which are observed in the PTD model and during recovery from ischemia. Dissociating the primary and secondary pathology and memory deficits will be a future challenge for animal models of amnesia induced by ischemia or thiamine deficiency.

What Can Animal Models of Amnesia Tell Us About Normal Memory?

Multiple Memory Systems

Most investigators today assume that the mammalian brain comprises multiple memory systems, which differ in terms of their anatomy and the kinds of information that they deal with. There is considerably less agreement about how many independent systems there are and how they should be characterized. For decades, these questions have been the focus of research and theorizing by cognitive scientists and neuropsychologists who study memory in humans, whereas others have explored the same general issues with lesion experiments in laboratory animals. For the most part, research has proceeded independently in these two domains, with each one generating its own terms and concepts and, not surprisingly, its own theories about multiple memory systems. Animal models of amnesia are squarely positioned between these two research lines, and thus they provide a conduit through which human and animal investigations influence each other.

The central issues related to multiple memory systems include questions about their anatomy, the functions of individual circuits, and their interactions. One way that animal models of amnesia have contributed to the investigation of memory systems is by introducing tasks for animals that ostensibly require the same abilities that are tapped by human memory tasks. For example, the DNMS task bears some resemblance to recognition tasks that are administered to humans. Historically, differences in the memory tasks that have been used with rodents and primates have obscured the extent to which their memory abilities, and the neural bases of these abilities, are similar. The adaptation of the DNMS task for use in rats, along with some of the other tasks used in monkey models of amnesia, broadens the comparative basis for studying the neural systems they engage. By virtue of requiring the subject to learn and retain information about objects, they complement the well-studied spatial memory tasks for rodents.

Some investigators today believe that the hippocampal formation and the rhinal cortex are two major components of a temporal lobe memory system, implying that these structures and their connections constitute a single functional system (e.g., Eichenbaum, Otto, & Cohen, 1994; Squire, 1992). A recent formulation of this idea proposes that the functions of the hippocampus are critically dependent on information that it receives through projections from the rhinal cortex (Eichenbaum et al., 1994). This interdependence predicts that it will be impossible to observe functional double dissociations after separate lesions of the rhinal cortex and the hippocampus. Yet such a result was recently observed: Rats with hippocampal lesions were impaired on a delayed-matching-to-place task, whereas rats with perirhinal cortex lesions performed normally. By contrast, the rats with lesions of the perirhinal cortex were impaired on the DNMS task, whereas rats with hippocampal lesions performed normally (Glenn & Mumby, 1996). Double dissociations of function also have been observed in monkeys with lesions of the hippocampal formation versus rhinal cortex (Meunier, Hadfield, Bachevalier, & Murray, 1996). The double dissociations suggest that these structures are better thought of as belonging to separate, functionally independent, memory systems rather than as multiple components of a single temporal lobe memory system. They may participate jointly to serve some memory abilities, but they each can be uniquely engaged by others. An important point is that the present dissociation would not have been discovered if the object-based DNMS task had not been adapted for use with rats.

The main challenge for researchers who seek to delineate memory systems is how to interpret deficits on the memory tasks that they use. Any memory task can be failed for more than one reason, so even if we know how a normal subject solves a particular task, this does not necessarily tell us why the brain-damaged subject fails. For example, it is clear from observations in patients with amnesia and from DNMS experiments in monkeys and rats that visual recognition abilities are impaired by lesions of the rhinal cortex. But knowing that recognition is impaired does not tell us what information-processing operations are disrupted. Several operations must be present and properly integrated for normal recognition to occur.

Interpretations are further complicated by the fact that most memory tasks potentially can be solved in more than one way. For example, the

DNMS task can be solved by explicitly remembering as a distinct episode the presentation of the sample object at the beginning of the trial and comparing that representation with the perceptions of the two objects present during the choice phase. Alternatively, the task can be solved without any explicit recollection of the sample presentation, by instead comparing the relative familiarity of the choice stimuli and selecting the one that feels less familiar. Different solutions require different component functions and therefore, presumably, different neural systems. By this scenario, one could disrupt the functions of a system that normally underlies DNMS performance yet fail to detect a disability because the task can still be solved a different way by using the functions of intact systems.

Seemingly minor changes to a task can drastically alter the way it is solved and, therefore, the neural circuitry that its solution depends on. For example, before the use of nonrecurring (i.e., trial-unique) stimuli on the DNMS task (Gaffan, 1974), conventional DNMS and DMS tasks used only a small number of stimuli, usually two, that recurred over several trials. As a result, the choice on each trial was between two equally familiar items, and thus the task required not only recognition but also a recency discrimination. The use of trial-unique stimuli removes the latter requirement and makes the task a more pure test of stimulus recognition. However, we must be cautious in assuming that rats, monkeys, and humans are solving the DNMS task in the same way, despite the superficial similarities between the versions that are administered to different species.

Retrograde Amnesia and Consolidation of Long-Term Memories

Investigators who use animal models have devoted considerably more attention to reproducing the phenomena of anterograde amnesia than those of retrograde amnesia. One feature of retrograde amnesia that has been the focus of a few studies is the temporal gradient of memory loss that is often observed, that is, the loss of recent memories with relative sparing of more remote memories.

One reported success in producing temporally graded retrograde memory loss in monkeys involved large medial temporal lesions that included the hippocampus, parts of the rhinal cortex, and the posterior temporal stem (Zola-Morgan & Squire, 1990). The question of what damage is responsible for the retrograde amnesia has not yet been answered. Mixed success has been obtained with animal models in rats with selective hippocampal lesions, where there have been reports of temporally graded (Sutherland, Arnold, & Rodriguez, 1987), ungraded (Bolhius, Stewart, & Forrest, 1994), and no retrograde amnesia (Morris, Shenk, Tweedie, & Jarrard, 1990). In the light of a growing awareness that the contribution of hippocampal damage to anterograde amnesia has been overstated, it is likely that attention will now turn elsewhere for an explanation of temporally graded retrograde amnesia in patients with medial temporal lesions.

Part of the motivation for attempts to model temporally graded retrograde amnesia is the belief that it will help us understand certain processes involved in normal memory. For instance, *consolidation* refers to the widely accepted notion that information becomes fixed in long-term memory only some time after its initial encoding. According to one view, the integrity of the medial temporal lobes is critical for the consolidation of long-term representations that are ultimately stored in the neocortex (Zola-Morgan & Squire, 1990). Remote memories are spared after medial temporal lesions because their neocortical representations are fully established in the neocortex and are now independent of the consolidation process involving medial temporal structures; recent memories, by contrast, are impaired because their neocortical representations have not yet been fully consolidated and are still dependent on medial temporal structures. According to this hypothesis, temporal gradients of retrograde amnesia reflect the time course of the consolidation process. Part of the difficulty in reaching any conclusions about the duration of the consolidation processes currently stems from the elusiveness of temporal gradients in animal models of retrograde amnesia. Even considering just those few studies that have reported temporal gradients, the period of time before surgery for which memory was affected ranged from a few days to several months, depending on the species, the treatment, and the memory tasks (reviewed in Squire, 1992). The wide-ranging estimates are not necessarily contradictory, because they may simply reflect the existence of different consolidation processes for different types of information. At the very least, they suggest that questions about temporally graded retrograde amnesia should specify the type of information in question.

The intended use of an animal model of retrograde amnesia has additional implications for the choice of task used to model the memory loss. For example, if the goal is to model as closely as possible the retrograde memory deficits displayed by amnesic patients, then a task that is learned over multiple trials may be more appropriate than a task that is learned on a single trial. The kinds of tasks that are used to assess retrograde amnesia in humans often involve information that a normal individual experiences on numerous separate occasions and in a variety of contexts; examples include tests of memory for famous persons or public events. Alternatively, if the primary objective is to determine the time course of consolidation, then a one-trial task is a better choice because it will permit a more accurate determination of when the critical information was originally registered.

Future Considerations

Until the past decade, most neuropsychologists studying brain lesions and memory in monkeys described their work as modeling amnesia. Meanwhile, lesion experiments in rats were seldom characterized this way. The important distinction between these two domains of research was not really the species involved, but rather the questions that motivated them during the 1970s and 1980s. Lesion studies in rats were mostly interested in questions like, "What are the normal functions of this structure?" whereas until recently, lesion studies in monkeys usually asked questions like, "What contribution does damage in this structure make to amnesia?" These questions are obviously related, but they are not simply redundant, and their answers provide complementary perspectives on brain–memory relations. This distinction between lesion studies in rats and monkeys has blurred considerably in recent years, with attempts to develop models of amnesia in rats and lesion experiments in monkeys that are aimed at understanding the normal memory functions of specific brain structures.

Slightly over 10 years ago, Richard Morris wrote a short article in which he argued eloquently and convincingly that it was "time to move on from too focused a preoccupation in animal lesion studies with modelling amnesia" (Morris, 1985, p. 452). One of his main arguments was that certain features of amnesia, such as the presence of normal intelligence in the face of severe memory loss and the ability of normal animals to engage in conscious (i.e., explicit) recollection, cannot be confirmed in animals. These difficulties remain, and they are not likely to be resolved in the near future. In recent years, studies in monkeys have in fact shifted focus slightly and generally appear to be motivated more by a desire to understand the neuroanatomy of normal memory than to develop theories of global amnesia. It appears, however, that the change in orientation has little to do with the concerns raised by Morris. The real reasons, I believe, have to do with the expansion and elaboration of ideas about multiple memory systems and an increase in the amount of attention given to lesion studies in rats by neuropsychologists who work with humans and non-human primates.

The growth of ideas about multiple memory system brings with it new perspectives, new problems, and new applications for animal models of amnesia. For example, one changing view stems from acknowledging that the DNMS and DMS tasks do not represent all of the memory abilities that are impaired in amnesia. This may explain why in recent years the term *amnesia* seems to be appearing less frequently in the titles and abstracts of studies that use the DNMS and DMS tasks; it is being replaced by phrases like *object-recognition deficit* or *impaired visual recognition*. There is a growing movement away from attempts to develop isomorphic models of amnesia that reproduce all of the features of human amnesia and toward models that reproduce only select aspects of amnesia. This is a desirable trend, because it acknowledges the evidence that global amnesia reflects multiple dissociable memory deficits, each resulting from damage in particular structures or from specific combinations of damaged structures.

This points to an important limitation of isomorphic models: If several structures need to be damaged to reproduce all of the core symptoms of global amnesia, then the animal model that is successful in doing so will not be very helpful in linking specific deficits to specific aspects of the damage. This objective will be better served by creating animal models that represent individual features of amnesia while keeping in mind the inescapable caveat that lesion experiments actually directly assess, not the functions of the damaged structures, but rather the functions of whatever structures remain undamaged.

Some of the major considerations of animal models of amnesia remain unchanged. In general, a model's potential to inform us about the facts of amnesia will depend to a large extent on its external validity, that is, how well it corresponds to the human condition. Would similar brain damage have the same psychological consequences in humans? What memory tasks should be used to demonstrate amnesia in animals? How similar is the neuropathology in alcoholic Korsakoff's disease patients and rats exposed to an acute bout of thiamine deficiency? One area that seems to have been largely neglected in models of amnesia is the importance of demonstrating the selectivity of the memory impairment. Yet this is an important feature that sets amnesia apart from other disorders that include memory impairment among other multiple symptoms, and it seems like it should, therefore, be an integral part of any animal model of amnesia.

There are also numerous questions about the internal validity of animal models, that is, how accurately the elements of the model have been characterized, such as the location and extent of the lesion or pathology or the memory abilities that are required to perform the tasks involved. Does DNMS really require recognition memory? The superficial similarities in the object-based memory tasks that are administered to humans, monkeys, and rats do not justify the assumption that all three species solve these tasks in the same way. At the very least, it is possible to think of ways that the DNMS task can be solved either with or without the use of explicit memory of the sample. If the DNMS task can be solved without explicit memory, are we justified in using it as a benchmark in animal models of amnesia? Are animals that display normal performance or only slight DNMS deficits after hippocampal lesions solving the task the same way that they solved it before surgery? One shortcoming is that animal models of amnesia have used only relatively few tasks. The problem is not that we do not have any good tasks, but rather that we do not have enough of them. For example, the list of spared memory abilities in amnesia has been increasing in recent years, yet there has been little effort to develop tasks that assess similar spared abilities in animal models of amnesia. These are important issues, but it is also important to avoid making the tasks the focus of inquiry. They are, after all, only tools that we use to index memory abilities and functions.

References

Aggleton, J. P., & Mishkin, M. (1983). Visual recognition impairment following medial thalamic lesions in monkeys. *Neuropsychologia, 21,* 189–197.

Aggleton, J. P., & Mishkin, M. (1985). Mammillary-body lesions and visual recognition in the monkey. *Experimental Brain Research, 58,* 190–197.

Aggleton, J. P., Nicol, R. M., Huston, A. E., & Fairbairn, A. F. (1988). The performance of amnesic subjects on tests of experimental amnesia in animals: Delayed matching-to-sample and concurrent learning. *Neuropsychologia, 26,* 265–272.

Aggleton, J. P., Shaw, C., & Gaffan, E. A. (1992). The performance of postencephalitic amnesic subjects on two behavioral tests of memory: Concurrent discrimination learning and delayed matching-to-sample. *Cortex, 28* 359–372.

Bolhuis, J. J., Stewart, C. A., & Forrest, E. M. (1994). Retrograde amnesia and memory reactivation in rats with ibotenate lesions to the hippocampus or subiculum. *Quarterly Journal of Experimental Psychology, 47B,* 129–150.

Cirillo, R. A., Horel, J. A., & George, P. J. (1989). Lesions of the anterior temporal stem and the performance of delayed match-to-sample and visual discrimination. *Behavioural Brain Research, 34,* 55–69.

Correll, R. E., & Scoville, W. B. (1965). Performance on delayed match following lesions of medial temporal lobe structures. *Journal of Comparative and Physiological Psychology, 60,* 360–367.

Drachman, D. A., & Ommaya, A. K. (1964). Memory and the hippocampal complex. *Archives of Neurology, 10,* 411–425.

Eichenbaum, H., Matthews, P., & Cohen, N. J. (1989). Further studies of hippocampal representation during odor discrimination learning. *Behavioral Neuroscience, 103,* 1207–1216.

Eichenbaum, H., Otto, T., & Cohen, N. J. (1994). Two functional components of the hippocampal memory system. *Behavioral and Brain Sciences, 17,* 449–518.

Gaffan, D. (1974). Recognition impaired and association intact in the memory of monkeys after transection of the fornix. *Journal of Comparative and Physiological Psychology, 86,* 1100–1109.

Glenn, M. J., & Mumby, D. G. (1996). Place- and object-recognition deficits following lesions of the hippocampus or perirhinal cortex in rats: A double dissociation. *Society for Neuroscience Abstracts, 22,* 1120.

Graf, P., & Schacter, D. L. (1985). Implicit and explicit memory for new associations in normal and amnesic subjects. *Journal of Experimental Psychology: Learning, Memory and Cognition, 11,* 501–518.

Harper, C. G., Kril, J. J., & Halloway, R. L. (1985). Brain shrinkage in chronic alcoholics: A pathologic study. *British Medical Journal, 290,* 501–504.

Holdstock, J. S., Shaw, C., & Aggleton, J. P. (1995). The performance of amnesic subjects on tests of delayed matching-to-sample and delayed matching-to-position. *Neuropsychologia, 12,* 1583–1596.

Horel, J. A. (1978). The neuroanatomy of amnesia: A critique of the hippocampal memory hypothesis. *Brain, 101,* 403–445.

Janowsky, J. S., Shimamura, A. P., Kritchevsky, M., & Squire, L. R. (1989). Cognitive impairment following frontal lobe damage and its relevance to human amnesia. *Behavioral Neuroscience, 103,* 548–560.

Langlais, P. J., & Savage, L. M. (1994). Thiamine deficiency in rats produces cognitive and memory deficits on spatial tasks that correlate with tissue loss in diencephalon, cortex and white matter. *Behavioural Brain Research, 68,* 75–89.

Mair, R. G., Anderson, C. D., Langlais, P. J., & McEntee, W. J. (1988). Behavioral impairments, brain lesions and monoaminergic activity in the rat following recovery from a bout of thiamine deficiency. *Behavioural Brain Research, 27,* 223–239.

Mair, R. G., Knoth, R. L., Rabchenuk, S. A., & Langlais, P. J. (1991). Impairment of olfactory, auditory, and spatial serial reversal learning in rats recovered from pyrithiamine-induced thiamine deficiency. *Behavioral Neuroscience, 105,* 360–374.

Meunier, M., Bachevalier, J., Mishkin, M., & Murray, E. A. (1993). Effects on visual recognition of combined and separate ablations of the entorhinal and perirhinal cortex in rhesus monkeys. *Journal of Neuroscience, 13,* 5418–5432.

Meunier, M., Hadfield, W., Bachevalier, J., & Murray, E. A. (1996). Effects of rhinal cortex lesions combined with hippocampectomy on visual recognition memory in rhesus monkeys. *Journal of Neurophysiology, 75,* 1190–1205.

Mishkin, M. (1954). Visual discrimination performance following partial ablations of the temporal lobe: II. Ventral surface vs. hippocampus. *Journal of Comparative and Physiological Psychology, 47,* 187–193.

Mishkin, M. (1978). Memory in monkeys severely impaired by combined but not by separate removal of amygdala and hippocampus. *Nature, 273,* 297–298.

Morris, R. G. M. (1985). Moving on from modelling amnesia. In N. M. Weinberger, J. L. McGaugh, & G. Lynch (Eds.), *Memory systems of the brain: Animal and human cognitive processes* (pp. 452–461). New York: Guilford Press.

Morris, R. G. M., Shenk, F., Tweedie, F., & Jarrard, L. (1990). Ibotenate lesions of the hippocampus and/or subiculum: Dissociating the components of allocentric spatial learning. *European Journal of Neuroscience, 2,* 1016–1028.

Mumby, D. G. (1992). *Development of a rat model of brain-damage-produced amnesia.* Unpublished doctoral dissertation, University of British Columbia, Vancouver, British Columbia, Canada.

Mumby, D. G., Mana, M. J., Pinel, J. P. J., Banks, K., & David, E. (1995). Pyrithiamine-induced thiamine deficiency impairs object recognition in rats. *Behavioral Neuroscience, 109,* 1209–1214.

Mumby, D. G., & Pinel, J. P. J. (1994). Rhinal cortex lesions and object recognition in rats. *Behavioral Neuroscience, 108,* 11–18.

Mumby, D. G., Pinel, J. P. J., & Dastur, F. N. (1993). Mediodorsal thalamic lesions impair object recognition in rats. *Psychobiology, 21,* 27–36.

Mumby, D. G., Pinel, J. P. J., Kornecook, T. J., Shen, M. J., & Redila, V. A. (1995). Memory deficits following lesions of hippocampus or amygdala in rats: Assessment by an object-memory test battery. *Psychobiology, 23,* 26–36.

Mumby, D. G., Pinel, J. P. J., & Wood, E. R. (1990). Nonrecurring-items delayed nonmatching-to-sample in rats: A new paradigm for testing nonspatial working memory. *Psychobiology, 18,* 321–326.

Mumby, D. G., Wood, E. R., Duva, C. A., Kornecook, T. J., Pinel, J. P. J., & Phillips, A. G. (1996). Ischemia-induced object-recognition deficits in rats are attenuated by hippocampal ablation before or soon after ischemia. *Behavioral Neuroscience, 110,* 266–281.

Mumby, D. G., Wood, E. R., & Pinel, J. P. J. (1992). Object-recognition memory is only mildly impaired in rats with lesions of the hippocampus and amygdala. *Psychobiology, 20,* 18–27.

Murray, E. A. (1996). What have ablation studies told us about the neural substrates of stimulus memory? *Seminars in the Neurosciences, 8,* 13–22.

O'Boyle, V. J., Murray, E. A., & Mishkin, M. (1995). Effects of excitotoxic amygdalo–hippocampal lesions on visual recognition in rhesus monkeys. *Society for Neuroscience Abstracts, 19,* 438.

Orbach, J., Milner, B., & Rasmussen, T. (1960). Learning and retention in monkeys after amygdala–hippocampus resection. *Archives of Neurology, 3,* 230–251.

Rothblat, L. A., & Hayes, L. L. (1987). Short-term object recognition memory in the rat: Nonmatching with trial-unique stimuli. *Behavioral Neuroscience, 101,* 587–590.

Scoville, W. B., & Milner, B. (1957). Loss of recent memory after bilateral hippocampal lesions. *Journal of Neurology, Neurosurgery, and Psychiatry, 20,* 11–21.

Squire, L. R. (1992). Memory and the hippocampus: A synthesis from findings with rats, monkeys, and humans. *Psychological Review, 99,* 195–231.

Squire, L. R., Zola-Morgan, S., & Chen, K. (1988). Human amnesia and animal models of amnesia: Performance of amnesic patients on tests designed for the monkey. *Behavioral Neuroscience, 11,* 210–221.

Sutherland, R. J., Arnold, K. A., & Rodriguez, A. R. (1987). Anterograde and retrograde effects on place memory after limbic or diencephalic damage. *Society for Neuroscience Abstracts, 13,* 1066.

Victor, M., Adams, R. D., & Collins, G. H. (1971). *The Wernicke–Korsakoff syndrome.* Philadelphia: Davis.

Witt, E. D., & Goldman-Rakic, P. S. (1983). Intermittent thiamine deficiency in the rhesus monkey: 2. Evidence for memory loss. *Annals of Neurology, 13,* 396–401.

Zola-Morgan, S., & Squire, L. R. (1985). Medial temporal lesions in monkeys impair memory on a variety of tasks sensitive to human amnesia. *Behavioral Neuroscience, 99,* 22–34.

Zola-Morgan, S., & Squire, L. R. (1990). The primate hippocampal formation: Evidence for a time-limited role in memory storage. *Science, 250,* 288–290.

Zola-Morgan, S., Squire, L. R., & Mishkin, M. (1982). The neuroanatomy of amnesia: Amygdala–hippocampus vs. temporal stem. *Science, 218,* 1337–1339.

15

Behavioral and Pharmacological Analyses of Memory: New Behavioral Options for Remediation

J. Bruce Overmier, Lisa M. Savage,
and Whitney A. Sweeney

On Animal Models and Applications

From the beginnings of scientific psychology, especially in the United States, psychologists have assumed that basic animal research would yield insights that could be applied to clinical and educational practice, despite the gulf between the research animal laboratory and the therapeutic clinic for human dysfunction (e.g., Pavlov, 1906; Watson, 1913). The metatheoretical bases for this assumption were the commonality of the underlying physiology and of psychological and associative mechanisms across species; any new basic principles and laws of behavior discovered were expected to have broad applicability.

So confident were the early scientists of this metatheoretical ground that they did indeed move quickly to apply newly discovered principles. Thorndike (1914) applied the law of effect in the classroom, as did Skinner (1954) with teaching machines. Others were concerned with psychiatric disorders: Their approach here was to model the behavioral dysfunction, synthesizing it using the newly discovered basic principles, and then, on the basis of the etiology or mechanisms revealed in this synthesis, to find therapeutic operations that remedied the dysfunction (see McDonald & Overmier, 1998; Overmier, 1992; Overmier & Patterson, 1988, on the nature of and use of models). An early and well-known example of this approach is Watson and Rayner's (1920) synthesis of a "phobia" in Little Albert from Pavlov's newly discovered laws of classical conditioning and their suggestion that Pavlovian counterconditioning would be an effective therapeutic technique—suggestions that Mary Cover Jones (1924) later tested. There are clear exemplars from the animal laboratory, too. For example, following Masserman's (1943) earlier lead, Wolpe (1952) studied "neurotic" behavior in the cat and deduced the therapeutic principles of reciprocal inhibition—a deduction that has provided much relief for hundreds of thousands of patients with phobias.

On the basis of the hopes and expectations generated by the early successful demonstrations and broad applications of general laws and theories of learning (e.g., Dollard & Miller, 1950), the study of learning theory became a central element of graduate training for all psychologists. With that training, additional successes were notable: Azrin, Krasner, and Lovaas successfully extended operant methods to hospitalized populations (see reviews in Neuringer & Michael, 1970), while Stampfl and Levis (1967) developed "implosive therapy" for phobias from animal laboratory studies of extinction of conditioned fear. But, alas, with the professionalization of clinical psychology training, fewer and fewer students took graduate training in the psychology of learning and—not incidentally—fewer and fewer findings from basic laboratory research on learning and its underlying mechanisms were translated into clinical applications.

There are some notable counterinstances to this trend, such as the rediscovery and elaboration of a basic behavioral phenomenon of stress-induced, proactive interference with coping behaviors—a phenomenon that Overmier and Seligman (1967) christened "learned helplessness" (p. 33). Seligman (1975), who not incidentally is a classically trained learning psychologist, went on to develop this observation into a model for depression (see Peterson, Maier, & Seligman, 1993, for a thorough review of this model and its applicability).

It has now been some time since a new learning principle was recognized and extended into the clinical domain. We believe that we are on the verge of having a new instance: *differential outcomes* phenomenon. This phenomenon appears to involve activation of a form of prospective memory, and it promises to aid those with learning and memory problems.

Differential Outcomes Effect

We now discuss a set of laboratory learning phenomena originally discovered in our laboratories at Minnesota (Overmier, Bull, & Trapold, 1971; Trapold, 1970) but now widely recognized (e.g., Goeters, Blakely, & Poling, 1992; McIlvane, Dube, Kledaras, deRose, & Stoddard, 1992). We believe that the finding provides a tool that is modestly useful in the teaching and training of learning- and memory-impaired individuals. The excursion from the laboratory to the clinic is an extended one. The path of discovery sprang from a reanalysis of the fundamental tenets of the law of effect and of the so-called two-process theories of learning (Trapold & Overmier, 1972).

According to the venerable and popular law of effect (Thorndike, 1914), when in the presence of a particular discriminative stimulus, a specific response occurs and this sequence is immediately followed by a reward; the reward "stamps in" or reinforces an association between the stimulus (S) and the response (R)—a so-called S–R association. Important for our discussion, the S–R association theory implies that the reward itself is not learned about, or is not part of the association, but rather is merely a catalyst for the S–R association. According to this view, the particular reward doesn't really matter; presumably, one should be able to use different rewards across successive trials and have the same reinforcing effect on the learning as would occur if one had always used the same reward after each trial. On reflection, that the reward is not learned about, or is not part of the association, seems awkward because one of the apparent features of instrumental behavior is that it is purposive and "reward seeking" (Tinkelpaugh, 1928).

According to the two-process theory, the occurrence of the reward actually results in two associations: one between the S and the R (S–R) and one between the S and the reward (S–S*); these two in concert determine and motivate, respectively, the response. Tests of this idea took the form of *transfer-of-control* experiments, in which a classical conditioned stimulus (CS) that had been paired with a reward was compounded with—or substituted for—the discriminative stimulus for a previously trained specific response reinforced by the same reward (see Overmier & Lawry, 1979, for several examples). The results were that the classical CS+ markedly facilitated and controlled the instrumental responding.

What was the mechanism of this control of the instrumental responding? Although the usual two-process view was that the pairing of the CS with the reward endowed the CS with general motivational properties (e.g., Rescorla & Solomon, 1967), Trapold and Overmier (1972) took a different view. They theorized that the embedded pairing resulted in the subject's learning something specific about the qualitative and quantitative properties of the reward, forming a *conditioned expectation* of the reward. According to this view, the classical conditioned response that arises when a cue stimulus is paired with a reward is merely the overt manifestation of this conditioned expectation of the reward. They further theorized that this conditioned expectation had functional stimuluslike or cue properties that guided specific acts rather than merely providing general motivation. Such conditioned expectations are a kind of *prospective memory*— a cue-elicited memory of which reward has come next in the past. In the case of differential outcomes, then, each discriminative cue elicits a different prospective memory of the scheduled reward that can combine with—or substitute for—the retrospective memory of the discriminative cue to better guide the animal in choosing correctly among responses.

On the basis of this theory, Trapold and Overmier (1972) began a series of experiments designed to demonstrate (a) that particular behaviors are guided by the prospective memories of the rewards that are consequent to the behaviors, (b) that classical conditioning is the mechanism for establishing these prospective memories that are specific to the reward, and (c) that independent evocation of these prospective memories can selectively cue behaviors that lead to that specific reward. In this, Trapold and Overmier focused on the study of choice behaviors because selection of a particular choice alternative is easily seen as guided or cued but is relatively difficult to interpret in terms of simple, general motivation.

To demonstrate that behaviors can be guided by prospective memories of to-be-earned rewards, Trapold and Overmier (1972) contrasted the learning of two virtually identical, discriminative, conditional choice tasks, as shown in Figure 15.1. The only difference was that in one procedure,

Standard Discriminative Conditional Choice

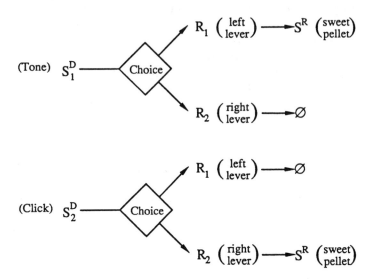

Differential Outcomes Discriminative Conditional Choice

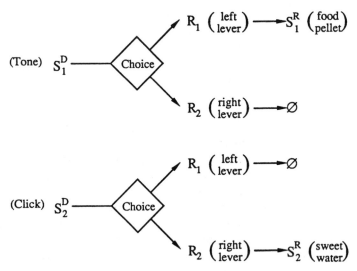

Figure 15.1.   A sketch of the standard common outcomes versus the differential outcomes paradigms for training conditional discriminations. The task to be learned in each is identical; only the reward contingencies differ between the paradigms. In the differential outcomes paradigm (bottom), each correct discriminative stimulus–choice alternative has its own unique reward. In this group, if the discriminative stimulus elicited a prospective memory–anticipation of the unique reward, it could help guide the choice. S = stimulus; R = response.

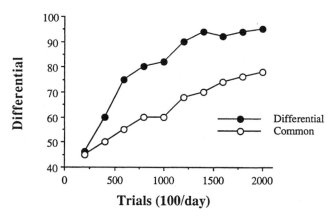

Figure 15.2. Rates of learning a conditional choice discrimination by rats in a two-choice lever box. Data from Trapold (1970).

called the *differential outcomes* procedure, each of the two correct S–R sequences was rewarded with its own unique reinforcer, whereas in the traditional standard procedure, both responses were followed by a *common outcome*.[1] According to the simple law of effect or even the two-process motivational view, this simple variation in training procedure should not matter substantially. But a theory that invokes specific prospective memories of to-be-earned rewards and hypothesizes that these prospective memories have unique cue properties must predict that the differential outcomes procedure should result in learning both faster and to a higher asymptote. Indeed, this is exactly what is found (e.g., Overmier et al., 1971; Trapold, 1970). These features are seen in Figure 15.2.

The next task was to demonstrate that classical conditioning is the mechanism for establishing these prospective memories that are specific to the reward and that evocation of these expectancies can selectively cue behaviors that lead to that reward. Kruse, Overmier, Konz, and Rokke (1983) did this experimentally, using a three-step transfer-of-control experiment: First, rats were trained in a conditional discriminative choice task with the differential outcomes procedure, as shown in the bottom of Figure 15.1; the second stage was carried out in a new context and was merely classical conditioning of a CS+ with one of the two rewards; the third stage was conducted in the choice context and consisted of presentation of the CS to test its power to directly induce the animal to make a specific choice. If the particular reward used is irrelevant, then choosing

---

[1]The common outcomes procedure is the usual laboratory arrangement for training conditional discriminations. The common outcomes procedure usually indicates the same reward after all responses, as is illustrated. However, when contrasted with the differential outcomes procedure, a variation of the common outcomes procedure is sometimes used in which each of the correct S–R sequences is followed randomly by either of the two rewards to control for the two different rewards that the other group is getting; this version of common outcomes is called *mixed* or *random outcomes*. In general, the results and phenomena we discuss are obtained without regard to kind of common outcomes procedure used, and we do not distinguish among them.

should be random. However, if the CS elicits a specific prospective memory that in turn has unique cue properties, then the CS should function to guide the animal into making the choice response that had previously produced that specific reward. That is exactly what occurred: The CS that had previously been paired with a food pellet later led to the animal's pressing the lever that had been reinforced with a food pellet, whereas the CS that had been paired with sweet water later led to its pressing the lever that had been reinforced with sweet water, even though the rats had never before made any choice responses in the presence of either CS. This result was taken as strong confirmation of the hypothesized cue properties of conditioned prospective memories and their response-guiding functions.

One might reasonably wonder which additional properties or functions these prospective memories might have. Are they an additional source of cues in conditional choice paradigms that might help the organism make correct choices even after a delay? A common strategy for assessing memorial function over relatively short delays involves variations on the matching-to-sample (MTS) paradigm, including symbolic-matching-to-sample (SMTS) and matching-from-sample (MFS; e.g., Zola-Morgan & Squire, 1986). These are all conditional discriminative choice tasks in which varying delays may be imposed between the occurrence of the discriminative stimulus and the opportunities to respond to the choice alternatives. Because in these conditional discriminations the choices are directed to alternative stimuli rather than to alternative locations, they are sometimes also referred to as *symbolic relation tasks*; an example is illustrated in Figure 15.3.

It is important for our discussion that all of these forms of discriminative choice may be taught with either the common outcomes or the differential outcomes procedure. Indeed, the learning of such conditional discriminations when delays are imposed has been studied with both procedures for rewarding behavior. The results with pigeons and rats uniformly are that the use of the differential outcomes procedure yields dramatically superior performance over delays and that this superiority actually increases with the delay (Brodigan & Peterson, 1976; Linwick, Overmier, Peterson, & Mertens, 1988; Peterson, Linwick, & Overmier, 1987). This is illustrated in Figure 15.4. That is, the differential outcomes procedure actually enables the animal to solve memory problems at delays at which they would otherwise fail!

The differential outcomes subjects can, in principle, solve these delay problems on the basis of either (a) their regular "retrospective" memory of what the discriminative stimulus was or (b) their elicited prospective memory—with its associated cue properties—of what the upcoming reward will be. The common outcomes procedure affords only one source of information: the retrospective recall of what the discriminative stimulus (sample) was. But, as Figure 15.4 makes clear, the retrospective memory can be very short lived, apparently diminishing to near zero strength within about 10 s in pigeons. Hence, we infer that after moderate delays in the differential outcomes procedure, choices are mediated and controlled solely by prospective memories of particular rewards. In addi-

Discriminative Conditional Choice as Symbolic Relation Learning

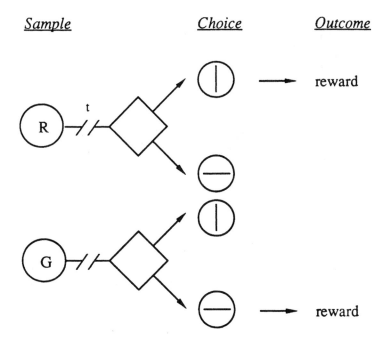

Sample   *Choice*   *Outcome*

t = delay between Sample and Choices as a test on Memory

Figure 15.3. An illustration of symbolic relation learning cast as a discriminative conditional choice task. The broken line and "t" refer to variable delays. The two rewards may be the same (common outcomes) or unique to the choice alternative (differential outcomes).

tion, one can infer that such prospective memories are more persistent than retrospective memories (see Linwick et al., 1988; Peterson et al., 1987).

On the basis of the evidence presented here, it is clear that the prospective memory elicited by the discriminative stimulus-to-reinforcer association is critical for facilitating choice accuracy in our differential outcomes procedure. It is possible that other associations created by virtue of the differential outcomes procedure may contribute to performance. For example, also embedded within the differential outcomes procedure is a perfect correlation between a particular choice alternative and its corresponding unique outcome. This relation may produce a response–outcome association that enhances performance (DeMarse & Urcuioli, 1993; Rescorla, 1992). However, a set of clever experiments by Sherburne and Zentall (1998) have demonstrated that this contribution, if any, is likely to be small.

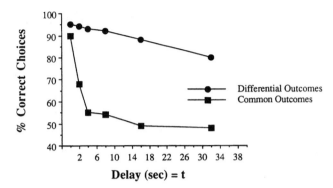

Figure 15.4. Performances on a discriminative conditional choice symbolic-matching task by pigeons as a function reward paradigm based on Linwick, Overmier, Peterson, and Mertens (1988).

Extension to Humans

When one finds a new powerful behavioral training technique for aiding learning and memory in animals, one begins to contemplate using that technique in applied situations with human populations in which the learning of discriminations and symbolic relations are a special challenge. Before one can embark on that, one needs to establish that the principles at hand are, in fact, general ones that apply to humans as well as animals. Maki, Overmier, Delos, and Gutmann (1995) demonstrated that 4- to 6-year-old children learned conditional symbolic discriminations more readily when taught with the differential outcomes procedure than with the common outcomes procedure. Indeed, they were able to learn problems under the differential outcomes procedure that were otherwise unlearnable (Experiment 1). On the basis of postexperimental query, this appeared to be because they had learned to expect the unique rewards for each symbolic relation. Moreover, parallel to the animal experiments, Maki et al. used a transfer-of-control test to show that a classical CS paired with one of the rewards could correctly control the previously trained discriminative choice behavior for that reward. These results demonstrated that prospective memories are conditioned in humans and that humans, too, can and do use the cue properties of these prospective memories to guide choice behavior.

This research was extended with a more challenged population, clients with Prader-Willi syndrome who suffer a congenital disorder that is associated with incomplete physical development, life-threatening obesity, and mild mental retardation or learning difficulties. Joseph, Overmier, and Thompson (1997) found that these clients more readily learned concepts and complicated equivalence relations when taught these using conditional discrimination training with the differential outcomes procedure than with standard common outcomes procedures. So it is clear that the differential outcomes procedure can serve as a training aid in at least some learning-challenged populations.

Potential for Application With Memory Disorders

The locus of the most powerful effect of the differential outcomes procedure is on memory-based performance rather than de novo learning. This consideration suggests that if one is interested in applications, one should focus on populations that show severe memory deficits, such as patients with senile dementia, Alzheimer's disease, or Korsakoff's disease. All of these diseases seem to have cholinergic dysfunction as at least one component. Experimental animal models of the memory deficits have commonly begun with manipulation of the cholinergic system (e.g., Bartus, Dean, Beer, & Lippa, 1982; Dawson, Heyes, & Iverson, 1992; McDonald & Overmier, 1998).

Therefore, Savage, Stanchfield, and Overmier (1994) undertook to confirm whether (a) moderate doses of scopolamine, a cholinergic antagonist and known amnestic agent, would impair performance on a conditional discriminative choice task with delays between the discriminative stimulus and the choice alternatives and whether (b) the degree of impairment would be modulated by training under the differential outcomes as opposed to the common outcomes procedure. One result is that a moderate dose of scopolamine (0.007 to 0.03 mg/kg in pigeons) did impair previously established asymptotic performances of >90% correct at 0-s delay. It is important for our purposes that the degree of impairment was greater when the birds had been trained under the common outcomes than under the differential outcomes procedure, and this difference was greater at the longer delays than at the shorter ones. The result is shown in Figure 15.5. In the presence of an amnestic process—here an anticholinergic drug— the differential outcomes procedure provided some degree of relief from memory impairment.

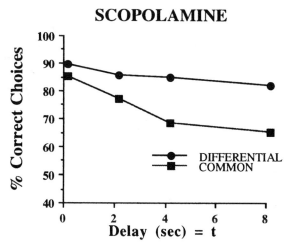

Figure 15.5. Postasymptotic performances on tests of matching-to-sample by pigeons in a two-key chamber under drug (averaged over three doses) as a function of training condition. Data from Savage, Stanchfield, and Overmier (1994).

Two Memory Systems?

An alternative and perhaps more theoretically focused way of describing the prior result is that retrospective memory appears to be substantially dependent on cholinergic mechanisms, whereas prospective memory is less so—perhaps even being independent of the cholinergic system. That is, we are implicitly claiming that there are two different memory systems that can be used to solve conditional discriminations that are trained under the differential outcomes procedure: a retrospective one and a prospective one.

Any claim of two different memory systems would be buttressed if one could provide a double dissociation between the two. We have already reported here that anticholinergic drugs impair performances that are based on retrospective memory, leaving performances presumably based on prospective memory relatively intact. Can we find a treatment that would do the opposite and, hence, provide the required double dissociation (Weiskrantz, 1968)?

Savage and Parsons (1997) appear to have done so. They used the matching-to-position form of conditional discrimination for which the differential outcomes procedure typically enhances choice performances after a delay interval. They have shown that the drug dizocilpine (MK–801), a noncompetitive N-methyl-D-aspartate (NMDA) antagonist at 0.18 mg/kg, has virtually no effect on delayed choice performance by rats trained under the common outcomes procedure, but it disrupts delayed choice performance of rats trained under the differential outcomes procedure. Figure 15.6 shows this new result. This is the opposite effect of scopolamine that we described earlier.

Together, these two results appear to provide the desired double dissociation that allows us to affirm that there are two neurochemically distinct memory systems. Delayed performances under the common outcomes procedure relies on one—retrospective memory—that is cholinergically mediated, whereas performances under the differential outcomes procedure relies on the other—prospective memory, that is glutamically mediated.[2]

Tests in an Animal Model of Korsakoff's Syndrome

Although anticholinergics have been widely used to model geriatric memory dysfunctions, more specific models of memory dysfunction are available. Korsakoff's syndrome is one clear example. Korsakoff's syndrome is

---

[2]Because of the different temporal loci of maximal effects of the two drugs, we have minor reservations about the adequacy of this double dissociation. The effect of scopolamine on performances under the common outcomes procedure seems to be most dramatic at longer delays, whereas that of dizocilpine under the differential outcomes procedure seems to be more dramatic at shorter delays. Both saline and dizocilpine performances under differential outcomes training are only modestly delay dependent. This may imply that the effect of dizocilpine is primarily on the discriminative cue elicitation of the prospective memory of the reward; to the degree it is elicited, it is as stable over delays as in the nondrug state.

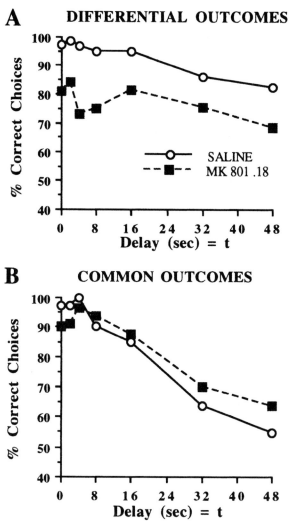

Figure 15.6. Performances on tests of matching-to-position by rats as a function of training conditions in a two-choice lever box under saline and under drug after learning to criterion when delays are imposed between the conditioned stimulus and the choice opportunity. This is based on data from Savage and Parsons (1997).

an amnestic disorder found in long-term alcoholics; it is attributable to thiamine deficiency from either malnutrition or malabsorption. The main cognitive characteristic of the disorder is that it affects memory (Kopelman, 1995; Oscar-Berman, Hutner, & Bonner, 1992).

Langlais (1992) has been developing a rat model of Korsakoff's syndrome based on the nutritional thiamine deficiency that accompanies chronic alcoholism. Rats treated with pyrithiamine until toxicity, about 2 weeks, develop central nervous system (CNS) lesions that parallel those seen in patients with Korsakoff's syndrome and, in addition, show permanent memory-based impairments in learning a matching-to-place conditional discrimination (Langlais & Savage, 1995). The natural question is whether application of the differential outcomes procedure can ameliorate the memory impairments seen in this rat model. Savage and Langlais (1995) addressed exactly this question. They trained control and pyrithiamine-treated rats to criterion using either the common outcomes or the differential outcomes procedure in the matching-to-place conditional discrimination. Although both training–reward regimes were equally effective for normal rats, allowing them to master the task in about 100 trials, this was not true for the Korsakoff-model rats. The "Korsakoff" rats trained with the common outcomes procedure required, on average, more than 180 trials to reach criterion, whereas those trained with the differential outcomes procedure required only about 130! That is, the differential outcome procedure substantially reduced the memory-based learning impairment in the Korsakoff rats—to within normal range! This is an exciting result.

To the extent that the animal model of Korsakoff's syndrome does model the human dysfunction, it suggests that application of the differential outcomes training protocol could help patients with Korsakoff's disease to overcome their learning and memory limitations. One particular limitation is learning the names of newly met people (Mayes, Downes, Symons, & Shoqeirat, 1994). Matching names to faces or vice versa is, in effect, a conditional discriminative choice task like those we have been discussing throughout this chapter. At the University of Minnesota, Bakke, Gershenson, Hochhalter, Overmier, and Sweeney are contrasting face–name learning under two different training regimes: common outcomes and differential outcomes. This application of the differential outcomes procedure to the teaching of a skill to human patients in the clinic follows directly from discoveries in the animal research laboratory. Confirmation of the effectiveness of this protocol with Korsakoff's patients would be one more confirmation of the continued clinical value of contemporary basic research with animals.

Summary

In this chapter, we have summarized the discovery in the research animal laboratory of a new principle of learning: Conditional choice tasks are learned faster and to a higher asymptote if the component-correct, discriminative stimulus-to-choice response sequences are reinforced with different rewards. This is called the differential outcomes effect. Moreover, we recapitulated the finding that an additional important feature of the differential outcomes effect is that it dramatically enhances discriminative choice performances under conditions of a delay between the discriminative stimulus and the choice opportunity. Theory and additional animal research suggests that this improved learning and the enhanced memory-based performances are attributable to an additional source of information that is available under conditions of training with the differential outcomes procedure. Specifically, the differential outcomes procedure allows for the conditioning of unique associations between the discriminative stimulus and the reward that can be elicited by the discriminative stimulus for the choice; this association is an expectation for the unique reward and is functionally a prospective memory with cue properties that can supplement—or even supplant—the memory of the discriminative stimulus itself, which is a retrospective memory.

Research with normal children confirmed these principles and inferences. A successful application of the differential outcomes teaching protocol to young adults with mild mental retardation confirmed its applied usefulness for enhancing learning by individuals with learning disabilities.

Double dissociation experiments with scopolamine and dizocilpine confirm that there are two possible sources of memory control, as implied. Scopolamine selectively disrupts common outcomes performances, whereas dizocilpine selectively disrupts differential outcomes performances.

Because scopolamine, a cholinergic antagonist, disrupts memory-based performances, we were led to ask whether persons with impaired cholinergic function, such as some geriatric patients, might benefit from the application of the differential outcomes teaching procedure. The development of an animal model of Korsakoff's syndrome was reviewed, and it was found that differential outcomes was "therapeutic" in remediating the learning deficit in these "Korsakoff" animals. An in-progress extension of the teaching protocol to clinical patients was discussed.

The general implication, then, is that to the extent that the memory deficits seen in various geriatric populations are at least in part attributable to disruptions of cholinergic-based functions, then the differential outcomes procedure may well be a useful therapeutic training regime. Teaching new tasks and discriminations with the differential outcomes procedure could allow these patients to circumvent the limitations imposed on them through a failing retrospective memory system by allowing them to call on a different, cholinergic-independent, less impaired, prospective memory system.[3]

References

Bartus, R. T., Dean, R. L., Beer, B., & Lippa, A. S. (1982, July). The cholinergic hypothesis of geriatric memory dysfunction. *Science, 217*, 408–417.

Brodigan, D. L., & Peterson, G. B. (1976). Two choice conditional discriminative performance of pigeons as a function of reward expectancy, prechoice delay, and domesticity. *Animal Learning & Behavior, 4*, 121–124.

Dawson, G. R., Heyes, C. M., & Iversen, S. D. (1992). Pharmacological mechanisms and animal models of cognition. *Behavioral Pharmacology, 3*, 285–297.

DeMarse, T., & Urcuioli, P. J. (1993). Enhancement of matching acquisition by differential outcome associations. *Journal of Experimental Psychology: Animal Behavior Processes, 19*, 317–326.

Dollard, J., & Miller, N. E. (1950). *Personality and psychotherapy.* New York: McGraw-Hill.

[3]We thank V. M. LoLordo and T. R. Zentall for their constructive comments.

Goeters, S., Blakely, E., & Poling, A. (1992). The differential outcomes effect. *Psychological Record, 42*, 389–412.

Jones, M. C. (1924). The elimination of children's fears. *Journal of Experimental Psychology, 7*, 382–390.

Joseph, B., Overmier, J. B., & Thompson, T. I. (1997). Food and nonfood related differential outcomes in equivalence learning by adults with Prader-Willi syndrome. *American Journal of Mental Retardation, 101*, 374–386.

Kopelman, M. E. (1995). The Korsakoff syndrome. *British Journal of Psychiatry, 166*, 154–173.

Kruse, J. M., Overmier, J. B., Konz, W. A., & Rokke, E. (1983). Pavlovian CS effects upon instrumental choice behavior are reinforcer specific. *Learning & Motivation, 14*, 165–181.

Langlais, P. J. (1992). Role of diencephalic lesions and thiamine deficiency in Korsakoff's amnesia: Insights from animal models. In L. R. Squire & N. Butters (Eds.), *Neuropsychology of memory* (pp. 440–450). New York: Guilford Press.

Langlais, P. J., & Savage, L. M. (1995). Thiamine deficiency in rats produces cognitive and memory deficits on spatial tasks that correlate with diencephalon, cortex, and white matter. *Behavioral Brain Research, 68*, 75–89.

Linwick, D., Overmier, J. B., Peterson, G. B., & Mertens, M. (1988). The interactions of memories and expectancies as mediators of choice behavior. *American Journal of Psychology, 101*, 313–334.

Maki, P., Overmier, J. B., Delos, S., & Gutmann, A. J. (1995). Expectancies as factors influencing conditional discrimination performance of children. *Psychological Record, 45*, 45–71.

Masserman, J. H. (1943). *Behavior and neurosis.* New York: Hafner.

Mayes, A. R., Downes, J. J., Symons, D. V., & Shoqeirat, M. (1994). Do amnesiacs forget faces pathologically fast? *Cortex, 30*, 543–563.

McDonald, M. P., & Overmier, J. B. (1998). Present imperfect: A critical review of animal models of the impairments in Alzheimer's disease. *Neuroscience and Biobehavioral Reviews, 22*, 99–120.

McIlvane, W. J., Dube, W. V., Kledaras, J. B., deRose, J. C., & Stoddard, L. T. (1992). Stimulus–reinforcer relations and conditional discrimination. In S. C. Hayes & L. J. Hayes (Eds.), *Understanding verbal relations: The second and third international institutes on verbal relations* (pp. 43–67). Reno, NV: Context Press.

Neuringer, C., & Michael, J. L. (1970). *Behavior modification in clinical psychology.* New York: Appleton-Century-Crofts.

Oscar-Berman, M., Hutner, N., & Bonner, R. T. (1992). Visual and auditory spatial and nonspatial delayed-response performance by Korsakoff and non-Korsakoff alcoholic and aging individuals. *Behavioral Neuroscience, 106*, 613–622.

Overmier, J. B. (1992). On the nature of animal models of human behavioral dysfunction. In J. B. Overmier & P. D. Burke (Eds.), *Animal models of human pathology* (pp. vii–xiv). Washington, DC: American Psychological Association.

Overmier, J. B., Bull, J. A., & Trapold, M. A. (1971). Discriminative cue properties of different fears and their role in response selection. *Journal of Comparative and Physiological Psychology, 76*, 478–482.

Overmier, J. B., & Lawry, J. A. (1979). Pavlovian conditioning and the mediation of behavior. In G. H. Bower (Ed.), *The psychology of learning and motivation* (Vol. 13, pp. 135–148). Hillsdale, NJ: Erlbaum.

Overmier, J. B., & Patterson, J. (1988). Animal models of human psychopathology. In P. Simon, P. Soubrie, & D. Wildlocher (Eds.), *Animal models of psychiatry* (pp. 1–35). Basel, Switzerland: Karger.

Overmier, J. B., & Seligman, M. E. P. (1967). Effects of inescapable shock upon subsequent escape and avoidance responding. *Journal of Comparative and Physiological Psychology, 63*, 23–33.

Pavlov, I. P. (1906). The scientific investigation of the psychical faculties or processes in the higher animals. *Science, 24*, 614–619.

Peterson, G. B., Linwick, D., & Overmier, J. B. (1987). On the comparative efficacy of memories and expectancies as cues for choice behavior in pigeons. *Learning & Motivation, 18*, 1–20.

Peterson, C., Maier, S. F., & Seligman, M. E. P. (1993). *Learned helplessness.* New York: Oxford University Press.

Rescorla, R. R. (1992). Response–outcome versus outcome–response associations in instrumental learning. *Animal Learning & Behavior, 22*, 27–33.

Rescorla, R. A., & Solomon, R. L. (1967). Two-process learning theory: Relationships between Pavlovian conditioning and instrumental learning. *Psychological Review, 74*, 151–182.

Savage, L. M., & Langlais, P. J. (1995). Differential outcomes attenuates spatial memory requirements seen in pyrithiamine-induced thiamine deficiency in rats. *Psychobiology, 23*, 153–160.

Savage, L. M., & Parsons, J. P. (1997). The effects of delay-interval, inter-trial interval, amnestic drugs, and differential outcomes on matching to position in rats. *Psychobiology, 25*, 303–312.

Savage, L. M., Stanchfield, M. A., & Overmier, J. B. (1994). The effects of scopolamine, diazepam, and lorazepam on working memory in pigeons: An analysis of reinforcement procedures and sample problem type. *Pharmacology, Biochemistry, and Behavior, 48*, 183–191.

Seligman, M. E. P. (1975). *Helplessness.* San Francisco: Freeman.

Sherburne, L. M., & Zentall, T. R. (1998). The differential outcomes effect in pigeons is not reduced by eliminating response–outcome associations: Support for a two-process account. *Animal Learning and Behavior, 26*, 378–387.

Skinner, B. F. (1954). The science of learning and the art of teaching. *Harvard Educational Review, 29*, 86–97.

Stampfl, T. G., & Levis, D. J. (1967). The essentials of implosive therapy: A learning theory based psychodynamic behavioral therapy. *Journal of Abnormal Psychology, 72*, 496–503.

Thorndike, E. L. (1914). *Educational psychology: Briefer course.* New York: Columbia University, Teachers College.

Tinkelpaugh, O. (1928). An experimental study of representative factors in monkeys. *Journal of Comparative Psychology, 8*, 197–236.

Trapold, M. A. (1970). Are expectancies based upon different positive reinforcer events discriminably different? *Learning & Motivation, 1*, 129–140.

Trapold, M. A., & Overmier, J. B. (1972). The second learning process in instrumental learning. In A. H. Black & W. F. Prokasy (Eds.), *Classical conditioning II: Current theory and research* (pp. 427–452.). New York: Appleton-Century-Crofts.

Watson, J. B. (1913). Psychology as the behaviorist views it. *Psychological Review, 20*, 158–177.

Watson, J. B., & Rayner, R. (1920). Conditioned emotional reactions. *Journal of Experimental Psychology, 3*, 1–14.

Weiskrantz, L. (1968). Some traps and pontifications. In L. Weiskrantz (Ed.), *Analysis of behavioral change* (pp. 415–419). New York: Harper & Row.

Wolpe, J. (1952). Experimental neuroses as learned behavior. *British Journal of Psychology, 43*, 243–268.

Zola-Morgan, S. M., & Squire, L. R. (1986). The primate hippocampal formation: Evidence for a time limited role in memory storage. *Science, 250*, 288–289.

16

Nonhuman Primates as Models of Hemispheric Specialization

Jacques Vauclair, Joël Fagot, and Delphine Dépy

As a result of his observation that the understanding of human cognition derives mostly from the study of human adults, Terrace (1993) called for the development of comparative psychology in the field of cognitive sciences. According to Terrace, "the study of cognitive processes in animals provides a unique opportunity to investigate the phylogeny and ontogeny of cognition" (Terrace, 1993, p. 162). There are several aspects of human cognition (e.g., list learning and imagery) that can be investigated by the use of nonverbal tasks. Psychologists' work with pigeons and monkeys (e.g., for chunking in memory, Terrace, 1987; for serial learning, Terrace, 1991; for imagery, Hollard & Delius, 1982; Neiworth & Rilling, 1987; Vauclair, Fagot, & Hopkins, 1993) has suggested that these complex cognitive skills are both independent from language and phylogenetically old. It is thus interesting to study animal cognition to understand the processes of human cognition that do not presuppose language and, more generally, to address the nature of nonverbal thought (Roitblat, 1987; Vauclair, 1996). In this context, nonhuman primates are worth studying because these species are closest to humans in their anatomy and physiology, as well as in their motor and perceptual processing. Nonhuman primates are also good candidates to test the phylogenetic validity of human-based models of cognition (see also Fujita, 1997).

The present chapter concerns the issue of hemispheric specialization for perceptual and cognitive processes. In spite of a long-lasting view that only humans are lateralized (e.g., Warren, 1980), there is now strong documentation for anatomical lateralizations, functional lateralizations, or both in several animal taxa, including birds, rodents, and nonhuman primates (see Bradshaw & Rogers, 1993; Hellige, 1993). We selectively report demonstrations from studies of nonhuman primates. After a short review of the evidence for structural (anatomical) lateralization, we describe the

Compliance with American Psychological Association standards for the ethical treatment of animals was adhered to during all phases of this research. Part of the work reported here was made possible with North Atlantic Treaty Organization Grant CRG950741. Correspondence concerning this chapter should be addressed to Jacques Vauclair, CNRS-CRNC, 31, Chemin Joseph-Aiguier, 13402 Marseille cedex 20, France. Electronic mail may be sent to vauclair@lnf.cnrs-mrs.fr.

methods used by neuropsychologists and psychologists to investigate functional lateralization in primates, and then we present some evidence for cerebral lateralization in monkeys and apes. Finally, we delineate the interests and limits of a primate model of cerebral asymmetry.

In the interest of space, we do not discuss motor asymmetries in detail here (see, for a review, Ward & Hopkins, 1993). Note, however, that although this topic remains controversial, several authors (e.g., Fagot & Vauclair, 1991; MacNeilage, Studdert-Kennedy, & Lindblom, 1987) reported the existence of population biases for hand preference in nonhuman primate species. Hopkins (1995, 1996) found a significant right-hand preference in a large sample of captive chimpanzees for bipedal reaching, bimanual feeding, throwing, and a coordinated bimanual task. These data suggest a phylogenetic continuity for handedness in primate species, at least between apes and humans.

Evidence for Neuroanatomical Asymmetries in Nonhuman Primates

Several left–right anatomical differences have been reported in apes and monkeys. For example, the left Sylvian fissure is longer than the right in chimpanzees (*Pan troglodytes*: Yeni-Komshian & Benson, 1976) and in macaques (*Macaca mulatta*: Falk, Cheverud, Vannier, & Conroy, 1986). Other asymmetries have been observed in the temporal planum and in the frontal lobe. Thus, the left planum of chimpanzees is, like that of humans, larger than the right (Gannon, Holloway, Broadfield, & Braun, 1998; Witelson, 1977). By contrast, there is in baboons (*Papio papio*: Cain & Wada, 1979), chimpanzees, gorillas (*Gorilla gorilla*), and humans (LeMay, 1976; Zilles et al., 1996) a protrusion of the right frontal lobe. In general terms, these studies suggest that anatomical asymmetries of nonhuman primates tend to be similar to those of right-handed humans, even though asymmetries are stronger in humans and apes than in monkeys. If the exact relation between structural and functional asymmetries remains unknown, it is likely that a connection exists between these two levels of asymmetry. Hence, it is probably more than a coincidence that the planum temporal is larger on the left side than on the right side of the human brain, as this structure on the left side includes the Wernicke area, which is involved in language comprehension.

Evidence for Functional Asymmetries in Nonhuman Primates

In this section we present empirical evidence for behavioral lateralization in nonhuman primates in visual and auditory tasks. In Japanese macaques (*Macaca fuscata*), a right-ear (left-hemisphere) advantage was found to discriminate vocalizations of conspecifics (Petersen, Beecher, Zoloth, Moody, & Stebbins, 1978). Implication of the left hemisphere for this kind of auditory discrimination was confirmed by lesion studies (Heffner

& Heffner, 1984). Because species different from Japanese macaques did not exhibit such asymmetries when they were tested with the Japanese macaques calls (Petersen et al., 1978), results suggest that signals have to convey signification to elicit cerebral lateralization.

Visuospatial tasks also revealed cognitive lateralization in primates. Thus, the left hemisphere of split-brain macaques was better than the right for discriminating line orientations (Hamilton & Vermeire, 1988). Jason, Cowey, and Weiskrantz (1984) observed that monkeys exhibited a left-hemisphere advantage when they had to report whether a dot was depicted in the center of a square. Evidence for a right-hemisphere advantage in visuospatial tasks comes from studies with split-brain macaques (*Macaca mulatta*) involving face discrimination (Hamilton & Vermeire, 1988). Morris and Hopkins (1993) used chimeric stimuli to demonstrate in two intact chimpanzees a right-hemisphere advantage for recognizing human and facial expressions ("happy" vs. "neutral" face). In addition, Ifune, Vermeire, and Hamilton (1984) found that split-brain macaques displayed more facial expressions toward video clips picturing humans and monkeys when the movies were presented to the right hemisphere. Finally, Hauser (1993) showed that facial expressions of fear and threat in rhesus monkeys were stronger on the left side of the face (primarily under the control of the right hemisphere) compared with the right (left hemisphere). In sum, the right hemisphere of monkeys appears to be specialized for perceiving emotional behaviors as well as for producing them. Similar right-hemispheric specializations for emotions were reported in humans (see Bradshaw & Rogers, 1993).

Which conclusion can be drawn from the literature on hemispheric lateralization? It appears that the existence of hemispheric asymmetries per se is neither specific to humans nor dependent on language. Consistent with this position, functional asymmetries (e.g., for face recognition) were found in human babies well before language acquisition (see references in Young & Ellis, 1989). Also, it is worth noticing that human and nonhuman primates show a remarkable convergence in their morphological and structural laterality. Thus, anatomical asymmetries of the Sylvian fissure are identical in apes and humans, although less pronounced in the former species.

At the functional level, face discrimination seems to be lateralized in the same way in several primate species. A consistent right-hemisphere advantage was found in monkeys, apes, and humans. Moreover, there is an advantage for the left hemisphere in Japanese macaques for processing communicatively significant auditory signals. Such a specialization evokes lateralization for speech processing in humans. Notwithstanding these similarities, there are some known differences between humans and other primates. For instance, Hamilton and Vermeire (1988) reported a left-hemisphere advantage for line orientation discrimination in split-brain macaques, a task that generally favors the right hemisphere in humans (Hellige, 1993). The demonstration of structural and functional asymmetries in primates (but also in other vertebrates; see Bradshaw & Rogers, 1993) corresponds to the idea that human laterality has phylogenetic roots. In fact, lateralization appears to represent a fundamental feature of the neuroanatomy and behavior in both animals and humans (Geschwind & Galaburda, 1985).

A Nonhuman Primate Model of Cerebral Asymmetry: Experimental Paradigms

In the study of cognitive hemispheric asymmetries in nonhuman primates, the traditional approach consists of either lesioning the brain unilaterally or splitting the two cerebral hemispheres by cutting the corpus callosum and accompanying posterior and anterior commissures. Such studies offer valuable data that complement the literature on brain-lesioned human participants. Nevertheless, they tell little about the intact brain and thus are of limited heuristic value for understanding its functioning. Consequently, there is a need for developing behavioral methods that would be adapted for the comparative investigation of intact human and nonhuman primates.

In the field of human vision, researchers interested in hemispheric lateralization have repeatedly used a tachistoscope (Hellige, 1993). The use of the tachistoscope implies, first, centration of the gaze on a fixation point and, second, the short display of a stimulus in either the left or the right visual half-field. Given the anatomy of the visual system, visual information presented with a sufficient eccentricity (more than 2.5°) relative to the fixation point is directed to the hemisphere that is opposite to the stimulated half-field (Bryden, 1982). It is thus possible with that method to selectively activate the left or the right hemisphere of the intact brain.

Following Washburn, Hopkins, and Rumbaugh (1989), we developed for humans and baboons a test procedure that has several characteristics in common with the use of a tachistoscope (Vauclair, Fagot, & Hopkins, 1993). During this procedure, primates are initially trained to manipulate a joystick, so as to displace a cursor in any direction on a computer monitor (see Figure 16.1). They are then tested in a matching-to-sample task in which the sample form is presented to either the left or the right of a fixation point for a duration shorter (e.g., 120 ms) than the latency to initiate a visual saccade (Wilde, Vauclair, & Fagot, 1994). To ensure that the sample form is presented in one visual half-field only, the researcher imposes fixation by having the subject place and maintain the cursor on the fixation point before the display of the sample form. Therefore, this technique is analogous to the tachistoscopic mode of stimulus presentation. It restricts the visual input to one visual half-field to transfer the information to the contralateral hemisphere.

This system is advantageous because it can be adapted for testing both human and nonhuman participants in strictly identical experimental conditions. Because there is no need for linguistic instructions, it is also ideal for participants, such as those with aphasia, whose language functions are deficient. In our experiments, humans and baboons are tested with the same stimuli and procedure. Use of identical procedures does not equate

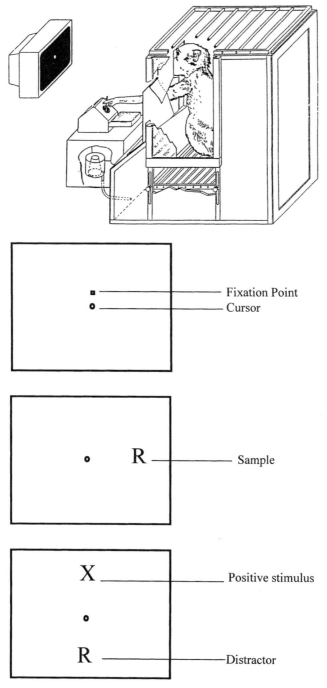

Figure 16.1. Illustration of the divided-field procedure and stimuli used during the comparative assessment of visual asymmetry in primates. Top: the apparatus used with monkeys. Bottom: the three phases of each testing trial: (a) presentation of the cursor and fixation point on the screen, (b) lateral presentation of the sample stimulus, and (c) presentation of the recognition display.

all the factors that may affect the results—for instance, the attentional, memory, and motivational factors. Nevertheless, testing humans and monkeys with similar procedures is a reasonable approach to tapping species' differences and similarities in hemispheric processing. Two sets of studies illustrate our approach and its heuristic value.

The first set of experiments was aimed at comparing the processing of local and global visual information in humans and monkeys. The perception of the global and local attributes of visual forms has led to a large literature on humans. For example, Navon (1977) presented humans with large Roman letters made of smaller letters (e.g., an *H* made up with small *H*s or *S*s). Participants had to report the identity of the letter depicted at the global or local stimulus level. Navon (1977) observed that response times were shorter on average for the global letters. On the basis of these results and others, Navon (1977) argued that humans perceive the global structure prior to the local one.

Several experiments were conducted to comparatively assess this phenomenon (Fagot & Deruelle, 1997; Deruelle & Fagot, 1997b). These experiments used the joystick system described above. In a first phase of each trial, a compound stimulus similar to that used by Navon was briefly presented in the left or right visual field of the participants. In a second phase, two comparison forms appeared on the screen after sample stimulus presentation. One of these two forms matched the sample at either the global or the local level, and the other was different from the sample at both levels. Baboons and humans were tested in this task with the same compound stimuli. Results from humans agreed with those found by Navon (1977) and demonstrated shorter response times for global than for local trials. By contrast, baboons showed shorter response times in the case of the local trials. Thus, it appears that the two species processed the forms differently. It is interesting to note, however, that both baboons and humans had a similar pattern of lateralization. For the two species, a right-hemisphere advantage was found for global trials, and a reversed but not significant left-hemisphere advantage was observed for local trials.

To better understand the processing strategy adopted by each species, researchers in other experiments (Deruelle & Fagot, 1997a, 1997b) used a visual search task in which participants had to detect a target among a variable number of distractors. According to attentional theories (e.g., Treisman & Gelade, 1980), a linear increment of response times as a function of display size suggests that an attentional (serial) search procedure is used for target detection. By contrast, flat search slopes reveal the use of preattentive (i.e., automatic) detection procedures. The experiments used compound stimuli as both targets and distractors.

In each trial, there were 4, 8, or 12 stimuli on the screen. In some trials, the target differed from the sample at the global level only. In other trials, targets and distractors differed at the local level only. Under both conditions, the participant had to move the joystick when the target was detected and to refrain from moving it when the target was absent. Flat search slopes were found in humans no matter what stimulus level they were to process (either global or local). In baboons, search slopes remained flat for the local trials, but, for the global trials, slopes linearly increased with display size. Thus, more attention is needed for the baboons than for humans to process the global targets. The fact that the two species showed the same right-hemisphere advantage for global processing (regardless of the amount of attention required for the task) suggests that lateralization in this task is rooted in early perceptual mechanisms.

The same joystick system as before was also used in a different theoretical context, with the aim of assessing lateralization for the processing of spatial relations in humans and baboons. The cerebral hemispheres of humans appear to be specialized to process spatial relations (Kosslyn, 1987). Studies involving normal and brain-damaged humans, or neural network simulations (see references in Kosslyn, 1994), converged to show a left-hemisphere superiority to categorize topological relations of the above or below type, and a right-hemisphere advantage to evaluate distances.

From an evolutionary standpoint, we questioned this left or right dissociation by using metric tasks. Indeed, nonhuman species are capable of processing distances (e.g., Fujita, 1997). However, to our knowledge, hemispheric specialization in the processing of distances has not yet been investigated with nonhuman primates. In our study (Dépy, Fagot, & Vauclair, 1998), baboons and humans were tested with the divided-field procedure and were required to decide whether a dot was near or far from a horizontal line. Using an arbitrary matching-to-sample task, participants had to select a red stimulus when the sample belonged to the "near" category and a green one when it belonged to the "far" category.

Results of this experiment suggest a left-hemisphere advantage for categorical treatments and a right-hemisphere advantage for distance processing. Findings are thus consistent with the predictions derived from Kosslyn's (1987) model. First, naïve human participants exhibited a right-hemisphere advantage in the early trials of the task. Second, this effect disappeared with practice. It can be hypothesized from these results that in the early trials of the task, the metric aspects of the stimuli predominated and induced a right-hemisphere advantage. With practice, categorical aspects of the task increased and overrode the metric aspects, thus inducing a greater involvement of the left hemisphere.

A Primate Model of Hemispheric Specialization: Implications

The experiments described above elucidate the importance of the comparative approach for understanding human cognition and the evolution of hemispheric specialization. In general, the comparative approach questions the validity of human-based models of cognition. As the human cognitive system is the product of evolution, there must be continuities between humans and other primates. Fundamental bases of human cognition can thus be searched for in nonhuman primates. This inquiry has an advantage over a human-based approach. It avoids anthropocentric biases for building models of cognition and stresses their biological significance.

From another perspective, the search for cognitive similarities between humans and nonhuman primate species permits us to evaluate the dependence of the cognitive functions vis-à-vis the functions that are considered as being typically human, such as language. Studies with nonhuman primates illustrate perfectly the importance of the comparative approach for understanding human lateralization. Following Broca's (1861) first observation of a case of lateralization, there was a pervasive view that lateralization was a typical characteristic of humans (Geschwind & Galaburda, 1985). The results presented above clearly challenge that view by showing that lateralization is independent from language. Also interesting is that the study of animal lateralization showed important similarities between humans and other primates—for instance, in the processing of faces or in the treatment of the global or local characteristics of the visual forms. It is thus presumed that instead of being primarily linked to language, lateralization actually emerged as a solution to either perceptual or motor demands.

One additional concern may be raised with regard to the validity of a nonhuman primate model of lateralization. Given that the brain of nonhuman primates shares many structural and functional features with that of humans, the species consistencies and differences observed in hemispheric specialization should indicate whether lateralization in these species is homologous (i.e., the trait has a common phylogenetic origin) or analogous (i.e., the trait has evolved independently in the two species). The need to uncover the origin of a given trait calls for an adequate choice of the species to compare. In this respect, more studies of the kind presented in this chapter should contribute significantly to solving this issue.

References

Bradshaw, L. S., & Rogers, L. J. (1993). *The evolution of lateral asymmetries, language, tool use, and intellect*. New York: Academic Press.

Broca, P. (1861). Remarques sur le siège de la faculté du langage articulé suivies d'une observation d'aphémie. *Bulletin de la Société d'Anatomie, 6*, 398–407.

Bryden, M. M. (1982). *Laterality: Functional asymmetry in the intact brain*. New York: Academic Press.

Cain, D. P., & Wada, J. P. (1979). An anatomical asymmetry in the baboon brain. *Brain Behavior and Evolution, 16*, 222–226.

Dépy, D., Fagot, F., & Vauclair, J. (1998). Comparative assessment of distance processing and hemispheric specialization in humans (*Homo sapiens*) and baboons (*Papio papio*). *Brain and Cognition, 38*, 165–182.

Deruelle, C., & Fagot, J. (1997a). Access to the global and local properties of compound stimuli in a visual search task: Effects of perceptual grouping in humans and baboons. *Psychonomic Bulletin and Review, 5*, 476–481.

Deruelle, C., & Fagot, J. (1997b). Hemispheric lateralization and global precedence effects in the processing of visual stimuli by humans and baboons (*Papio papo*). *Laterality, 2*, 233–246.

Fagot, J., & Deruelle, C. (1997). Processing of global and local visual information and hemispheric specialization in humans (*Homo sapiens*) and baboons (*Papio papio*). *Journal of Experimental Psychology: Human Perception and Performance, 23*, 429–442.

Fagot, J., & Vauclair, J. (1991). Laterality in nonhuman primates: A distinction between handedness and manual specialization. *Psychological Bulletin, 109*, 76–89.

Falk, D., Cheverud, J., Vannier, M. W., & Conroy, G. D. (1986). Advanced computer graphics technology reveals cortical asymmetry in endocasts of rhesus monkeys. *Folio Primatologica, 46*, 98–103.

Fujita, K. (1997). Perception of the Ponzo illusion by rhesus monkeys, chimpanzees and humans: Similarity and difference in the three primate species. *Perception and Psychophysics, 59*, 284–292.

Gannon, P. J., Holloway, R. L., Broadfield, D. C., & Braun, A. R. (1998, January 9). Asymmetry of chimpanzee planum temporale: Humanlike pattern of Wernicke's brain language area homolog. *Science, 279*, 220–222.

Geschwind, N., & Galaburda, A. M. (1985). *Cerebral lateralization: Biological mechanisms, associations and pathology.* Cambridge, MA: MIT Press.

Hamilton, C. R., & Vermeire, B. A. (1988, December). Complementary hemispheric specialization in monkeys. *Science, 242*, 1691–1694.

Hauser, M. D. (1993). Right hemisphere dominance for the production of facial expressions in monkeys. *Science, 261*, 475–477.

Heffner, H. E., & Heffner, R. S. (1984, October). Temporal lobe lesions and perception of species-specific vocalizations by macaques. *Science, 226*, 75–76.

Hellige, J. B. (1993). *Hemispheric asymmetry: What's right and what's left.* Cambridge, MA: Harvard University Press.

Hollard, V. D., & Delius, J. D. (1982, November). Rotational invariance in visual pattern recognition by pigeons and humans. *Science, 218*, 804–806.

Hopkins, W. D. (1995). Hand preferences for a coordinated bimanual task in 110 chimpanzees (*Pan troglodytes*): Cross-sectional analysis. *Journal of Comparative Psychology, 109*, 291–297.

Hopkins, W. D. (1996). Chimpanzee handedness revisited: 54 years since Finch (1941). *Psychonomic Bulletin and Review, 3*, 449–457.

Ifune, C. K., Vermeire, B., & Hamilton, C. (1984). Hemispheric differences in split-brain monkeys viewing and responding to videotape recordings. *Behavioral and Neural Biology, 41*, 231–235.

Jason, G. W., Cowey, A., & Weiskrantz, L. (1984). Hemispheric asymmetry for a visuo-spatial task in monkeys. *Neuropsychologia, 22*, 777–784.

Kosslyn, S. M. (1987). Seeing and imagining in the cerebral hemispheres: A computational approach. *Psychological Review, 94*, 148–175.

Kosslyn, S. M. (1994). *Image and brain.* Cambridge, MA: MIT Press.

LeMay, M. (1976). Morphological cerebral asymmetries of modern man, fossil man and nonhuman primates. *Annals of the New York Academy of Sciences, 280*, 349–366.

MacNeilage, P. F., Studdert-Kennedy, M. G., & Lindblom, B. (1987). Primate handedness reconsidered. *Behavioral and Brain Sciences, 10*, 247–301.

Morris, R. D., & Hopkins, W. D. (1993). Perception of human chimeric faces by the chimpanzees: Evidence for a right hemisphere advantage. *Brain and Cognition, 21*, 112–122.

Navon, D. (1977). Forest before the tree: The precedence of global feature in visual perception. *Cognitive Psychology, 9*, 353–383.

Neiworth, J. J., & Rilling, M. E. (1987). A method for studying imagery in animals. *Journal of Experimental Psychology: Animal Behavior Processes, 13*, 203–214.

Petersen, M. R., Beecher, M. D., Zoloth, S. R., Moody, D. B., & Stebbins, W. C. (1978, October). Neural lateralization of species-specific vocalizations in Japanese macaques (*Macaca fuscata*). *Science, 202*, 324–327.

Roitblat, H. L. (1987). *Introduction to comparative cognition.* New York: Freeman.

Terrace, H. S. (1987). Chunking by a pigeon in a serial learning task. *Nature, 325*, 149–151.

Terrace, H. S. (1991). Chunking during serial learning by a pigeon: 1. Basic evidence. *Journal of Experimental Psychology: Animal Behavior Processes, 17*, 81–93.

Terrace, H. S. (1993). The phylogeny and ontogeny of serial memory: List learning by pigeons and monkeys. *Psychological Science, 4*, 162–169.

Treisman, A., & Gelade, G. (1980). A feature integration theory of attention. *Cognitive Psychology, 12,* 97–136.

Vauclair, J. (1996). *Animal cognition: Recent developments in modern comparative psychology.* Cambridge, MA: Harvard University Press.

Vauclair, J., Fagot, J., & Hopkins, W. D. (1993). Rotation of mental images in baboons when the visual input is directed to the left cerebral hemisphere. *Psychological Science, 4,* 99–103.

Ward, J. P., & Hopkins, W. D. (Eds.). (1993). *Primate laterality: Current behavioral evidence of primate asymmetries.* New York: Springer-Verlag.

Warren, J. M. (1980). Handedness and laterality in humans and other animals. *Physiological Psychology, 8,* 351–359.

Washburn, D. A., Hopkins, W. D. & Rumbaugh, D. M. (1989). Automation of learning set testing: The video task paradigm. *Behavior, Research Methods, Instruments & Computers, 12,* 38–45.

Wilde, J., Vauclair, J., & Fagot, J. (1994). Eye movements in baboons performing a matching-to-sample task presented in a divided-field format. *Behavioural Brain Research, 63,* 61–70.

Witelson, S. F. (1977). Anatomic asymmetry in the temporal lobes: Its documentation, phylogenesis, and relationship to functional asymmetry. *Annals of the New York Academy of Sciences, 299,* 328–354.

Yeni-Komshian, G., & Benson, D. A. (1976, April). Anatomical study of cerebral asymmetry in the temporal lobe of humans, chimpanzees, and rhesus monkeys. *Science, 192,* 387–389.

Young, A. W., & Ellis, H. D. (Eds.). (1989). *Handbook of face processing.* Hillsdale, NJ: Erlbaum.

Zilles, K., Dabringhaus, A., Geyer, S., Amunts, K., Meishu, Q., Schleicher, A., Gilissen, E., Schlaug, G., & Steinmetz, H. (1996). Structural asymmetries in the human forebrain and the forebrain of non-human primates and rats. *Neuroscience and Biobehavioral Reviews, 20,* 593–604.

Part V

Aggression

17

Animal Aggression:
A Model for Stress and Coping

Jaap M. Koolhaas, Sietse F. de Boer,
Anne J. H. de Ruiter, and Bela Bohus

A considerable part of our present understanding of human biology has been acquired through the extrapolation of knowledge obtained from animal experiments. Animal research has strongly enhanced our understanding of neurochemical, neuroendocrine, and genetic factors in the normal and pathological functioning of human beings. However, the role of animal research in the study of human behavior and psychiatry is still controversial, despite, for example, the frequent use of animal experimentation in the preclinical screening of psychoactive substances. This controversy is mainly due to an overemphasis of the direct relevance of animal models. Before embarking on a description of the usefulness of animal aggression models in stress research, it is necessary to first discuss the rationale of animal models and their limitations. The evaluation of animal models needs to be closely linked to the major purpose of developing the model. In a description of the use of animal models in the study of human affective disorders, McKinney (1989) discusses four categories of animal models: (a) *behavioral similarity models*, which are developed to simulate a specific sign or symptom of the human disorder; (b) *theory-driven models*, which are developed to evaluate etiological theories of human psychopathology; (c) *mechanistic models*, which are developed with the primary purpose of studying underlying mechanisms; and (d) *empirical validity models*, which are developed to permit preclinical evaluation of treatment methods.

Although researchers' observations suggest that the contribution of social and physical environmental stress to the development of disease has a common biological basis in animals and humans, one may criticize the validity of many of the current animal models for stress research. Most are mechanistic models, empirical validity models, or both. Many of these models fail particularly with respect to their face validity, which means that the animal models fail to sufficiently mimic both the etiology and the symptomatology of human stress-related disorders. For example, most of the animal models use stressors that bear little or no relationship to the biology of the species, that is, to the situations an animal may meet in its everyday life in a natural habitat. If psychologists want to improve their knowledge of the causal mechanisms of stress-related disorders, behavioral similarity models and theory-driven models that allow an experimental analysis of the etiology and the symptomatology of the disease are essential.

This chapter argues that animal models based on intraspecies aggressive behavior may combine all four types of models, as mentioned above. The arguments are based on a more fundamental insight into the biological basis of aggressive behavior and its causes and consequences.

Social Stress in Nature

The individual capacity to deal with everyday problems in the natural environment is considered to be one of the driving forces of evolution and speciation. Organisms have adapted to a dynamic and complex natural environment in which they have to find their food, deal with conspecifics, or react to changes in climate. Within a species, the capacity to cope with environmental challenges largely determines the individual survival in the natural habitat. In the course of evolution, animals have developed a wide variety of defense mechanisms to deal with such environmental challenges. Several studies in free-ranging social groups of animals indicate that the social capacities of individuals play an important role in the maintenance of stable social groups, whereas the failure of social adaptive capacities may lead to serious forms of stress pathology. Under natural circumstances, many animal species live in rather complex social structures in which individuals differ in their social relations to other group members.

Several studies have demonstrated a relationship between position in the social hierarchy and incidence of certain stress pathologies. The first studies on the relationship between social position and stress pathology mainly concentrated on cardiovascular disease. For example, in mice (Ely, 1981; Henry & Stephens-Larson, 1985; Lockwood & Turney, 1981), rats (Henry et al., 1993; Fokkema, Koolhaas, & Gugten, 1995), and monkeys (Manuck, Kaplan, & Clarkson, 1983) research has demonstrated that hypertension and cardiovascular abnormalities are more frequent in socially unstable groups and occur predominantly in the dominant and subdominant males of the social group. Stomach ulcers are mainly found in social outcasts of colonies (Calhoun, 1962; Barnett, 1987). Similar observations in rats were reported with respect to excessive alcohol intake (Wolffgramm, 1990) and to immune system mediated diseases. A rather extreme example of this latter phenomenon is found in a naturalistic study on the relationship between stress, disease, and mortality in a small Australian marsupial (Barker, Beveridge, Bradley, & Lee, 1978; Barnett, 1973). It is suggested that aggression induces a state of stress during the mating season, which is exacerbated by the fall of corticosteroid binding globulin concentration. This results in a rise of free corticosteroids leading to the suppression of the immune- and inflammatory systems. The death is caused by gastrointestinal hemorrhage and infections due to parasite and micro-organism invasions (Bradley, McDonald, & Lee, 1980). Such a field study clearly demonstrates that the extreme use and failure of natural defense mechanisms may lead to various forms of stress pathology. Observations in rat colonies (Bohus, Koolhaas, Ruiter, & Heijnen, 1991) and groups of pigs (Hessing, 1994) confirm the general idea that animals with a different position in the social hierarchy differ in the state of the immune system and consequently differ in the vulnerability to immune-system-mediated diseases. Recent studies by Blanchard et al. (1994) have indicated that subordinate male rats living in colonies with a relatively large number of aggressive males show several of the main symptoms of depression, such as reduced eating, reduced sexual and social interest, reduced movement celerity, and altered sleep cycles. Hence the study of more naturalistic animal models based on natural defenses may provide animal models of stress pathology with sufficient face validity. Ideally, these animal models should be based on the epidemiology of stress-related disorders in (semi-) natural populations. Unfortunately, few other recent field studies are available.

Despite the relative lack of data, it is evident that under (semi-) natural environmental conditions, adaptive mechanisms may be seriously challenged and may even fail, resulting in a variety of stress-related disorders that are common in a human population as well. Therefore, a closer analysis of social relationships and its consequences with animal models seems to be highly relevant in understanding the etiology of stress-related disorders. Clearly, under (semi-) natural social conditions, not all group members develop pathology, and the type of pathology seems to be some-how related to the social position. Therefore, a major advantage of social stress models is that they allow an experimental approach to the factors involved in individual vulnerability to stress pathology. After all, under-standing individual vulnerability is one of the most important research goals of human psychopathology.

To understand factors involved in individual vulnerability to stress pathology, we follow two lines of laboratory research using aggressive behavior of male rats and mice. First, we study the long-term dynamics of the behavioral and physiological responses to social stress. Second, we focus on the individual differentiation in coping with environmental (social) stressors.

Social Stress

A number of studies indicate that loss of behavioral control of the environment is the major factor inducing stress pathology (Brown, 1993). Also, in humans, stress is considered a major factor in the etiology of several psychiatric disorders, such as depression (Victor & Mark, 1995). Stress in a social setting might mean loss of social control, that is, social defeat. Social defeat by a male conspecific induces an acute increase in heart rate, blood pressure, and body temperature, strong neuroendocrine responses in plasma catecholamines, corticosterone, prolactin, and testosterone (Bohus et al., 1987), as well as changes in central nervous serotonergic neurotransmission. These responses, including the behavioral reaction (flight and immobility), can be considered as part of the classical response to an acute stressor. More important, however, is the time course of these stress responses and to what extent these changes can be considered as a reflection of a pathological state of the animal. Recent studies with more chronic recordings indicate that the various stress parameters have a different time course. Whereas the cardiovascular and catecholaminergic response to a 1-hr social defeat diminishes within 1 or 2 hr after the defeat, the corticosterone response lasts for more than 4 hr. After an initial rise, plasma testosterone drops below baseline levels and remains at extremely low levels for at least 2 days. A single social defeat appears to induce a reduction in the circadian variation in body temperature, growth, sexual interest, open-field exploration, and food preference (carbohydrate and fat intake) that may last from 2 to 10 days after the social stress (Meerlo, Boer, Daan, Koolhaas, & Hoofdakker, 1996; Meerlo, Overkamp, Benning, Koolhaas, & Hoofdakker, 1996; Meerlo, Overkamp, Daan, Hoofdakker, & Koolhaas, 1996). Miczek, Thompson, and Tornatzky (1990) found changes in opiate analgesia that even last for at least 1 month after the defeat.

Although many of these changes can be considered as part of the symptomatology of human depression, we want to emphasize that social defeat induces changes in a variety of physiological and behavioral parameters, each of which may have different temporal dynamics. This notion has important theoretical consequences that are schematically illustrated in Figure 17.1. The different temporal dynamics of the various stress parameters imply that the physiological and behavioral states change over time. At $t = 1$, the state or the syndrome of the animal will be different from the state or the syndrome measured at $t = 2$. Moreover, as a consequence of these different states, the vulnerability to subsequent stressors may be different at these points in time after the first stressor as well. However, direct animal experimental evidence that the vulnerability to stressors changes over time, after the social defeat, is not available so far.

A few studies demonstrate a sensitization to subsequent stressors. In a study on the long-term behavioral consequences of social defeat, Koolhaas et al. (1990) used the behavioral response to a mild environmental

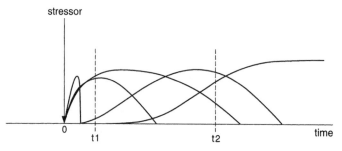

Figure 17.1.   Schematic representation of the differential temporal dynamics of stress parameters.

stressor as a challenge test that can be repeated daily or weekly without showing habituation in the response. They observed a progressive increase in immobility behavior in the defeated animals, reaching a maximum at 3 weeks after the defeat. Dijken, Heyden, Mos, and Tilders (1992) obtained similar results with the same time course, using the same challenge test after a brief session of inescapable footshock. The progressive change observed in these two studies suggests a gradual sensitization to environmental stimuli developing in the course of weeks after the single stress experience.

From the observations described above, we may conclude that the social stress model allows a further analysis of the time domain of factors involved in the development of changes in vulnerability to stress pathology. By manipulating the frequency, intensity, and type of previous social experiences, one can obtain insight into the way in which experiential factors determine (social) adaptive capacity.

Individual Variation in Aggression and Coping

Aggressive behavior has been the subject of many behavioral and neurobiological studies. Most of these studies were interpreted with the assumption that aggressive behaviors reflect the action of a motivational system for aggression. However, on the basis of our recent studies of aggression in rats and mice, we have developed a more instrumental view on aggression in which aggressive behavior is considered as a way of actively coping with environmental challenges. Although this view is not entirely novel, it has opened new vistas with respect to interpretation of experimental results in terms of social stress and adaptation.

Many of our animal studies were aimed at the hypothesis that the individual level of aggressive behavior—that is, the tendency to defend the home territory—is related to the way individual male subjects react to environmental challenges in general. Benus, Bohus, Koolhaas, and Oortmerssen (1991b) tested the hypothesis, using house mice that were genetically selected for either a short attack latency (SAL) or a long attack latency (LAL). Also, when other indexes of aggressive behavior are taken into account, the SAL male subjects are considered extremely aggressive, whereas the LAL male subjects have very low levels of intermale aggressive behavior (Oortmerssen & Bakker, 1981). The results of a series of experiments not only in mice but also in an unselected population of laboratory-bred wild rats are summarized in Table 17.1. Clearly, the individual level of aggressive behavior, as measured by the tendency to attack a conspecific intruder in the home territory, is correlated with the performance in a variety of challenging conditions.

Several conclusions can be drawn from these correlations. First, the individual level of aggressive behavior predicts the way in which the animals react to a wide variety of environmental challenges. Second, the results obtained in the active avoidance test (Schulteis & Koob, 1993), the defensive burying test (Treit, Pinel, & Fibiger, 1981), and the nest building

Table 17.1. Summary of the Behavioral Differences Between Aggressive and Nonaggressive Male Rats and Mice

| Test | Behavioral characteristics | | Reference |
	Aggressive	Nonaggressive	
Attack latency	Low	High	Oortmerssen and Bakker (1981)
Active avoidance	High	Low	Benus, Bohus, Koolhaas, and Oortmerssen (1989)
Defensive burying	High	Low	Koolhaas, Everts, Ruiter, Boer, and Bohus (1999)
Nest building	High	Low	Sluyter, Bult, Lynch, Oortmerssen, and Koolhaas (1995)
Routine formation	High	Low	Benus, Koolhaas, and Oortmerssen (1987)
Cue dependency	Low	High	Benus et al. (1987)
Conditioned immobility	Low	High	Bohus et al. (1987)

paradigm suggest that aggressive male rodents have a more active type of behavioral response, whereas nonaggressive male rodents tend to accept the situation as it is. Third, the data obtained in various maze experiments (cue dependency) suggest that aggressive male rodents develop routines, which means that behavior, once triggered, is very little affected by environmental stimuli. The behavior of nonaggressive male rodents, however, seems to be guided more by environmental stimuli (Benus et al., 1991b; Benus, Koolhaas, & Oortmerssen, 1987; Benus, Den Daas, Koolhaas, & Oortmerssen, 1990). This latter aspect is, in our opinion, one of the most fundamental differences between aggressive and nonaggressive male rodents, which may explain the differential adaptive values of the two responses as well.

An important fundamental question is whether the two types of behavior patterns can be considered to represent two styles of coping (Koolhaas & Bohus, 1989). In psychology, the term *coping* refers to the subject's belief that he or she has strategies available to keep the situation under control (Ursin & Olff, 1995). However, such positive outcome expectancies are hard to measure in animals, and one needs a more operational definition of coping. Coping can be defined as the behavioral and physiological processes necessary to reach homeostasis. In this view, *control* can be defined as successful coping. Several experiments indicate that the different behavior patterns can indeed be considered as coping styles aimed at environmental control (Koolhaas & Bohus, 1989). This can be demonstrated, for example, in the defensive burying paradigm with domesticated wild rats. This strain of rats shows a large individual variation in aggressive behavior similar to the variation in wild house mice. After being tested for their tendency to defend the home cage against unfamiliar male conspecifics, the male rats were tested in a shock prod defensive burying test. In this test, the animal is confronted with a small electrified prod in its home cage. Because this prod is a novel object, the experimental animal will explore it by sniffing the object. Consequently, the animal receives a mild but aversive shock. As soon as it has experienced the shock, the animal has two options to avoid further shocks. It either may hide in a corner of the cage to avoid further contact with the shock prod or may actively bury the shock prod with the bedding material of the cage. Under these free-choice conditions, aggressive male rats spend much more time burying than nonaggressive male rats. However, the two types of responding are equally successful in avoiding further shocks. In this particular test, *successful coping* can be defined operationally as avoidance of further shocks. This leads to the conclusion that both the burying and the im-mobility response are equally successful. This observation again supports our conclusion that the individual variation in aggressive behavior represents a variation in coping style that is expressed in a wide variety of environmental challenges (Bohus et al., 1987; Koolhaas & Bohus, 1989). However, this conclusion contrasts with the original idea by Henry and Stephens (1977): They considered the more passive conservation withdrawal response as a form of pathology induced by a loss of control. Although loss of control induces a form of passivity or depressive symptoms indeed, our studies indicate that the natural variation in ag-gressive behavior reflects a biologically functional variation in coping style.

So far we have used the terms *active* and *passive coping* to indicate the differences between the two styles. However, the more we learn about the nature of the individual variation, the more we realize that these terms are inadequate to fully characterize the two coping styles. As men-tioned above, one of the most fundamental differences seems to be the degree in which behavior is guided by environmental stimuli. Aggressive male rodents develop routines and seem to anticipate the situation, whereas nonaggressive male rodents react to environmental stimuli all the time. This creates a differential degree of flexibility and may explain why aggressive male rodents are more successful under stable colony con-ditions, whereas nonaggressive male rodents do better in variable envi-ronmental conditions—for example, during migration (Fokkema, Kool-haas, & Gugten, 1995; Oortmerssen & Busser, 1989). We prefer to use the terms *proactive coping* rather than active coping and *reactive coping* rather than passive coping.

Physiology of Coping Styles

Behavior is the product of a wide variety of central nervous, neuroendo-crine, and peripheral physiological processes. Hence, the existence of individual differences in coping behavior implies the existence of differ-ences in accompanying physiology as well. In the original model, Henry and Stephens (1977) already suggested that the two coping styles not only differ in behavior but also in some of the associated periph-eral neuroendocrine and central nervous mechanisms. Table 17.2 sum-

Table 17.2. Summary of the Neuroendocrine Differences Between Aggressive and Nonaggressive Rats

	Physiological characteristics		Reference
	Aggressive	Nonaggressive	
Plasma testosterone	High	Low	Schuurman (1980)
Sympathetic reactivity	High	Low	Fokkema, Smit, Gugten, and Koolhaas (1988)
Parasympathetic reactivity	Low	High	Bohus et al. (1987)
HPA axis reactivity	Low	High	Koolhaas and Bohus (1989)

marizes the state of the art with respect to the differences in neuroendocrinology.

It is important to realize that this table is only a qualitative summary of the available data and does not offer conclusions at which level of organization the differences are located (i.e., in the brain, in the periphery, or both). However, several studies show a widespread central nervous differentiation between the two coping styles, for example, at the level of the peptidergic modulation of the central nucleus of the amygdala (Roozendaal, Wiersma, Driscoll, Koolhaas, & Bohus, 1992), the vasopressinergic neurons in the bed nucleus of the stria terminalis and its innervation of the lateral septum (Compaan, Buijs, Pool, Ruiter, & Koolhaas, 1992), the suprachiasmatic nucleus (Bult, Hiestand, Van der Zee, & Lynch, 1993), the hippocampal mossy fibre system (Cools, Brachten, Heeren, Willemen, & Ellenbroek, 1990; Lipp et al., 1989), and striatal dopaminergic mechanisms (Benus, Bohus, Koolhaas, & Oortmerssen, 1991a; Cools, Brachten, Heeren, Willemen, & Ellenbroek, 1990). These differences seem to reflect differences in the state of brain mechanisms in terms of number of neurons, degree of arborization of neurons, hormonal and neurotransmitter receptor binding capacity, and so on, which in concert may determine the tendency to cope either actively or passively with environmental challenges.

Implications for Stress Pathology

In the previous sections, we have shown that animals that differ in their style of coping with environmental challenges also differ with respect to the state and reactivity of a variety of central nervous and neuroendocrine mechanisms. We briefly discuss the fact that this differentiation may have important implications to the individual vulnerability to stress pathology. Several of these physiological mechanisms are causally involved in the development of pathologies. For example, the pituitary adrenocortical system and the sympathetic branch of the autonomic nervous system are important mediators in the communication between the brain and the immune system (Dantzer & Kelley, 1989; Carlson & Felten, 1989). For this reason, these mechanisms play an important role in the control of immunocompetence. Similarly, the autonomic nervous system is heavily involved in cardiovascular control and hence in the development of cardiovascular pathology as well (Victor & Mark, 1995).

On the basis of these behavioral and physiological arguments, one may predict a differentiation in vulnerability to stress pathology in relation to coping style. Indeed, a number of studies in different species show such a differential vulnerability under conditions of severe environmental challenge (Hessing, 1994; Wiepkema & Adrichem, 1987; Fokkema, Smit, Gugten, & Koolhaas, 1988; Fokkema, Koolhaas, & Gugten, 1995).

With respect to these environmental challenges, in most animal experimental studies, the occurrence of pathologies such as stomach ulcers and immune deficiencies is related to conditions that involve lack or loss of control (e.g., inescapable shock or restraint). From a behavioral point of view, the term *coping style* already implies a differential capacity to reach homeostasis in different environments. In other words, controllability depends on the individual capacity to cope. Although the concept of controllability has strongly contributed to the present knowledge and insights into the development of stress pathology, we would like to remark on the experimental limitations of the concept of controllability. First, in most experiments, controllability is operationally defined as a two-stage situation (i.e., full control or loss of control). However, in everyday life situations, controllability seems to be graded from absolute control through threat to control to loss of control. Few studies consider the importance of a different degree of control in the development of stress pathology. Experiments aimed at understanding the development of hypertension indicate that the threat to control rather than the loss of control is the crucial factor. In a series of experiments, Fokkema (1985) showed that proactive coping males are sympathetically more reactive, which is considered to be a risk factor in the development of hypertension. Subsequent experiments in colony situations showed that these proactive coping males indeed develop high blood pressure, but only when the animals are in a situation of continuous threat to control (Koolhaas & Bohus, 1989). This threat to control may occur when the aggressive male takes a subdominant position in the social structure, or when the dominant male has difficulties to maintain its dominant position.

A second problem with the concept of controllability concerns its relationship with the two coping styles. Control cannot be separated from the aims and goals of the individual (i.e., what and how the animal wants to control). By definition, proactive and reactive coping animals have different ways to reach control, but in the proactive coping individual, successful coping seems to result in a form of objective control. In other words, the proactive coping individual actively masters the situation. This is far more difficult to assess in the reactive coping animal, which, from a behavioral point of view, seems to accept the situation as it is more readily, leading to a kind of perceived control. This has direct consequences to what we consider to be a threat to or a loss of control. Challenges that may be uncontrollable for the proactive coper may be controllable for the reactive coper, and vice versa. Further physiological and neuroendocrine measurements are required to assess the cognitive appraisal of a certain environmental challenge by different individual animals and to prove that the differentiation in coping style is causally involved in a differential disease vulnerability.

Conclusion

In this chapter, we have provided evidence that animal models based on the biology of the species (i.e., using the social adaptive capacities of individuals) allow an experimental approach to some factors that determine the individual vulnerability to stress pathology. These factors include not only the individual stress history but also the individual coping style. In view of the fact that almost all vertebrate species, including human beings, are social creatures, it is conceivable that the social stress processes and the coping styles as observed in rats and mice and several other species are somehow a primitive reflection of similar processes in humans. For example, epidemiological studies in humans have also indicated the importance of major life events in the development of a variety of human stress pathologies, including depression (Shrout et al., 1989), cardiovascular disease (Natelson, 1983), anxiety disorders (Angst & Vollrath, 1991), and immune-system-related disorders (Vandvik, Høveraal, & Fagertun, 1989). These life events are often of a social nature. Although the study of life events in a human population is full of pitfalls (Dohrenwend, Dohrenwend, Dodson, & Shrout, 1984), the literature shows unequivocally that the experience of a single major stressor enhances the vulnerability to stress-related disorders. This suggests that major life events may have long-term consequences ultimately leading to a higher incidence of disease in humans. This notion is supported by recent data on human posttraumatic stress disorder (PTSD) indicating that the experience of even a single traumatic life event may have serious and long-lasting consequences to physical and psychic health (Friedman & Schnurr, 1995). However, the processes involved in the enhanced vulnerability to stress pathology are far from understood and require the experimental support of animal models.

It is tempting to consider the possibility that the phenomenon of coping styles in rats and mice relates to personality factors and coping styles in humans as well. In view of the differences in cognitive capacities between animals and humans, this does not seem to be a very fruitful discussion. However, we want to emphasize that individual differences in coping style can be found in a wide variety of species throughout the animal kingdom. Apparently, an individual differentiation in coping with environmental challenges is a rather basic biological phenomenon. From this point of view, animal models may contribute to our basic understanding of the role of coping styles in stress pathology and their genetic and developmental basis.

References

Angst, J., & Vollrath, M. (1991). The natural history of anxiety disorders. *Acta Psychiatrica Scandinavica, 84,* 446–452.

Barker, I. K., Beveridge, I., Bradley, A. J., & Lee, A. K. (1978). Observations on spontaneous stress-related mortality among males of the dasyurid marsupial *Antechinus stuartii* Macleay. *Australian Journal of Zoology, 26,* 435–444.

Barnett, J. L. (1973). A stress response in *Antechinus stuartii* Macleay. *Australian Journal of Zoology, 21,* 501–513.

Barnett, S. A. (1987). *The rat: A study in behavior.* Chicago: University of Chicago Press.

Benus, R. F., Bohus, B., Koolhaas, J. M., & Oortmerssen, G. A. v. (1989). Behavioral strategies of aggressive and nonaggressive male mice in active shock avoidance. *Behavioral Processes, 20,* 1–12.

Benus, R. F., Bohus, B., Koolhaas, J. M., & Oortmerssen, G. A. v. (1991a). Behavioral differences between artificially selected aggressive and nonaggressive mice: Response to apomorphine. *Behavioral Brain Research, 43,* 203–208.

Benus, R. F., Bohus, B., Koolhaas, J. M., & Oortmerssen, G. A. v. (1991b). Heritable variation in aggression as a reflection of individual coping strategies. *Experientia, 47,* 1008–1019.

Benus, R. F., Den Daas, S., Koolhaas, J. M., & Oortmerssen, G. A. v. (1990). Routine formation and flexibility in social and nonsocial behavior of aggressive and nonaggressive male mice. *Behavior, 112,* 176–193.

Benus, R. F., Koolhaas, J. M., & Oortmerssen, G. A. v. (1987). Individual differences in behavioral reaction to a changing environment in mice and rats. *Behavior, 100,* 105–122.

Blanchard, D. C., Spencer, R. L., Weiss, S. M., Blanchard, R. J., McEwen, B., & Sakai, R. R. (1994). Visible burrow system as a model of chronic social stress: Behavioral and neuroendocrine correlates. *Psychoneuroendocrinology, 20,* 117–134.

Bohus, B., Benus, R. F., Fokkema, D. S., Koolhaas, J. M., Nyakas, C., Oortmerssen, G. A. v., Prins, A. J. A., Ruiter, A. J. H. d., Scheurink, A. J. W., & Steffens, A. B. (1987). Neuroendocrine states and behavioral and physiological stress responses. In E. R. De Kloet, V. M. Wiegant, & D. De Wied (Eds.), *Progress in brain research* (pp. 57–70). Amsterdam: Elsevier.

Bohus, B., Koolhaas, J. M., Nyakas, C., Steffens, A. B., Fokkema, D. S., & Scheurink, A. J. W. (1987). Physiology of stress: A behavioural view. In P. R. Wiepkema & P. W. M. Adrichem (Eds.), *Biology of stress in farm animals: An integrative approach* (pp. 57–70). Dordrecht, The Netherlands: Martinus Nijhoff.

Bohus, B., Koolhaas, J. M., Ruiter, A. J. H. d., & Heijnen, C. J. (1991). Stress and differential alterations in immune system functions: Conclusions from social stress studies. *Netherlands Journal of Medicine, 39,* 306–315.

Bradley, A. J., McDonald, I. R., & Lee, A. K. (1980). Stress and mortality in a small marsupial (*Antechinus stuartii* Macleay). *General and Comparative Endocrinology, 40,* 188–200.

Brown, G. W. (1993). Role of life events in the etiology of depressive and anxiety disorders. In S. C. Stanford, P. Salmon, & J. A. Gray (Eds.), *Stress: From synapse to syndrome* (pp. 24–50). London: Academic Press.

Bult, A., Hiestand, L., Van der Zee, E. A., & Lynch, C. B. (1993). Circadian rhythms differ between selected mouse lines: A model to study the role of vasopressin neurons in the suprachiasmatic nuclei. *Brain Research Bulletin, 32,* 623–627.

Calhoun, J. B. (1962). *The ecology and sociology of the Norway rat.* Washington, DC: U.S. Government Printing Office.

Carlson, S. L., & Felten, D. L. (1989). Involvement of hypothalamic and limbic structures in neural–immune communication. In E. J. Goetzl, & N. H. Spector (Eds.), *Neuroimmune networks: Physiology and diseases.* (pp. 219–226). New York: Alan R. Liss.

Compaan, J. C., Buijs, R. M., Pool, C. W., Ruiter, A. J. H. d., & Koolhaas, J. M. (1992). Differential lateral septal vasopressin innervation in aggressive and nonaggressive male mice. *Brain Research Bulletin, 30,* 1–6.

Cools, A. R., Brachten, R., Heeren, D., Willemen, A., & Ellenbroek, B. A. (1990). Search after neurobiological profile of individual–specific features of Wistar rats. *Brain Research Bulletin, 24,* 49–69.

Dantzer, R., & Kelley, K. W. (1989). Stress and immunity: An integrated view of relationships between the brain and the immune system. *Life Sciences, 44,* 1995–2008.

Dijken, H. H., Heyden, J. A. M. v., Mos, J., & Tilders, F. J. H. (1992). Inescapable footshocks induce progressive and long-lasting behavioral changes in male rats. *Physiology & Behavior, 51,* 787–794.

Dohrenwend, B. S., Dohrenwend, B. P., Dodson, M., & Shrout, P. E. (1984). Symptoms, hassles, social supports, and life events: The problem of confounded measures. *Journal of Abnormal Psychology, 93,* 222–230.

Ely, D. L. (1981). Hypertension, social rank, and aortic arteriosclerosis in CBA/J mice. *Physiology & Behavior, 26,* 655–661.

Fokkema, D. S. (1985). *Social behaviour and blood pressure. A study of rats.* Doctoral thesis, University of Groningen, Haren, The Netherlands.

Fokkema, D. S., Koolhaas, J. M., & Gugten, J. v. (1995). Individual characteristics of behavior, blood pressure, and adrenal hormones in colony rats. *Physiology & Behavior, 57,* 857–862.

Fokkema, D. S., Smit, K., Gugten, J. v., & Koolhaas, J. M. (1988). A coherent pattern among social behavior, blood pressure, corticosterone, and catecholamine measures in individual male rats. *Physiology & Behavior, 42,* 485–489.

Friedman, M. J., & Schnurr, P. P. (1995). The relationship between trauma, posttraumatic stress disorder, and physical health. In M. J. Friedman, D. S. Charney, & A. Y. Deutch (Eds.), *Neurobiological and clinical consequences of stress: From normal adaptation to PTSD* (pp. 507–524). Philadelphia: Lippincott.

Henry, J. P., Liu, Y. Y., Nadra, W. E., Qian, C. G., Mormede, P., Lemaire, V., Ely, D., & Hendley, E. D. (1993). Psychosocial stress can induce chronic hypertension in normotensive strains of rats. *Hypertension, 21,* 714–723.

Henry, J. P., & Stephens, P. M. (1977). *Stress, health, and the social environment: A sociobiological approach to medicine.* Berlin, Germany: Springer-Verlag.

Henry, J. P., & Stephens-Larson, P. (1985). Specific effects of stress on disease processes. In G. P. Moberg (Ed.), *Animal stress* (pp. 161–173). Bethesda, MD: American Physiological Society.

Hessing, M. (1994). *Individual behavioral characteristics in pigs and their consequences for pig husbandry.* Doctoral thesis, Agricultural University, Wageringen, The Netherlands.

Koolhaas, J. M., & Bohus, B. (1989). Social control in relation to neuroendocrine and immunological responses. In A. Steptoe & A. Appels (Eds.), *Stress, personal control, and health* (pp. 295–304). Brussels, Belgium: Wiley.

Koolhaas, J. M., Everts, H. G. J., Ruiter, A. J. H. d., Boer, S. F. d., & Bohus, B. (1999). Coping with stress in rats and mice: Differential peptidergic modulation of the amygdala-lateral septum complex. In J. J. A. Urban, J. P. H. Burbach, & D. de Wied (Eds.), *Progress in brain research* (pp. 437–448). New York: Elsevier.

Koolhaas, J. M., Hermann, P. M., Kemperman, C., Bohus, B., Hoofdakker, R. H. v.d., & Beersma, D. G. M. (1990). Single social interaction leading to defeat in male rats induces a gradual, but long-lasting behavioral change: A model of depression? *Neuroscience Research Communications, 7,* 35–41.

Koolhaas, J. M., & Oortmerssen, G. A. v. (1989). Individual differences in disease susceptibility as a possible factor in the population dynamics of rats and mice. *Netherlands Journal of Zoology, 38,* 111–112.

Lipp, H. P., Schwegler, H., Crusio, W. E., Wolfer, D. P., Leisinger-Trigona, M. C., Heimrich, B., & Driscoll, P. (1989). Using genetically defined rodent strains for the identification of hippocampal traits relevant for two-way avoidance behavior: A noninvasive approach. *Experientia, 45,* 845–859.

Lockwood, J. A., & Turney, T. (1981). Social dominance and stress induced hypertension: Strain differences in inbred mice. *Physiology & Behavior, 26,* 547–549.

Manuck, S. B., Kaplan, J. R., & Clarkson, T. B. (1983). Behaviorally induced heart rate reactivity and atherosclerosis in cynomolgous monkeys. *Psychosomatic Medicine, 45,* 95–108.

McKinney, W. T. (1989). Basis of development of animal models in psychiatry: An overview. In G. F. Koob, C. L. Ehlers, & D. J. Kupfer (Eds.), *Animal models of depression* (pp. 3–17). Cambridge, MA: Birkhauser.

Meerlo, P., Boer, S. F. d., Daan, S., Koolhaas, J. M., & Hoofdakker, R. H. v. (1996). Changes in daily rhythms of body temperature and activity after a single social defeat in rats. *Physiology & Behavior, 59*, 735–739.

Meerlo, P., Overkamp, G. J. F., Benning, M. A., Koolhaas, J. M., & Hoofdakker, R. H. v. (1996). Long-term changes in open-field behavior following a single social defeat in rats can be reversed by sleep deprivation. *Physiology & Behavior, 60*, 115–119.

Meerlo, P., Overkamp, G. J. F., Daan, S., Hoofdakker, R. H. v., & Koolhaas, J. M. (1996). Changes in behavior and body weight following a single or double social defeat in rats. *Stress, 1*, 21–32.

Miczek, K. A., Thompson, M. L., & Tornatzky, W. (1990). Short- and long-term physiological and neurochemical adaptations to social conflict. In S. Puglisi-Allegra & A. Oliverio (Eds.), *NATO ASI Series D: Behavioral and social sciences.* (pp. 15–30). Dordrecht, The Netherlands: Kluwer.

Natelson, B. H. (1983). Stress, predisposition and the onset of serious disease: Implications about psychosomatic etiology. *Neuroscience & Biobehavioral Reviews, 7*, 511–527.

Oortmerssen, G. A. v., & Bakker, T. C. M. (1981). Artificial selection for short and long attack latencies in wild *Mus musculus domesticus. Behavior Genetics, 11*, 115–126.

Oortmerssen, G. A. v., & Busser, J. (1989). Studies in wild house mice III: Disruptive selection on aggression as a possible force in evolution. In P. F. Brain, D. Mainardi, & S. Parmigiani (Eds.), *House mouse aggression: A model for understanding the evolution of social behavior* (pp. 87–117). Chur, Switzerland: Harwood.

Roozendaal, B., Wiersma, A., Driscoll, P., Koolhaas, J. M., & Bohus, B. (1992). Vasopressinergic modulation of stress responses in the central amygdala of the Roman high-avoidance and low-avoidance rat. *Brain Research, 596*, 35–40.

Schulteis, G., & Koob, G. F. (1993). Active avoidance conditioning paradigms for rodents. In E. Sahgal (Ed.), *Behavioural neuroscience: A practical approach* (pp. 57–122). Oxford, England: IRL Press.

Schuurman, T. (1980). Hormonal correlates of agonistic behavior in adult male rats. In P. S. McConnel, G. J. Boer, H. J. Romijn, & N. E. Van de Poll (Eds.), *Progress brain research* (pp. 415–420). Amsterdam: Elsevier.

Shrout, P. E., Link, B. G., Dohrenwend, B. P., Skodol, A. E., Stueve, A., & Mirotznik, J. (1989). Characterizing life events as risk factors for depression: The role of fateful loss events. *Journal of Abnormal Psychology, 98*, 460–467.

Sluyter, F., Bult, A., Lynch, C. B., Oortmerssen, G. A. v., & Koolhaas, J. M. (1995). A comparison between house mouse lines selected for attack latency or nest-building: Evidence for a genetic basis for alternative behavioral strategies. *Behavior Genetics, 25*, 247–252.

Treit, D. Pinel, J. P. J., & Fibiger, H. C. (1981). Conditioned defense burying: A new paradigm. *Pharmacological Biochemistry Behavior, 15*, 619–626.

Ursin, H., & Olff, M. (1995). Aggression, defense, and coping in humans. *Aggressive Behavior, 21*. 13—19.

Vandvik, I. H., Høveraal, H. M., & Fagertun, H. (1989). Chronic family difficulties and stressful life events in recent onset juvenile arthritis. *Journal of Rheumatology, 16*, 1088–1092.

Victor, R. G., & Mark, A. L. (1995). The sympathetic nervous system in human hypertension. In J. H. Laragh & B. M. Brenner (Eds.), *Hypertension: Pathophysiology, diagnosis, and management* (pp. 863–878). New York: Raven.

Wiepkema, P. R., & Adrichem, P. W. M. v. (1987). *Biology of stress in farm animals.* Dordrecht, The Netherlands: Martinus-Nijhoff.

Wolffgramm, J. (1990). Free choice ethanol intake of laboratory rats under different social conditions. *Psychopharmacology, 101*, 233–239.

18

Mouse Genes and Animal Models of Human Aggression

Stephen C. Maxson

Genetic research on intraspecific aggression in male mice began with two studies of differences in attack behaviors among inbred strains (Ginsburg & Allee, 1942; Scott, 1942). One purpose of these studies and subsequent ones was the development of animal models at the behavioral and biological levels for aggression in humans (Maxson, 1992a). For example, a pair of strains (NC900 and NC100) selected for differences in aggression of male mice has been used to construct animal models at the behavioral level; these have been used to develop hypotheses as to ontogenetic and experiential influences on aggression in humans (Cairns, 1996). Another pair of strains (SAL and LAL) selected for differences in male aggression has been used to construct animal models at the biological level; these have been used to develop hypotheses for the role of testosterone levels and sensitivity in aggression of humans (Benus, Bohus, Koolhaas, & van Oortmerssen, 1991). Such strains differ in many genes. For these, it is difficult to identify gene effects on biological systems or their relation to aggression in mice and, thereby, of each to aggression in humans. Strains differing in a single gene with effects on aggression in mice would help to solve some or all of this problem.

There is now some evidence for effects of 11 genes on the offense type of attack in male mice. The genes are Ar (androgen receptor), CamK2a (α-calcium/calmodulin Kinase II), Enk (enkephalin), Estr (estrogen receptor), H1r (histamine 1 receptor), Htrlb (5-HT1B receptor), Maoa (monoamine oxidase A), Nos1 (nitric acid synthase), Sts (steroid sulfatase), Sry (sex determining region on the Y), and Tgfa (transforming growth factor α). There are congenic or coisogenic strains differing in alleles for each gene. These genes are referenced and listed with chromosome location (if known) in Table 18.1. Table 18.1 also gives the human gene symbol and chromosome location, if known. This identifies homologous genes in humans and animals.

Elsewhere, I have discussed genetic, experiential, and testing issues that must be considered to firmly demonstrate effects of gene variants on offense or any other type of aggression in mice (Maxson, 1992b, 1998). For the didactic purposes of discussing issues in constructing and using animal models, I consider that these genetic, experiential, and testing is-

Table 18.1. Homologous Genes and Aggression

Mouse gene	Chromosome	Human gene	Chromosome
Ar[a]	X	AR	X
CamK2a[b]	18		
Enk[c]			
Estr[d]	10	ESR	6
H1r[e]			
Htr1b[f]	9	HTR_{1B}	6
Maoa[g]	X	MAOA	X
Nos1[h]	5		
Sry[i]	Y	SRY	Y
Sts[j]	X/Y PAR	STS	X
Tgfa[k]	6	TGFa	2

Note. Ar = androgen receptor; CamK2a = α = calcium/calmodulin kinase II; Enk = enkephalin; Estr = estrogen receptor; H1r = histamine 1 receptor; Htr1b = 5-HT1B receptor; Maoa = monoamine oxidase A; Nos1 = nitric acid synthase; Sry = sex determining region on the Y; Sts = steroid sulfatase; PAR = pseudoautosomal region; Tgfa = transforming growth factor α. Blank spaces indicate no homologue gene known. [a]Ohno, Geller, and Young Lai, 1974. [b]Chen, Rainnie, Greene, and Tonegawa, 1994. [c]Konig et al., 1996. [d]Ogawa, Lubahn, Korach, and Pfaff, 1997. [e]Yanai, Watanabe, Inque, and Watanabe, 1996. [f]Saudou et al., 1994. [g]Cases et al., 1995. [h]Nelson et al., 1995. [i]Maxson, 1996b. [j]Roubertoux et al., 1994. [k]Hilakivi-Clarke, 1994.

sues have been properly resolved for the genes listed in Table 18.1. However, the reader should consult the individual publications to obtain the details for each gene.

Genic Models

Animal models may be at the genic level (Maxson, 1992a, 1996a). When a gene has been identified as causing variation in a human characteristic, variants of the homologous gene in mice may be used as a model at the genic level. Genic models are used to develop hypotheses for the mechanism by which a gene affects the trait in humans. These are based on the similarities of a trait and its biology in humans and mice. So far, about 1,500 genes have been proposed as homologous in mice and humans (Graves, 1996). Two of these genes appear to affect some aspect of impulsive aggression in humans; I have described this in more detail in the next section. The human genes are TH (tryptophan hydroxylase; Nielsen et al., 1994) and MAOA (monoamine oxidase A; H. G. Brunner, Nelen, Breakefield, Ropers, & van Oost, 1993; H. G. Brunner, Nelen, van Zandvoort, et al., 1993). There is an allelic variant in mice for Maoa. In both mice and humans, one allele for MAOA produces a functional protein, and the other allele produces a nonfunctional protein.

There is a Dutch kindred with a null mutant for MAOA on the X chromosome (H. G. Brunner, Nelen, Breakefield, et al., 1993; H. G.

Brunner, Nelen, van Zandvoort, et al., 1993). Eight affected men with the null mutant show mental retardation and both aggressive and sexual impulsivity. These men have had repeated episodes of aggression, often unprovoked and sometimes violent. Some of them have also attempted rape and committed arson. There are also behavioral effects of a null mutant in the C3H inbred strain of mice (Cases et al., 1995). The homozygous mutant mice have shorter attack latency and inflict more wounds in a resident–intruder test of the offense type of aggression than do the homozygous wild types. The mutants also show more grasping of nonestrous females, spend more time in the center of an open field, have decreased swim-time immobility, and have some motor incoordination. There are clear behavioral differences, and there appear to be behavioral similarities for male mice and humans with the null variant of MAOA. It has been suggested that the behavioral effects of the mouse mutant on aggressive and sexual behavior are a possible animal model for the effects of the human mutant on these behaviors. However, at the behavioral level, careful comparisons of the similarities and differences need to be considered. This issue is discussed more in the next section.

Regardless of the issues at the behavioral level for using the Maoa null mutant of mice as a genic model, there are parallels at the biological level for the MAOA mutants of mice and humans. In humans, there is increased urinary excretion of monoamine substrates and products of monoamine oxidase; in mice, there are higher brain levels of 5-HT (5-hydroxytryptamine), NE (norepinephrine), and 5-HIAA (5-hydroxyindoleacetic acid). Perhaps, this disturbance in monoamine metabolism is either developmentally or immediately causal to the behavioral disturbances in humans and mice. In mice, there are neuroanatomical effects of the null mutant. The barrel field of the somatosensory cortex is disturbed. This may be due to prenatal exposure to altered levels of substrates and products for MAOA. In rats, prenatal exposure to inhibitors of MAOA and MAOB affects the structure of the neocortex (Whitaker-Azmitia, Zhang, & Clarke, 1994). As I discuss in a subsequent section, tracing the exact pathway from gene to behavior is a necessary step in the development of a homologous gene as a biological model. This is needed because homologous genes may have different biological and behavioral effects in mice and humans (H. G. Brunner, 1996; Erickson, 1989).

Behavioral Models

Homologous genes may also be used to develop animal models at the behavioral levels. Such behavioral models can be used to develop hypotheses about effects of developmental or immediate experience on human behaviors. These behavioral models will always be, at best, similar and different to the human phenomenon. Therefore, careful attention should be given to the similarities and the differences between mouse and human behaviors in developing the models and in generating hypotheses with them. Here, I focus on proposals that individual genes with effects on offense in male mice may be behavioral models for *impulsive aggression* in humans. Impulsive aggression in humans has been characterized as that which is not premeditated, is not provoked, and is associated with irritability, frustration, and impulsiveness (Coccaro, 1992). Also, injury due to attacks is often severe and may be lethal.

It has been suggested that mutants in mice with shorter attack latency for offense than that of wild types may be animal models for impulsive aggression in humans. Attack latencies are lower for mutants as compared with wild types for the Enk, Htrlb, Maoa, and Nosl genes. This is a face validity proposal. Two aspects of impulsivity, including that for aggression, are quick response time and decreased response inhibition. This proposal also assumes that impulsive aggression of humans is of the offense type. This proposal needs to be evaluated by detailed comparison of impulsive and offensive aggression.

It has been suggested that offensive attacks across many mammalian species are rarely if ever lethal (Blanchard & Blanchard, 1984). In contrast, the attacks of impulsive aggression are often lethal. There is a strain of mouse with a very short latency for offensive attacks, which can and do kill opponents (van Oortmerssen & Bakker, 1981), but it has not been reported that offensive attacks by Enk, Hrtlb, or Maoa mutant mice are ever lethal. Although attacks by the Nosl mutant are lethal, they appear to resemble those seen in predation rather than offense. This raises the issue of whether gene effects on attack latency of male mice in tests of offense are valid models for impulsive aggression in humans. Also, in animals, offensive attack is used to obtain and retain resources, and it has been suggested that in humans, offensive attack is used to establish and maintain rights (Blanchard & Blanchard, 1984, 1989). The unprovoked aspect of some acts of impulsive aggression in humans does not appear to be consistent with these adaptive functions for offense and, therefore, with the effects of mouse genes on the attack latency of male mice in tests of offense as a valid behavioral model for impulsive aggression in humans. I suggest that more detailed comparisons of impulsive aggression in humans and of offense in mice are needed before using genetic variants of offense in mice as valid models for this human behavior. Other possibilities at the behavioral level should also be considered in the search for genetic variants in mice as animal models of impulsive aggression in humans.

Alternatively, it has been suggested that enhanced active avoidance, deficits in passive avoidance, and open field "freezing" may be impulsive responses in rats and that for genetic selection, brain lesion, neurochemical, and neuropharmacological studies, these responses are associated in rats with an increase in aggression (Eichelman, 1995). Here, the aggressive behavior is pain or shock-induced fighting. It has been proposed that this type of fighting is defensive rather than offensive (Blanchard & Blanchard, 1984). Often, defensive attacks of animals as well as humans are lethal. Also, pathological forms of human defense, identified by some as rage, seem frequently to be unprovoked. Together, these are consistent with, but do not prove, the hypothesis that genetic variants for defense in mice could be a valid model for impulsive aggression. Also, it has recently been suggested but not fully established that all intraspecific aggression of humans is defensive (Albert, Walsh, & Jonik, 1993). Variants for only 1 of the 11 genes in Table 18.1 have been assessed in resident–intruder tests of defense. The null mutants for CamK2a decrease offensive and defensive attacks relative to the wild type (Chen, Rainnie, Greene, & Tonegawa, 1994). Again, further comparisons of impulsive aggression in humans and defense in mice are needed to decide whether genetic variants of defense in mice are valid models of this human behavior.

Both offense and defense are adaptive forms of aggressive behavior. Mak, de Konig, Mos, and Olivier (1995) suggested that impulsive aggression of humans may be pathological or at least nonadaptive and that animal models based on adaptive types of aggression, such as offense and defense, may not be relevant to impulsive aggression of humans. A possible type of nonadaptive aggression in mice is that facilitated by irritability or frustration. There are well-known behavior tests for irritable aggression in rodents (Moyer, 1976); these include situations with reward denial on successful trials and reward extinction. Because a characteristic of impulsive aggression is that it may occur in frustrating or irritable situations, genetic variants in mice for irritable aggression may be suitable animal models at the behavioral level. Again, more detailed comparisons of impulsive aggression in humans and irritable aggression in mice are needed before deciding whether genetic variants of irritable aggression in mice could be valid animal models of this human behavior. So far, no single gene variant of mice has been tested for irritable aggression.

However, it is not clear from the literature on impulsive aggression in humans that this is a distinct type of attack behavior. Rather, it may be that individuals with poor impulse control have problems in controlling many kinds of behavior and that aggression is just one of them (Plutchik & van Praag, 1995). Here, offensive, defensive, or irritable aggression of mice would not be valid animal models for the human behavior. Also, if this hypothesis is valid, genetic variants with effects on impulsivity in mice might be a better starting point for developing animal models at the behavioral level. Tests of impulsivity in rodents are being developed (D. Brunner, Hofer, Buhot, & Hen, 1996; Evenden, 1996). These include learning tests varying reward size, delay, and so forth. For this approach, mutants that were impulsive on these tests would then be screened for effects on different types of aggression. This would be the basis for identifying animal models at the behavioral level on the basis of genetic variants of mice.

The null mutant of MAOA in humans affects impulsive aggression, and the null mutant of Maoa in mice affects offense. The effect of the null mutant on offense in mice is a valid model at the behavioral level only if impulsive aggression is offense. As we have seen, there are other possibilities for the classification of impulsive aggression of humans. Hence, effects of the null mutant for Maoa in mice should also be determined for the defensive and irritable attack as well as for impulsivity in other situations.

I believe that the development of valid animal models at the behavioral level based on single gene variants requires close collaboration among those doing animal and human research on aggression. For the animal research, different types of aggression have been clearly defined by mechanism, function, and motor patterns (Maxson, 1992a). These need to be critically related to the disparate phenomenon described as human aggression, including those involving impulsivity.

Biological Models

Homologous genes can be used to develop animal models at the biological level. For such models, some part of the pathway from gene to behavior must be identified and characterized. These models are useful for developing hypotheses about how a biological system is involved in the aggression of humans. Here, mouse genes with effects on offense and on some aspect of the 5-HT system in the brain are used to consider some issues in developing animal models at the biological level for impulsive aggression. For didactic purposes, it is assumed that gene effects on offense of mice are, in fact, valid animal models at the behavioral level for impulsive aggression of humans.

It has long been hypothesized that in humans, decreased serotonin function in brain is related to impulsive aggression (Coccaro, 1989). Many measures of impulsive aggression or impulsivity per se in humans are associated with lower levels of 5-HIAA in the CSF (cerebrospinal fluid). Also, similar associations are reported among increased risk taking, impulsiveness, and severe aggression and decreased 5-HIAA in the CSF of macaque monkeys (Doudet et al., 1995; Mehlman et al., 1994). In some but not all instances, the association between low 5-HIAA in CSF and impulsive aggression in humans may be due to a variant for the gene for tryptophan hydroxylase (Nielsen et al., 1994). Mouse mutants with effects on other aspects of the 5-HT system of the brain may suggest hypotheses about the role of other parts of the 5-HT pathway in lowered 5HT and 5-HIAAA levels of humans. Four mouse mutants have effects on an aspect of the 5-HT brain system and on offense.

The mutant of the CamK2a gene has no effect on the 5-HT receptor response of the 5-HT transporter reupake but does affect the 5-HT release in neurons of the dorsal raphe. The decreased release of 5-HT might result in lower 5-HIAA levels in the brain. However, this decreased release of 5-HT and these potentially low levels of 5-HIAA are associated with a decrease in offense and defense behaviors. If a decrease in 5-HT and 5-HIAA levels is associated with increased offense of mice, this increase would appear to occur in neurons other than those of the dorsal raphe.

Rather, this increased offense may involve other neurons in the brainstem. Male mice carrying a transgene for Tgfa and consequently with high levels of TGFα (transforming growth factor alpha) have a lower 5-HIAA/5-HT ratio, indicating a lower 5-HT turnover in the brainstem (Hilakivi-Clarke et al., 1995). Also, male mice with a high level of TGFα are more aggressive in resident–intruder tests of offense than are those with low levels. 5-HT reuptake inhibitors reduced offensive attack in these male mice (Hilakivi-Clarke & Goldberg, 1993). Thus, it may be that a decrease in 5-HT turnover in the brainstem neurons other than those of the raphe are associated with an increase in offense of male mice.

The 5-HT_{1B} receptor in this or other regions may be involved in regulating levels and turnover of the transmitter in relation to aggression. There are autoreceptors involved in regulating presynaptic release of serotonin or other neurotransmitters in the brain. A knockout mutant for 5-HT_{1B} lacks the receptor throughout the brain and has lower latency to offensive attack and higher frequency of offensive attacks than do wild-type mice. It has been suggested that the lack of the 5-HT_{1B} receptor might result in a decreased 5-HT turnover and in lower 5-HIAA levels and that this might be causal to the increase in offense (H. G. Brunner, 1996).

The three genes described so far suggest the following hypothesis. Low 5-HT turnover in the brainstem is associated with increased offensive behaviors of male mice, and there is more than one genetic pathway to a decrease in 5-HT turnover. To the extent that impulsive aggression of humans is of the offense type, the Tgfa and Htr1b mutants may be relevant biological models for developing hypotheses about the effects of reduced 5-HT function on it. Further research is necessary to determine the causal relation, if any, of low 5-HT and 5-HIAA levels to offense in these mice.

However, this does not appear to be the pathway for the effect of the Maoa gene on offense in mice. Here, high levels of brain 5-HT, norepinephrine, and 5-HIAA are associated with increased offensive aggression. The monoamine levels may be related to the behavior in three ways.

1. Elevated brain levels of 5-HT might developmentally down regulate 5-HT receptors such as 5-HT_{1B}. This would be a genocopy of the null mutant for 5-HT_{1B}, which has increased offensive aggression. This hypothesis also implies that the effect of changing the functional level of 5-HT_{1B} receptors on offensive aggression is not entirely mediated by consequent changes in levels of 5-HT, 5-HIAA, or 5-HT turnover.

2. The null mutant of mouse has higher brain levels of NE. Because adrenergic antagonists suppress offensive attack in mice (Al-Maliki & Al-Hammood, 1993), this may be a pathway by which the Maoa mutant affects offense in mice.

3. Alternatively, the disturbed monoamine metabolism in Maoa mutants of mice affects the neuroanatomy of the nervous system. This change in neuroanatomy may be causal to the increase in offense behaviors of the Maoa mutant.

To the extent that impulsive aggression of humans is of the offense type, these different pathways for the effects of the Maoa mutant on offense in mice may be useful as part of genic models at the biological level for the effects of the null mutant of human MAOA on impulsive aggression.

These four genes illustrate the advantages and the limitations of mutants as biological models. Convergent and divergent effects of mutants on a neurotransmitter system, such as 5-HT, are advantages, as shown for the hypothesis developed with the CamK2a, Tgfa, and Htrlb genes. Experimental manipulations are, of course, needed to test these hypotheses. Pleiotropic effects of a gene, as with Maoa, are a disadvantage. These yield several different hypotheses about the pathway from gene to behavior. Experimental manipulations are required to determine the separate role of each. Another disadvantage of genetic variants is that a gene may act at different times and in different tissues, rendering it difficult to trace the pathway, even in part, from gene to behavior. However, techniques are now available for determining when and where a gene has its effects. These include antisense DNA (Ogawa & Pfaff, 1996) and inducible gene targeting (Tsien et al., 1996).

Conclusion

Genic models are initially easy to identify. One has only to show that the genes in mice and humans are homologous. Once that is done, their development encounters the same difficulties as animal models per se at behavioral or biological levels. There are two requisites for animal models at the behavioral level. Research must show that the type of aggression in mice and humans are the same and that the similarities and differences for the aggression of mice and humans are carefully and critically identified. Unfortunately, this has not yet been done for any of the genes with effects on offense of male mice. There are other requisites for animal models at the biological level. At least part of the pathway from gene to behavior must be established. This involves determining the time and the site of a gene's relevant transcription and separating relevant from nonrelevant pleiotropic effects of the gene. The convergent and divergent effects of different genes are useful for this, as are techniques of molecular biology. Again, this has yet to be done fully for any of the genes with effects on offense of male mice. Thus, much research needs to be done with known genes to fulfill the promise of individual gene variants as animal models for impulsive or other types of human aggression. The same must be done for genes yet to be identified as having an effect on any type of aggression in mice. I expect that the number of known genes with effects on offense and other types of aggression will grow very rapidly.

References

Albert, D. J., Walsh, M. L., & Jonik, R. H. (1993). Aggression in humans: What is its biological foundation? *Neuroscience and Biobehavioral Reviews, 17,* 405–425.

Al-Maliki, S. J., & Al-Hammood, M. H. (1993). Effects of alpha and beta adrenergic antagonists on aggressive behavior in male mice. *Aggressive Behavior, 19,* 361–367.

Benus, R. F., Bohus, B., Koolhaas, J. M., & van Oortmerssen, G. A. (1991). Heritable variation for aggression as a reflection of individual coping strategies. *Experientia, 47,* 1008–1019.

Blanchard, D. C., & Blanchard, R. J. (1984). Affect and aggression: An animal model applied to human behavior. In R. J. Blanchard & D. C. Blanchard (Eds.), *Advances in the study of behavior* (Vol. 1, pp. 1–62). New York: Academic Press.

Blanchard, D. C., & Blanchard, R. J. (1989). Experimental animal models of aggression: What they say about human behavior. In J. Archer & K. Browne (Eds.), *Human aggression: Naturalistic approaches* (pp. 94–121). New York: Routledge.

Brunner, D., Hofer, M., Buhot, M.-C., & Hen, R. (1996). Do 5HT$_{1B}$ knockout mice display impulsive behavior in food reward choice task? *Society for Neuroscience Abstracts, 22,* 609.

Brunner, H. G. (1996). MAOA deficiency and abnormal behavior: Perspectives on an association. In G. R. Bock & J. A. Goode (Eds.), *Genetics of criminal and antisocial behavior* (pp. 155–164). New York: Wiley.

Brunner, H. G., Nelen, M., Breakefield, X. O., Ropers, H. H., & van Oost, B. A. (1993). Abnormal behavior associated with a point mutation in the structural gene for monoamine oxidase A. *Science, 262,* 578–580.

Brunner, H. G., Nelen, M. R., van Zandvoort, P., Abeling, N. G., van Gennip, A. H., Wolters, E. C., Kuiper, M. A., Ropers, H. H., & van Oost, B. A. (1993). X-linked borderline mental retardation with prominent behavioral disturbances: Phenotype, genetic localization, and evidence for disturbed monoamine metabolism. *American Journal of Human Genetics, 52,* 1032–1039.

Cairns, R. (1996). Aggression from a developmental perspective: Genes, environment, and interactions. In G. R. Bock & J. A. Goode (Eds.), *Genetics of criminal and antisocial behavior* (pp. 45–60). New York: Wiley.

Cases, O., Seif, I., Grimsby, J., Gasper, P., Chen, K., Pournin, S., Muller, U., Aguet, M., Babinet, C., Shih, J. C., & de Maeyer, E. (1995). Aggressive behavior and altered amounts of brain serotonin and norepinephrine in mice lacking MAOA. *Science, 268,* 1763–1766.

Chen, C., Rainnie, D. G., Greene, R. W., & Tonegawa, S. (1994). Abnormal fear response and aggressive behavior in mutant mice deficient for a-calcium-calmodulin kinase II. *Science, 126,* 291–294.

Coccaro, E. F. (1989). Central serotonin and impulsive aggression. *British Journal of Psychiatry, 155*(Suppl. 8), 52–62.

Coccaro, E. F. (1992). Impulsive aggression and central serotonergic system function in humans: An example of a dimensional brain–behavior relationship. *International Clinical Psychopharmacology, 7,* 3–12.

Doudet, D., Hommer, D., Higley, J. D., Andreason, P. J., Moneman, R., Soumi, S. J., & Linnoila, M. (1995). Cerebral glucose metabolism, CSF 5-HIAA levels, and aggressive behavior in rhesus monkeys. *American Journal of Psychiatry, 152,* 1782–1787.

Eichelman, B. (1995). Animal and evolutionary models of impulsive aggression. In E. Hollander & D. J. Stein (Eds.), *Impulsivity and aggression* (pp. 59–69). Chichester, England: Wiley.

Erickson, R. P. (1989). Why isn't a mouse more like a man? *Trends in Genetics, 5,* 1–3.

Evenden, J. (1996). The effects of alcohol and benzodiazepines on tests of impulsivity in the rat. *Society for Neuroscience Abstracts, 22,* 699.

Ginsburg, B. E., & Allee, W. C. (1942). Some effects of conditioning on social dominance and subordination in inbred strains of mice. *Physiological Zoology, 5,* 485–506.

Graves, J. M. (1996). Comparative genome organization in vertebrates: The first international workshop on comparative genome organization. *Mammalian Genome, 7,* 717–734.

Hilakivi-Clarke, L. A. (1994). Overexpression of transforming growth factor α in transgenic mice alters nonreproductive, sex-related behavioral differences: Interaction with gonadal hormones. *Behavioral Neurosicence, 108,* 410–417.

Hilakavi-Clarke, L. A., & Goldberg, R. (1993). Effects of tryptophan and serotonin uptake inhibitors on behavior in male transgenic transforming growth factor α mice. *European Journal of Pharmacology, 237,* 101–108.

Hilakivi-Clarke, L. A., Corduban, T.-D., Taira, T., Hitri, A., Deutsch, S., Korpi, E. R., Goldberg, R., & Kellar, K. J. (1995). Alterations in brain monoamines and GABA$_A$ receptors in transgenic mice overexpressing TGFα. *Pharmacology, Biochemistry, & Behavior, 50,* 593–600.

Konig, M., Zimmer, A. M., Steiner, H., Holmes, P. V., Crawley, J. N., Brownstein, M. J., & Zimmer, A. (1996). Pain responses, anxiety, and aggression in mice deficient in preproenkephalin. *Nature, 383,* 535–538.

Mak, M., de Konig, M. M., Mos, J., & Olivier, B. (1995). Preclinical and clinical studies on the role of 5-HT receptors in aggression. In E. Hollander & D. J. Stein (Eds.), *Impulsivity and aggression* (pp. 289–311). Chichester, England: Wiley.

Maxson, S. C. (1992a). Potential genetic models of aggression and violence in males. In P. Driscoll (Ed.), *Genetically defined animal models of neurobehavioral dysfunctions* (pp. 174–188). Cambridge, MA: Birkhauser Boston.

Maxson, S. C. (1992b). Methodological issues in genetic analyses of an agonistic behavior (offense) in male mice. In D. Goldowitz, D. Wahlsten, & R. E. Wimer (Eds.), *Techniques for genetic analysis of brain and behavior: Focus on the mouse* (pp. 349–373). New York: Elsevier.

Maxson, S. C. (1996a). Issues in the search for candidate genes in the mice as potential animal models of human aggression. In G. R. Bock & J. A. Goode (Eds.), *Genetics of criminal and antisocial behavior* (pp. 21–30). New York: Wiley.

Maxson, S. C. (1996b). Searching for candidate genes with effects on an agonistic behavior (offense) in mice. *Behavior Genetics, 26*, 471–476.

Maxson, S. C. (1998). Homologous genes, aggression, and animal models. *Developmental Neuropsychology, 14*, 143–156.

Mehlman, P. T., Higley, J. D., Faucher, I., Lilly, A. A., Taub, D. M., Vickers, J., Soumi, S. J., & Linnoila, M. (1994). Low CSF 5-HIAA concentrations and severe aggression and impaired impulse control in nonhuman primates. *American Journal of Psychiatry, 151*, 1485–1491.

Moyer, K. E. (1976). *The psychobiology of aggression*. New York: Harper & Row.

Nelson, R. J., Demas, G. E., Huang, P. L., Fishman, M. C., Dawson, V. L., Dawson, T. M., & Snyder, S. H. (1995). Behavioral abnormalities in male mice lacking neuronal nitric acid synthase. *Nature, 378*, 383–386.

Nielsen, D. A., Goldman, D., Virkkunen, M., Tokola, R., Rawlings, R. & Linnoila, M. (1994). Suicidality and 5-hyroxyindoleacetic acid concentration associated with a tryptophan hydroxylase polymorphism. *Archives of General Psychiatry, 51*, 34–38.

Ogawa, S., & Pfaff, D. (1996). Application of antisense DNA method for the study of molecular basis of brain function and behavior. *Behavior Genetics, 26*, 279–292.

Ogawa, S., Lubahn, D. B., Korach, K. S., & Pfaff, D. W. (1997). Behavioral effects of estrogen receptor gene disruption in male mice. *Proceedings of the National Academy of Sciences, USA, 94*, 1476–1481.

Ohno, S., Geller, L. N., & Young Lai, E. V. (1974). Tfm mutation and masculinization versus feminization of the mouse central nervous system. *Cell, 3*, 235–242.

Plutchik, R., & van Praag, H. M. (1995). The nature of impulsivity: Definitions, ontology, genetics, and relations to aggression. In E. Hollander & D. J. Stein (Eds.), *Impulsivity and aggression* (pp. 7–24). Chichester, England: Wiley.

Roubertoux, P. L., Carlier, M., Degrelle, H., Haas-Dupertuis, M.-C., Phillips, J., & Moutier, R. (1994). Co-segregation of intermale aggression with pseudoautosomal region of the Y chromosome in mice. *Genetics, 136*, 225–230.

Saudou, F., Amara, D. A., Dierich, A., LeMeur, M., Ramboz, S., Segu, L., Buhot, M.-C., & Hen, R. (1994, September 23). Enhanced aggressive behavior in mice lacking the 5-HT$_{1B}$ receptor. *Science, 265*, 1875–1878.

Scott, J. P. (1942). Genetic differences in the social behavior of inbred mice. *Journal of Heredity, 33*, 11–15.

Tsien, J. K., Chen, D.-F., Gerber, D., Tom, C., Mercer, E. M., Anderson, D. J., Mayford, M., Kandel, E. R., & Tonegawa, S. (1996). Subregion- and cell type-restricted gene knockout in mouse brain. *Cell, 87*, 1317–1326.

van Oortmerssen, G. A., & Bakker, T. C. M. (1981). Artificial selection for short and long attack latencies in wild *Mus musculus domesticus*. *Behavior Genetics, 11*, 115–126.

Whitaker-Azmitia, P. M., Zhang, X., & Clarke, C. (1994). Effects of gestational exposure to monoamine oxidase inhibitors in rats: Preliminary behavioral and neurochemical studies. *Neuropsychopharmacology, 11*, 125–132.

Yanai, K., Watanabe, T., Inque, I., & Watanabe, T. (1996). Reduced aggressiveness and impaired exploratory behaviors in mice lacking histamine H1 receptors. *Society for Neuroscience Abstracts, 22*, 2064.

19

Ethological and Welfare Considerations in the Study of Aggression in Rodents and Nonhuman Primates

Augusto Vitale and Enrico Alleva

This chapter deals with the study of aggression in two groups of mammals: rodents and nonhuman primates. We do not intend here to underline the importance of studying aggression in animals to improve our understanding of the origins and forms of aggressive behavior in humans (see, in this respect, chap. 20 by Blanchard, Hebert, & Blanchard and chap. 17 by Koolhaas, de Boer, de Ruiter, & Bohus, in the present volume). Instead, we emphasize both the ethological value of studies in this field, given the importance of agonistic behavior in socially organized groups of animals, and the welfare of the animal models involved.

Because we believe that the study of aggression is a valid means to improve our knowledge of the biology of particular species, as we discuss later, the real question is the following: "Why should we be concerned about the ethical aspects of experiments involving aggression?" One of the considerations underlying the answer to this question is that the scientist is part of society. Science, like any other productive activity, is wholly integrated into and influenced by the structure of society. It follows that the growing concern of the general public for the welfare of animals used in experimental biology cannot be dismissed as irrelevant. We both acknowledge and approve the public's increasing concern regarding animal experimentation, which is shared by part of the scientific community, in which the activity of ethologists has been crucial. It is enough to mention the seminal work of Mariam Stamp Dawkins (e.g., 1990) in successfully attributing scientific dignity to the study of animal welfare: This issue is now the topic of conferences, workshops, and monographs (Appleby &

We would like to thank the anonymous reviewers who helped to improve the quality of our manuscript. In particular, they were essential in pointing out to us that some of our statements gave the impression that we underestimate the complexity of the issues related to animal experimentation. We would also like to thank Francesca Cirulli for her final, and resolvent, touches to the manuscript. Finally, we thank Margaret Wayne for editing our English.

Hughes, 1997; Dols, Kasanmoentalib, Lijbach, Rivas, & van den Bos, 1997). As Dawkins (1998) rightly pointed out, ethology has nowadays "come of age" and can address the issue of subjective feelings in animals in a scientifically valid manner as a means to setting the problem of animal welfare in an appropriate perspective. Although these studies have to date not supplied a completely satisfactory definition of "pain" when referred to laboratory animals, they have indicated that animals can suffer in a comparable manner to humans, both physically and psychologically. These indications have to be kept in mind when performing experiments, not only when studying aggression, obviously, but also when involved in any kind of experiment that limits the freedom of choice of the animal model.

The question of animal welfare in laboratory animals is a complex one. First of all, the very meaning of the concept is highly debatable. As indicated by Duncan and Fraser (1997), three main approaches can be identified. The first defines animal welfare in terms of subjective feelings and aims to promote comfort in laboratory animals. A second approach emphasizes the importance of the animals' satisfactory biological functioning and, therefore, uses characteristics such as longevity, health, and reproductive success as parameters. Finally, the third suggests that animals be raised in conditions that suit the natural characteristics of each species and that allow each individual to perform the full behavioral repertoire. These approaches can lead to the same results; in this chapter, we refer to all three.

A proper approach to the issue of animal welfare surely calls for the contribution of experts from different fields. Hence, the arguments put forward by philosophers and social scientists are very useful in helping animal researchers to analyze their work more comprehensively (see, e.g., Arluke, 1990; Rachels, 1990; Singer, 1990). Experimental scientists should attempt to include ethical considerations in the planning of their experimental protocols. This is one of our aims in this chapter. We do not offer simple answers to very difficult questions: That would be hypocritical. Instead, we offer some suggestions concerning particular protocols, which may contribute to reaching an honorable compromise between the needs of the scientist and those of the animal model.

The first part of the chapter focuses on rodents (mice and rats are the most commonly used animals in the study of aggression; Archer, 1988); these are followed by some considerations on the study of aggression in nonhuman primates. Finally, we make a number of proposals aimed at reconciling the needs of scientifically valid, but also ethically improved, experiments involving animals.

Ethological and Welfare Considerations in the Study of Aggression in Rodents

In recent years, researchers have become increasingly aware of the needs of animals used in experimental studies, forcing us to rethink our experimental procedures. Behavioral biologists are increasingly concerned about using vertebrates in experiments that involve pain and distress. Numerous guidelines for the ethical use of rodents in research have been established by scientific associations, funding agencies (European Science Foundation, National Science Foundation, National Institutes of Health, European Community, American Psychological Association, etc.), and increasing numbers of intramural ethical committees, some of which are open to members from outside the scientific community (e.g., lawyers, general practitioners, and representatives of the World Wildlife Fund).

In an article published by the Association for the Study of Animal Behaviour, Huntingford (1984; but see also Elwood, 1991) addressed important ethical issues raised by the study of aggression and provided guidelines. This article stresses that when studying aggressive interactions, it is important to record the behavior accurately, to reduce the duration of the experiments to the minimum, to use the smallest number of animals necessary, and to use information available from studies conducted in other laboratories (e.g., World Wide Web information is increasingly available and should be used for this purpose).

If scientists take for granted that it is ethical to use animals in research, one key problem is that precautionary measures need to be taken to prevent animals from hurting each other during aggressive encounters. Sensitivity of animals to pain, which is not an unavoidable outcome of experiments in which animals express aggressive behavior (although fences or wire-mesh grids may exclude physical contact between individuals; Alleva, Petruzzi, & Ricceri, 1995), has to be a primary concern, as discussed by Bateson (1991; but cf. Bateson, 1986). We strongly recommend that psychologists refer to these articles and adopt their suggestions for practical, ethically grounded, experimental objectives. Bateson's analysis started from a bidimensional model in which animal suffering was weighed against scientific achievement. A few years later, in a second phase that probably reflected the increased concern of the general public and of the scientific community, the bidimensional model was refined and became tridimensional, with the addition of the variable "certainty of medical benefits."

Rodents are used mainly as animal models to study the neural basis of emotional behavior. A good example is represented by the attempts to establish a new animal model of the effects of serotoninergic drugs.

In behavioral studies involving aggression between rodents in an artificial setting, the experimenter should endeavor to reduce injury, or even the death, of the subjects by following some of the suggestions listed in Exhibit 19.1.

Obviously, these suggestions are not compulsory and should be compatible with the current state-of-the-art studies on aggression. For example, studies aimed at assessing the effects of different degrees of familiarization and involving either physical cues or social stimuli (Corridi, Chiarotti, Bigi, & Alleva, 1993) should use experimental protocols in which the subjects have, as a matter of fact, different degrees of familiarization or contrasting social experiences. In particular, these suggestions should be taken into account when hormone treatment, lesions, or genetic manipulations create conditions of high interspecific aggressiveness. In any case, a balance should be sought between the needs of the experimenters and those of the experimental subjects, although we are aware that such a balance is by no means easily determined.

As well as the items indicated in Exhibit 19.1, different kinds of housing conditions also influence the physiological and behavioral conditions of both male and female rodents (Brain & Nowell, 1971a, 1971b; Brain & Stanislaw, 1988). In mice, in particular, individual housing (social isolation) leads to a higher propensity to attack when these subjects are used in an experimental context. A factor to be taken into account in this case is the possible existence of a sensitive period for the effects of isolation on the level of aggressiveness of certain individual subjects (Cairns, Hood, & Midlam, 1985). Furthermore, both the size and the group composition of a mouse colony must be monitored and planned in advance. For example, in socially established mouse colonies, residential mice respond differently to intruders with different fighting experience (Burg & Slotnick, 1983; Crawley, Schleidt, & Contrera, 1975). Daily monitoring of the physical condition of single subjects, especially right after the formation of a new group, can be checked against wound maps (for mice and other rodents, see Pellis & Pellis, 1988; for rats, see Alleva, 1993, particularly for ultrasound signaling of male "subordination"). In ritualized agonistic interactions, bites are directed toward specific target areas, and the detection of wounds outside such areas indicates an overaggressive situation with a potentially fatal outcome. Furthermore, although it is relatively easy to observe the overt fighting between aggressive male mice, a reliable and conspicuous indicator of the establishment or reestablishment of a dominant–subordinate relationship, the behavioral relations occurring in

Exhibit 19.1.   Suggestions to Minimize the Possibility of Dangerous Attacks in Captive Rodents

---

Adequately large size of the testing environment

Use of opponents of similar body size

Use of subjects with similar previous reproductive experience (to avoid the use of subjects with different behavioral profiles)

Use of subjects with similar degree of familiarization with testing environment

Use of subjects with similar degree of familiarization with the procedures of handling

Use of laboratory-born subjects of similar social experience (e.g., males being caged together since preweaning)

Continuous supervision of the experiment by an experienced human observer, particularly taking into account the likelihood of dangerous outcomes, such as the eating of the pups in a female mouse nest-defending paradigm, to evaluate female aggression (use of a female intruder is highly recommended)

Presence of hiding places to avoid being seen by the repeatedly attacking "dominant" individual[a]

---

[a]To avoid a common cause of death in the case of long-duration sessions involving highly aggressive subjects.

the apparently quiet social environment of a group of two or three male rats is much more elusive. However, when challenged with a drug or a social stimulation, the neurobehavioral or neuroimmune response of a dominant rat is quite different from that of a subordinate partner. It is also useful to point out that the observation of dominance and its correlates in a socially stable group of mice or rats does not produce the same results as those obtained in a neutral territory involving acquainted subjects.

Ethological techniques to study psychoactive drug effects are widely used in studies of aggressive behavior in rodents (see, e.g., MacKintosh, Chance, & Silverman, 1977). As a result of these extensive investigations, a variety of data are now available on treatment with a number of drugs (see, e.g., Miczek & Krsiak, 1979). These data should be used to select drug dosage and regimen to avoid excessive side effects, such as the appearance of stereotypic patterns of behavior or marked changes in locomotor activity, which could interfere with species-specific expressions of aggressive behavior. It is important that researchers are aware of these possibilities when planning protocol and always attempt to minimize the risk of injuries, weighing the specific goal of the study against the psychophysical welfare of the rodents.

An example of an alternative experimental protocol aimed at reducing the likelihood of physical injuries is the case in which intermale aggressive behavior can be used as a variable to cause changes in specific mouse central nervous system (CNS) areas, for example, leading to changes in gene expression (Spillantini et al., 1989). A possible stepwise approach is to ask whether something less dangerous than overt aggression (male aggressive patterns can include violent repetitive biting on the rump and back between the two contestants) could achieve the aims of the study as well or better. For example, male rodents could be simply exposed to social odor cues, such as wood shavings soaked in the urine, secretions from sex glands (which reportedly have a high communicative value in intraspecific agonistic interactions), or fur debris from another male subject. An even more sophisticated procedure might be to expose the mouse to a particular amount of secretion from the preputial gland of a dominant conspecific to elicit the coping reaction that leads to the required changes at the CNS level. These last two protocols also have the advantage of avoiding the contamination of the experimental data with unwanted variables because of the physical exhaustion of the contestants.

The increased use of genetically engineered rodents, particularly mice, is generating a number of new problems such as hyperaggressive strains, not an uncommon result of genetic modification. For example, abnormal fear responses and altered aggressive behaviors in mutant mice have been found in mice deficient in alpha-calcium-calmodulin kinase II (Chen, Rainnie, Grene, & Tonegawa, 1994). These knockout (KO) mice, in which one gene is inactivated, provide a promising model to link behavioral and cellular abnormalities with a targeted molecular lesion. The behavioral syndrome of heterozygous animals (KO gene + one wild-type "normal" gene) consisted primarily in a lowered fear response and a correspondingly higher level of defensive aggression in the absence of cognitive deficits. At variance with heterozygotes, the homozygous mice (both genes inactivated) displayed widespread abnormal behavior patterns in different types of experiments. In particular, heterozygotes reacted by freezing briefly and less than normal mice in contrast to homozygotes who did not freeze. Moreover, the pain threshold of heterozygotes was normal, whereas that of the homozygotes was increased. Unusually frequent fighting occurred among heterozygotes. When a resident–intruder paradigm was used, heterozygotes showed more defensive attacks against residents than against controls. The heterozygous intruder often counterattacked rapidly by biting the resident, whereas the wild-type intruder assumed the upright defensive posture or fled. The homozygous intruder provoked a lower amount of fighting episodes than either the wild-type or the heterozygous mice and fled when attacked by the resident. Fearlessness in approaching the resident in a nonaggressive fashion, even after being repeatedly attacked, was shown by homozygous intruders, whereas wild-type intruders rarely exhibited such confidence. In general, marked changes in agonistic confrontations were evident after genetic modification.

To define the role of serotonin receptor subtypes in controlling mouse agonistic behavior, Saudou et al. (1994) produced mutant animals lacking one serotonin receptor. These animals did not show any developmental or major behavioral alterations. However, the administration of a specific receptor agonist (RU24969) failed to produce the usual hyperlocomotor effect, indicating that this effect is mediated by $5\text{-}HT_{1B}$ receptors. More interesting, when confronted with a male intruder, mutant mice attacked the intruder faster and more vigorously than did wild-type controls, suggesting that $5\text{-}HT_{1B}$ receptors are involved in intraspecific agonistic patterns. The number of tail rattlings preceding the attacks was also higher in the case of mutant residents. The level of aggressiveness was higher in a second social confrontation test, consistent with reports that aggression increases with fighting experience (Lagerspetz, 1964).

Mutations of the p75 low-affinity NGF receptor gene lead to marked changes in the peripheral sensory nervous system (Lee et al., 1992). Homozygous mutant mice were viable, fertile, and lacked wild-type receptor mRNA and protein. Peripheral neuropathy was evident, as shown by a substantial reduction in skin innervation. A resulting heat insensitivity of homozygous mutants was observed in a hind-paw retraction test.

These examples represent cases in which experimental protocols should be checked against regulations governing experimentally induced contexts resulting in suffering or pain in genetically altered vertebrates. Significant changes in agonistic patterns may well emerge as a by-product of genetic modification, and researchers should consider this possibility.

Ethological and Welfare Considerations in the Study of Aggression in Nonhuman Primates

Primatology is positioned on a scientific, philosophical, and moral borderline. The main reason for this particular intellectual location is the evolutionary proximity of human and nonhuman primates. This biological proximity carries with it sentimental and evocative, as well as scientific, implications. As Donna Haraway so eloquently stated, "[M]onkeys and apes, and human beings as their taxonomic kin, exist on the boundaries of so many struggles to determine what will count as knowledge" (Haraway, 1989, p. 13). Modern primatologists should consider that the feelings, motivations, and cultural and social perspectives of the observer affect his or her construction of a natural reality through observation of behavior.

These issues are particularly important because, as already mentioned, monkeys and apes are our closest relatives in evolutionary terms and, for this reason, are in many ways considered an appropriate model for the study of humans. Robert Hinde (1987) has indicated that the study of nonhuman primates can contribute to an understanding of human beings in two principal ways. First, this type of study can improve our knowledge in such areas as anatomy, pathology, and physiology because of the characteristics shared by human and nonhuman primates. Second, the methodologies and principles derived from behavioral studies of nonhuman primates can be applied to human ethology. In the latter case, important results have been obtained from studies comparing aggression in animals and humans (de Waal, 1989; Potegal & Knutson, 1994).

Because of the complexity of their nervous system, which allows for the attribution of humanlike feelings and emotions, nonhuman primates occupy a special niche in the concerns of people who care about the well-being of animals. As a matter of fact, nonhuman primates, perhaps more than other animals, are a privileged object of our moral perceptions. (Interesting in this regard is the concept of *commitment by affinity*, proposed by the Dutch philosopher Tjard de Cock Buning, 1995.) For example, the International Primate Protection League, a society dedicated to the protection of nonhuman primates around the world, founded by Shirley McGreal in 1973, has been successful in stopping cases of illegal trading of and cruelty to these animals. Also noteworthy is the campaign promoted by Peter Singer and Paola Cavalieri (1993) to include the apes in the *community of equals*. As far as legislation is concerned, since 1992, animal experimentation in Italy has been regulated by a legislative decree (n.116/92) derived directly from the related European Community directive. The Italian decree bans experimentation on nonhuman primates, with permission being granted only after a specific request for exemption. However, various associations, such as the Eurogroup for Animal Welfare, are pushing for a gradual total elimination of painful experiments on animals. Others, such as the Royal Society for the Prevention of Cruelty to Animals, call for amendments that substantially improve the housing and maintenance of nonhuman primates used in biomedical research.

We believe that the study of aggression in nonhuman primates, like the study of other behavioral traits, is affected by all these considerations. On the one hand is the primatologist, with his or her cultural, political, and scientific background and expectations; on the other hand is the scientific community and a society that rightly demands the humane treatment of animals used in research. The monkey sits in the middle.

Other studies of aggression in higher mammals are specifically aimed at understanding how sociality is structured, its natural history and its rules, how social roles are acquired and lost, and how changes in social structure may lead to psychopathology. These kinds of study, although aimed at analyzing the social behavior of a given species, are nonetheless used as an attempt to understand the social relationships of humans.

Most primates live in complex social systems. It has been suggested that these social systems can be better seen as the results of the patterning of the relationships between different individuals; relationships are the results of the patterning of the interactions between these individuals (Dunbar, 1988; Hinde, 1976). The interactions between individuals are sex and age related and environmentally contextual. Nonhuman primates who live in a society benefit in different ways, from communal rearing of infants (Nicolson, 1987; Whitten, 1982) to improved defense from predators (Seyfarth, Cheney, & Marler, 1980). However, communal living also implies conflict. Within a primate group, conflicts between individuals arise from competition for resources such as food, shelter, and mates. Competition for mates, in particular, can lead to physical aggression. Naturally, as with many other animals, nonhuman primates are quite capable of avoiding potentially dangerous physical contact when competing for a limited resource. One of the most obvious cases of this avoidance is the establishment of a hierarchical structure and its recognition by other members of the social group. High rank confers priority to access limited resources and, at least for the dominant individuals, decreases the probability of involvement in aggressive interactions (although the generality of this statement is challenged by a variety of observations in both natural conditions and captivity). When discussing aggressive interactions, the primatologist Robin Dunbar (1988) indicated three different factors that competitors have to take into account: (a) the value of a given resource for the two contestants in particular ecological circumstances; (b) the assessment, by each of contestant, of the probability of winning the contest; and (c) the cost to each of a possible escalation of the contest into a fight. This appears to summarize a very complex behavioral phenomenon well.

Much has been written and debated on the issues of aggression and dominance in primate societies. The concept of dominance itself has been heavily criticized (Hinde, 1978; Rowell, 1974). In relation to this point, we refer to a new interpretation of the concept proposed by Frans de Waal (1982) and colleagues at the beginning of the 1980s. Before moving to the United States, the Dutch primatologist observed for many years the chimpanzee (*Pan troglodytes*) community of the Arnhem zoo in The Netherlands. On the basis of these observations, de Waal described the forging and plasticity of political alliances, resulting in changes at the top of the hierarchy. This experience pervades a seminal article in which de Waal (1986) proposed a new interpretation of dominance in primate societies. His interpretation no longer emphasized social dominance in the context of competition for resources, but social dominance in terms of affiliative bonding and interactions. Instead of writing about competition, de Waal wrote about trading and sharing. The result of this approach is his proposal of a new model to represent the dynamics underlying social hierarchies. The *reconciled hierarchy model* is based on the view that relationships of dominance have an affective component. Social mechanisms between individuals, such as *conditional reassurance* and *formalization*, promote cohesion, harmony, and stability, whereas *status striving* leads to dynamism and tension. The message is that researchers do not need to identify the actors involved in social dynamics as only selfish competitors.

Obviously this is only one, albeit fascinating, possible interpretation of aggressive behavior. In studying this subject, the researcher should feel free to adopt any theoretical approach. What is important to remember is that any new idea implies a particular experimental protocol aimed at substantiating it, and the researcher should be aware of the ethical aspects of any new experimental protocol he or she might think of following.

The study of aggression and reconciliation in primates remains, as we have shown, a very fruitful topic of research. There are two fundamental principles to be kept in mind when dealing with the problem of aggression in captive populations on nonhuman primates: (a) Groups of nonhuman primates should be housed in such a way as to minimize conflict, regardless of the object of the research; (b) if the experimental protocol is likely to influence the social interactions between participants, as when aggression itself is the object of the study, one must always be able to intervene to control the level of aggression or to stop it completely.

One must remember that every social group of primates comprises individuals and that, as mentioned before, the degree of stability within any group will be determined by interactions among the individuals of the group. The tendency for certain individuals to form both alliances and possible alterations in the social hierarchy must be monitored constantly. The social needs of different individuals obviously differ, and the same need may be expressed in varying ways by different individuals. Furthermore, knowledge of the temperament and social disposition of each individual can be acquired and communicated otherwise than by assuming a neutral and objective scientific attitude. Feelings, emotions, and empathy with a particular monkey are useful tools to gain such knowledge. Empathetic caretakers and technicians are absolutely crucial in this process (Wemelsfelder, 1993; but see also Davis & Balfour, 1992). The information concerning the social disposition of each individual should then be integrated with that concerning the species-specific social behavior. This highly recommended twofold approach can only be pursued through constant and careful observation of the captive colony's behavior. *Know your animals* must be the maxim.

In studies concerning aggressive behavior in captive colonies, the inclusion of particular individuals in the experimental protocol must depend on the known temperament of each candidate. The actual protocol should naturally be designed to prevent any kind of physical contact among contestants that could lead to injuries. (However, behavioral journals, such as *Animal Behaviour*, have an ethical committee that screens protocols to verify the risks to the animals involved.) Useful examples of protocols that do not let contestants injure each other come from studies of the social behavior of different species belonging to the *Callitrichidae* family. The behavior of these small New World monkeys is characterized by aggressive reactions toward intruders (Anzenberger, 1985; *Saguinus Oedipus*: French & Snowdon, 1981; *Callithrix jacchus*: Harrison & Tardif, 1988). In particular, Jeffrey French and colleagues (French, Schaffner, Shepherd, & Miller, 1995) studied these interactions in black tufted-ear marmosets (*Callithrix kuhli*) to investigate the hypothesis that familiarity with conspecifics outside the family might affect their reactions toward intruders. The experimental protocol never allowed intruders to be fully in contact with members of a different family: A small wire-mesh cage protected the intruder from possible injurious aggressions, and no "intruder phase" ever lasted for more than 10 min. At the Istituto Superiore di Sanità in Rome, we performed a number of experiments aimed at investigating the dominant role of female adults over other individuals in families of common marmosets in an environment in which food was a limited resource. Some instances of aggression among members of the families were observed, but fortunately these were never serious enough to warrant interrupting the experiments. Moreover, by the end of the sessions, the aggressive individuals were fraternizing and showing a playful attitude toward their "victims" (which takes us back to Frans de Waal's interpretation of social dominance dynamics). However, our sessions were also limited to no more than 10 min, and the cage in which we carried out the experiments had an escape route that could be opened instantaneously in the event any individual became the object of dangerous attacks.

Toward Qualitatively and Ethically Improved Animal Experimentation

In this final section, we summarize some of the key aspects underlying both the quality of research and the welfare of the research animals.

1. It is the duty of any scientist carrying out experiments on living organisms with a nervous system complex enough to provide even indirect evidence of the capacity to feel pain to minimize the suffering of the animals involved. In practice, this implies the need to establish a critical threshold at which the need to match the data with the questions asked and the physical and psychological welfare of the experimental subjects can be satisfied. There is a point in the preparation of a specific experimental protocol in which the two tendencies should meet. In any case, provided that there is a reduction of overfighting, the researcher should be free to follow a valid protocol, depending on the specific aim of the research.

2. The welfare and quality of life of animals used in laboratories must be considered both before and after as well as during the actual experiments. As already mentioned, when possible, it is advisable to assess the social status of each socially housed individ-

ual. For instance, when male rodents are caged in groups, their behavioral, neuroendocrine, and neuroimmune profiles may differ widely from those of similar animals housed individually. The identification and monitoring of the continuous rearrangement of social relationships in groups of both rodents and nonhuman primates can prevent unnecessary injuries, or even killing, among cage-mates.

3. In the past, the fear of overindulging anthropomorphic interpretations of animal behavior led to a playing down of the importance of an empathic knowledge of the psychological state of individual animals. Today this approach has become more respectable. The importance of the inevitable bond being formed between the human experimenter and the subject has been emphasized for different taxonomic groups, including reptiles (Bowers & Burghardt, 1992) and birds (Pepperberg, 1992). The most common problem generated by an uncaring caretaker is the unpreventable fear the animal might associate with a capturing or handling procedure that is too harsh. This can easily result in the animal's avoiding human experimenters and in a *response competition effect*, with possible quantitatively and, more dangerously, qualitatively effects on the full expression of an intraspecific agonistic pattern. When the hasty caretaker is not the same person who performs the experiments, a transfer of the avoidance reactions toward human beings in general may occur.

4. For any experimental protocol, the selection of a particular animal model must be appropriate. It is important that there is a logical connection between the question asked, the experimental model chosen, and the expected results. The choice of an alternative model other than nonhuman primates for a particular experimental protocol, for example, must be justified not only on the basis of ethical considerations but also with an eye to the suitability of the model to the aims of the research. It should be possible for "ethically" improved experimental science to remain comfortably within the theoretical and methodological boundaries that define today what is known as "good science."

References

Alleva, E. (1993). Assessment of aggressive behavior in rodents. *Methods in Neurosciences, 14*, 111–137.

Alleva, E., Petruzzi, S., & Ricceri, L. (1995). Evaluating the social behaviour of rodents: Laboratory, semi-naturalistic and naturalistic approaches. In E. Alleva, A. Fasolo, H. P. Lipp, L. Nadel, & L. Ricceri (Eds.), *Behavioural brain research in naturalistic and semi-naturalistic settings* (pp. 359–374). Dordrecht, The Netherlands: Kluwer Academic.

Anzenberger, G. (1985). How stranger encounters of common marmosets (*Callithrix jacchus jacchus*) are influenced by family members: The quality of behavior. *Folia Primatologica, 45*, 204–224.

Appleby, M. C., & Hughes, B. O. (Eds.). (1997). *Animal welfare*. Wallingford, UK: Cab International.

Archer, J. (1988). *The behavioural biology of aggression*. Cambridge, England: Cambridge University Press.

Arluke, A. (1990). The significance of seeking the animal's perspective. *Behavioral and Brain Sciences, 13*, 13–15.

Bateson, P. (1986). When to experiment on animals. *New Scientist, 20*, 30–32.

Bateson, P. (1991). Assessment of pain in animals. *Animal Behaviour, 42*, 827–839.

Bowers, B. B., & Burghardt, G. M. (1992). The scientist and the snake: Relationships with reptiles. In H. Davis & D. Balfour (Eds.), *The inevitable bond* (pp. 250–263). Cambridge, England: Cambridge University Press.

Brain, P. F., & Nowell, N. W. (1971a). Isolation versus grouping effects on adrenal and gonadal functions in albino mice: I. The male. *General and Comparative Endocrinology, 16*, 149–154.

Brain, P. F., & Nowell, N. W. (1971b). Isolation versus grouping effects on adrenal and gonadal functions in albino mice: II. The female. *General and Comparative Endocrinology, 16*, 155–159.

Brain, P. F., & Stanislaw, H. (1988). A reevalutation of the effects of differential housing on physiology and behaviour in male and female mice. *Aggressive Behavior, 8*, 130–132.

Burg, D. R., & Slotnick, B. M. (1983). Response of colony mice to intruders with different fighting experience. *Aggressive Behavior, 9*, 49–58.

Cairns, R. B., Hood, K. E., & Midlam, J. (1985). On fighting in mice: Is there a sensitive period for isolation effects? *Animal Behaviour, 33*, 166–180.

Chen, C., Rainnie, D. G., Greene, R. W., & Tonegawa, S. (1994, October 14). Abnormal fear response and aggressive behavior in mutant mice deficient for alpha-calcium-calmodulin kinase II. *Science, 266*, 291–294.

Corridi, P., Chiarotti, F., Bigi, S., & Alleva, E. (1993). Familiarity with conspecific odor and isolation-induced aggressive behavior in male mice (*Mus domesticus*). *Journal of Comparative Psychology, 107*, 328–335.

Crawley, J. N., Schleidt, W. M., & Contrera, J. F. (1975). Does social environment decrease propensity to fight in male mice? *Behavioral Biology, 15*, 73–83.

Davis, H., & Balfour, D. (Eds.). (1992). *The inevitable bond*. Cambridge, England: Cambridge University Press.

Dawkins, M. S. (1990). From an animal's point of view: Motivation, fitness, and animal welfare. *Behavioral and Brain Sciences, 13*, 1–61.

Dawkins, M. S. (1998). Book reviews. *Animal Behaviour, 54*, 1575.

de Cock Buning, T. (1995). What apes teach us about ethics. In R. Corbey & B. Theunissen (Eds.), *Ape, man, apeman: Changing views since 1600* (pp. 385–394). Leiden, The Netherlands: Leiden University.

de Waal, F. B. M. (1982). *Chimpanzees politics. Power and sex among apes*. London: Unwin Paperbacks.

de Waal, F. B. M. (1986). The integration of dominance and social bonding in primates. *Quarterly Review of Biology, 61*, 459–479.

de Waal, F. B. M. (1989). *Peacemaking among primates*. Cambridge, MA: Harvard University Press.

Dols, M., Kasanmoentalib, S., Lijbach, S., Rivas, E., & van den Bos, R. (Eds.). (1997). *Animal consciousness and animal ethics. Perspectives from the Netherlands*. Assen, The Netherlands: Van Gorcum.

Dunbar, R. I. M. (1988). *Primate social systems*. Ithaca, NY: Cornell University Press.

Duncan, I. J. H., & Fraser, D. (1997). Understanding animal welfare. In M. C. Appleby & B. O. Hughes (Eds.), *Animal welfare* (pp. 19–31). Wallingford, UK: Cab International.

Elwood, R. W. (1991). Ethical implications of studies on infanticide and maternal aggression in rodents. *Animal Behaviour, 42*, 841–849.

French, J. A., Schaffner, C. M., Shepherd, R. E., & Miller, M. E. (1995). Familiarity with intruders modulates agonism towards outgroup conspecifics in Wied's black-tufted-ear marmoset (*Callithrix kuhli*: Primates, *Callitrichidae*). *Ethology, 99*, 24–38.

French, J. A., & Snowdon, C. T. (1981). Sexual dimorphism in responses to unfamiliar intruders in tamarin, *Saguinus oedipus*. *Animal Behaviour, 29*, 822–829.

Haraway, D. (1989). *Primate visions*. London: Verso.

Harrison, M. L., & Tardif, S. D. (1988). Kin preference in marmosets and tamarins: *Saguinus oedipus* and *Callithrix jacchus* (*Callitrichidae*, Primates). *American Journal of Physical Anthropology, 77*, 377–384.

Hinde, R. A. (1976). Interactions, relationships and social structure. *Man, 11*, 1–17.

Hinde, R. A. (1978). Dominance and role: Two concepts with dual meaning. *Journal of the Society of Biological Structure, 1*, 27–38.

Hinde, R. A. (1987). Can nonhuman primates help us understand human behavior? In B. B. Smuts, D. L. Cheney, R. M. Seyfarth, R. M. Wrangham, & T. T. Struhsaker (Eds.), *Primate societies* (pp. 413–420). Chicago: University of Chicago Press.

Huntingford, F. A. (1984). Some ethical issues raised by studies of predation and aggression. *Animal Behaviour, 32*, 210–215.

Lagerspetz, K. M. (1964). Studies on the aggressive behaviour of mice. *Annales Academiae Scientiarum Fennicae (Series B), 131*, 3–21.

Lee, K. F., Li, E., Huber, L. J., Landis, S. C., Sharpe, A. H., Chao, M. V., & Jaenish, R. (1992). Targeted mutation of the gene encoding the low affinity NGF receptor p75 leads to deficits in the peripheral sensory nervous system. *Cell, 69*, 737–749.

MacKintosh, J. H., Chance, M. R. A., & Silverman, A. P. (1977). The contribution of ethological techniques to the study of drug effects. In L. L. Iverson, S. D. Iverson, & S. H. Snyder (Eds.), *Handbook of psychopharmacology* (Vol. 7, pp. 3–35). New York: Plenum Press.

Miczek, K. A., & Krsiak, M. (1979). Drug effects on agonistic behavior. In T. Thompson & P. Dews (Eds.), *Advances in behavioral pharmacology* (pp. 87–162). New York: Academic Press.

Nicolson, N. A. (1987). Infants, mothers, and other females. In B. B. Smuts, D. L. Cheney, R. M. Seyfarth, R. M. Wrangham, & T. T. Struhsaker (Eds.), *Primate societies* (pp. 330–342). Chicago: University of Chicago Press.

Pellis, S. M., & Pellis, V. C. (1988). Identification of the possible origin of the body target that differentiates play fighting from serious fighting in Syrian golden hamsters (*Mesocricetus auratus*). *Aggressive Behavior, 14*, 437–449.

Pepperberg, I. M. (1992). Social interaction as a condition for learning in avian species: A synthesis of the disciplines of ethology and psychology. In H. Davis & D. Balfour (Eds.), *The inevitable bond* (pp. 178–204). Cambridge, England: Cambridge University Press.

Potegal, M., & Knutson, J. F. (Eds.). (1994). *The dynamics of aggression*. Hillsdale, NJ: Erlbaum.

Rachels, J. (1990). *Created from animals: The moral implications of Darwinism*. Oxford, England: Oxford University Press.

Rowell, T. (1974). Contrasting adult male roles in different species of nonhuman primates. *Archives of Sexual Behavior, 3*, 143–149.

Saudou, F., Amara, D. A., Dierich, A., LeMeur, M., Ramboz, S., Segu, L., Buhot, M. C., & Hen, R. (1994, September 23). Enhanced aggressive behavior in mice lacking 5-HT receptor. *Science, 265*, 1875–1878.

Seyfarth, R. M., Cheney, D., & Marler, P. (1980). Vervet monkey alarm calls. *Animal Behaviour, 28*, 1070–1094.

Singer, P. (1990). *Animal liberation*. London: Cape.

Singer P., & Cavalieri, P. (1993). *The great ape project*. London: Fourth Estate.

Spillantini, M. G., Aloe, L., Alleva, E., De Simone, R., Goedert, M., & Levi-Montalcini, R. (1989). Nerve growth factor mRNA and protein increase in hypothalamus in a mouse model of aggression. *Proceedings of the National Academy of Sciences, USA, 86*, 8555–8559.

Wemelsfelder, F. (1993). *Animal boredom: Towards an empirical approach of animal subjectivity*. Unpublished doctoral dissertation, University of Leiden, Leiden, The Netherlands.

Whitten, P. L. (1982). *Female reproductive strategies among vervet monkeys*. Unpublished doctoral dissertation, Harvard University, Cambridge, MA.

20

Continuity Versus (Political) Correctness: Animal Models and Human Aggression

D. Caroline Blanchard, Mark Hebert, and Robert J. Blanchard

One of the sadly enduring themes in aggression research is the inability of animal and human researchers to make meaningful impressions on each other's understanding of the behaviors on which they focus. This problem is not restricted to aggression research, but it appears to be more strongly expressed in this area than in the study of most other behavioral phenomena. New findings in animal research on aversive conditioning, sexual behavior, eating, drug addiction, and so forth are typically regarded as at least potentially relevant by researchers dealing with human aspects of these problems, whereas new human phenomena in these areas may be used to guide the direction of animal research. In contrast, researchers of animal or human aggression have tended to remain aloof, separate from, and disdainful of each other, even while attending and participating in the meetings of a single, dedicated, society: the International Society for Research on Aggression.

Needless to say, this situation has actively interfered with the development of any sort of unified view of aggression that applies to both humans and nonhuman animals. It has thus been one of several major problems that have hindered progress in aggression research during a period in which many other somewhat similar areas—for example, the neurobiology of defense and its relationship to human emotionality—have made considerable advances.

Aggression research does have some relatively unique problems in terms of the establishment of bridges between animal and human behavior. A particular problem is that the concept of aggression as a phenome-

Preparation of this chapter was supported in part by National Science Foundation Grant IBN95-11349. We would like to acknowledge the help of two anonymous reviewers, each of whom provided criticism and information that was extremely useful to this chapter. Although their contributions are hinted at in the two footnotes, these do not begin to encompass the many helpful suggestions they made. These reviewers strengthened both our arguments and our resolve.

non with substantial biological underpinnings is widely perceived as running counter to many worthy social and political views. The characterization of this family of views as worthy is not ironic: These positions are both well-meaning and certainly more likely to produce good results (or to avoid damage) than is adherence to their diametric opposite: a belief that aggression does represent some sort of biological imperative. Moreover, the assumption underlying a distancing of many of the proponents of such views from too close contact with animal aggression research is correct: Animal work often suggests that aggressive behavior has extensive roots in biology, and it is quite likely that exposure to such research may raise questions about the modulation of human aggression that are difficult to answer from the perspective that there is no direct biological influence on this behavior.

These antibiological views encompass a variety of concepts, ranging from the position that war, specifically, has no biological underpinnings to one that decries any direct involvement of biology in the substantial interindividual (socioeconomic, ethnic, subcultural, gender, age, etc.) variation in violence and violent crime. Because individual differences in human as well as animal aggression are undeniable on a phenomenological level—and these so often seem to be associated with factors that clearly relate to biology, such as gender and age—one can acknowledge the possibility of interactions between biology and experience. Thus gender differences may be interpreted as reflecting greater opportunity for aggression or greater reinforcement of aggressive behaviors for boys and men as opposed to girls and women because of either cultural norms (interpreted as a relatively "biology-free" explanation) or differences in gender-typical group composition or social activities (which suggests, but does not dwell on, a biological origin for these differences). In a similar fashion, interpretations with a strong focus on personal self-esteem and social skills as modulators of aggression may acknowledge that these reflect an interaction of personality factors such as behavioral inhibition (increasingly viewed as having an important biological component; see Rosenbaum et al., 1991) with specific experience. Nonetheless, although some acknowledge the possibility of such interactions, the existence of biological differences directly relating to aggression is often denied, minimized, or ignored in human research.[1]

---

[1] We gratefully acknowledge the cogent criticisms of a reviewer who noted that the above paragraphs appear to fall into the trap of accepting a dichotomy between biological and nonbiological (e.g., experiential) factors in aggression. The reviewer points out that experience has no effect on behavior unless it acts through biological structures (i.e., the brain and body of the organism), altering those structures in a manner that, although often hard to measure directly and typically imperfectly understood, is nonetheless "biological." The reviewer goes on to point out that the dichotomization of factors influencing behavior into "biological" and "nonbiological" represents an artificial division imposed by social science, and one that has the odd effect of conceptualizing the experiencing and learning organism as a sort of "spook"—a nonbiological, noncorporeal entity. We agree completely with this point and had hoped that the immediately preceding paragraph would suggest, through a reductio ad absurdum, our skepticism about the scientific value of the convoluted logic that has been advanced to encompass the obvious phenomenological impact of factors such

A second problem in the acknowledgment of a relationship between human and animal aggression involves the cognitive distance between humans and other animals. In the past couple of decades, researchers have shown great interest in the analysis of intelligence, linguistic abilities, or both in such nonhuman animals as dolphins, great apes, and parrots. Although the results of such work have suggested that earlier (say, pre-1970) conceptions of intelligence and potential for language use in these and other nonhuman species were far too limited, nonetheless, there appears to be a relatively well-developed consensus that no known nonhuman species has cognitive or linguistic capabilities that are close to those of humans. The difference is highly relevant to the study of aggression because many instances of human aggression are so clearly accompanied (triggered? modulated?) by complex cognitions or are expressed in terms of mechanisms that rely on cognitive and technological achievements.

These may have no direct parallels in nonhuman species' behavior. For example, the use of technology can ensure that the damage resulting from a particular human act of aggression is quite disproportionate to what would have resulted from an otherwise similar scenario without the technology. This is an important factor, and one that is often overlooked in terms of specific differences between animal and human research. It may be very much involved in a discrepancy between human and animal research findings on the effects of alcohol consumption on aggression: In a range of nonhuman animals, alcohol sometimes increases aggression at low to moderate dose levels but almost always reduces it at higher doses, above about 1.2 g/kg (see Berry & Smoothy, 1986, for review). Neither the human literature involving direct administration of different alcohol doses in an aggression-relevant context nor the criminological and sociological literature on alcohol intake in those who have committed violent crimes provides evidence of such a monotonic relationship. However, aggression in animals requires good coordination to be effective or even recognizable, whereas in contrast, heavily inebriated, poorly coordinated, and even partially sedated humans can perform highly damaging aggressive actions by use of a weapon. In addition, much human aggression is expressed verbally, and the damage potential of this type of aggression is little reduced by the motoric and sedative consequences of a high alcohol load. Thus the disruptive effects of higher alcohol doses on aggression in animals may not be seen in people. This potentially high-magnitude difference may obscure similar alcohol effects on emotional, motivational, or cognitive systems modulating aggression in both animals and humans.

There are other consequences of the cognitive and technological gap between man and nonhuman animals. A major, perhaps pivotal, aggression-related term—*war*—is defined in terms of both the aggressive action and the social organization and tactical capabilities of the opponent groups, as

---

as gender and age in human aggression without admitting any role for "biology" in this effect. These convolutions would not be necessary if one recognized that all of the factors that determine behavior act through their impact on biological organism and through interactions with the existing features of that organism.

applied to these aggressive acts. If these organizational and tactical capabilities are inadequate, then the aggressive behavior, no matter how
focused or how damaging or how clearly it involves groups rather than
individuals, does not represent war. Thus some undoubtedly aggression-
linked behaviors displayed by humans will certainly not be seen in nonhuman animals. Is this important? How important? Does, in a similar
fashion, the inability of nonhuman animals to write sonnets or to make
other verbal declarations of sexual interest or love call into question the
essential continuities between animal and human sexual behavior, or of
an important biological substrate for much of this continuity?

Regardless of what intellectual or emotional comforts may ensue from
treating animal and human aggression as fundamentally different and
unrelated phenomena, unless they genuinely have no significant connections, the tactic is scientifically counterproductive. It removes the possibility of comparative analysis and cross-fertilization of hypotheses between the two realms. It deprives human-focused researchers of an
extensive literature with experimental methodologies to investigate aggression phenomena, whereas those animal researchers who ignore the
human literature inevitably fail to learn of findings that could open up
new and fruitful areas of investigation with nonhuman animals. Given the
present and established situation—that the attitudes with which human
and animal aggression researchers regard each other show only a limited
range, from lack of interest to distrust to horror—is there any way that
this situation can be defused and common grounds found for serious consideration of phenomena with which both human and animal researchers
are deeply involved?

Heterogeneity of Animal Aggression

Words are artificial creations without any necessary, direct, or specific connection to the realities of the phenomenological world. Although this point
is obvious, it is often ignored. Words that are valued in everyday communication over long periods of time tend to acquire an aura of established
validity: to project the belief not only that they are useful and (through
repeated use) psychologically meaningful but also that they represent an
optimum conceptualization of reality.

With reference to the needs of science, this last impression is seldom
correct—for example, *aggression*. Although the term can be used with apparently acceptable levels of mutual understanding in ordinary conver-
sation, it has so many different meanings and is so difficult to conceptualize satisfactorily that Benjamin (1985) selected it (with possible
alternatives: *intelligence* and *self-esteem*) as a particularly egregious example with which to demonstrate the difficulties of concept analysis, for
use in a suggested psychology classroom exercise with a questionnaire and
subsequent class discussions.

Offensive Attack

Analyses from the animal literature suggest one important reason that a single and universally accepted scientific definition of aggression has been difficult to establish: Several different phenomena are encompassed by the term. The distinction between "offensive" and "defensive" forms of adult aggression has received a good deal of systematic attention (e.g., R. J. Blanchard & Blanchard, 1977; D. C. Blanchard & Blanchard, 1984), with both of these typically being differentiated from play fighting (Pellis, 1988) or from predation. *Offensive aggression* occurs in the context of a resource (including territory) or dominance dispute; it involves a set of species-typical behaviors that enable the aggressive animal to approach and con-tact particular body sites on the opponent where bites or blows are deliv-ered; its successful outcome is the termination of the resource–dominance dispute, typically involving flight by the opponent, or the appearance of behaviors of the opponent indicating that it has been defeated. These fea-tures are found in a number of different mammalian species, and elegant analyses are available of both the target sites for offensive attack and the behaviors that permit the offensive or aggressive animal to reach this species-specific target site on the body of its conspecific opponent (e.g., Pellis & Pellis, 1989, 1992a). Many of these actions were interpreted as aggressive display behaviors prior to the realization that they have a very crucial function in enabling the attacker to deliver a bite or blow at this targeted site or as submission postures before it was recognized that these actions help the attackee to conceal specific target sites for attack on its own body.

Defensive Attack

In contrast, *defensive attack* occurs in the context of immediate threat to the subject, from either a conspecific or nonconspecific such as a predator. To clarify a point that continues to confuse researchers, defensive attack is seen only when the subject is defending its own body, not when it is attacking another animal to "defend" a disputed resource. The latter sit-uation involves offensive attack. Defensive attack involves a set of species-typical behaviors that are very different from those seen in offensive attack (R. J. Blanchard, Kleinschmidt, Fukunaga-Stinson, & Blanchard, 1980; R. J. Blanchard, Flannelly, & Blanchard, 1986). Two features of this behavior pattern are particularly relevant. Defensive attack includes a salient threat component (not seen in offensive attack) with loud vocali-zations and displays of weapons such as teeth or claws. The bites or blows delivered tend to be made on different body sites on the opponent (typi-cally, to the face of the attacker) than on those contacted or injured in offensive aggression. The latter, targets of offensive attack, are somewhat variable from one species to another but tend to involve the back and flanks in most species studied (see R. J. Blanchard, Blanchard, Takahashi, & Kelley, 1977; Pellis, 1997, for views of the head as an additional target of offensive attack). The successful outcome of defensive aggression is discouragement of the body-threatening conspecific or predator and discontinuation of its attack. This can occur prior to the defensive attack, as the result of defensive threat, or following the delivery of a bite or blow, particularly to the sensitive eye or snout sites that are the targets of defensive attack. Although relatively little field research has been done on the effectiveness of defensive threat and attack, the strong inhibitory effect of fear on predation suggests that defensive threat may serve as a considerable deterrent (Pellis, O'Brien, Pellis, & Teitelbaum, 1988).

Play Fighting

Play fighting is common among the young of many mammal species, dropping off in frequency, but sometimes not disappearing, after sexual maturity is attained (Pellis & Pellis, 1991b). The behaviors involved in play fighting have considerable structural similarity to those of adult attack and defense in that a species-typical attack pattern is used to approach and make contact (nondamaging in the case of play fighting) with a specific site on the body of the opponent while the defender uses species-typical behaviors to make that body site unavailable to the attacker. In addition, across-species studies suggest that as in adult fighting, attack and defense in play fighting are motivationally distinct behavior patterns (Pellis & Pellis, 1991a). However, both the contact site and the behaviors used to attain (by the attacker) and conceal (by the defender) this site may differ in play fighting from those of adults of the same species during serious fighting (Pellis, 1988); the play-fighting attack target may instead be similar to an important contact target on the female that is used in adult male sexual behavior. This suggests that play fighting, at least for males, may be more linked to adult sexual behavior than to adult fighting, a view that is supported by the finding that deprivation of play fighting has more of a deleterious effect on the latter than on the former (Pellis, Pellis, & Whishaw, 1992). In addition, play fighting defenses in female juveniles may involve some of the responses that later become useful in fending off the sexual advances of males. Consonant with the view that juvenile fighting is not an important preparation for adult fighting (as opposed to sexual behavior), the transition from juvenile play fighting to adult fighting does not appear to involve a continuity in individual levels of attack tendency from one to the other: Males that show the highest attack rates during play fighting tend to become subordinates rather than dominants (Pellis & Pellis, 1992b; Smith, Field, Forgie, & Pellis, 1996).

Predation

Phenomena related to predation are also often subsumed under the rubric of aggression. The most commonly used animals in aggression research are rats and mice; many rats kill and eat mice, a phenomenon that, in part because of the apparent similarities of rats and mice, suggests conspecific aggression. Mouse hunting and mouse killing by rats does not depend on exposure to other mouse-killing rats (Rylov & Kozyrev, 1985), and it increases in food-deprived rats (Rylov, 1985) as one might expect for a predation pattern. In those rats that do kill mice, this is a very stable behavior that has been investigated extensively (see Karli, 1991, for review), particularly in the context of a response to physiological manipulations. However, predatory (as opposed to conspecific) attack can occur in species even more closely related and more similar than rats and mice: Grasshopper mice kill and eat laboratory mice (and other small mammals in their natural habitat), and both the target sites for attack and the behaviors typical of the attack pattern are different during predatory (toward laboratory mice) and conspecific attacks by grasshopper mice (Pellis & Pellis, 1992a). These findings indicate that predatory attack can and should be differentiated from conspecific attack, even when the combatants involved are closely related and (to human eyes) very similar animals.

In addition to the differences in stimuli, response patterns, target sites for contact, and outcome of the various aggressive behavior patterns, recent work on the anatomic and neurochemical systems associated with some of these strongly suggests that the physiology of the systems is also different (e.g., Bandler & Shipley, 1994). Most of the work on the neurobiology of aggressive behaviors has actually involved defensive threat and attack, with a relatively substantial literature also on *quiet biting attack* (which likely corresponds to predation). In addition, the pharmacology of offensive and defensive aggression appears to be different, with the former (Olivier, Mos, & Miczek, 1991) but not the latter (D. C. Blanchard, Takushi, Blanchard, Flannelly, & Kemble, 1985) responding dramatically to a class of "serenics," with effects at various serotonin-receptor subtypes. Motivational variables also produce differential effects on these behaviors, with fear reducing offensive attack (R. J. Blanchard, Blanchard, Flannelly, & Hori, 1988) and predation (Pellis et al., 1988) but not altering defensive attack (R. J. Blanchard et al., 1980).

Heterogeneity of Human Aggression

A variety of coherent and differentiable behavior systems, each of which either directly results in damage to an opponent or (play fighting) involves a somewhat similar site-contact-focused behavior pattern but without producing damage, has been found in every nonhuman mammal in which they have been sought. Examination of the human literature suggests that this work also frequently involves attempts to differentiate various types of aggression, although these attempts have little correspondence to the major categories used in animal research.

For example, Buss (1961) proposed three dimensions of aggression— physical–verbal, active–passive, and direct–indirect—that are still often applied to the analysis of human aggressive behavior. Thus Baron and Richardson (1994) noted that "these dimensions yield eight possible categories into which most, if not all, aggressive actions can be divided" (p. 10). What is interesting in the present context is that only one of the eight combinations (physical–active–direct) has any important representation in most laboratory animals. It might be argued that aggression in primate groups does sometimes involve other combination categories, reflecting increasingly subtle, complex, and sophisticated relationships among individuals within groups (e.g., Silk, 1992). Nonetheless, in terms of current understanding of aggression in nonhuman mammals, it seems clear that the description *physical–active–direct* is applicable to the vast majority of incidents and thus has no ability to provide useful differentiations among these actions that might be reflected in human phenomena. The obvious corollary is that the distinctions among different types of aggression in animals must have no ability to differentially project onto the remaining seven categories of the Buss schema. Thus, this set of dimensions has little relevance to attempts to forge links between human and animal aggression. This situation would seem unpromising for those who believe that human and animal aggression are, in fact, related, but this is true only to the degree that the eight combination-category schema is seen as representing a meaningful and dynamic analysis of human aggression rather than a simple combination of characteristics that might apply to most behaviors.

Another common differentiation in human research is made between "instrumental" and "hostile" or "emotional" aggression. Although this concept was included in a schema that was to be applied to both human and animal aggression (Moyer, 1981), it has been used much more extensively in human analyses, perhaps reflecting that a good deal of human violence does occur as a component of crimes involving gain or, perhaps, that people are so good at observational learning, including learning of aggressive-type behaviors (Hall & Cairns, 1984; Huesmann, 1988; Parker & Rogers, 1981), even in situations in which there is relatively little elicitation of aggression-related emotions or motivations.

Does this ability to use aggression as an instrumental response represent a relatively unique human capacity or tendency? Certainly the concept *crime of gain* has no clear animal parallel, but this is because the concept *crime* is inappropriate, not the concept *gain*. Across mammalian species, aggression is importantly involved in obtaining and holding resources and other prerogatives. In fact, resource disputes constitute one of the major elicitors of offensive attack. In direct tests of the role of status (based on aggression) in determining access to various resources, dominant males made the majority of copulations and tended to gain differential access to preferred foods—but not to water—after single, short, deprivation periods (D. C. Blanchard et al., 1984). In fact, there are a number of classic studies (e.g., Flannelly & Lore, 1977; Thor & Carr, 1979) providing either direct or indirect evidence that priority of access to females is a major outcome of aggression in rat groups, that is, consonant with the view that the aggressive behavior involved in the acquisition of dominance has a general instrumental function. In addition, male attacks increase consistently when females are placed in a group and copulation is allowed (for rats, see Flannelly, Blanchard, Muraoka, & Flannelly, 1982; for mice, see O'Donnell, Blanchard, & Blanchard, 1981). Although the data on food sequestering by dominant rats are equivocal, dominant pigs do obtain a greater share of food (Hansen, Hagelso, & Madsen, 1982), a difference that either may be related to specific conditions of the studies (e.g., deprivation times and durations) or may represent a species difference. Moreover, one might anticipate that fighting over food would be easier to demonstrate in species that obtain food in large, widely scattered chunks (e.g., in carnivores) because in such chunks, the resource—as with a territory or females—would be more sequestrable. This suggests that the use of rodents, or even pigs, as subjects would lead to an underestimation of the role of aggressive behavior in obtaining food for mammalian species.

If the function of much offensive aggression in animals is precisely this—to obtain and hold some sequestrable resource—then both instrumental and emotional aspects of attacks may commonly be involved in the same situations. We have elsewhere (D. C. Blanchard & Blanchard, 1984) argued that the emotion of anger reflects a response to challenge regarding some resource for which the angry individual has a claim. The nature of that claim is interesting. Data (Wilson & Daly, 1992) on violence resulting from "love triangles," or the violence of men on women relating to some real or imagined sexual or love relationship, suggest that many male humans are capable of establishing or maintaining a claim on the affections or persons of particular women that go far beyond the degree of encouragement or acquiescence that has been afforded them. Violence in the context of female claims on a man has also received considerable recent attention, but jealous women may be less likely than jealous men to express this in damaging violence (e.g., Campbell, 1995; Paul, Foss, & Galloway, 1993); this phenomenon may reflect gender differences in the propensity to cause damage as much as (or possibly more than) in the propensity to be jealous. Aggressive actions in the context of jealousy are clearly linked to attempts to discourage challenges to the perpetrator's relationship to and control over the love-object, regardless of whether the latter, or a third-party challenger, serves as victim.

In this context, it is clearly simplistic to contrast instrumental and emotional forms of human aggression. The same action is both. However, the prototypical example of instrumental aggression involves a professional (or at least well-practiced) thief or killer who feels no anger in the event. Such examples conveniently omit the significant element of challenge. Offensive aggression in animals occurs in the context of a challenge to resource control, not merely in the obtaining of resources. Although it is certainly plausible that "emotionless" aggression (or any other action of which humans are capable of acquiring voluntary control) may be learned as an instrumental response to obtain resources, does this aggression remain "emotionless" if the aggressed-upon individual actually presents a significant challenge? We are skeptical.

Further indication that the category of purely instrumental aggressive acts is rather small may be found in Katz's (1988) discussion of the subjective rewards of criminal and violent behavior. This suggests that the "resources" gained by violence often involve status, access to particularly valued women, and other status symbols rather than money or goods per se and that the achievement of these ends for many habitually violent individuals is associated with strongly positive emotions. A challenge successfully overcome is seen as contributing to the intensity of this subjective experience, with greater reward from victory over more able challengers. This, of course, fits a definition of instrumentality in that the complex of emotional and material sequelae is the anticipated reward, but the anticipated positive emotion, and also anger at the possibility of frustration through defeat, are important components of the incitement toward violence. This analysis is couched in terms that may seem uncomfortable when applied to animals, and indeed the linking concepts have not been adequately defined to be applicable to both realms; however, one might consider that for violent offenders and—for example, resident male rats—the stimuli and situations eliciting aggression and the consequences of successful and unsuccessful aggression are very similar.

These considerations also suggest why a challenge is so frequent and potent a stimulus to elicit human aggression. As Daly and Wilson (1988) have pointed out, this is particularly true in populations of young men (who, notoriously, account for a disproportionate share of crimes of violence; e.g., D. C. Blanchard & Blanchard, 1983; Campbell, 1995) in which failure to respond to a challenge may have real consequences for the status of the individual in the group and for his ability to command important resources, such as access to young women. The common supposition that such challenges and the responses to them reflect aberrant social skills and inadequate self-esteem may have some basis in reality (one reason for this may be that individuals with poor social skills and self-esteem have less success and greater levels of frustration in acquiring status and resources).[2] However, it misses the point that the paradigm "challenge elicits aggressive response" is a common feature of mammals, particularly young postpubertal male mammals, and that the specific challenge involved is typically either to the status of the individual within the group or, directly and indirectly, to his access to female mammals or other important and sequestrable resources. Higher primates have added to this paradigm in

---

[2]A second reviewer points out that in addition to the view that aggressive individuals may be low in self-esteem, there is a recent analysis by Baumeister, Smart, and Boden (1996) arguing that unrealistically high self-esteem may be related to aggression, the mechanism being that this elevated view of oneself is challenged by reality. The concept *self-esteem*, is, for us, very difficult to deal with because it obviously depends on subjective experience and some form of self-report, a complex that is impossible to apply meaningfully to nonhuman animals and pretty slippery in the context of human research as well. However, as we read it, the relationships of low or unrealistically high self-esteem to aggression may be similar, in that the individual is frustrated in achieving status and its accoutrements through socially approved activities and so may be particularly prone to anger and aggression when confronted by status challenge.

that other group members may get involved either as seconds (Pereira, 1989; Silk, 1992) or in an attempt to control and defuse the situation (Reinhardt, Dodsworth, & Scanlan, 1986), and humans have contributed the factor that challenges may be purely verbal (and often quite inventive). They have also invented a very encompassing form of sequestrable resource: money. The paradigm, however, remains, and it is a mammalian (vertebrate? chordate?) pattern—not one that merely reflects dysfunctional human social groups.

Defensive Attack

These considerations suggest that many instances of human aggression involve close parallels to what is called offensive aggression in the animal literature. What about defensive attack? Although the definition of defensive attack is simple and clear because the concept is defined in terms of response to relatively intense threat or pain to the subject, it is all but impossible to create a laboratory situation that adequately models these stimuli and elicits this mode of attack in humans. Even observing such an event in the real world without attempting to intervene might involve an ethical problem. This effectively limits research on defensive attack either to retrospective reports or to the creation of scenarios in which participants are asked to describe how they would feel or respond—or to indicate their agreement or disagreement with various suggested feelings and actions—in situations involving immediate threat and intense fear. The value of retrospective reports may be further compromised by an oddity in recall: When asked to recall an incident in which she or he attacked a strongly threatening person, participants tended to recall the fear but not the attack itself (D. C. Blanchard & Blanchard, 1983). A typical description was the following: "I was so scared that I just went berserk." However, defensive attack, unlike resource dispute situations, appeared to involve screaming, biting, and clawing at the threat stimulus, and considerable damage to the opponent was sometimes reported. (It might be noted that the oddity in recall may not be so odd after all but may possibly be related to other experiential or memory anomalies related to traumatizing situations.) These are possibly related to analgesic effects during the traumatic event (see review by Rodgers, 1995) or to glucocorticoid effects on memory systems involving the hippocampus (McEwen & Sapolsky, 1995).

The creation of scenarios designed to model situations involving defensive (vs. offensive) attack represents another, albeit also less than perfect, method of investigating the subjective–behavioral differences in the two types of attack. Fukunaga-Stinson (unpublished study reported in D. C. Blanchard & Blanchard, 1983) asked 119 male or female students to respond to scenarios involving a resource dispute or a physical threat (attack by a stranger in an isolated spot) by indicating the likelihood of specific actions or subjective feelings. These were, as predicted, very different for the two scenarios, with feelings of anger predominating in the former and fear in the latter. In addition, the first-choice action for the fear situation was to leave as soon as possible, followed by (for women) looking around for something with which to hit the attacker, and with "hit to harm" also among the first five choices for both sexes. None of these hitting-related choices was among those selected as likely in the resource dispute situation, although a strong desire to attack the challenger was often cited. Physical and physiological responses to the two situations also differed, with "freezing" and becoming "stiff" or showing "nervous breath" used to describe the fear situation, whereas becoming "hot" or "burning" was associated exclusively with the resource dispute situation: "clinching fist," "staring at," and "adrenalin surge" were also used to describe the latter. What is important is not only that these two scenarios elicited a variety of strongly differentiated physiological responses and subjective feelings but also that they were both associated with a perceived tendency either to attack or to want to attack the opponent. Moreover, attack in the fear situation appears to have been less inhibited than in the anger situation, as the latter produced a strong desire to attack but no actual attack response.

These studies were aimed at the immediate reactions to a strong threat stimulus. A history of experience with high-level threat or fear also appears to be associated with unusual aggression in at least some individuals. Studies of traumatizing events ranging from childhood sexual abuse to experience in a prisoner of war camp and other disasters have pointed to enhanced aggression as a relatively consistent component of the post-traumatic stress disorder (PTSD) syndrome (e.g., Browne & Finkelhor, 1986; Ehrensaft, 1992; Glover, 1988; Ollendick & Hoffmann, 1982; Russell, 1984). Clearly, this is one response among many that are associated with PTSD, and it can provide little evidence of a specific connection. However, such reports are sufficiently common that they suggest that aggressive or violent behavior may be one component of a syndrome that is produced by trauma and involves strong, residual, defensive behaviors.

Play Fighting

Play fighting obviously occurs in children as well as in the young of most other mammalian species. Prepubertal boys (Boulton, 1993; Honig, Douthit, Lee, & Dingler, 1992; Maccoby & Jacklin, 1980), like prepubertal rats (Pellis & Pellis, 1990), participate more often in fights than do comparable females. Moreover, play fighting and serious fighting in children are different (e.g., Boulton, 1991a, 1993; Blurton-Jones, 1967; P. K. Smith, 1989), and this difference reflects the actions involved as well as factors such as facial expression or the evaluated intent of the participants (Boulton, 1991a). All these provide some possible parallels to play fighting in nonhuman species, but it is not known how far the parallels may extend. Is there, for example, a target site for attack? Observations in nursery school children suggest that this may be the case (Margaret Manning, personal communication, June 1980), although other studies (Aldis, 1975) have indicated a goal of controlling the partner's movement rather than contacting a specific body site. Is playful attack reinforced by the defensive response of the opponent (see Pellis & McKenna, 1995), and does the over-all intensity of play fighting depend on the strong tendency of the attackee to reciprocate, such that the behavior appears to be "contagious" (see Pellis & McKenna, 1992)? Attempts to initiate play fighting do appear to be met by a play-fighting response in a significant number of instances (Boulton, 1991a), but the influence of this in maintaining the initial or subsequent interactions of the dyad is not known.

The literature does contain suggestions of potential differences be-tween the play fighting of prepubertal children in comparison to that of rats. In rats, the animal that proves in adulthood to be the subordinate rather than the dominant initiates most of the attacks (Pellis & Pellis, 1992a; L. K. Smith et al., 1996), whereas play fighting in middle-school children tends to involve partners who like each other more than chance and tend to be closely matched in strength, with both weaker or stronger children (than their partners) initiating bouts (Boulton, 1991a, 1991b). Another area of potential difference is that serious fighting, although not so frequent as play fighting, is common enough in prepubertal children to be of concern (Boulton, 1996), whereas serious fighting, in terms of adult targets for bites and associated movement patterns, is seldom observed in prepubertal rats (L. K. Smith et al., 1996). Some component of this differ-ence may reflect specific learning: Notably, many of the specific behaviors (e.g., karate chop, back kick, and scissor kick) seen in play fighting but not in serious fighting in a study of middle-school English children rep-resent actions that are likely to have been learned through observa-tion and imitation, perhaps, of television programs. Notably, the last two did not occur in play fighting among Zapotec children—who did, how-ever, show some different behaviors of their own, such as burro kick and knuckle rap (Fry, 1987)—suggesting that the form of play fighting in 8- to 12-year-olds already may have been greatly altered by culture-differentiated practices.

Predation

Predation seems to be the least studied of human aggressive behaviors, at least in its present context, as opposed to speculation concerning its possible role in the evolution of early hominoids. There do appear to be some substantial differences between predation in most predator species and in humans, but these may be very understandable in terms of major features of human evolution. First, there is the use of technology, a more or less universal factor in human predation (i.e., hunting and fishing and, perhaps, the killing of domesticated animals for food?). Second, among most mammalian predator species, both sexes show predatory behavior, and females are at least as likely as males to engage in this activity. This is quite different to the human situation, with, for example, many more male than female hunters and fishermen. This phenomenon may reflect the suggested early development of gender-differentiated roles during human evolution (Eals & Silverman, 1994), or it may reflect a more general primate phenomenon (e.g., Anderson, 1986).

The view that human predation has a biological link to that of closely related mammals is supported by findings that a variety of primates predate and consume other vertebrates, including mammals (e.g., Anderson, 1986; Kudo & Mitani, 1985). Such predation may be more common among large primates and those that are adapting to reduced food supplies as a result of climate change. This is consonant with the above-mentioned speculation as to the role of hunting in human evolution, suggesting that human evolution may have involved an increased tendency to kill and consume other vertebrates. In addition, primates appear to be among the few mammals (carnivores may be similar) that also seek out and kill animals of species that predate them or that serve as important resource competitors with reference to prey (Hiraiwa-Hasegawa, Byrne, Takasaki, & Byrne, 1986); this suggests that primate hunting is by no means limited to animals that are to be consumed. Thus, the hunting of large and dangerous animals not meant for food, a feature of virtually every society that has lived in proximity to such animals, also has a clear parallel in nonhuman mammalian behavior.

Animal and Human Aggressions: Parallel Biobehavioral Systems?

This brief glimpse at several of the rubrics that have been included in analyses of animal or human aggression (or, infrequently, both) is designed to suggest a selective approach to the concept of aggression. Rather than trying to establish a basic parallel between animal and human aggression per se, it might be advantageous to look at the concept of aggression as consisting of a number of different neurobehavioral systems, at least some of which show considerable evidence of continuity between nonhuman mammals and people.

This is not to say that everything included under the human aggression rubric will have a direct parallel in other mammals: Obviously the "aggressive" investor or lawyer or businessman has no direct correspondent in infrahuman mammals, but, as noted above for "crimes of gain," this may be because the nouns are inappropriate, not the adjectives (if the noun were *politician*, the phrase might have an enhanced correspondence). All of these designations reflect a common theme of actions and attitudes that seek to expand claims to resources, rights, or influence in a variety of relevant arenas. Although physical attack is extensively used by both humans and nonhuman mammals, primate behaviors appear to provide a bridge between the largely direct and individual physical nature of aggression in most mammals and its more subtle manifestations in people. For example, in captive vervet monkeys, group males may show mutual facilitation of aggression toward intruding males, interpreted as cooperative behavior in repelling competitors for the group females (Schuster, Raleigh, McGuire, & Torigoe, 1993). Also, among free-ranging olive baboons, dominant males may or may not be the most aggressive animals of the group, and dominance is often maintained by stratagems other than direct attack (Sapolsky, 1990). De Waal and others (Aureli & Van Schaik, 1991; de Waal & Johanowicz, 1993; de Waal & Yoshihara, 1983; Judge, 1991) have reported that many, but not all (Kappeler, 1993), primates show post-aggression "reconciliation" behaviors toward the aggressive animal. All these represent complexities added to the basic mammalian offensive aggression mode and may represent something of a transition to the undoubtedly even more complex set of behaviors and stratagems that make up human aggression in the context of resource disputes.

When particular aggression paradigms are individually examined, there may be either parallels that might be overlooked when an undifferentiated "aggression" behavior is considered or transitions in the organization of that specific aggression paradigm as larger brained mammals with more complex social organizations and technical capabilities are examined. For some aggression paradigms, such as defensive attack, human research is difficult and will likely continue to be difficult because the eliciting stimuli are so traumatic as to be outside the range of events that researchers can ethically manipulate or even observe. For others such as play fighting and predation, however, there are many opportunities for observation and measurement of behavior. Play fighting, in particular, has been extensively analyzed in children and even more extensively analyzed in the young of a variety of nonhuman mammalian species. Evaluation of the degree to which this activity reflects continuity of a biobehavioral system across mammals would be greatly facilitated by some attention of researchers in these two arenas to the methodologies and findings of the other.

These considerations offer the possibility that real breakthroughs may be possible in relating specific human aggression phenomena to their nonhuman mammalian parallels. What is likely to continue to be a stumbling block has been there all along: that aggression is one of the most value-laden terms in any language and is likely to continue in this role. Thus, although aggression can be a "good" thing in the context of pursuit of a valued goal, even here it carries the baggage of implying activity encroaching on the rights of others; the tendency is to label precisely the same actions as "defense" of the desired goal, making the other guy the aggressor. As the old saying goes, "virtually every country in the world has a ministry, bureau, or department of defense and not one has a bureau of aggression."

The problem, in short, is that many researchers of aggression are afraid of the term and of the concepts that it represents. In particular, students of human aggression are afraid of some of the implications of the view that human aggression is essentially similar to aggression in other mammals. Among these implications are that some instances of aggression, and the situations and stimuli that elicit these, are imbedded in normal circumstances of life for people as well as for most nonhuman mammals. In this sense, some aggressive behaviors may be legitimate and normal. Another such implication is that—again, some instances of or tendencies toward—aggression may be evolutionarily adaptive for the individual. If this is true, then these individuals, aggressive under particular circumstances, may leave more descendants, and these descendants would be expected to express, to varying degrees, that tendency. From the perspective of animal research, these implications seem to be undeniable, although the various mechanisms involved are in need of a great deal more analysis, as is the issue of the equally undeniable relationship of aggression to experience, and to the interaction of experience, with a host of genetic, gender, hormonal, and brain neurochemical factors. Finally, although some aggressive tendencies, in some situations, may be normal and adaptive, an emphasis on different types of aggression and on their relationship to specific eliciting circumstances indicates that violent acts that do not agree with these guidelines may be neither normal nor adaptive. Clearly, maladaptive aggressive behaviors, such as those of the occasional male rat that kills females and even related young, do sometimes appear in nonhuman mammals as well, to the detriment of both the individual and its companions.

Set against some of the past and contemporary horrors of human history, acceptance of the view that aggression is basically an adaptive behavior pattern involving a variety of complex biological systems interacting with experience, even if this is true, may be interpreted as political naiveté. We take this point. In opposition, however, is another point of view. The truth may not make you free, but it does make you somewhat better equipped to cope with reality. Acceptance of important continuities in stimulus, organismic, response, and outcome components of particular aggressive behaviors between nonhuman mammals and people promotes a deeper and more comprehensive understanding of human aggression. The goal of science is to understand, to predict, and to control phenomena. To improve the last two of these, the first is required.

References

Aldis, O. (1975). *Play fighting*. New York: Academic Press.

Anderson, C. M. (1986). Predation and primate evolution. *Primates, 27*, 15–39.

Aureli, F., & Van Schaik, C. P. (1991). Post-conflict behaviour in long-tailed macaques (*Macaca fascicularis*): II. Coping with the uncertainty. *Ethology, 89*, 101–114.

Bandler, R., & Shipley, M. T. (1994). Columnar organization in the midbrain periaqueductal gray: Modules for emotional expression? *Trends in Neurosciences, 17*, 379–389.

Baron, R. A., & Richardson, D. R. (1994). *Human aggression* (2nd ed.). New York: Plenum Press.

Baumeister, R. F., Smart, L., & Boden, J. M. (1996). Relation of threatened egotism to violence and aggression: The dark side of high self-esteem. *Psychological Review, 103*, 5–33.

Benjamin, L. T. (1985). Defining aggression: An exercise for classroom discussion. *Teaching of Psychology, 12*, 40–42.

Berry, M. S., & Smoothy, R. (1986). A critical evaluation of claimed relationships between alcohol intake and aggression in infrahuman animals. In P. F. Brain (Ed.), *Alcohol and aggression* (pp. 84–137). London: Croon-Helm.

Blanchard, D. C., & Blanchard, R. J. (1983). Violence in Hawaii: A preliminary analysis. In A. Goldstein & M. Segal (Eds.), *Global perspectives on aggression* (pp. 159–192). New York: Pergamon Press.

Blanchard, D. C., & Blanchard, R. J. (1984). Affect and aggression: An animal model applied to human behavior. In R. J. Blanchard & D. C. Blanchard (Eds.), *Advances in the study of aggression, Vol. I* (pp. 1–58). New York: Academic Press.

Blanchard, D. C., Fukunaga-Stinson, C., Takahashi, L. K., Flannelly, K. J., & Blanchard, R. J. (1984). Dominance and aggression in social groups of male and female rats. *Behavioural Processes, 9*, 31–48.

Blanchard, D. C., Takushi, R., Blanchard, R. J., Flannelly, K. J., & Kemble, E. D. (1985). Fluprazine hydrochloride does not decrease defensive behaviors of wild and septal syndrome rats. *Physiology and Behavior, 35*, 349–353.

Blanchard, R. J., & Blanchard, D. C. (1977). Aggressive behavior in the rat. *Behavioral Biology, 21*, 197–224.

Blanchard, R. J., Blanchard, D. C., Flannelly, K. J., & Hori, K. (1988). Ethanol effects on freezing and conspecific attack in rats previously exposed to a cat. *Behavioral Processes, 16*, 193–201.

Blanchard, R. J., Blanchard, D. C., Takahashi, T., & Kelley, M. (1977). Attack and defensive behavior in the albino rat. *Animal Behaviour, 25*, 622–634.

Blanchard, R. J, Flannelly, K. J., & Blanchard, D. C. (1986). Defensive behaviors of laboratory and wild *Rattus norvegicus*. *Journal of Comparative Psychology, 100*, 101–107.

Blanchard, R. J., Kleinschmidt, C. F., Fukunaga-Stinson, C., & Blanchard, D. C. (1980). Defensive attack behavior in male and female rats. *Animal Learning and Behavior, 8*, 177–183.

Blurton-Jones, N. (1967). An ethological study of some aspects of social behavior of children in nursery school. In D. Morris (Ed.), *Primate ethology* (pp. 347–368). London: Weidenfeld & Nicolson.

Boulton, M. J. (1991a). A comparison of structural and contextual features of middle school children's playful and aggressive fighting. *Ethology and Sociobiology, 12*, 119–144.

Boulton, M. J. (1991b). Partner preferences in school children's playful fighting and chasing: A test of some competing functional hypotheses. *Ethology and Sociobiology, 12*, 177–193.

Boulton, M. J. (1993). Aggressive fighting in British middle school children. *Educational Studies, 19*, 19–39.

Boulton, M. J. (1996). Lunchtime supervisors' attitudes towards playful fighting and ability to differentiate between playful and aggressive fighting: An intervention study. *British Journal of Educational Psychology, 66*, 367–381.

Browne, A., & Finkelhor, D. (1986). Impact of child sexual abuse: A review of the research. *Psychological Bulletin, 99*, 66–77.

Buss, A. H. (1961). *The psychology of aggression*. New York: Wiley.

Campbell, A. (1995). A few good men: Evolutionary psychology and female adolescent aggression. *Ethology and Sociobiology, 16*, 99–123.

Daly, M., & Wilson, M. (1988). *Homicide*. New York: Aldine de Gruyter.

de Waal, F. B., & Johanowicz, D. L. (1993). Modification of reconciliation behavior through social experience: An experiment with two macaque species. *Child Development, 64*, 897–908.

de Waal, F. B., & Yoshihara, D. (1983). Reconciliation and redirected affection in rhesus monkeys. *Behaviour, 85*, 224–241.

Eals, M., & Silverman, I. (1994). The hunter–gatherer theory of spatial sex differences: Proximate factors mediating the female advantage in recall of object arrays. *Ethology and Sociobiology, 15*, 95–105.

Ehrensaft, D. (1992). Preschool child sex abuse: The aftermath of the Presidio case. *American Journal of Orthopsychiatry, 62*, 234–244.

Flannelly, K. J., Blanchard, R. J., Muraoka, M. Y., & Flannelly, L. (1982). Copulation increases offensive attack in male rats. *Physiology and Behavior, 29*, 381–385.

Flannelly, K. J., & Lore, R. (1977). The influence of females upon aggression in domesticated male rats (*Rattus norvegicus*). *Animal Behaviour, 25*, 654–659.

Fry, D. P. (1987). Differences between playfighting and serious fights among Zapotec children. *Ethology and Sociobiology, 8*, 285–306.

Glover, H. (1988). Four syndromes of post-traumatic stress disorder. *Journal of Traumatic Stress, 1*, 57–78.

Hall, W. M., & Cairns, R. B. (1984). Aggressive behavior in children: An outcome of modeling or social reciprocity? *Developmental Psychology, 20*, 739–745.

Hansen, L. L., Hagelso, A. M., & Madsen, A. (1982). Behavioural results and performance of bacon pigs fed "ad libitum" from one or several self-feeders. *Applied Animal Ethology, 8*, 307–333.

Hiraiwa-Hasegawa, M., Byrne, R. W., Takasaki, H., & Byrne, J. M. (1986). Aggression toward large carnivores by wild chimpanzees of Mahale Mountains National Park, Tanzania. *Folia Primatologica* (Basel), *47*, 8–13.

Honig, A. S., Douthit, D., Lee, J., & Dingler, C. (1992). Prosocial and aggressive behaviours of preschoolers at play in secular and church-based day care. *Early Child Development and Care, 83*, 93–101.

Huesmann, L. R. (1988). An information processing model for the development of aggression. *Aggressive Behavior, 14*, 13–24.

Judge, P. G. (1991). Dyadic and triadic reconciliation in pigtail macaques (*Macaca nemestrina*). *American Journal of Primatology, 23*, 225–237.

Kappeler, P. M. (1993). Reconciliation and post-conflict behaviour in ringtailed lemurs, *Lemur catta* and redfronted lemurs, *Eulemur fulvus rufus. Animal Behaviour, 45*, 901–915.

Karli, P. (1991). *Animal and human aggression.* London: Oxford University Press.

Katz, J. (1988). *Seductions of crime.* New York: Basic Books.

Kudo, H., & Mitani, M. (1985). New record of predatory behavior by the mandrill in Cameroon. *Primates, 26*, 161–167.

Maccoby, E. E., & Jacklin, C. N. (1980). Sex differences in aggression: A rejoinder and reprise. *Child Development, 51*, 964–980.

McEwen, B. S., & Sapolsky, R. M. (1995). Stress and cognitive function. *Current Opinion in Neurobiology, 5*, 205–216.

Moyer, K. E. (1981). Biological substrates of aggression and implications for control. In P. F. Brain & D. Benton (Eds.), *The biology of aggression* (pp. 47–67). Rockville, MD: Sythoff & Nordhoof.

O'Donnell, V., Blanchard, R. J., & Blanchard, D. C. (1981). Mouse aggression increases after 24 hours of isolation or housing with females. *Behavioral and Neural Biology, 32*, 89–103.

Olivier, B., Mos, J., & Miczek, K. A. (1991). Ethopharmacological studies of anxiolytics and aggression. *European Neuropsychopharmacology, 1*, 97–100.

Ollendick, D. G., & Hoffmann, M. (1982). Assessment of psychological reactions in disaster victims. *Journal of Community Psychology, 10*, 157–167.

Parker, D. R., & Rogers, R. W. (1981). Observation and performance of aggression: Effects of multiple models and frustration. *Personality and Social Psychology Bulletin, 7*, 302–308.

Paul, L., Foss, M. A., & Galloway, J. (1993). Sexual jealousy in young women and men: Aggressive responsiveness to partner and rival. *Aggressive Behavior, 19*, 401–420.

Pellis, S. M. (1988). Agonistic versus amicable targets of attack and defense: Consequences for the origin, function, and descriptive classification of play-fighting. *Aggressive Behavior, 14*, 85–104.

Pellis, S. M. (1997). Targets and tactics: The analysis of movement-to-movement decision making in animal combat. *Aggressive Behavior, 23*, 107–129.

Pellis, S. M., & McKenna, M. M. (1992). Intrinsic and extrinsic influences on play fighting in rats: Effects of dominance, partner's playfulness, temperament and neonatal exposure to testosterone propionate. *Behavioural Brain Research, 50*, 135–145.

Pellis, S. M., & McKenna, M. M. (1995). What do rats find rewarding in play fighting?—An analysis using drug-induced non-playful partners. *Behavioural Brain Research, 68*, 65–73.

Pellis, S. M., O'Brien, D. P., Pellis, V. C., & Teitelbaum, P. (1988). Escalation of feline predation along a gradient from avoidance through "play" to killing. *Behavioral Neuroscience, 102*, 760–777.

Pellis, S. M., & Pellis, V. C. (1989). Targets of attack and defense in play-fighting of the Djungarian hamster *Phodopus campbelli*: Links to fighting and sex. *Aggressive Behavior, 15*, 217–234.

Pellis, S. M., & Pellis, V. C. (1990). Differential rates of attack, defense, and counterattack during the developmental decrease in play fighting by male and female rats. *Developmental Psychobiology, 23*, 215–231.

Pellis, S. M., & Pellis, V. C. (1991a). Attack and defense during play fighting appear to be motivationally independent behaviors in muroid rodents [Special issue: Ethoexperimental psychology of defense: Behavioral and biological processes]. *Psychological Record, 41*, 175–184.

Pellis, S. M., & Pellis, V. C. (1991b). Role reversal changes during the ontogeny of play fighting in male rats: Attack vs. defense. *Aggressive Behavior, 17*, 179–189.

Pellis, S. M., & Pellis, V. C. (1992a). Analysis of the targets and tactics of conspecific attack and predatory attack in northern grasshopper mice *Onychomys leucogaster. Aggressive Behavior, 18*, 301–316.

Pellis, S. M., & Pellis, V. C. (1992b). Juvenilized play fighting in subordinate male rats. *Aggressive Behavior, 18*, 449–457.

Pellis, S. M., Pellis, V. C., & Whishaw, I. Q. (1992). The role of the cortex in play fighting by rats: Developmental and evolutionary implications. *Brain, Behavior and Evolution, 39*, 270–284.

Pereira, M. E. (1989). Agonistic interactions of juvenile Savanna baboons: II. Agonistic support and rank acquisition. *Ethology, 80*, 152–171.

Reinhardt, V., Dodsworth, R., & Scanlan, J. (1986). Altruistic interference shown by the alpha-female of a captive troop of rhesus monkeys. *Folio Primatologica* (Basel), *46*, 44–50.

Rodgers, R. J. (1995). Neuropharmacological aspects of adaptive pain inhibition in murine "victims" of aggression. *Aggressive Behavior, 21*, 29–39.

Rosenbaum, J. F., Biederman, J., Hirshfeld, D. R, Bolduc, E. A., Faraone, S. V., Kagan, J., Snidman, N., & Reznick, J. S. (1991). Further evidence of an association between behavioral inhibition and anxiety disorders: Results from a family study of children from a non-clinical sample. *Journal of Psychiatric Research, 25*, 49–65.

Russell, J. F. (1984). The captivity experience and its psychological consequences. *Psychiatric Annals, 14*, 250–254.

Rylov, A. I. (1985). Change of predator intraspecies aggression of male rats under food deprivation. *Zhurnal Vysshei Nervoi Deyatel'nosti, 35*, 875–878.

Rylov, A. I., & Kozyrev, S. A. (1985). Correlation of genetic and environmental factors in manifestation of predatory reactions in rats. *Zhurnal Vysshei Nervoi Deyatel'nosti, 35*, 480–486.

Sapolsky, R. M. (1990). A. E. Bennett Award paper. Adrenocortical function, social rank, and personality among wild baboons. *Biological Psychiatry, 28*, 862–878.

Schuster, R., Raleigh, M. J., McGuire, M. T., & Torigoe, D. (1993). Rank, relationships, and responses to intruders among adult male vervet monkeys. *American Journal of Primatology, 31*, 111–127.

Silk, J. B. (1992). The patterning of intervention among male bonnet macaques: Reciprocity, revenge, and loyalty. *Current Anthropology, 33*, 318–324.

Smith, L. K., Field, E. F., Forgie, M. L., & Pellis, S. M. (1996). Dominance and age-related changes in the play fighting of intact and post-weaning castrated male rats (*Rattus norvegicus*). *Aggressive Behavior, 22*, 215–226.

Smith, P. K. (1989). The role of rough-and-tumble play in the development of social com-
     petence: Theoretical perspectives and empirical evidence. In B. H. Schneider, G. Attili,
     J. Nadel, & P. P. Weissberg (Eds.), *Social competence in developmental perspective* (pp.
     239–255). Dordrecht, The Netherlands: Kluwer Academic.
Thor, D. H., & Carr, W. J. (1979). Sex and aggression: Competitive mating strategy in the
     male rat. *Behavioral and Neural Biology, 26*, 261–265.
Wilson, M., & Daly, M. (1992). The man who mistook his wife for a chattel. In J. H. Barkow,
     L. Cosmides, & J. Tooby (Eds.), *The adapted mind: Evolutionary psychology and the
     generation of culture* (pp. 289–322). New York: Oxford University Press.

Author Index

Numbers in italics refer to listings in the reference sections.

Frazier, L. L., 121, *137*
Freedman, D. X., 107, *113*
Fregnac, Y., 149, *154*
French, J. A., 292, *294*
Frenk, S., 148, *155*
Freund, T. F., 199, 209, *211, 213*
Friedman, M. J., 268, *270*
Friedman, R., 92, *102*
Frijda, N. H., 48, *54*
Friston, K. J., *156*
Frommer, G. P., 92, *97*
Fry, D. P., 309, *314*
Fujita, K., 247, 253, *255*
Fukuda, Y., 149, *155*
Fukunaga-Stinson, C., 301, *313*
Fulker, D. W., *171*
Fuster, J. M., 52, *54*

Gaffan, D., 200, 201, *212*, 224, *228*
Gaffan, E. A., 218, *228*
Gagnon, R., 124, *137, 138*
Gal, G., *98*
Galaburda, A. M., 250, 254, *255*
Galaverna, O., 131, *140*
Gallhofer, B., 104, *113*
Galloway, J., 305, *314*
Gallup, G. G., Jr., 175–190, *191–194*
Gannon, P. J., 248, *255*
Gantt, W. H., 16, *22*
Gardner, C. R., 63, *71*
Garety, P. A., 90, *98*
Garrett, M., 179, 184, *192*
Gasper, P., *281*
Gautheron, B., *139*
Gazzaniga, M. S., 199, *213*
Gelade, G., 252, *256*
Geller, L. N., 274, *282*
Gellhorn, A., 122, *138*
George, F. W., 159, *171*
George, P. J., 219, *228*
Gerber, D., *282*
Gerhardt, K. J., 123, 124, 128, *136, 138, 140*
Gershon, S., 91, *97*
Geschwind, N., 250, *255*
Gewirtz, J. C., 88, 89, 95, *99*
Geyer, M. A., 88, *101*, 103–112, *112–116*
Geyer, S., *256*
Giarman, N. J., 107, *113*
Gibbons, R. D., 67, *71*
Gibert-Rahola, J., 66, *71*
Gilbert, C. D., 150, *154*
Gilissen, E., *256*
Gimbrett, R., 79, *85*
Ginsberg, M. D., 199, *211*
Ginsburg, B. E., 273, *281*
Gjerde, P. F., 88, *98*

Gladue, B. A., 159, 160, 167, *170, 171, 174*
Glenn, M. J., 207, *212*, 223, *228*
Glick, I., *112*
Globisch, J., 104, *116*
Glover, H., 308, *314*
Gobaille, S., *100*
Goedert, M., *295*
Goeters, S., 232, *244*
Gogan, F., 159, *171*
Gold, G., 130, *142*
Goldberg, R., 279, *281*
Goldman, D., *282*
Goldman-Rakic, P. S., 17, *22*, 52, *54*, 221, *229*
Good, M., 92, *99*
Goodrich, L. V., *39*
Gooren, L. J. G., 166, 169, *173, 174*
Gordon, J. H., 159, *171*
Gorski, R. A., 159, 161, 166, 167, *169, 171, 172*
Gosselin, O., 92, 94, 95, *98, 101*
Gottlieb, G., 119, 120, 133, 136, *138*
Götz, F., 163, *171*
Goy, R. W., 157, 159, 163, *171–173*
Graeff, F. G., 83, *84, 100, 101*
Graf, P., 198, *212*, 220, *228*
Graham, C. H., 147, *154*
Graham, D. L., 199, *211*
Graham, F., 104, *113*
Grahame, N. J., 88, *96, 98*
Grandy, D. K., *115*
Grangé, D., 96, *100*
Granier-Deferre, C., 127, 128, 133, 134, *138, 139, 141*
Granier-Deferre, J. P., 135, *137*
Graves, J. M., *281*
Gray, J. A., 51, *54*, 88, 90, 91, 96, *98, 99, 101, 102*
Gray, L., 133, *141*
Gray, N. S., 88–90, *98*
Graziano, M. S. A., 149, *154*
Green, J. A., 133, *138*
Green, S., 21, *22*
Greene, R. W., 274, 277, 281, 287, 291, *294*
Griebel, G., 76–78, 80, 81, *84, 85*
Griffiths, S. J., 124, *138*
Griffiths, S. K., 124, *140*
Grigorian, G. A., *98*
Grillon, C., 103, 104, 108, *112–114*
Grimsby, J., *281*
Grimwade, J. C., *142*
Gueubelle, F., 125, *138*
Gugten, J. V., 260, 265, 267, *270*
Guimaraes, F. S., 83, *85*
Gunther, L. M., 88, 96, *98, 100*
Gusak, O., *98*
Guterman, Y., 89, *99*

Subject Index

About the Editors

Marc Haug, PhD, is director of research at the Université Louis Pasteur, Strasbourg, France. He coproduced, among other books, *Heterotypical Behaviour in Man and Animals*, *The Aggressive Female*, and, also with Dr. Richard E. Whalen, *The Development of Sex Differences and Similarities in Behavior*. A fellow of the New York Academy of Science, the Harry Frank Guggenheim Foundation, as well as of the European Neuroscience Association, Dr. Haug is serving as an adviser to the vice president for international affairs of the Université Louis Pasteur to promote higher education links with universities in the United States.

Richard E. Whalen, PhD, is professor emeritus at the University of California and is currently affiliated with the University of California, Riverside. He has taught and conducted research at the University of California, Los Angeles, the University of California, Irvine, and the State University of New York, Stony Brook. A cofounder, with Frank A. Beach, of the journal *Hormones and Behavior*, Dr. Whalen has coedited many books during his academic career and has published extensively in a wide range of other journals, including *Science, Nature,* the *Journal of Comparative and Physiological Psychology, Psychological Review, Brain Research,* and *Endocrinology.*

DATE DUE

~~DEC 1 0 2000~~			
~~APR 2 6 2003~~			
			Printed in USA